SYNTHEISM
CREATING GOD
IN THE INTERNET AGE

ALEXANDER BARD & JAN SÖDERQVIST

SYNTHEISM

CREATING GOD IN THE INTERNET AGE

STOCKHOLM TEXT

STOCKHOLM TEXT
www.stockholmtext.com

Syntheism – Creating God in the Internet Age
Swedish title: *Synteism – Att skapa Gud i Internetåldern*
Alexander Bard & Jan Söderqvist © 2014
© Stockholm Text 2014
Translation: John Wright
Cover: Per Gustafsson/pgustafsson.com
Author photo: Niclas Brunzell

ISBN 978-91-7547-183-9

Index

Everything is religion

Does God exist?

Many people regard this question as almost ludicrously simple, and thus also as provocative and confrontational. But the problem is that major and polarising discord remains concerning the answer. Some say that the answer to this simple question obviously is a resounding no: Of course there is no God! All talk of a God is an expression of a tenaciously persistent superstition that has stuck with humanity throughout all of known history, ever since the rain dances of the first shamans. A superstition that in all likelihood will wither away and die as our knowledge of the nature of physics at the macro and micro levels grows sufficiently to be able to refute the many foolish notions of religion and document how these are tied to various sociocultural conditions.

But as we know, some others are as unshakeably convinced that God not only exists with the greatest certainty, but also that this God painstakingly keeps track of all of our sins as well as our good deeds. And as if that were not enough, this same

God created our planet and all its innumerable life forms at the dawn of Time. This God, who thus exists, permeates every aspect of our existence, and not believing in Him and admitting this is something that sooner or later will incur punishment. Possibly for all eternity. But the matter is complicated further by the lack of agreement among these many people who are convinced of His existence as to exactly which god really does exist, and throughout history this has given rise to innumerable conflicts – battles and wars that have claimed countless human lives in the name of God. So how could God *not* exist?

So in fact, this seemingly simple question must be nuanced and made more specific, at least somewhat, in order for us to be able to discuss it in a meaningful way. What the answer will be – and what the question actually means – depends, of course, partly on what we mean by "God", and partly on what we mean by "exist". Let us start with the latter, which might perhaps be the most convenient place to start. A beautiful poem, untitled, one of the very last authored by the Portuguese poet Fernando Pessoa – the manuscript is dated as November 19, 1935 – reads as follows:

There are sicknesses worse than any sickness;
There are pains that don't ache, not even in the soul,
And yet they're more painful than those that do.
There are anxieties from dreams that are more real
Than the ones life brings; there are sensations
Felt only by imagining them
That are more ours than our very own life.
There are countless things that exist
Without existing, that lastingly exist
And lastingly are ours, they're us…
Over the muddy green of the wide river
The white circumflexes of the seagulls…
Over my soul the useless flutter

Of what never was nor could be, and it's everything.
Give me more wine, because life is nothing.

(Translation: Richard Zenith. From Fernando Pessoa, *A Little Larger Than the Entire Universe*, Penguin Books 2006.)

In the poem several assertions are made; assertions about the texture of existence. The poem states that things are this way and that way. There are sicknesses that are worse than any sickness and therefore are also something *other* than sickness (although they are, nonetheless, sicknesses), and the anxieties from dreams are more real than those that afflict us in what we call life or reality (which means that the concepts "dream" and "reality" must be challenged), and so on. Sicknesses, anxieties, a hint of elusive hopes and a significant measure of resignation. If we were to attempt to identify some sort of all-encompassing feature of Pessoa's poem, we might perhaps agree that it encapsulates a frame of mind, even an acquired outlook on life. And that this frame of mind and this outlook are coloured by an increasingly lucid sadness.

But exactly where does this sadness exist? Well, not on the piece of paper or on the screen where the poem is available to us. For there, if we are going to be picky, only a set of abstract, graphic symbols in various combinations exists. That these combinations of something that we call letters come together to produce something we call words, and that moreover these "words" mean something and have a context-specific value, depends entirely on a social contract that most of us subscribe to through learning, because it is comforting and in many respects also enriching. We look at the symbols and conjure up various perceptions. Which means that the question of where this sadness actually exists, to the extent that it actually *does* exist, remains unanswered, unless it exists on the piece of paper or on the screen.

And we may take this one step further: Does art exist? Most people do not question that a whole host of physically tangible objects that purport to be art actually exist, although there are many who would energetically deny the unique experience of art that others testify to more or less loquaciously and eloquently. This concept of art actually being an organised hoax, orchestrated for the purpose of enriching all those who participate in this racket while making them appear to be extremely high-minded, is a philistine concept, deeply rooted and difficult to address. Where people do not participate in the social contract they do not quite understand what it is all about, and consequently assume that it must be some sort of fraud. Someone is fooling you and all the others are either pretending that everything is as it should be, or are allowing themselves to be convinced without being able to see through the hoax. This applies, by the way, to a large degree also to philosophy which, outside certain protected reserves, is considered a rather dubious activity. Maybe it does not exist either.

But returning to Pessoa's sadness – where does it exist? For we maintain that it does. And the answer closest at hand is surely that it is we as readers who create it. With the ardent support of the author himself of course. He and we create it together with the aid of that set of social contracts that is literature and poetry, in exactly the same way that we create a multitude of other things that exist in and through language with the aid of various other social contracts: nations, ideologies, communities of various kinds. This in turn means that most of us who are either reading or writing this book, and who now and then reflect on existential and ontological problems, are carrying around a relatively flexible definition of what it actually means that something "exists". There is a lot that does not exist, but that actually does exist – in language. The sadness of Pessoa, or rather the sadness of the poem, does not exist in the same sense that the saucepan that is standing over there on the kitchen stove exists, which we can touch and measure and weigh and photograph, and whose existence is irrefutable since the meat stew inside it would certainly spill onto the stove if the saucepan did not actually exist. But we know nevertheless with great certainty that the sadness of the poem actually does exist and that we ourselves are particularly well equipped to vouch for this very fact, since we have participated in creating it. Thus we also know that there exists, just as Pessoa writes, so much that does not exist, but that *does* exist – in fact, that lingers there.

The German philosopher Martin Heidegger constructs *existentialism* on this basic distinction. He categorises the saucepan on the stove and all other indisputably physically existing phenomena within the idea of *the ontic*. But what else "exists" in a broader sense, outside and beyond the ontic – such as the sadness we read into Fernando Pessoa's late poem – Heidegger sums up in the idea of *the ontological*. Heidegger's point is that the existential human being does not simply live within a *Sein (being)* in the ontic world, but belongs just as much in the ontological world, in a *Dasein (being there or existence as it is generally translated in English)*. Being there and experiencing *Dasein* is, according to Heidegger, about being fully human. Thus, the human being is much more than merely a *physical* being. The world is more than just saucepans. Heidegger's existentialist idea of *Dasein* is a *metaphysical* state.

Naturally, at least in theory, you could choose to stand outside all linguistic contracts that you do not understand. You could simply not participate, and you could, as Lewis Carroll's Humpty Dumpty once did, in a contemptuous tone of voice maintain that when one uses a word, it means exactly what one chooses it to mean – neither more nor less. And with the word "exists" you therefore merely mean that something that actually does exist must exist in the same ontic and apparently indisputable way that the saucepan exists on the stove in the kitchen, and that if it does not exist in this way, it does not exist at all. However, one should also bear in mind that Humpty Dumpty fails to communicate anything of interest at all in his conversation with an increasingly frustrated Alice.

The problem with this kind of language philosophy desperado is namely that your existence becomes rather boring and lonely amid the saucepans. At the same time one should stress in this context that this "being" definitely does not constitute a guarantee of quality, and that the cosmic vacuum we call "nothing" in everyday parlance has proven to be anything but empty in the classical sense. It is in fact out of this apparent "nothing" that the Universe has been created, which the cosmologist and physicist Lawrence Krauss argues convincingly for in his book entitled just that: *A Universe from Nothing.* That something exists in an ontic sense is, in other words, not very remarkable. So do *E. coli* bacteria, and in large numbers, too. While being the only thing that assuredly does not exist, "nothing" is something that even physics barely wants to acknowledge nowadays.

With this flexible understanding of the various nuances of the concept of "being", and with Pessoa's and Heidegger's insights that there exists so much which does not exist in the ontic sense, but which nonetheless does exist, we are cautiously approaching the concept of "God" and posing questions such as how we should understand this concept fairly correctly – or at least in a way that is reasonable – and whether what is accommodated within the definition we finally settle on actually does exist in an ontic or an ontological sense. Or are we merely talking about hot air here? The handling of the issue becomes somewhat easier however when it dawns on us that the ontological question in all likelihood answers itself, since God – whatever this turns out to be – is something we humans have created ourselves. Throughout history, there has never existed a human society where religion was not exercised in some form. At any rate, there have been no research findings of any kind anywhere indicating the tiniest trace of the presence of human collectives of any significance that did not have a religious community. This is indisputable. Even our dead cousins the Neanderthals buried their near and dear ones under ritual forms that indicate the presence of some kind of religion. From this, one may then draw a number of different conclusions.

One of the conclusions that was particularly frequently and eloquently proposed around the millennium shift was that God – and here we are speaking mainly about the Christian God and his Almighty colleagues within Judaism and Islam – is pure delusion. This is in fact the title of the central work of the radical atheist genre, *The God Delusion* by Richard Dawkins, a celebrated evolutionary biologist and pugnacious atheist. Many other titles by others who share Dawkins' views develop fairly similar arguments. The common and recurring idea is one that describes how, roughly up until now, human beings have been so ignorant and superstitious that it became necessary to invent sundry varieties of religion in order to extract various useful things such as solace, community morals, and something that might resemble a pattern in, and a meaning for, a gloomy existence filled with privation and suffering.

In connection with this, one might argue – and indeed not without reason –that with the passing of time, religion turns into the story that those in power tell to the people in order to legitimise the prevailing order and thereby also, conveniently enough, their own privileges. Those in power promise abundant rewards in the afterlife to obedient subjects who pay taxes and without complaint accept their subservient places in this life on this Earth. In this way, the emperor gets his way without fuss and in practice at really no cost at all. In this way, religion becomes both the opiate that keeps the people asleep and the pretext with which one commandeers people into war whenever it benefits the interests of those in power. Whoever succeeds in usurping the office of God's spokesperson here on Earth need not risk being contradicted to any greater extent, at least not within his or her own faith community. And what the others – the infidels – have to say by definition is of little or no value at all. For it is with them that one makes war, it is them one hounds from places that one considers sacred, it is them one plunders and torments the life out of with God's clear blessing. That the infidels believe in the wrong god conveniently enough makes it possible to strip them of all humanity.

Hardly anyone would deny that hideous atrocities and cruelties have been committed in the name of this or that god throughout history: the examples are innumerable and a complete catalogue of all the crimes carried out under a religious banner would require a book of its own. Nor is this in any way a unique speciality of the Abrahamic religions. In Polynesia, prisoners of war and heretics were sacrificed to the gods. The Aztecs refined human sacrifice to an activity that was carried out on a near-industrial scale, administered by the state and clergy in an effective symbiosis. Dispatched soldiers carried out raids on the neighbouring peoples in order to bring home prisoners in great quantities, after which these prisoners, courtesy of the clergy, were sacrificed to the great god Huitzilopochtli by cutting the hearts out of their living bodies, which subsequently, not quite as alive, were rolled down the steps leading up to the altar.

But when it comes to the extent of these types of crimes, most particularly in the present era, although there are Hindus making war on Muslims with great energy in India for example, the Abrahamites occupy an unchallenged position of prominence. Militant Islamists terrorise other Muslims along with the rest of us with an intensity that affects all of our lives and communities: how we travel and move across national boundaries, whom we choose to trust and interact with, what we dare to write and publish, and what we allow ourselves to say in public. A significant measure of self-censorship is exercised in both Islamic countries and in the West because of an unbridled fear of the physical attacks of religious fundamentalists. What one can and must ask oneself in this context is, however, what the causative links actually are, and to what extent these religions as such are culpable in the exercise of violence and the atrocities that are carried out in the name of various gods.

It is of course possible to find calls for cruelty towards the impure of faith in both the Bible and the Quran, as well as in other religious scriptures, but it is also possible to find calls for loving kindness. The programmatic inconsistencies in religious scriptures is part and parcel of their nature, since they are a collage produced from a multitude of various texts, written by various people on various occasions and under various conditions for completely separate purposes, which means that one may find support for almost any position by quoting various Bible verses and Qur'anic suras. And it is with this painstakingly selective citing of scripture – or alternatively without any support whatsoever in any significant source at all – that various groups invoke God's blessing for their acts of violence directed at dissidents. Which ought to invite a certain caution when pointing the finger at this or that religion as responsible for this or that act of violence.

While it is certainly true, to take a much talked about example, that the triggering factor when it came to the murder of Dutch film director Theo van Gogh was a film, *Submission*, which critically discusses the oppression of women that is religiously tinged; and while it is true that the murderer himself confirmed the connection between the deed and his own fanatical interest in protecting the true faith, it is also true that this kind of aggressive and confrontational practice of religion is rejected by many, if not most, Muslims. Thus one might imagine that religion has been made to serve, and throughout history continuously has served, as a fancy excuse for dogmatic fanatics and the unscrupulously powerful who, for various strategic reasons, or because the violence quite simply was addictively intoxicating, chose to terrorise real and imagined enemies. As an example, the conflict between the Israelis and the Palestinians in the Middle East is political and social rather than religious in any real sense, in spite of them choosing to fight about so-called *holy places* – strictly *symbolic assets* – from time to time when it is expedient for turning up the rhetorical heat. The same applies to the civil war in Northern Ireland, where the designations "Catholics" and "Protestants" fail to tell us anything relevant whatsoever about wherein the historical and multidimensional conflicts really have lain, and to a certain extent still lie.

In addition, one might ask oneself whether it really is sport that should be held accountable when organised groups of football hooligans clash, or if it isn't more a question of people who simply want to engage in collective violence subject to certain rituals, and that this function that has been imposed on football in this context should be regarded as purely symbolic. For the various teams that are pitted against one another on the field encapsulate, formalise and discipline this aggression within very strict limits. After the game, opponents offer each other a friendly handshake and exchange shirts with each other. Sport in itself brings people together, at least in terms of its practitioners. That the hooligans actually want nothing more than to fight before, during and after the game – and that people actually enjoy both engaging in collective violence and the freedom from responsibility and the intoxication that comes with surrendering to the collective will that places itself above all of society's formal laws and regulations, irrespective of what cause or group identity one claims to be fighting for – has an extremely negligible connection to the practice of sport *per se*.

In large part, this reasoning may be transferred to the question of the excesses and crimes carried out in the name of God.

God is innocent, to the extent he actually exists: it is we humans who are guilty. Thus, we cannot blame religion with any degree of preserved credibility, and maintain that it was religion that forced us to act brutally towards our neighbour, when the truth is that – countless times throughout the course of history and under every possible pretext – we have tortured and massacred people who in some sense have belonged to a group other than ourselves, quite voluntarily and with great enthusiasm. We just don't like strangers or what is different: this is deeply rooted in us. The cure is *civilisation*, but it is far from all-embracing and probably never will be. Nevertheless, all of these ecclesiastical sins and crimes are one of articulated atheism's two principal arguments against religion as it has been manifested thus far.

The other argument – which we regard as considerably stronger – is traditional religion's demands for special treatment in the form of a completely unique reverence and respect vis-à-vis other ideological systems. Thus, not infrequently religion regards itself per definition as above every kind of questioning. Aside from the more or less opaque declarations concerning its existence that traditional religion itself chooses to make, it should be under no obligation to explain itself. Criticising religion, or just studying it like any kind of natural and social phenomenon, amounts to desecrating the holy doctrine and offending an entire world of believers. On this theme, the American philosopher Daniel Dennett has written an astute atheist manifesto, *Breaking the Spell,* where he observes that the *Enlightenment* is buried and forgotten and that the gradual secularisation of modern society – which could long be observed and which it was thought would soon be complete – is now crumbling away before our very eyes. Religion is more important than ever. But religion evades serious study, Dennett complains: it only allows itself to be enticed into something that has the semblance of a dialogue on its home turf, surrounded by smoke and mirrors, where it uses suggestion to produce murky connections between faith in, for example, the sacred soul's immortality on the one hand, and on the other hand the believer's moral refinement. But it never clarifies what these connections actually consist of.

In so far as this sort of nonsensical reasoning is gaining ground, there is of course good reason to criticise religion. Anything of this kind sooner or later inevitably leads to a more or less brutal oppression of dissenting opinion, which in turn leads to a wholesale destruction of knowledge in the name of God. Which of course unarguably implies that ignorance in important areas is a necessary prerequisite for at least some types of religion. When, for example, Christian fundamentalists try to launch *creationism* under the ridiculous label of *intelligent design* as an alternative on an equal footing with Darwin's theory of evolution – that is, as a sufficiently respectable alternative in order for it to be part of the curriculum in American schools – this is in fact a case of intellectual sabotage of the worst kind. Genuine knowledge is pitted here against bizarre nonsense. Anyone who seriously claims that "intelligent design" is an adequate "theory", deserving of being discussed in the same halls of learning in which the evolutionary process through natural (and sexual) selection is studied – which according to this reasoning also is just a "theory" – does not know what actually constitutes a theory, and refuses to understand what the theory of evolution actually says and explains.

A religion that, in a similar way to Abrahamic monotheism's many variants, largely rests on contrafactual fairy tale material may choose to either water itself down to the point of self-annihilation and proclaim that all the old dogmas and convictions that are in conflict with accepted knowledge should be seen as historically conditioned parables that are meant to be interpreted allegorically and not literally; or else walk down the path of complete denial and fight real knowledge by any means at its disposal in order to safeguard its own survival. The latter alternative becomes considerably easier to carry out if the individual not only wields religious but also political power, which of course is the case in many countries rule by Islam where religion and law go hand in hand. But even in the democratic USA, where freedom of speech is protected under the Constitution, many Christian communities successfully choose the path of denial and the destruction of knowledge, which probably, and paradoxically, is something that is being facilitated by the network dynamics that have developed on the Internet.

Whereas previously one could be in at least reasonable agreement concerning certain basic facts and then argue about how to interpret these, nowadays it is quite possible for various groups to maintain exclusive sets of facts that are determined by, and tally well with, their own fixed faith. The reason is that most people, if it were up to them, would prefer to be embraced by, and to associate in confidence with, the people they agree with rather than to be contradicted and questioned. And this they may well do. What enables this development towards an escalating social *polarisation*, both politically and in terms of outlook on life, is that on the Internet one tends to choose the sources of information that say exactly what one wants to hear and which confirm one's own world view. And this occurs while one effectively isolates oneself from those with divergent opinions, with whom one quite simply refrains from engaging in debate, and with whom a meaningful conversation in principle is always impossible, since one does not even agree on the basics and game rules. Thus, the Internet has not developed into one big global village where everyone communicates with everyone else in a way that reflects mutual understanding and trust – which many digital pioneers naively had hoped it would. Instead, the landscape that emerges on the Web is an all too vast archipelago of closed communities without fixed connections between them.

Capitalism's fixation with *exploitation* is therefore being followed by informationalism's obsession with its counterpart, *imploitation*, that is, a maximisation of the value of information by means of the community's deliberate delimitation, rather than a naive openness towards the outside world (see *The Netocrats*). Within such a closed collective, one might claim unchallenged that "intelligent design" is a "theory" that is broadly superior to the theory of evolution, or anything at all as long as it wins the approval of the collective's intersubjective liking. To the extent that the protests and indignation of the outside world seep through these walls, they rather tend to strengthen the sense of community, since this concern from the outside easily can be dismissed as propaganda from the enemy. And the more bizarre the ideas proclaimed by a religious community or a sect, the more robust the resistance they trigger in the hostile outside world, and the more they strengthen the sense of internal community and the production of *social identity*.

But let us now return to our initial question: does God exist? We are talking here about the God of Christianity that Friedrich Nietzsche pronounced dead as early as the 19th century. The atheist Dennett answers both yes and no to this question. What does not exist is the supernatural, omniscient and all-seeing God of which the Bible speaks, the God that created our world and everything else, and who sent his only son to our Earth for him to die a sacrificial death on the cross and thereby, in a transaction which in many ways is utterly unclear, purchase our liberation from our dreadful sins (that God himself thus takes no responsibility for despite the fact that he apparently created us as the wretched sinners that we are). At least this is what Dennett says, with reference to, among other things, the worthlessness of the "evidence" for God. Take for example Anselm of Canterbury's *ontological argument*, according to which God quite simply has to exist by logical necessity since God by definition is above all else, which means that God cannot lack existence, since this unthinkable scenario would make God incomplete and in at least one important respect inferior to all that indisputably does own existence, such as that saucepan on the stove containing the stew. And according to our accepted idea of God, God must then be above all else, in particular saucepans.

This argument runs, as can be seen, in a tight little circle, and Dennett is not impressed. According to the same logic, everything that is said to be perfect and complete also must exist, and this is of course not something we can accept. And if this applies only to God, it is hardly the kind of logic to write home about. Nor does *the cosmological argument* – according to which everything must have a cause and everything that is created must have a creator, and that this creator is what we call God – appear particularly convincing on closer inspection. The idea here is that the causative link cannot stretch back in all eternity: this appears unreasonable. But if God in some way has created himself out of nothing and has no underlying cause, what is actually stopping the *Universe itself* from having created itself out of nothing? As we know nowadays, there is absolutely nothing to preclude this. What we know about the Universe actually indicates precisely that it did create itself out of what through ignorance we used to think of as nothing, but which instead turns out to be very much something.

There are, according to Dennett, no good reasons to believe that this God exists, and there are an almost infinite number of good reasons to believe that he does *not* exist. This prompts Dennett to view himself as an atheist. But he also claims, with an argument borrowed from Dawkins, that all of us, even the most devout and literal believers among theists in our cultural sphere, are in fact radical atheists when it comes to all those other gods that the rest of humanity believe in or have believed in once upon a time: Baal and the Golden Calf, Thor and Wotan, Poseidon and Apollo, Mithras and Amun-Ra, and so on. Theists around the world thus don't just believe in one god or the other, but also in their fantastic luck that the god they believe in within their particular congregation, and that they have been raised to believe in – as long as they do not happen to be converts – just happens to be the only god that actually exists, as opposed to all the other false gods, who thus do not exist.

However, what really exists without a doubt, according to Dennett, is the *idea of God*. What could be more obvious? One can believe in that idea and fill it with any number of different values without actually believing that only the Christian God (or Baal or the Gold Calf) actually exists. Dennett calls this *belief in belief*. You can believe that a religious faith supplies various commodities, and thus you can, which many do, believe in this faith without thereby necessarily believing in what the faith community for this religion believes in. You can also observe how the content of the idea of God has gradually changed almost beyond recognition from the old days of the folk religions up until the present day. This was brought to light as early as towards the end the 18ᵗʰ century by David Hume in *The Natural History of Religion*, where he calls the polytheists "superstitious atheists", since they do not recognise any phenomenon that is in accordance with "our idea of a deity".

Dennett argues that no idea has ever undergone such a dramatic transformation act as that of "God". On the one hand, this naturally creates a large measure of uncertainty. Many protest a faith in one and the same idea, but in actual fact they believe in completely different things, and if one expands the definition of God to comprise whatever it was that created life on Earth, it might turn out that God is, or at least could be, Darwin's natural selection, in which case all atheists are in principle ardent believers in God. But that the idea of God has kept its name through all these shifts in meaning – from human-like jealous monsters and autocratic avengers to a diffuse kind of higher being with fuzzy boundaries – does mean, on the other hand, that religion and the religious attitude have co-opted large parts of, if not all of, existence; and that the God brand has retained a strong and extremely valuable loyalty, courtesy of its long history.

Consequently, we have every reason to expect that the idea of God will undergo additional transformation acts, because social structures continue to change, and because consequently believers will continue to demand more useful things from God. It is precisely these that are the foundations of this book. Voltaire writes that "If God did not exist, it would have been necessary to invent him" ("*Si Dieu n'existait pas, il faudrait l'inventer*"). And that is exactly what we humans invariably do: invent God anew, filling this flexible and robust idea with ever-new dreams and desires. Syntheism is quite simply the name of the next revolutionary phase in this development without end.

Sigmund Freud, the great father of psychoanalysis, regarded religion as an "illusion", a thought that he developed in the book *An Illusion and Its Future* from 1927. His ambition was to let psychoanalysis offer its contribution to the understanding of religion, which is part of the culture whose main task it is, through various instructions and coercive measures, to defend humans against frightening, and in many ways cruel and dangerous, Nature. These instructions are held aloft, above criticism and questioning, by dint of their being accorded a divine origin. "In this way", writes Freud, "a treasure trove of concepts born of the need to make human helplessness bearable is gathered, based on a fabric of memories of childhood helplessness, one's own helplessness and that of the human race." Thus religion is born: an increasingly systematic wishful thinking about superior and threatening forces that are endowed with the features of the father figure precisely because of the experienced helplessness that is associated with the solitary child's vulnerability. That this illusory construction then grows to be so strong is related to the strength of this wishful thinking. The relief that it offers is as substantial as it is welcome: the difficult questions about the genesis of the world and the soul's relationship to the body are conveniently answered and the fear of many of life's dangers is allayed through divine providence. The acute terror which is caused by helplessness is eased through a carefully crafted illusion that responds to our collective and personal yearning for the father.

Freud is careful to stress that illusion does not need to be the same as delusion. Fallacies and delusions always contradict the truth, which is not necessarily the case with an illusion. What is characteristic of an illusion is the dominant element of wish fulfilment. We yearn for a father figure and find him up there in Heaven. A typical illusion, infused with wishful thinking, is also that the child is a pure and innocent creature without sexuality, according to Freud. Without taking a pronounced stand on the truth value of religion – for the designation 'illusion' is primarily linked to psychological mechanisms – Freud argues that religion corresponds to the neurotic phase that the human child must undergo in its development towards a cultural being with a fully developed superego. The human race itself also ought to be able to undergo this development and leave the childhood neurosis of religion behind – this is what Freud hopes – since science is continually advancing and displacing ignorance. There is no reason for us modern human beings to take over the faith of previous generations without reservation: we know better than to believe in what they believed in. From this arch-atheist perspective, the human race ought to be on the road to maturity and thereby becoming capable of basing its thoughts and actions on rational considerations. The question is whether more naive and illusory wishful thinking than this has ever existed.

The French historian François Furet chooses the same designation as Freud – *illusion* – when he studies and passes judgement on Communism in his book *The Passing of an Illusion* from 1995. This book primarily discusses the Russian Revolution with its aftermath and consequences, and Furet speaks throughout about this artfully orchestrated political illusion in religious terms. To all intents and purposes Bolshevism is a religious sect: it reflects and very consciously shrouds itself in a mythical inheritance from the French Revolution. It celebrates the dictatorship of the Committee of Public Safety from 1793 to 1794, and it legitimises its own power-consolidating terror with the same kind of sweeping reference to the threat from the counter-revolution as the Jacobites did in their rule of terror. Lenin is naturally depicted as a latter-day Robespierre, and just as incorruptible. Through this reflection and identification, the myth of the Russian Revolution grew ever stronger. And it is in this way that it becomes possible to combine the advantages of the shockingly new with the seductiveness of a glorious past. In a ravaged and war-weary Europe, the October Revolution willingly and with remarkable success took on as its own the well-established utopia of the arrival of the new human being.

"What happens in Russia in 1917 and the following years when the people of Europe make their way home from the war are only outwardly Russian events," writes Furet. "What counts is that the Bolsheviks proclaim the universal revolution. Out of a successful coup in Europe's most backward country carried out by a Communist sect headed by an audacious leader, the political situation creates an exemplary event that will steer the course of history in the same way as France of 1789 did in its time. As a consequence of the general war-weariness and rage of the vanquished people, the illusion that Lenin created out of his own theses and actions came to be shared by millions of people." The revolution constitutes a promise of a future kingdom of good fortune for the new human being. Inconvenient facts melt away in the brutal heat generated by the radical rhetoric. This incompletely secularised salvation doctrine means that politics takes over religion's claim to totality. "Revolutionary fervour wants everything to be politics," writes Furet. Politics produces its own clergy as well as its heretics, and it thereby becomes impossible to separate it from religion, in terms of both expression and content. It is not enough that religion cunningly takes on another guise and meaning when necessary; it can also change name and label itself something completely different. Not infrequently politics, for example. Or just anything.

"War is merely a continuation of politics by other means," writes the German General Carl von Clausewitz in his book *On War* from 1832. This is his answer to the question: What is war? Similarly, if we ask ourselves what politics really is, the answer is that politics is merely a continuation of religion by other means. And it definitely not only applies to Bolshevism or to other more or less doctrinal and airy-fairy movements with distinct features of sectarianism. Activities in the modern capitals of Western democracies do not constitute exceptions to this rule, whatever many secularised men and women in government and opposition would like to believe.

An interesting example that sheds light on this is the bitter resistance that was mobilised against President Barack Obama's health care reform – the Affordable Care Act – during his second term in office. It was a resistance that finally led to a ruling in the U.S. Supreme Court which, by a margin of a single vote, established that the law in question does not violate the Constitution and consequently cannot be repealed. What is interesting is the following: what the Republican resistance focused on, what they claimed with great energy was incompatible with the Constitution, was the principle of an *individual mandate*, that is, that the responsibility for insurance rests in the end on the individual citizen, instead of, for example, on the employer. What is particularly curious and odd in this matter is then that the idea of an individual mandate – a requirement that people protect themselves through insurance, rather like the way in which by law they must protect themselves with a safety belt when they are travelling by car – as the foundation for a health care bill was initially proposed by the Republicans themselves after having been originally launched by the conservative think-tank The Heritage Foundation in 1989.

Consequently, the individual mandate was the basis of the system that Obama's rival Mitt Romney implemented as Governor of Massachusetts, and also of the Republican alternative to the bill that Bill Clinton once failed to steer through Congress, and which was built on the principle of employer responsibility (which Clinton in hindsight regards as a decisive mistake). All the chopping and changing in the Republican establishment's dramatic turnaround from love to hate in terms of an individual mandate are depicted in an extremely illuminating essay by the journalist and blogger Ezra Klein in *The New Yorker* magazine (June 25, 2012). Barack Obama had no intention of repeating Bill Clinton's mistake by proposing a law that his political opponents detested on the grounds of principle. Therefore, he based his health care act on an idea that the Republicans themselves had introduced once upon a time and had repeatedly expressed their support for: the individual mandate. Obama himself was one of the last Democrats to concur with this Republican idea. So what happens? Lo and behold, in a vote in December 2009 all Republican senators voted against the law and in favour of declaring it unconstitutional precisely because of the construct based on an individual mandate that they themselves had championed for 20 years.

Thus the parties had exchanged positions with each other and were struggling hard not to give the game away. What until recently was considered exemplary and heartily embraced by the Republicans is suddenly not only rash and reprehensible in general, but also something that in addition actually defaces the holy vision of the special case of America that the Founding Fathers had formulated once and for all time – a turnaround fully comparable to Josef Stalin's embracing of the concept of *socialism in one country* instead of Lenin's and Trotsky's ambitions to export the Bolshevik revolution across all of the industrialised world. But where Stalin, to make absolutely certain, uses purges, intrigues and liquidations to maintain party discipline, it is sufficient for the members of the Republican resistance to rely on psychological turncoat mechanisms and loyalty to the collective with which one identifies – and which guarantees one's status and support. Soon enough the unthinkable – that Obamacare might be the subject of a Supreme Court ruling *because* of the principle of the individual mandate – is not only thinkable, but a reality. It is sufficient that a few key people in the legislative body change their opinions for the entire flock to trot obediently along behind them, eagerly cheered on by their supporters in the media. And suddenly the Republicans are also enthusiastic advocates for an activist Supreme Court, on which all their hopes of victory are now pinned, which is also an entirely new, and almost revolutionary experience for the party.

But how is this possible? Even if we choose to disregard the fact that politics often thinks of itself as dealing with rational deliberations on thoroughly analysed matters of fact – while it actually primarily revolves around primitive antagonisms, loyalty to one's own group and resolute non-questioning in order to preserve the religious community – there is of course generally a price to be paid for this sort of turnaround, that is, unless one has a police force of one's own with which one can terrorise all one's critics into silence. In this particular case with Obamacare, the price was that the Republicans were forced to present themselves as a party that, for two decades, had advocated measures that violated the Constitution. But this pain was considerably relieved by highly developed denial and repression mechanisms. Our actions and thinking in critical situations – and as a matter of fact in all possible situations – is actually not governed by conscious reasoning or rational deliberations. Instead, we react immediately and instinctively, only to subsequently delegate to our consciousness the task of legitimising the decision we have already made and producing at least a passably coherent explanation for our actions. Consciousness may also be likened to the officious press secretary of our emotional and instinctual life: assuredly eloquent and astute in every way, but lacking all real influence over the policy decisions that we continuously make emotionally and instinctively.

This means that we are still not measuring up to Sigmund Freud's lofty expectations. And there is precisely nothing to indicate that we will ever do so. At a basic level, we feel and act *religiously*, not least those of us who incessantly allow ourselves to be convinced by our own officious little press secretary. We tie ourselves knots in order to motivate the most absurd positions and actions with common sense. And the overall pattern of all these hastily improvised decisions that require more or less laboured defences is solicitude for the group and its cohesion, as well as one's own position within the group, or in other words, exactly what religion basically is all about and is concerned with. It is, as psychology professor Jonathan Haidt maintains in his book *The Righteous Mind*, impossible to understand the human being – as well as politics and religion – if we do not realise and bear in mind that our ancestors could not have survived and procreated with any success unless they had been extremely adept at belonging to groups. This is what people do and devote their lives to. We are, as Haidt writes, no saints, but sometimes we are really good team players. "Religion is loyalty to the world", as the forefather of syntheism Alfred North Whitehead puts it.

In order to function as good team players, we require a sound ability to assess what our own group believe in and, when the need arises, to defend this belief with convincing quibbling just like a clever little press secretary (and you always convince others far better if you are yourself convinced). To support this ability, we use something psychologists call *motivated reasoning*, which means that you first of all adapt all interpretations of incoming information to the perception you have of what will serve your own interests in general and the group's interests in particular.

These mechanisms have been documented in lots of clinical experiments. We relate to events and statements in accordance with what we experience to be the wishes of group leaders and authorities. As long as it is to the good, we deny facts that are easy to check, and accept evident fallacies without it chafing our intellect too much. We search high and low for reasons to believe in something that appears to confirm what we already believe that we know, and we easily find reasons to dismiss anything that challenges our beliefs.

We all constantly act like believers in our everyday lives. And how could we act otherwise? Even Daniel Dennett himself reasons thus. We are all laymen in all conceivable subject areas that lie outside our own professional fields. We have first-hand knowledge of extremely little of everything that lies at the core of our existence and our societies. Accordingly, we choose our authorities on more or less arbitrary grounds, and we then choose to believe in what they claim without being able to investigate the matter to any extent at all. Dennett uses the formula $e=mc^2$ as an example. Do we believe in it? Many of us have heard about it, and many believe they know it to be accepted by a number of experts within physics, which makes it appear truthful and plausible. But few of us can actually explain in any detail why, because few of us can be said to understand the formula in any reasonable sense of the word "understand". So how can we believe in something we do not understand?

What we do, according to Dennett, is believe that anything asserted about the formula $e=mc^2$ is actually true. But in truth we do not know. And for this reason, it is impossible to attain anything even resembling consensus on, for example, the issue of the climate crisis. What opinion the layman has about it depends largely on what authorities he chooses to believe in, which in turn is governed by his political positions on issues that pertain to economic growth and government regulation, among other things. We believe in what agrees with what we already believe in. *We are religious.* For this reason, the tough atheists' criticism of religion misses the mark completely, however brilliantly formulated it actually may be in lengthy paragraphs. The God one is kicking is already long dead, and to once more joke about the old proofs of God's existence is entirely pointless.

The new, rational human being, freed from superstition and systematic self-delusion by the sciences that are making heroic progress, is a completely unrealistic utopia without any foundation in what research actually tells us about how people really function. We are religious, whether we understand it or not. We believe, and believe that we know much more than we actually do know. And actually it really does not matter at all what content is proclaimed from pulpits or in scripture. The person who enters into a discussion about the apparent self-contradictions or absurdities in a religious doctrine is barking up the wrong tree. Some believe in God X, endowed with certain attributes and preferences, while others believe in something else, which is either called God or something else. What is important and interesting is whether, and in that case how, religion actually works. Trying to understand religion's tenacity and fervour by studying various ideas of God is, writes Jonathan Haidt, like trying to understand the attraction of football games to their audience by studying how the ball moves on the pitch.

Religion has developed through cultural evolution, just like all other social-collective phenomena. Today we can reject a number of features of the content of many religions – it would be strange if it were not so – but we can hardly deny that they have served certain purposes under certain historically determined sets of conditions; and nor can we reasonably deny that they have in fact served these purposes with considerable success; otherwise religions would have perished without leaving many traces. But they did not. Along with psychologists such as Haidt and anthropologists such as Scott Atran and Joe Henrich we argue that the main reason is that this cultural innovation increased the coherence within groups and made them cooperate better internally compared to other groups. This did not necessarily mean that the other groups were outcompeted, but rather that they allowed themselves to be absorbed by the more effective religions.

The crucial point of having a god is that the god is said to reward loyalty and cooperation, while punishing selfishness and mendacity. An all-seeing god is particularly effective in such a context, since people cheat less when they feel that they are being watched. Common sacrifices and collective rites increase coherence, which creates the trust within the group that enables intimate and trusting cooperation outside the circle of family members. According to Haidt with support from Charles Darwin and the French sociologist Emile Durkheim, the main function of religion is that it produces groups whose coherence makes them function like organisms. The biologist David Sloan Wilson writes in his book *Darwin's Cathedral* that religions primarily exist in order for it to be possible for people to accomplish together what they cannot accomplish on their own.

This productive coherence exercises a powerful allure for reasons that we need not address further. We humans are social creatures who experience well-being by doing things together with others, and its contrast – alienation and isolation – is not something on which one can build dynamic and prosperous societies. This in turn means, as Haidt points out, that in the sense of being modern people, enlightened and rational, we can choose to reject organised religion, but even if we do so, we cannot emancipate ourselves just like that from the basic religious psychology that we are concerned with here. However, we can, as stated, always manipulate the terminology and imagine that religion is something other than religion, because we have decided to call it something else, if this makes us feel modern and clear-thinking.

Thus we have actually answered our opening question. God does exist. At least and without a doubt in an ontological sense. We have ourselves created the idea, just as we have created the ideas of democracy and art and a host of others. Religion lives, even among those who believe they have left it. Everything is religion and everyone is a believer. Anyone claiming the opposite, is truly, literally speaking, *blinded by their faith*. The really interesting question which thereby opens up is what to do with God and religion in the Internet age, when all the basic assumptions of our lives and existence are changing. How can God and religion become relevant, credible and engaging concepts for us and for future generations? That is the question which *Syntheism* seeks to answer.

The three dramatic revolutions of the Internet age

The term *religion* stems from Medieval French where it signified the strong and heartfelt sense of community that prevails within a collective, a group of people who make up a congregation through establishing this loyalty to each other. This French term in turn originates from the Latin *re-ligare*: to reconnect with somebody or something, to connect again with those who, for some reason or other, have lost contact with each other but who ought to, and/ or want to, belong together. So if we follow this term back to its source, we find that in its original sense religion ought to be seen as a social practice, organised with the purpose of creating strong and enduring ties between people, an affinity that in some cases, but far from always, also includes affinity between people and a set of gods, a theism.

According to the Austrian monk David Steindl-Rast, religious practice starts with doctrine, which is followed by ethics and finally consummated in ritual – all with the purpose of creating a *social emergence*, to unite people around an entity that they experience as greater than themselves individually, and greater than the sum of the group of individuals. This is definitely something worth bearing in mind: the original point of religion was to create affinity and loyalty within a dynamic collective. In this context, God is no more than the arbitrarily chosen name for the sense of belonging that people seek. Nowhere is this usage of God as a productive object of projection clearer than in the person who has failed in life in his or her own mind and is bravely struggling for self-restitution. When Bill Wilson founds Alcoholics Anonymous in the United States in the 1930s for example, it was with the unshakeable conviction that religion – in whichever form it appears, as long as it preaches a sense of belonging that is greater and mightier than the small, cramped prison, which is how the addict experiences his/her own subjectivity – is the best possible springboard out of alcohol addiction. Religion is *that within us which is greater than ourselves* and for precisely this reason it is closer to our hearts than our fragile little egos.

Note that *philosophy is religion* according to the definition we are now putting forward. It follows from this that religion can also be philosophy. In this context, it is important to understand that reality is not quite as real as we are biologically and socially programmed to believe. While philosophy tries to come as close to the truth as possible in life's chaos of information, religion transforms this information and formulates its own particular truth based on this approximation. When truth is thus regarded as an active endeavour, by definition philosophy should be regarded as truth, while religion is philosophical truth manifested in practice. Syntheology constantly returns to this concept of *truth as an act*. The passion for activism is the very foundation of syntheist ethics.

Philosophy is founded on metaphysics, and metaphysics in turn is founded on theology. However solid the logic in a world view may seem, its logic is nonetheless based on a metaphysical assumption that is a functional but blind *fai-*

th and definitely not any form of *knowing*. Under the primitivism of hunting and gathering, the tribe's presumed primordial father and mother constituted the theological foundation for the collective's *ancestor worship*. Primordial fathers are definitely not just any people at all, since unlike all others they lack parents – accordingly they must be a form of primitive god with extraordinary power. Under feudalism, God took over the role of the metaphysical foundation. God is the common primordial father of all tribes, the primordial father of primordial fathers. In this way, the particular stories of small tribes are bound up with the *universal* stories concerning human beings of larger regions and the forces that wreak havoc in their lifeworld. *Monotheism* is born.

With the Cartesian revolution in the 17th century, the metaphysics of individualism arrived on the scene, with Man gradually replacing God as the theological foundation, even if this revolutionary change was kept hidden as far as possible in order to avoid outbursts of ecclesiastical rage. God is thus not dead to start with; God has only gone to bed and fallen asleep. But ultimately, what role does His potential presence play when His creation is perfect anyway? The main thing for the individualists is that God has become superfluous, which enables the individual to slowly but surely take His place. It soon became evident that *humanism* fitted perfectly as the religion for the new capitalist and industrialist paradigm, and society clung to humanism and its individualist and atomist ideal right up until the late 20th century, when the network society emerged with full force and the idea of *the network* as the new metaphysical foundation caught on. *Syntheism is the metaphysics of the Internet age.* A shift is necessary because the philosophy of every paradigm must have its own blind but nonetheless relevant faith as a basic axiom. The masters of informationalism – the *netocrats* – quite simply perceive the network as the most striking metaphor for the necessary metaphysical foundation of the paradigm.

This requirement of a – conscious or subconscious – underlying metaphysics as a platform for all philosophical argumentation means that all speculation must start from an occasionally declared but at times concealed theological assumption. The two main alternatives that crystallise out from Antiquity and onwards are laid bare in the antagonism that arises between the Greek philosophers Plato and Aristotle, where Plato launches the *dualist tradition,* which prizes cosmos over chaos, the idea over matter, and also foreshadows thinkers such as Paul, Saint Augustine, René Descartes, Immanuel Kant, and among contemporary thinkers Alain Badiou; while Aristotle represents the *monist tradition,* where chaos precedes cosmos and matter is primal in relation to the idea, and foreshadows thinkers such as Baruch Spinoza, Gottfried Wilhelm Leibniz, Friedrich Nietzsche, Alfred North Whitehead, Martin Heidegger and Gilles Deleuze. Dualism postulates that the idea itself is divine and as such separate from the worldly, and thereby secondary, matter; while monism postulates that *the One*, that which binds together everything in the Universe, and within which all difference is comprised of discrete attributes within one and the same substance, is the divine. Of course equivalent conflicts can be found in the history of ideas outside Europe. A clear and illustrative example is the Chinese antagonism between the followers of the dualist Confucius and the monist Lao Tzu.

It is important here to make a distinction between religion and *theism*, that is, faith in the existence of one or more gods. Since most people throughout history have believed that gods in various guises actually exist, it is totally plausible that most of the metaphysical systems that have been developed have also been theist: *monotheistic* systems are based on a faith in only one god, while *polytheistic* systems are based on a faith in many gods coexisting in parallel and more or less peacefully. *Pantheistic* systems, on the other hand, presuppose that the Universe and God in one way or another are one and the same thing, while what we now call *syntheistic* systems assume that all gods are necessary, human constructs; historically determined projections on existence that engender supra-objects that are shaped by and adapted to the social situation.

In addition, there are also many widespread religions that are *atheist*, that is, they devote no energy at all to theist questions. Taoism in China and Jainism in India are well-known examples. Even many forms of Buddhism, such as Zen in Japan and Chan in China, lack a belief in God. Brahmanism in India and Zoroastrianism in Central Asia both lack active deities – while it is true that they are pantheist, they are centred on human rather than divine religious activity, which means that even these religions in practice are atheist. Insofar as God exists, if anything this entity is present through its absence, and accordingly these religions are deist. Note that syntheism is fully compatible with both pantheism (God is created by Man, as a sacralising projection onto the Universe) and atheism (God has not created the world, in all likelihood does not exist today in any philosophically interesting sense, but is fully possible in the future, in particular if the idea is regarded as a human invention).

Beyond the ongoing paradigm shift from capitalism to informationalism (see *The Netocrats*) we need a new *metaphysics*, a *new religion,* a new common arena for collective *spirituality* in the Internet age. Without a credible metaphysics – no philosophy and no meaning either. Man is the meaning-generating animal constantly scanning his environment for patterns that indicate and keep confirming various causative links that engender a feeling of security. And if we do not find any such patterns, we don't hesitate to quite simply invent them. With a utopia on the horizon, we give our lives a direction and a context. God is another name for *utopia,* and utopia is another name for God. The productive and fruitful response to atheism is not to indifferently accept the death of God, but to instead realise that it was a mistake to place God in the past as the ageless progenitor of us and the cosmos. We have already killed the God of the past by producing and accumulating large quantities of knowledge with which this divinity is not compatible. God as a functional utopia is instead the name of what we dream of creating; God is *Syntheos*, the created rather than the creating God. *God is not (any longer) dead, since (we have now realised that) God has never been born: God belongs to us because God belongs to the future, and we already live in the future.* The French philosopher Quentin Meillassoux expresses the syntheist passion in the words: "God is too important a concept to be left in the hands of the religious." Or to quote the American novelist William Gibson: "The future is already here – it's just not very evenly distributed."

Most people take for granted that they themselves and the world they live in exist in exactly the same way that they have learnt to apprehend and reproduce. Even if we humbly admit that we are constantly being forced to correct our ideas of self and the world, we still remain stuck in the feeling of *all of a sudden I have finally realised how everything hangs together.* We tend to regard the present state of our knowledge as final; it is most comfortable that way. Thus we do not need to exhaust ourselves with further counter-intuitive thinking. This default state is best summed up in René Descarte's famous tweet from the 17th century: "I think, therefore I am". Nothing is certain except one thing, thus: I exist because someone has to think the thought that is materialising itself (Descartes presumes that thoughts cannot think themselves). This thinking 'I' cannot exist alone in a vacuum: the phrase "I think, therefore I am" presumes both a sender and a receiver, and just as indisputably there is also a world where this thinking and communicating 'I' is and acts.

Thus, Descartes considers himself to have established an original subject, to which he connects a corresponding object.

With this as an indisputable axiom, he reckons that he can quickly think into existence more and create more subjects and objects. However, a *faith* – a faith by its nature is subjective as well as arbitrary and transient – is not the same thing as a *truth*. A truth is assumed, by definition, to be objectively verifiable, proven by examination and valid for all time. What we are forced to accept, whether we like it or not, is that the foundation of ideas of both the self and the world is always a more or less cohesive faith and never pure knowledge. We believe ourselves to be practising science when the subject observes the Universe. *We know that we are practising religion when the subject experiences that the Universe is peering back at the subject.* But actually, neither the inner subjects nor the outer objects that we believe that we are perceiving, and which we use as building blocks when constructing our image of the world – our paradigm – exist.

The Cartesian subject – which we intuitively perceive as so unproblematic, it is always there waiting for us when we wake up – is in itself a skilfully orchestrated illusion, a kind of cunning fraud of the brain and body (see *The Body Machines*) with the purpose of economising with precious resources and creating an illusory but functional model of life. But in a scientific sense there are only fields, particles, energies and relationships. The belief systems that we construct and utilise in order to be able to navigate at all a life that is constantly becoming increasingly complex are, if anything, historically determined narratives whose *memetic* survival is considerably more concerned with actual relevance, the attractiveness of the narrative and social arbitrariness than with any objective degree of truth in the dogmata themselves, to the extent that anything of this kind is even possible to document. Man is the animal that is constantly on the lookout for meaning, and in the absence of results creates for himself *patterns* in an overwhelming flow of information, *fictives* that will, as far as possible, elucidate the causative links of existence. And the meaning that we succeed in producing in one way or another, we ascribe mentally and socially to *the great Other*, the guarantor and ultimate originator of meaning, fully in line with the Cartesian view of thinking and the thinker who must exist since the thought exists.

Our subconscious is constantly driven by the idea that there is someone else out there in an inaccessible dimension outside our physical universe who sees and knows all and senses the meaning of all the toil and pain we go through in our short lives. This also applies to the most entrenched atheists. Even if the atheist's consciousness does not believe in *the great Other,* his or her subconscious refuses to accept that this great Other does not exist. Even in the most die-hard atheist, little thoughts and behaviours constantly float up to a conscious level in daily life; thoughts and behaviours that remind us that *the real,* the subconscious depth under the conscious surface, will never accept the absence of the great Other. Psychoanalyst Jacques Lacan calls all of these sudden, revealing outbursts *sinthomes.* The sinthome is quite simply the event or behaviour that does not fit with the individual's current fantasy of his or her ideas of self and the world. Thus, the sinthome is also the event or the behaviour around which the human being is forced to construct new, altered ideas of self and the world when the old fantasies collapse. The sinthome is the deepest truth about oneself that a human being can be aware of.

God is just one of the infinite number of conceivable forms of revelation of *the great Other* throughout history. The primordial father, the chieftain, the feudal lord, the priest, the monarch, the saint, the president, the boss, the manager, even the subject's own parents, are all examples of figures who, through history, people have fantasised about as being the great Other. And even if the most die-hard atheists actually succeed in eliminating all these figures from their fantasy worlds, there is still a great Other that they never succeed in fleeing from: the fantasy of themselves (the subject) as the object of their own submission. The phenomenon of *the great Other* is thus an integral and extremely important part of the experience of being a subject. The father of psychoanalysis, Sigmund Freud, takes this thesis to its ultimate conclusion. He argues that the ego, constantly in terror, experiences the superego as *the great Other par excellence.*

We humans are not only powerfully attracted to *anthropocentrism*: a slightly grotesque tendency to constantly exaggerate our own position, power and importance in the Universe; a grandiose overestimation of ourselves that we have grappled with, without respite, throughout history. Unfortunately, the problem is even more serious than this. Our personal *individuation* – as individuals, our demarcation from the social flock – is namely actually dependent on a process that we term *internarcissism:* it is through constantly seeking validation of our own identity with other people, other beings of our own species – who accordingly find themselves in exactly the same existential dilemma as ourselves – that for a fleeting moment we can experience ourselves as happily liberated from our narcissistic prison, the pathological self-centeredness that is our constant companion.

This incessantly and obsessively repetitive self-validation process is mostly an empty ritual and really only hides our narcissism behind a kind of collective Potemkin village of no real substance. We simply replace conscious narcissism with an every bit as unfounded, subconscious internarcissism. Simply put: two people who no longer have the energy to worship themselves, instead worship each other for each other through mutual, pathological back-scratching. This means that, subconsciously rather than consciously, we are still as frustrated as before. This situation engenders a constantly growing inability to see things clearly – "Why does everything just get and feel worse even though I'm doing everything right?" – which leads to a burdensome, stupefying alienation. And there we are. What the contemporary secularised person finds it hard to see for obvious reasons is that religion, according to its syntheological definition, is the effective and necessary remedy for this alienation. Only through religion can we undergo a *dividuation* and acquire a liberating dividual rather than an imprisoned individual identity. A human being is not a solid indivisible entity. A human being is many divisible entities collaborating with each other.

The philosophical discipline that deals with, compiles, compares and makes us aware of our existential stories is *metaphysics*: the branch of philosophy concerning our pictures of ourselves and of the world which are fundamental to our personalities and the collective. To be a metaphysician is to formulate and articulate the largely unarticulated ideas of the self and the world and thereafter propose changes in these that render them more relevant and productive for the agent in question. If physics deals with everything that can be measured and transformed into mathematics, metaphysics is preoccupied with precisely all the important things that *cannot* be measured nor transformed into mathematics. Metaphysics thus comprises everything within ontology, phenomenology and epistemology which cannot be converted into numbers.

History shows that people cannot live without metaphysical explanatory models. Therefore, human history is predominantly a history of metaphysics. The existential experience is in itself metaphysical. At the same time as we experience ourselves as something *emergent*, something more than the molecules in our bodies; as something inside, over and above, or beyond the physical body; we have removed ourselves and our experience as subjects from the world of physiology to the world of metaphysics. All human beings and societies constantly produce enormous amounts of metaphysics. The question is not whether metaphysics has any place in our lives or not, but rather whether the metaphysics in question is relevant or irrelevant for the conditions that prevail in the society in question. There is every reason to fear a considerable lag, particularly when the rapid development of technology is driving social change at a hectic pace. And so the question is: Is the generally embraced metaphysics capable of reflecting the current paradigm? Does it provide people with the requisite instruments to take charge of their own lives, or does it leave people helpless by rendering them incapable of creating comprehensible causative links and credible meaning?

Because there is in fact considerable power attached to controlling the production of metaphysics. Whoever exercises a decisive influence over the former will also sooner or later be able to control the society in question in important respects. Therefore, it is especially important to investigate whether metaphysics is conscious or only subconscious. What metaphysics succeeds in communicating subconsciously is in fact the most powerful thing of all. Metaphysics is fundamentally a narrative of who has, or rather ought to have, the power in any given society and why. The figure who is emphasised in the metaphysical narrative, who according to the narrative brings together the world into a comprehensible cosmos rather than a threatening chaos in order to the benefit of all the others, is also the person who is entrusted with the real power by the narrative's devotees in any given society – the person who is assigned the role as *the great Other*.

To a considerable extent, metaphysics is in fact the story of power and of who is to exercise it. We can see how this fact applies to the troika of the monarch, the aristocrat and the priest under the feudal paradigm, and it is repeated in the same way for the troika of the politician, the entrepreneur and the university professor under the capitalist paradigm. When all is said and done, metaphysics will always be about power, and it will always use the prevailing symbolic, economic and truth-producing power in these three main roles in the paradigm's narratives. Because the storytellers work in the service of the prevailing holders of power, their prime task is to depict the prevailing holders of power in a glorified light, to incorporate them into a tailor-made story and thus treat the prevailing power structure as if it were the most natural thing in the world. The storytellers incorporate all of this adeptly, at every possible turn, into *the collective subconscious* for the greatest possible effect. There is a considerable measure of circular argumentation in this scheme of things, but this only makes it even more impenetrable. Only the most eccentric deviants doubt the latent *ideology* of a social order, which by definition is inaccessible to rational criticism since it is built into the very perspective through which a society contemplates its history and development.

Because of this dramatic efficacy, metaphysical storytelling is not random, but of the highest priority for those in power. It can only be consigned to the person who is best suited to be the truth producer of the prevailing paradigm and who thereby also has the strongest incentive to preserve the *status quo*. Responsibility for metaphysics falls to either an already powerful institution in the society, such as the Church in relation to the monarchy and the aristocracy under feudalism. Otherwise a new institutional elite is constructed to formulate the new, emerging paradigm's conception of the world – naturally at the expense of the old paradigm – such as when the universities expanded and acquired enormous power under capitalism, because the university formulated the *individualism* and the *atomism* that the bourgeoisie used in order to sweep away the Churches' monotheist explanatory models and to take power from the aristocracy. Without popes we would never have seen any kings, and without university professors the world would never have beheld any industrialists either. The cardinals dined on pheasant with the nobility, and the academics eat steak with the entrepreneurs for good reason. They divide up and balance *the power* in the prevailing paradigm between themselves.
It is important to have clear this fundamental understanding of the historical terms of the production of metaphysics when we are confronted by the fact that no less than *three dramatic re-*

volutions exploded concurrently at the start of the third millennium. These three interactive and synergistic revolutions are the Internetisation of planet Earth, the relationalist revolution that is moving from physics to philosophy, and the chemical liberation within physiology. Taken together, these three epoch-making developments laid the foundation for a new superparadigm in the history of humanity. Power structures, the world view and the view of humanity were radically and fundamentally changed all at once in one of the most dramatic social upheavals humanity has ever seen.

In only a few decades, the revolution in communication technology has connected billions of people and the innumerable machines around them with each other, globally and in real time. The world was digitised, globalised, virtualised and became interactive. The inadequacy and unfitness of the Cartesian individual as a basic concept in the new cyber world has resulted in the individual dying – summarily dismissed by neurophysiology and research into consciousness (see *The Body Machines*) – and being replaced by *the network* as the fundamental metaphysical idea. The human being is transformed from an individual chained to his or her narcissistic ego to an open and mobile *dividual* in an all-encompassing, gigantic network that is acting more and more like a single *emergent phenomenon*, like a single, global, coherent *agent*. We call this agent, with its historically speaking divine proportions and characteristics, *the Internet*.

Since syntheism is the metaphysics that, so to speak, is already built into interactive technologies, it has already invented itself. The Internet has gone from being a *virtual god* to becoming plainly a potential god, all in accordance with the radically new meaning that Quentin Meillassoux gives the concept of God, as something belonging to the future rather than the past. *Syntheism is the religion that the Internet created.* The dedicated political struggle for a free and open Internet is based on the blind faith that the network has a *sacred potential* for humanity. The Internet is thereby transformed from a technological into a *theological phenomenon.* The Internet is the God of the new age, and furthermore extremely appropriate for an age characterised by an unlimited faith in the possibilities of *creativity.* Thus, the Internet is a god that even those who regard themselves as atheists can devote themselves to. Syntheologically, we express this state of affairs as that the *Internet is a manifestation of Syntheos,* the new god that we humans are creating rather than the old god which, according to our ancestors, is said to have created us once upon a time in a distant past.

Without utopias, idea-wise we can cling to all and sundry types of cynical and/or pragmatic ideologies, from socialism on the left via liberalism in the middle to conservatism on the right. But when the syntheist utopia emerges as the new metaphysical axiom, all the ideological work must be redone from scratch. With the *theologisation* of the Internet follows a necessary repudiation of all other previous political ideologies with direct links to the abandoned paradigm, in favour of *theological anarchism.* First of all, this is the only ideology that is compatible with the belief that another better world can be born of itself, appearing as a suddenly emergent phenomenon in history. It is moreover the only ideology that can *accumulate a creative resistance* vis-à-vis a society so complex that no one can take it all in any longer. This is because theological anarchism does not require the omnipotent overview nor the political and moral control of human expression that all other ideologies have had as a fundamental condition. It is the syntheist utopia's predecessor in the present and is driven by *enjoyment of the multiplicity of expression.*

Theological anarchism is described exhaustively by the British philosopher Simon Critchley in his book *The Faith of The Faithless,* and it is of course completely synonymous with syntheism. And syntheism maintains that, precisely because everything of value is transient, unique, finite and mortal, it seeks *existentiality* and *intensity*. Thus, syntheism is the religion of immanence and multiple finitudes, and the radical opposite of the Abrahamic religions' worship – contemptuous of reality – of another transcendental world and singular eternity. For how could anything at all enjoy its existence and be maximised in its existence, if it were not simultaneously aware of its own finality and limitation in the physical realm?

The burgeoning netocracy, the elite that is succeeding the bourgeoisie in the new paradigm being driven by digitisation and interactivity, obviously represented a special interest group when it initially marketed the *anarcho-libertarian ideology* as the metaphysics of the Internet age. If *truth is an act*, and if truth will set us free, it follows that *if the Internet is allowed to be free, it will also set us free.* There is here of course an ill-concealed intention to use noble motives as a pretext for the seizure of power. The netocracy is thus acting in exactly the same way that the feudal aristocracy did when it embraced monotheism, and in the same way as the capitalist bourgeoisie did when it embraced humanism. These specific metaphysics developed as the dominant stories – and they worked! – during their respective paradigms, for the very reason that they appointed the emerging social classes as the social theatre's new protagonists.

The Internet is – like so many previous technological revolutions – an attractive surface on which to project every kind of fantasy and variant of wishful thinking. For the capitalist, the Internet is the dream of prodigious profits. But in reality the Internet is more of a virtual slaughterhouse for masses of dreamed-up cash cows and pseudo-monopolies. In fact, the Internet has a tendency to destroy old corporate colossi, at least initially, rather than to further new business models. The result is clear from reading the business press: old market leaders perish in no time, and the turnover period of the biggest listed corporations is tremendously short. For the narcissistic individualist, the Internet is the dream of finally getting the big breakthrough, the dream of finally being seen and appreciated by a broad audience. But when all actors attempt to take the stage at the same time – and no one is sitting in the auditorium any more – the effect becomes the opposite: the audience disappears. When everyone wants to be a sender there are no longer any receivers. What we call the My Space syndrome – after a well-known example that should be a lesson for all – occurs: the individualist's dream of a permanent, successful performance in front of a complete, receptive world inevitably comes crashing down once and for all. Everyone's frenetic babbling over the top of everyone else kills the experience.

The disappointment is not even about the audience not wanting to see individualist X or Y *per se*. Rather, it is about individualism as such having become vulgar and boring and that no one wants to see any individual at all any longer. To the extent that there is any audience at all for anything at all in the old media, preferences are firmly oriented towards sundry variants of ironic freak show. This is the anxiety-relieving evening and weekend entertainment of consumtarians made passive (see *The Netocrats*) The truth is that only a small minority, the *netocracy*, understand and have mastered the Internet and can utilise the medium to their own advantage. This is in spite of the fact that almost the entire population of the world are already living their lives in the new social arena. In his book *Average Is Over* the American economist Tyler Cowen estimates that approximately 15 per cent of the American population will succeed in the transition to netocrats in a productive interaction with the Internet and the torrents of newly automated processes in society, while the remaining 85 per cent of the population will establish themselves as just a *consumtariat*, the fast-growing underclass in a social, cultural and also increasingly economic sense.

In 2013 statistics were made public revealing that the gaps in the socio-economic classes in the Unites States had returned to the same levels as in 1917. An entire century of energetic political attempts to level out class differences with egalitarian taxation, allowances and educational measures had come to nothing. Even in other parts of the world, these gaps are widening, and regrettably there is nothing either to suggest that they will decrease once the full power of the Internet revolution comes into effect. And then we have not even touched on the even more dramatic social and cultural class differences that are being created in the *attentionalist* society that is replacing the capitalist society online (see *The Netocrats*). Only a handful of Twitter users have access to hundreds of thousands of followers, but they are sitting on the *netocratic megaphone*, they really have *attentionalist power*. Meanwhile the great mass of people are pseudo-babbling on Twitter straight out into the void without any of the people in power caring at all. This goes on until they tire and, having given up, are forced to accept their powerlessness and total lack of influence in their capacity as faceless biomass in the great, vegetating consumtariat.

If there is anything we can say with certainty, it is that *alienation* in the new network society will increase dramatically. A growing alienation is the price we pay for every increase in the technological and social complexity that we are experiencing now and for years to come. With the Internet's breakthrough, it is literally exploding. And there is only one functional weapon against alienation, namely its opposite: *religion*. Traditional religion's mistake was to place the name of its longing for another world, *God*, in the past (*theism*, belief in a preordained God), when the logically correct and only reasonable manoeuvre of course is to place the object of all human longing, God, in the future (*syntheism*, the belief in a God that man himself creates).

The atheism that denies longing – between theism and syntheism – has played out its role as the necessary antipole between thesis and synthesis. For in its lack of content, and as pure negation, atheism is completely meaningless as the goal of the dialectical process. This acute lack of essence explains why atheists have never succeeded in building any cathedrals or anything at all except vapid paper monuments to their own excellence. It is like a philosophical temperance movement: you meet and are sober together, totally oblivious of the ecstatic party that is going on somewhere else entirely. Classical atheism can only say what it is not, but not *what it de facto is*. This purely negative and in essence substance-less doctrine is quite simply a worthless weapon against alienation. It consoles no one and explains nothing.

It is hardly tone-deaf atheism that inspires us most. Rather it is Spinoza's pantheism that is philosophically consummated through a further development of *syntheism*. God is no longer only the final *idealisation* of Spinoza's pantheism, *God as the subject of the Universe;* rather, God acts as humanly produced idealisations even on other planes, among which the *Internet as a theological realisation* is a typical example in our time. If divinities both can and should be created through idealisations necessary for survival – why then, like Spinoza, settle for *Pantheos*, the Universe, as the only god? In particular since the Internet actually has its own agenda, controls us rather than lets us control it and, to put it bluntly, is beginning to assume divine proportions. Moreover, there is a long list of idealisations available to *the syntheologists* to develop into divinities in order to then make themselves into their memetic host organisms and preachers and thereby contribute to their dissemination. In this book, we are concerned with the four most basic idealisations from the world of metaphysics: the void, the Universe, the difference and the utopia.

The conflict over the metaphysics behind physics – clearly illustrated in Albert Einstein's and Niels Bohr's passionate correspondence from the mid-1930s – finally gets its resolution through *experimental metaphysics,* also called *the second quantum revolution*; a long list of complicated scientific experiments from the 1980s onwards, the results of which have had dramatic consequences for metaphysics. The results of this development strengthen Bohr's position considerably in the above-mentioned conflict, which is why both Newtonian and Einsteinian metaphysics with their requirements of timeless, universal laws seem increasingly passé. Bohr's *indeterministic relationalism* overshadows Einstein's *deterministic relativism.* The constant of physics is time, not space. Time is not an illusory dimension of space, but highly real. Mathematics does not precede the Universe: mathematics is never anything more than an idealised approximation in hindsight of constantly dynamic Nature, an arbitrary and anthropocentric *eternalisation* of a genuinely mobilist reality (see *The Global Empire*).

This results in *agential realism* defeating *atomist individualism* as the foundation of metaphysics. The network is not only a useful metaphor for understanding social relationships; the Universe is basically one large physical network in itself, where all *phenomena,* beside the fact that they themselves constitute constantly higher complexities of constantly lower sublevels, are universally entangled with each other. *The entanglements* are thus the fundamental, not the illusory, objects. Nothing occurs independently of something else. The result is a physics and a universe of fields, probabilities, energies and relationships, without any preordained laws or discrete objects. Thus all support for Kant's fantasy of *the holy object* localised in a law-bound, determinist universe disappears. Kant, Newton and Einstein: all of them now appear to have been left behind. Time is real and the future is open and totally controllable.

Nothing ever happens twice, since every moment is completely unique and the relationships that surround a phenomenon at a specific moment are constantly in a state of flux, and they will not either ever reappear in the same configuration again. In the enmity within philosophy that has existed between mobilists and totalists ever since disciples of the mobilist Heraclitus clashed with the totalist Plato's adherents in Ancient Greece in the 5th century BC, it is now Heraclitus' successors who appear to be our contemporaries. The results from experimental metaphysics that are based on the ideas of Niels Bohr indisputably place themselves on the side of mobilist relationalism. Plato's world of ideas is nowhere to be found outside of his own neurotic fantasies. Thus the universal laws that Kant, Newton and Einstein presume to be primary in relation to the Universe's physical existence do not exist either. In reality, habits that resemble laws arise in and with the Universe and physics. There is quite simply no mysterious set of rules built into physics before its genesis, since no external prehistoric builder of such laws exists.

As if this revolutionary advance were not enough, Bohrian quantum physics also shows that the Universe is *an existential necessity*: some kind of non-existence has never been an alternative. Regardless of whether a universe within a multiverse is born out of a virtual fluctuation, or, for example, out of a black hole, it nevertheless always arises sooner or later in quantum physics' *active void*. Similar but never identical events then occur again and again. A perfectly balanced Universe in terms of energy can expand indefinitely as long as the positive energy from its matter is counterbalanced by exactly the same amount of negative energy from gravity, as is precisely the case in our 93 billion light-years wide universe. There is simply no lack of basic resources within physics, in contrast to the limited assets that constantly constitute the framework for all activity on planet Earth, which is in every respect limited.

In relationalist physics, the existence of the Universe is far more than a possibility, it is in fact a *necessity*. And with this necessity there is no longer any other metaphysical alternative than pantheism. The existence of the Universe is not an external by-product, *it is de facto internal inside and comes from the essence of the Universe*. The Universe exhibits a will to exist that emerges from out of the very foundation of physics. This means that the Universe has a clear existential substance, however bizarre and alien this highly non-human will to exist may seem. The Universe definitely has no consciousness in the way that we humans have, or even anything that we could speak of as any kind of cosmic equivalent to human consciousness. The Universe needs no awareness, but it *is* definitively something and it *does* many different things. For the simple reason that nothing else would be physically possible.

Accordingly, the entire basis of classical atheism disappears. Existence is no mistake. The existence of existence is wondrous in its *indeterminist necessity* rather than in any kind of supposed determinist randomness. A non-existence in the sense of a balance without energies – the only non-existence that physics can even contemplate – is the only really bizarre and impossible probability in this context. Everything in the Universe, including its seemingly enormous void, is boiling with a constant, intense, virtual activity. Its imagined non-existence is, like its (at some time in the future anticipated) cessation, nothing other than anthropocentric fantasies with a metaphorical origin in mankind's own intrusive thoughts around our own mortality and impermanence. However, this human mortality has in fact nothing at all to do with the world of physics.

The *will to exist* is not only a by-product of human eagerness to survive, funnily enough it is the Universe's own *raison d'etre* in relation to itself. Just as much as mankind, the Universe is a product of Darwinian evolution, where continuing and expanding existence constantly accrues to the phenomenon that happens to be best adapted to the current situation, while competing phenomena disappear. This means that the Internet age's syntheistic metaphysics focuses on *survival* and not on *immortality*. Syntheism entails a worship of this intensity and of indeterminist existence rather than a death worship and determinist illusion. The Platonic cult of death, from the ancient Greeks via Christianity to Newton's and Einstein's fixed, atomist world views, loses all its credibility.

Totalist thinking cannot deflect attacks from the mobilist alternative, its constantly questioning shadow, where Leibniz's time-bound and open world view defeats Kant's timeless and closed world view. Pragmatism triumphs over idealism. The law loses its overwhelming, metaphorical power. Laws are created by humans in order to control otherwise chaotic societies, in order to impose power from above and benefit social masochism at the expense of creative freedom. But in nature there have never been any preordained laws. The regularity that science finds in nature is nothing other than similarities within the framework for the preordained conditions between different processes. But there are no preordained *laws that nature must subject itself to* in the same way that slaves are expected to yield to their masters. There is nothing timeless and predetermined outside our contingent and open universe. *The law* has exercised a magical power over people's world views ever since it arose in a theology that was functional at the dawn of civilisations, but it now stands exposed as an empty myth.

The sexual revolution under capitalism was followed by *the chemical liberation* during informationalism (see *The Global Empire*). The development of a post-atheist religiosity, which is built around the need for a new metaphysics, spurred on by globally collaborative, syncretist and religio-social practices, and not least by the exploding plethora of entheogenic substances, laid the foundation for a resolution of the conflict between *theism* and *atheism* which, in a Hegelian dialectics, has grown into *syntheism* as the metaphysics of the Internet age. This occurred at the same time as the sexual revolution was rejected when its unavoidable flip side, the *hypersexualisation* of the individual, was exposed as the underlying engine of capitalist consumption society; the sexual revolution ended up being a *straitjacket of the superego* where the chemical liberation offered a possible way out.

This does not mean that we lose free sexuality to some kind of renaissance of asceticism and abstinence. We merely gain access to the sacred tools that enable us to start taming and mastering it to our long-term advantage. Indirect *desire* can thereby finally gain control over the directly instinctual *drive*. What Slavoj Zizek calls late capitalism's moral imperative, the superego's command *to enjoy*, is converted into its opposite: attentionalism's imperative to *confront the meta-desire on its own terms*. Syntheism's entire driving force is its offer of a kind of sanctuary and protection against capitalist and consumptive stress, its utopic vision of a new and radically different way of thinking and *continuing to exist*.

The netocratic *dividual* uses the enormous offering of new chemicals to constantly change his/her many personalities. This occurs in part as a late-capitalist adaptation strategy vis-à-vis the demands and expectations of one's environment, and in part also as a subversive netocratic and revolutionary tactic to overthrow capitalism's limited *status quo*. When the chemicals set the classical, genetic constants of intelligence, gender and sexual orientation in motion, the foundation of the stale *myth of the sober individual* (see *The Body Machines*) is demolished, and is therefore forced into a final hyperphase as an increasing *consumtarian underclass phenomenon* (see *The Netocrats*). The consumtarian therefore strives right to the very end to constantly try to improve him/herself, to invoke an allegedly genuine and underlying *I-essence*, accompanied by tabloid culture's demands for consumption-generating frustration with the self. Career choice, gym sessions, fashion diets, partner hunting: all these are flagrant examples of vulgar hyperindividualism. On the other hand, the netocrat has long stopped believing in the coherent *individual,* and instead cultivates hundreds of different personalities within his/her new ideal *dividual* (see *The Body Machines*), often invoked and expedited by carefully designed chemical cocktails.

The modernist social structure was aggressively questioned in the 20th century, first by the Frankfurt School and later by post-structuralism, and collapsed under both external and internal pressure. A philosophical renaissance was begun by thinkers such as Gilles Deleuze, Michel Foucault, Jacques Derrida, Manuel De Landa, Thomas Metzinger and Karen Barad with *The Death of Man* as a starting point – which can be compared with how 18th century philosophers launched the project *The Death of God* – and with this development a fundamental shift from the anthropocentric to *the universocentric world view* was initiated, which is being realised by the post-structuralists' heirs in the 3rd millennium, with empirical support from *experimental metaphysics.*

The syntheistic mission receives its eschatological fuel from the approaching *ecological apocalypse*, which in itself is an unavoidable consequence of a world without faith in a relevant divinity. Only through a new syntheistic meta-narrative, constructed on the utopian conviction that humanity's only possible salvation is through its creation of Syntheos, can the ecological apocalypse be avoided. It is not possible to preserve human life on the planet with any amount of politics. For politics is subservient to the capitalist death drive – there is no chance of becoming a leading politician without first becoming dependent on the statist-corporativistic power structure – which does its utmost to grind on relentlessly with its ruthless plundering of resources until the planet is uninhabitable and lifeless. The planet can only be saved for continued human life with the aid of *a new religion*, a metaphysics driven by a utopia concerning a physically functional future for our children and their children.

The French philosopher Alain Badiou divides metaphysics into four disciplines, from which the human being produces the meaning of her existence. These four activities are *politics, love, science* and *art*. Metaphysics binds these four disciplines together into a cohesive conception of the world. From the point of view of syntheology, religion then emerges as *metaphysics in practice* and is therefore reflected in the prevailing ideals of the four activities. Religion is thus *the execution of the paradigm's metaphysical truth*, and syntheology is constructed in an intimate interaction with religious practice as the theoretical foundation for other types of ideology production. According to Badiou, it is symptomatic of our meaning-depleted, hyperindividualist existence that precisely the timeless ideals that ought to represent the four disciplines have been set aside by the collective death drive, which is riding us humans in an evermore hysterical hunt for absolutely nothing.

Badiou maintains for example that politics should be driven by *revolution* as an ideal, but instead it is driven nowadays by a kind of administrative micromanagement; politics has become entirely a matter of *management*. Love should be driven by *passion* as an ideal, but is instead driven by *sexuality*. Science ought to be driven by *invention* as an ideal, but is instead driven by *technology*. Art ought to be driven by *creation* as an ideal, but is instead driven by *culture*. All of these dislocations expose *the hypercynical Zeitgeist*, which moreover has the ironic audacity to dress itself up as non-ideological. The only way to expose this dense, destructive ideology-building and to overcome its concomitant hypercynicism is to patiently offer a new *syntheological metaphysics* which can be the inspiration for a new *syntheist religion*. There are no other credible ways out of our cultural deadlock.

Religion can be summed up as various practices carried out by people in search of meaning in their lives. This is so, no matter whether the religion in question takes that meaning as preordained, as something revealed, or as something that is to be sought and created within the framework of religion. Building a credible religion is primarily about long-term thinking and enormous patience. It is the only intellectual discourse that does not allow itself to become the object of *tendentiousness*. Religion can never be a fashion. Regardless of whether religion is theist, atheist or syntheist, it is of the utmost importance that it is kept separate from *the secular*. Politics goes deeper than markets, but religion goes deeper than politics. *And theology invariably rests deep down underneath philosophy.*

The problem with humanism is that it is basically Christianity without Christ. Humanism is an attempt to keep Christian moralism alive, while it pretends that there is no need for Christ in order to maintain this desired conception of the world. Simply put, the humanist tries to keep the illusion of the *individual* – there are only human bodies, there are no individuals other than in the humanist's fantasies – alive in the same way that the Church tried to keep the illusion of God alive during the previous paradigm shift. This is never clearer than within Communism with its atheist Christianity, with its blind faith in the human being's own mystically predetermined realisation of the Christian paradise. Without underlying religious conviction, a theological foundation, Communism is an impossibility; it lacks the engine that can engage the activists. Therefore it continually decays into corruption and hypocritical dreams of a capitalist feast of consumption.

That the consummation of humanism as the socialist project lacks a firm footing in a post-atheist world is the theme driving both Slavoj Zizek's *Less Than Nothing* and Simon Critchley's *The Faith of The Faithless* as well as Quentin Meillassoux's *L'inexistence divine*. The way forward for Zizek, Critchley and Meillassoux therefore is a return to theology; certainly not back to Abrahamic theology, but to theology in its deepest form, as philosophical metaphysics. The problem for Zizek is that his return does not go deeper than to the Enlightenment's romanticised idea of the bloody revolution as deliverance for everything. However, in contrast to Zizek, Critchley seeks to return to the origin of religion and finds there a *mystical anarchism* in constant opposition to the patriarchal, ecclesiastical power hierarchies.

According to Critchley, mystical anarchism is the true engine starter for the genuinely revolutionary project. Critchley's mystical anarchism is of course synonymous with the syntheism we are talking about and advocating in this book. The already established syntheist Meillassoux sees in his distinction between *the potential* and *the virtual* the possibility for an *event* where God suddenly appears in history as the metaphysical *justice*, where justice arrives with the same importance as *existence*, *life* and *thought*, the previous virtualities that have been shockingly and dramatically realised through history. Meillassoux argues that God as justice is the missing fourth virtuality that is now waiting to be realised. Syntheologically we express this as a focus on the oscillating axis between Entheos and Syntheos in *the syntheological pyramid*.

Since it is Kant's philosophical contributions that pave the way for the death of humanism and the individual, it is scarcely wrong to regard Kant as *the last humanist*. When Hegel and Nietzsche arrived on the scene in the 19th century, the anti-humanist revolution was already in full swing. With Nietzsche and his concept of *The Death of God* – which Michel Foucault half a century later finally accomplishes by also proclaiming *The Death of Man* – nothing whatsoever remains any longer of the humanist paradigm. Hegel's religiosity is found in *Atheos* while we place Nietzsche's spirituality with *Entheos* in the syntheological pyramid.

After Hegel's and Nietzsche's revolution, *rationalism*, blind faith in man's ability to solve all the mysteries of life through his reasoning, had to be replaced by *transrationalism*, a rationality that realises its own limitations as an intersubjective discourse within the phenomenology that mankind is reduced to (see *The Global Empire*). For rationalism is based on a logical 'optical' illusion: within itself rationality is consistent and looks convincing. However, the problem is that when rationality is viewed from outside, it falls down completely since *it is not founded on anything that in itself is rational*, it is based only on blind faith and nothing else. Kant's problem is that he wanted to place *rationality* above reason, but he never succeeded in stating logically how this would be possible. Kantian rationalism is thus not founded on anything other than Kant's own highly personal, autistic temperament. Blaise Pascal argues for a *transrationalist epistemology* as early as the 17th century, long before Kant, but it was not until the American and European pragmatists at the end of the 19th and the early 20th century that transrationalism acquired its formulation in detail.

Bodies are real. And reason defeats rationality, since reason is based on the body while rationality lacks a foundation outside its own tautological loops. No thoughts exist separate from the body. Every thought is drenched in and impossible to distinguish from the chemicals and hormones that at the time in question are infesting the body in which the thought is being thought and where the words are being articulated. Reason is represented by a highly real, active *actor*, while rationality is represented only by a highly illusory, passive observer. This insight reduces the *individual*, Descarte's and Kant's transcendental subject, to the object of its own dominance and colonisation. The result is the chain of psychotic reactions that are fundamental to the Cartesian subject.

The discrepancy between the observer and the actor leads to *paralysis*. This paralysis is experienced by the subject as *impotence*. This impotence is in turn transformed into a forceful reaction of denial to its opposite: omnipotence. And the omnipotence triggers a whole host of compensatory fixations and behaviours in order to keep *the Cartesian subject's fundamental lie* alive. It was no coincidence that Kant's followers in 19th century Europe embarked on colonisation campaigns around the world. And who is the clearest Kantian, the most devoted individual, if not Napoleon, the organisational forefather of modernist society? *What you cannot find within yourself as an individual, you attempt with compensatory zeal to find out in the world instead*, even if the entire world ends up in flames because of your futile search.

For this reason, syntheism necessarily arrives after humanism. Syntheism is the logical response to the crisis of humanism. Man cannot replace God, since man is every bit as much of an illusion as God ever was. The protosyntheist Martin Heidegger and his follower Jacques Derrida wrestle in their work with metaphysics as an idea and claim to be working for the death of all metaphysics. However, they end up instead becoming *metaphysicists par excellence*, proponents of precisely what we call *the eternally postponed end of metaphysics*. The more forcefully you try to flee from metaphysics, the more deeply entangled you become in its yarn. So what syntheism does is that it places *God, Man* and *the network* next to each other and says: we know that these illusions have never existed in any physical sense. Nonetheless we have learned pragmatically from history that we cannot live without them. A life without *the great Other* is both a phenomenological and psychological impossibility. These entities are essential for a world view to be coherent. The consequence is that we choose to include the three black holes – God, Man and the network – concurrently in our new world view, as the black holes they actually are, that is, as *culturally productive voids*.

The dependence of bodies on each other is real. We know that dopamine, serotonin and oxytocin hold people together in a collective that accords pleasure to those in the group, and in this pleasure a meaning arises, produced by and for ourselves. Therefore we have arrived at the historical juncture when theism and atheism must be consummated as dialectical opposites, not through some kind of hybrid, but through us seeing and accepting their *historically consummated interconnection as a unit* and being able to push this unit aside and go forth in history, into syntheism. Today's fusion between our historical understanding of the fact that when all is said and done our cohesiveness is what is most holy to us, and the exploding, genuinely new virtual connection between people thanks to the arrival of the Internet, interacts with and is creating the foundation for the new era's syntheist metaphysics. *God* (theism) and *Man* (atheism) are quite simply followed by *the network* (syntheism) as the fundamental event of metaphysics.

The question is what is possible. Lacan makes a distinction between *alienation* and *separation*. Alienation is the experience of a dramatic distance between ourselves and the society in which we live. The society is no longer experienced as our own. We do not belong in our own time. Separation means that the crisis is deepened further: now there is not just a dramatic distance between ourselves and our contemporary society, but *society itself has cracked open*, it no longer appears cohesive, not even to itself. When separation gets the upper hand, the paradigm crumbles. We must withdraw in order to try to construe a new paradigm. First and foremost we must create a world view that is cohesive in a credible manner. The separation that has occurred opens the way for the possibility of attacking the preceding alienation: Why should we settle for piecing together a new world view when we have the chance of placing ourselves and the class we belong to at the centre of the new world view, now that we are initiating the revolution that is changing the world view by questioning and shifting its very foundations anyway?

It is of the utmost importance here to distinguish between *living religion* and *dead religion*. Quite irrespective of whether a metaphysical explanatory model is in any way true, or just merely functional and relevant for its own time, it is either living or dead in its practice. The modern human being is under the impression that previous generations really *believed*. The myth of the classical faith is incredibly tenacious, not least as a backdrop to the myth of the modern human being's *non-faith*. The Austrian, syntheist philosopher Robert Pfaller shows in his book *Illusionen der Anderen* that this is a double falsification of history. It is the modern human being who really believes, and this, in contrast to previous generations, *without any distance whatsoever*. Therefore, it is only in modern society that *fundamentalism* is possible. Religious fundamentalism is based on the conviction that *God is dead,* that God is active only in the past, which is why the fundamentalist must act without God's help and so to speak force life back to the time when God was still alive. Syntheism's response to fundamentalism is of course as brilliant as it is self-evident; it instead runs in the opposite direction, towards the God and the religion that has never existed, but which we only now are able to create. You could not get further away from religious fundamentalism than syntheism.

The four paradigms in the history of metaphysics

Since information technology is the most important instrument of power in existence, it is both productive and in every respect correct – particularly in connection with the transition to an informationalist paradigm – to divide the history of humanity into four, distinct information technology paradigms. So forget the Stone Age, the Bronze Age, the Iron Age and the other mythological constructions of industrialism, produced for precisely the purpose of writing history so that it culminates in the smoking factories of industrialism. Let us instead regard all societies in all forms and stages of development as various kinds of information societies, and let us view history as a story of the battle for power over the means of communication. Because whoever controls the channels for communicating truth and ideas also can be said to own and dictate the truth and the ideas.

The pattern which emerges in *the information technology writing of history* tells how spoken language, written language, the printing press, and the Internet have each created the foundations for their paradigm, and that these technologies, once they have had time to have an impact and play all their cards, have formed social structures that differ in important respects from what the world has shown before (see *The Netocrats*). We distinguish the four paradigms from each other by the sudden, revolutionary shifts between the different systems for information processing and different forms of communication that have occurred throughout history, and which have resulted every time in dramatically altered living conditions, power structures, social models, world views and what constitutes the human ideal.

For each and every one of these four information technology complexes has increased the quantity of information available in a given society to a revolutionary extent, which in turn has created entirely new social hierarchies with entirely new parameters for metaphysics and its assumptions and consequences. A pervasive social change means exactly this: not more of the old, but a qualitatively tangible change of an emergent nature. The old feudal Europe plus the printing press meant, after this epoch-making technology had been operating for long enough, not the same old Europe plus an interesting machine, but a completely new Europe that gave birth to industrialism, parliamentarism and the colonisation of the rest of the world. These new metaphysical narratives in turn radically changed both the world view and the human ideal, and thereby the entire power structure.

For reasons that we have detailed extensively in *The Netocrats*, these four information technology paradigm shifts should be regarded as the genuine revolutions that have driven history; created by the radically increasing amount of information available and the unique impact of their accompanying metaphors. The seemingly dramatic events that follow on from these paradigm shifts ought rather to be viewed as symptoms of the underlying, genuine revolution, which has its basis in radically changed material conditions and thereby also dramatically changed power structures. For what would capitalism be, for example, without the printing press as a metatechnology and without the *watch* (timepiece) as a metaphor? It is impossible to imagine the factories of industrialism and all the other capitalist institutions that emerged during the powerful expansion of capitalism in the 19th century without their armies of literate office workers and without the clock on the factory wall and the fob watches in the factory managers' waistcoat pockets that divided the working day up into clearly delimited and measurable units.

Ideas of revolt and other seemingly sudden and dramatic changes are merely secondary by-products that followed on from these changing material conditions, rather than some kind of *originating event*. For example, the French Revolution of 1789 cannot be viewed as a genuine revolution *per se*, but rather as a *symptom* of an underlying genuine revolution, namely the printing press, which was invented in Germany just over 300 years earlier. The printing press set in motion a gigantic feedback loop by making books cheap and generally available, thus creating a mass audience for texts, which in turn paved the way for an explosive production and consumption of knowledge and abstract ideas. Thanks to France being the first country in Europe with widespread literacy – and also with an increasingly urbanised economy – the French Revolution became the first *event* of its kind and, as stated, in many respects is exemplary in political mythology. It constitutes the first sudden, dramatic evidence of the reality of the printing press revolution, and thereby in hindsight a clear dividing line between the feudalist and capitalist paradigms, often referred to as the new era's *emergent moment*. But let us for the sake of clarity keep these revolutions separate from their symptoms.

The French historian Fernand Braudel quite correctly describes *the art of writing* as the definitive technology. Both the *Enlightenment* and the *Reformation* were built on the printing press revolution; they both rest heavily on words and text, which had of course suddenly became available in cheap, mass circulation. The cost of producing a single book fell from tens of thousands of pounds to just a pound or so per copy, converted into today's money value. Thus the Enlightenment and the Reformation exploited the advantages of the printing press to such an extent that *they transform words and text per se into metaphysics*. The book, the newspaper and the banknote as well as the later electronic, one-directional printing press derivatives for communicating, namely radio and television, acquire a fetishistic status under capitalism.

The Enlightenment constructs a new humanist mythology in opposition to Feudalism's monotheism – with *the individual* as the bourgeoisie's substitute for the aristocracy's *God* – while the Reformation constitutes religion's backlash against the Enlightenment's criticism of religion. Here, the hybrid between the God of feudalism and the new individual emerges when the Protestant theologians position *the suddenly established direct dialogue between God and the individual* at the centre of metaphysics. The Reformation quite simply recasts God as the perfect bourgeois individual, the atomistic God, *Jesus*. These consequences – fatal for the Catholic Church – of the printing press putting cheap, mass-produced, vernacular editions of the Bible into the hands of the people, were probably not something that Gutenberg, a pious Catholic, could reasonably have conceived of, which once again underlines that every dominant metatechnology plays out its hand regardless of any intentions of its inventor and other serious stakeholders. The Internet is going to do the same.

Paradigm shifts entail dramatic conflicts, since for obvious reasons the prevailing power structure strives to preserve the *status quo* at any price for the purpose of defending its own privileges against the new, burgeoning elite. Therefore, with both violence and moralising nostalgia, the old power structure tries to keep the society fixed in the old paradigm for as long as humanly possible. That somebody voluntarily gives up the advantages bestowed on them by virtue of their class is a rare occurrence indeed. But the ice floe in the rapids on which civilisation to date has been standing eventually becomes so small that civilisation must migrate to another ice floe. With this sooner or later inevitable jump, the power structure and its writing of history changes radically, because everything must be hastily adapted to the new conditions for survival that are linked to and built into the new ice floe. Therefore it is always the new and not the old rulers – those who have most to gain and absolutely nothing to lose from the altered prioritisations within the new metaphysics – who are the fastest to change ice floes and adapt to the new rules for survival. The new metaphysics forces the pace, and the leap between the ice floes thus accelerates the rate of the shift of power between the elites of the two paradigms.

Every paradigm is accompanied by its own narrative, its own production of truth, circling around an essential starting point for its metaphysics. Each and every one of these narratives in turn contains three components: a *cosmology*, a *romance* and a linear *history* of the formative events in the past of the new paradigm, determined after the fact. As Hegel points out, these components are characterised throughout *metahistory* by an underlying requirement of *necessity*. What is metahistorically radically new in the case of *syntheism* – the metaphysics of the Internet age – is that it is based on *contingency* rather than necessity as its principle. Syntheism is indeterministic, not deterministic.

The information technology metahistory began with the tribe's oral camp fire stories about itself in the spoken word society (*mythos*). Thereafter followed the painstakingly documented story of God's fate and adventures in the written word society (*logos*), which in turn was followed by the printed story of the idolised human being in the mass media society (*ethos*). The corresponding transition in our time means that we now gather around the narrative – spread at lightning speed – of the holy network in the Internet society (*pathos*). The paradigm shifts are supremely material; the suddenly increased quantities of available information enable a powerful expansion of complexity and specialisation in human relations. Simultaneously, the new forms and extent of communication in our society are dictating a radical qualitative change in the conditions of the cultural ecosystem. This results in the older paradigm collapsing, and with it also its outmoded narrative and power structure. The old story must be replaced by a new, more credible *metanarrative*, which contains and popularises the allegories and metaphors that are relevant for the new paradigm. Above all, the new history must reflect the new power structure and its assumptions, or else it will not achieve acceptance or be spread.

The new power structure is strengthened by a new metaphysical narrative and vice versa. In this way, history repeats itself at every information technology paradigm shift. The tribe's story is the foundation of *paganism* and its primitivist power structure. The story of God's creation and control of the world forms the foundation of *monotheism* and the feudal power structure. The story of the genesis and perfection of Man as a rational being is the foundation of *individualism* and the capitalist power structure, while the story of how networks give content and meaning to everything in existence forms the foundation for *syntheism* and the informationalist power structure. Paganism uses *survival* as a metaphysical engine, while monotheism's metaphysical engine is *eternity* and that of individualism is *progress*. Syntheism's metaphysical engine is *the event* (see *The Global Empire*).

Primitivism is the first paradigm; it is based on the revolutionising emergence of spoken language and is characterised by nomadism, hunting, fishing and gathering. Primitivist metaphysics is based on reverence for one's ancestors and respect for the tribe's oldest members, since these are the collective's most reliable and resource-rich knowledge bank, and thus also the key to *survival*, the engine of primitivist metaphysics. The narrative of nomadism revolves around the concept of history as circular with the regular return of the seasons as its dominant symbol. Existence is not linear, has no direction, time instead runs in recurring cycles; there is no development, everything is instead repeated *ad infinitum*. To be a human being is to be a member of a tribe, and within the limits of the tribe's structures, to take responsibility for ensuring that this perpetual repetition is maintained. Strangers constitute competitors for the tribe's resources, wherefore one either flees from them or beats them to death when one happens upon them. The human being who does not belong to the tribe is therefore not a human being at all, but an animal that can basically be treated as nonchalantly or brutally as one pleases.

Feudalism is the second paradigm, which starts from the emergence of written language and is characterised by permanent settlements, land ownership, agriculture and the domestication of livestock. Society's focus lies on the domestication of animals and plants and a low-intensity class struggle between the aristocrats and the peasants. Written language was invented and started to develop as early as more than 5,000 years ago by the Sumerians in Mesopotamia, after which it arose in three other places (Egypt, the Indus Valley and China) roughly simultaneously and independently of each another. But it exploded in use over the entire Eurasian landmass during the period that the German philosopher Karl Jaspers calls the *Axial Age* (*Achsenzeit* in German) between 800 and 200 B.C. The Chinese, Indian, Iranian, Mesopotamian, Egyptian and Greek cultures flourished during the Axial Age, since for the first time it became possible to build empires (an order from the administrative centre of the empire could be expected to arrive un-garbled and be implemented as intended out in the provinces), and it was at this time the world was also blessed with the first formalised world religions – for example Zoroastrianism, Brahmanism, Buddhism, Jainism, Taoism and Judaism – and the first documented philosophy. It might be added that additional advanced civilisations in for example Italy, Ethiopia and Peru developed soon thereafter.

Written language, which by this point in time was technically very advanced, was quickly disseminated across the Eurasian landmass. It soon proved to be an extremely efficient instrument of power in the form of keeping accounts and spreading propaganda for its – at least initially – few users and their masters. This is never clearer than when its most important product becomes widely accepted: the magical *law*. In conjunction with the arrival of the law, a metaphysics was produced in which all forms of social mobility were presented as an anarchical threat to the cohesion of the society, a danger that must be combated. For example, Zoroaster devotes half of his holy scripture *Gathas* – which was authored orally in Central Asia as early as 1700 BC, to be written down only many generations later – to praising enterprising settlers and condemning irresponsible nomads.

Feudal metaphysics achieved the intended effects by preaching totalism and dualism to enable the unimpeded formulation of *eternal truths* as the foundation for the law. Steadfastness and obedience are everything, there is no room left for openness or questioning of the prevailing order of any kind. The state is presented as founder, upholder and guarantor of the holy law and all the good values that it claims to represent, in the same way that monotheist religion preaches that God is founder, upholder and guarantor of existence as a whole. Paul is therefore quite right when he builds his Christian theology on the premise that *the law is the manifesto of the death drive*, an assertion of the death drive with the aim of restricting and economising with the intensity of life. This becomes all the more clear when the metaphysical ideal of feudalism, *the law-abiding citizen*, is asserted as a personification of the death drive itself.

What is brilliant about the law is that it is based on a clear representation of the divine. Although it pays homage to God – to pay homage to someone who anyway never interferes with anything costs nothing, and it is therefore also the oldest metaphysical trick in the book – but what is important is to whom the law pays homage, but that it is based on something physically absent so that, with the homage as camouflage, it can furtively hand over the actual power to the (self-appointed) *representative* of the object of homage. The monarch who is present therefore becomes the representative on Earth of the absent god (with ancient Egypt's *pharaoh* as the most flagrant example). To obey the monarch is thus in practice to obey God, which must be seen as a powerful incentive. Power thereby ends up with the monarch and his allies, the landed *aristocracy* and their common truth producer, *the monotheistic religion*. The feudal paradigm's triangle of power is thus complete. The monarch, the aristocrat and the High Priest can sit down to an expensive and well-prepared dinner in peace and quiet together and in complete understanding share the power and the glory between themselves.

The law's external and eternal values are pitted against the internal and arbitrary values of chaos. And the idea follows on from the principle, which says that the values of metaphysics must be external and eternal in order for the narrative to hang together, that mankind must be offered the possibility of *becoming one with the law*, that mankind should be able to become external and eternal in relation to the internal, mental limitation and physiological transience that she/he experiences existentially every day of the week. The idea of *eternal life as the reward for the law-abiding citizen* for his/her demonstrated fidelity and reliability throughout life is born, and with this essential prerequisite in place, monotheistic metaphysics, which revolves around the idea of eternity, arrives with full force. Previously every tribe had had its own mythological progenitor, but with monotheism all tribes – since they have begun to trade and communicate with each other whenever this can be more profitable than, each according to his abilities, killing each other – get one and the same progenitor, *God*. Hinduism in India keeps its local subordinate deities and Catholicism in Europe cultivates its saint myths, but all feudal metaphysics is based on a solid monotheistic foundation where *God is the personification of the law*. It turns out to be a metaphysical necessity in order for feudal society to be able to maintain its cohesiveness and endure over time.

Capitalism is the third paradigm in the information technology writing of history. It emanates from the multifarious offshoot effects of the printing press and is characterised by the mass media, urbanisation, capital accumulation, mass education, industrialisation, globalisation and a class struggle between the bourgeoisie and the workers. The Reformation expresses the definitive *deification* of the printed word. With this deification, monotheism's blind faith in the possibilities of *the manifestation* is replaced by individualism's blind faith in the potential of the *proclamation*. Capitalism is the golden age of the printed and mass-distributed ideologies. And since new proclamations can be constructed on top of old proclamations – when yesterday's objectives in the factory have been attained, they are replaced by today's new and loftier objectives for tomorrow –a metaphysics evolves out of the magic of the proclamation around *progress* as an idea. Similar to the way in which eternity is portrayed in monotheistic metaphysics, progress is portrayed in individualist metaphysics – regardless of whether it concerns liberalism's evolving, individual person, or socialism's five-year plan, collective society – as *the manifestation of the indivisible*, as something external and eternal in relation to all of life's obvious transience.

When the Enlightenment eliminates God as the cohesive factor for metaphysics – either, as the deists do, by anaesthetising Him, or as the *atheists* do, by killing Him off – the focus is shifted onto *the individual*, the idea of Man himself as *the existential atom* and the very cornerstone of existence and the social model. Thus, metaphysics no longer allows any angels who come to prophets to hand down the truth, which is already perfectly formulated by God, from God to Man. Man must instead construct his own metaphysics, and Man reckons that this is best done by deriving *the truth* directly from his/her own lifeworld, by basing a world view on empirical facts and defending it with logical arguments. However, this ambition requires in itself an unfounded and illogical faith in Man's innate ability to take in and understand all of life with his limited intellect and imperfect access to information. This blind faith is *rationalism* – the irrational core of individualist metaphysics that gives the individual divine qualities. The individual is made into a being that suddenly grasps, comprehends and has mastered absolutely everything in her own wishful thinking.

This blind faith becomes irresistible when the capitalist paradigm's eponymous engine, that is, *capital*, is set in motion after the breakthrough of the banknote press in the 17th century. With the arrival of capital, for the first time in history *the symbol* becomes even more important than what it claims to represent. And with this *representationalism*, this worship of the symbol, follows social homogeneity as the norm. It is a fact that the search for homogeneity dominates the entire capitalist paradigm. An example of this is that it becomes near-impossible to maintain *neurodiversity* – the rich flora of various personality types developed under millions of years of nomadic tribal life that *de facto* distinguishes humanity biologically – as an ideal once capitalism becomes generally accepted. From the late 18th century, neurodiversity is scorned by all available means, and instead a steady stream of *pathological diagnoses* is produced, based solely on suddenly realised, presumed dysfunctional relationships to capitalism's constantly shifting production ideal.

Everything that deviates from capitalism's two human ideals – different forms of the capitalist himself as master and different forms of the factory worker as slave – is branded as an expression of psychological disease that must be remedied or, in the worst case, eliminated altogether from the social body (with Nazism's and Stalinism's mass purges during the 20th century as an entirely logical consequence of this reasoning). This is because capitalism's industries not only necessitate demands for a constantly increasing level of education among the general public, but also the medical treatment of a steady stream of newly created psychopathologies as a normatively necessary practice. In their study *Dialectic of Enlightenment* Max Horkheimer and Theodor Adorno show how this constantly growing production of pathology ultimately degenerates into skull measuring and the race theories of the Nazis and the Fascists in the 20th century. Fascism and Nazism are, according to Horkheimer and Adorno, quite simply rationalism taken to its ultimate conclusion. With blind faith as a foundation, one can place on top of it any logic at all; sooner or later the result will always be socially (self-)destructive madness.

According to Kant and his followers, *rationalism* is a necessary linchpin in individualist mythology. Individualism requires blind faith in Man's own thinking – given time and necessity – being able to understand and solve all the world's riddles and problems. While rationalism does accept that the individual is not omnipotent today, for the individual is evidently a mortal being, but with the individual's *omnipotence* – since she actually is a latent god – according to rationalism, the solution to the problem can only be a matter of time. From the early 19th century onwards, individualist metaphysics becomes as conveniently as it is effectively self-fulfilling: individualism is proclaimed from the universities, and at the same universities, professors and researchers are also organised as *individuals*, encased in increasingly specialised subject area *atoms*, where they devote their days to quoting one another within closed coteries under the pretext that they are engaging in some sort of objectively true knowledge production. And as long as one stays within the mythology of individualist metaphysics – and why wouldn't you, if you are part of the elite that reap the full rewards of it – it is hard to see the individualised human being in relation to the atomised world in any other way. The external signals that interfere with the generally held mythology are of course immediately removed by the system itself.

It is only when the *Internet* arrives with full force towards the late 1980s and early 1990s that society is endowed with an environment where *holism* and *generalism* are fostered at the expense of the academic world's *atomism* and *specialism*. It is also only after the advent of the Internet that criticism of the individualist axiom begins to grow. The new paradigm with its new power structures requires a new mythology; a new narrative of *the developing information, communication and network society in the Internet age.* The informationalist paradigm is characterised by *interactivity* as the dominant form of communication, *the cyber world* as the geographical arena, *attention* rather than capital as the driving force socially, as well as the production, consumption and above all social reproduction of *media* as the main occupation (we have written about all of this extensively in *The Netocrats*). Informationalism is driven by *the event* as its metaphysical horizon, and is dominated by the conflict between the new classes, the small but wholly dominant *netocracy* and the considerably larger but in every respect subordinate *consumtariat.*

If we have learnt anything from history, there is no reason to believe that the academic world will be relevant as a producer of truth in the developing network society to any greater extent than the clergy of the monotheistic religions were as producers of truth for the industrial society. Which is another way of saying that universities are a thing of the past in all other respects than when it comes to pure networking: at best, one learns to run projects and come into contact with attentionally valuable people during one's student years. On the other hand, truth production is automated, and itself becomes a network effect. Under informationalism, it is quite sufficient to use collectively generated and freely available sources of knowledge on the web (such as Wikipedia) in order not to have to consult academic experts if one wishes to formulate a socially acceptable truth. Nowadays, it is the Internet that is the arbiter (for better or worse). The universities' power over truth production peaked as early as the mid-20th century in the same way that the power of the Church over truth production peaked as early as the 15th century. With the advent of informationalism, newer and more creative institutions take over. Through the increasingly marked independence of physical geography, the syntheistic monastery can act as the central agent for truth production in the Internet society in both the physical and the virtual world.

According to the information technology writing of history, the capitalist and industrialist paradigm was enabled by the arrival of the printing press in the mid-15th century. The publication of books and newspapers in Europe gradually increases and at an ever-increasing pace, an increasing number of readers entail an increasing number of authors, and vice versa; and from the 17th century onwards the banknote presses also start running. The new paradigm then becomes widely accepted during the 18th century, which is clearly manifested by the French Revolution, for example, which was initiated by the storming of the Bastille in 1789. The streets of Paris filled with the burgeoning bourgeois class, which was united in its newly-acquired literacy, its books, newspapers and banknote presses, and in its hatred of the old feudal paradigm's aristocratic superiority. An entirely new power structure – consisting of the politicians, the bourgeoisie and the universities – emerged and took over, while the old power troika – consisting of the monarchy, the aristocracy and the Church – was caught off guard to the extent that it never succeeded in recovering again. The social conditions that had brought the old troika to power quite simply no longer prevailed, and consequently monarchy, aristocracy and Church were reduced to museum exhibits: curiosities from a nostalgically glowing past, robbed of all power and all influence and relegated to a growing capitalist tourist industry, which exploits them with considerable success.

The capitalist and industrialist paradigm was taken to a whole new level when *Napoleon's army* tore across Europe in the early 19th century. No one personifies the World Spirit (in German: *der Weltgeist*) – which Hegel seeks in his magnum opus *Phenomenology of Spirit* (1807) – with the same force and clarity as the ruthless Napoleon, who the year before had plundered and ravaged Hegel's own home town of Jena in eastern Germany. Napoleon's army becomes the emblem of the literally murderously effective and finely honed organisations constructed by the literate masses – compartmentalised into productive hierarchies, where both responsibility and authority are extremely clearly defined – with the capacity to receive and pass on written instructions on an industrial scale and over distances that had previously been overwhelming. Soldiers and factory workers who can read and write are quite simply dramatically much more effective at carrying out their orders than illiterates. Not just because they can assimilate and relay information and knowledge in a totally new way, but also because they can express and clarify their own situations and teach it to others much better within the system at hand. This escalates the accumulation of information and knowledge dramatically.

By building a maximally functional hierarchy of literate soldiers – even the cannon-fodder at the front lines were educated before waging war in Napoleon's army – with himself in the function as God's all-seeing eye at the very top of the hierarchy, Napoleon created a fascinating killing machine of a kind never beheld before. Subsequently, all the institutions of industrialism were built in the 19th century with Napoleon's army as a shining example:

the nation state and all its bureaucrats, the company and its factories, the police, the prison, the school, the hospital, the colony on the other side of the ocean: organisationally they are all direct copies of Napoleon's feared and admired army. According to Isaac Newton, the father of classical physics, *history* is a kind of perfect machine that grinds away in a completely deterministic manner without the smallest departure from preordained laws and rules. Newton's idea of the Universe as a (by God) wound-up clock that ticks on forever inspired both Napoleon's *organisational architecture* and Hegel's *historicism*.

It does not take long before the history of humanity is rewritten. If the purpose of being human is *to one day build a factory full of obedient worker soldiers*, history must be the story of a long line of increasingly sophisticated domestications of various physical (and initially unwieldy) materials. Consequently the concepts – with time highly successful – of the Stone Age, the Bronze Age and the Iron Age are invented once industrialism becomes widely accepted in the 19th century. These are manufactured by historians financed by the industrialists, that is, precisely the gentlemen who have created and assumed the leading positions within the new era's nation states and big corporations. Thus, the old feudalist writing of history, from Adam's and Eve's trouble with the talkative serpent in Paradise and onwards, can be tossed onto the mythological rubbish heap. The Abrahamic religions are reduced from highly esteemed knowledge to an entertaining fairy tale for the not so bright and for young children.

René Descartes opened the way to individualism by penning the 17th century's most famous tweet: *I think, therefore I am.* But what consummates individualism's metaphysics is Immanuel Kant's transcendentalism a century later. By isolating *the subject* from *the object*, Kant makes it possible for the subject to both deify the object and simultaneously plan for its material and sexualised seduction, conquest and colonisation. History repeats itself: God created the world in order to be able to deify and then seduce, conquer and colonise it. Now it is the 18th century's growing bourgeois middle class of patriarchal Enlightenment philosophers, scientists, industrialists, capitalists and colonists that see and grab the opportunity when *the new individualist and atomist metaphysics* lends support to their ambitions. Bourgeois ambitions are quite crassly transformed into *the individualist ideal.*

By adhering to *a correlationist narrative* around the subject's and the object's absolute isolation and delimitation, both from each other and from the surrounding world, the bourgeoisie succeeds in building an attractive identification with the subject, and the fantasy connected thereto of the conquest of the object as the perfection of history. Note that the subject is an individual and that the object is an atom: which are isolated, delimited, indivisible entities. Thus is individualism born, and with it also *capitalist patriarchy.* The individualist and atomist ideology is on fertile ground among the new elite, which it validates, and it rapidly becomes axiomatic and remains so right up until the arrival of the Internet age in the late 20th century. This is because *individualism* and its running-mate *atomism* are both tailor-made to promote the burgeoning bourgeoisie's interests and hegemonic aspirations.

Kant is unarguably the prophet of individualism *par excellence.* His individual is a tragic solipsist who – precisely because of her solipsism – is free to act as a ruthless egoist. Kant's radical subjectivism – with its emphasis on free will, dominance, abstract inner experiences and strict, soldier ethics – is built around *the subject's transcendental separation from the object,* which means that the object can be deified undisturbed, to be later conquered, colonised and plundered. Individualism is a master ideology. The individual has taken over God's place as the only thing that is certain in life according to Descartes' basic tenet *I think, therefore I am,* which Kant later develops to perfection. *Humanism* and *representation-*

alism grow rapidly out of and presuppose individualism and atomism as metaphysical axioms. Through its *prioritisation of the representation over the represented*, representationalism suits exploding capitalism right down to the ground. With its actively observing subject and passively observed object – this object merely exists because the subject must have something to relate to – representationalism is a sublime expression of *capitalist ideology*. Society is based on strong, active, expanding subjects. Around them flock weak, passive, delimited objects, pining for the subject's gaze and attention. These objects are to be hunted, conquered, tamed, exploited and finally discarded before the entire process is repeated with ever-new objects as targets.

Representationalism is not just the perfect narrative for colonialism, slavery and the rampant, ruthless exploitation of natural resources; it also comprises the necessary foundation for the narrative of *patriarchal sexuality* with the man as the active subject and the woman as the passive object. That women in this narrative are put on a par with exploited mines and colonised continents should therefore come as no surprise. Nor is it particularly surprising either that representationalism limits human sexuality to a power-hungry and validation-thirsty man hunting for a passive female body, who in turn longs for and is begging for the man's gaze, and who demands nothing more than to submit to the man and please him. The racist perspective from Europe vis-à-vis the aboriginal peoples of Asia, Africa, the Americas and Australia functions according to precisely the same pattern. Consequently, 19th century public discourse is permeated by a set of bizarre axioms that can claim things like Africans cannot learn to read and write and women lack a sex drive; these delusions and propaganda lies are all consequences of the same twisted, ideological basic premise. This representationalism finally becomes an aggressive hyper-condition in the form of the 20th century's fascism with the worship of the one leader as the perfect individual (Benito Mussolini as *Il Duce*, Adolf Hitler as *Der Führer*, and so on).

There is, however, an object that the patriarchal gaze can never get enough of; an object that constantly evades the observer's vain attempts at conquest, colonisation and plundering, and that is the object which finally gives its name to the entire paradigm in question, namely *capital*. Since capital constantly shuns patriarchal lust – no individual can ever be rich enough; somewhere there is always more money to be made, bigger profits to extract, increased growth to produce for anyone who simply gets a grip and refuses to be idle – individualism is strengthened by a tremendously potent metaphysical engine: *progress*.

Through the essential but subtle shift from the Cartesian subject focus to the Newtonian object fixation in Kant's transcendentalism, individualism is extended into capitalism. And with the march of capitalism across the world, there also followed the markedly superstitious belief in *the invisible hand* as an eternal guarantor of never-ending growth. Exactly how naive this notion really is has now dawned on thinking people across the world as the crises-ridden nation states, one after another, drift away towards the precipice while impotent politicians and bureaucrats sit in fruitless meetings dreaming of a dramatic increase in growth that never eventuates. The Western welfare state, which is based on precisely such institutionalised wishful thinking about strong and continuous growth, is looking more and more like a cynical pyramid scheme. Future generations are welcomed with gigantic debts and badly eroded benefits. Not to mention the escalating environmental problems that arise as a result of capitalism's intemperate, ruthless exploitation of the planet.

Capitalism's genius lies primarily in its constant postponement of the reward, not just for the bourgeoisie's sadistic patriarchy, but also for the working class's masochistic submission. Progress promises reward for today's toil only for future generations. *Your children will be better off than you are.* But it is also in the nature of capitalism to constantly borrow from the future only to subsequently destroy the real value behind the capital in conjunction with the repeated and dramatic crises that are unavoidable; crises that capitalism's supporters constantly, and without any provision for doing so whatsoever, promise to cure as soon as the business cycle starts to soar again towards the heavens, something which one deludes oneself is fated to be. The system offers hopes that cannot be fulfilled, and if, contrary to expectations these are fulfilled, the reward must be packaged as pure luck. This desire-driven fantasy keeps the big capitalist middle class firmly in place. The perfect example is of course *the American dream*; the fantasy of being richly rewarded through obedience and industry with living the care-free middle class life that you can see on television, which is cultivated by and thrives among the potentially socially mobile everywhere capitalism has penetrated.

The university is individualism's truth producer and this institution's most important role is to moderate enjoyment among citizens. However, it continuously fails in its task, since enjoyment is only maximised in *transgression*, and transgression presupposes a host of prohibitions against crossing the boundaries for the taboos that the Church was much more adept at producing than the university. In this context, the university is reduced to the paltry imperative of identifying and subsequently maximising the individual's enjoyment. Therefore, individualism's complicated relationship with enjoyment is characterised by a fundamental *envy of religion*. In the 20th century, individualism was developed by the universities into *cultural relativism*, Kantianism's ideological waste dump and its logical endpoint, where all that remains are unfounded solipsistic credos, the quality of which, because of a growing political hypersensitivity, it is forbidden to compare. This qualifies cultural relativism as syntheism's ideological arch-enemy at the paradigm shift from capitalism to informationalism.

With the advent of informationalism, a freedom arises to organise the rapidly-growing, expanding social networks in accordance with the long-neglected desires of our genes. The optimal size of a tribe of nomads or the newly-established, permanent settlement of around 150 adult members as a genetically determined ideal resurfaces constantly as the ideal size for these virtual networks. When this ideal can be reproduced without costly opposition over and over again from the advent of the network society and onwards, what musician Brian Eno calls *technological primitivism* arises, a kind of high-tech return to the primitivist tribe community. The virtual subcultures on the Internet replace the Church's and nation's identity-bearing functions from the previous paradigms (see *The Netocrats*). The Internet is a digital jungle filled with dividual-driven subcultures in vast quantities.

Informationalism's view of mankind can crassly be described as a mobile phone surrounded by fat and muscle. The paradigm shift is rapid; as early as December 2012 traffic on Google's search engine to the *attentionalist* left-hand column – which one cannot buy into but instead must deserve one's prominent placement in by *maximizing one's attention*, that is, making oneself interesting and attractive to the Internet's users – passed 99% for the first time, while traffic to the *capitalist* right-hand column dipped below 1%. This fact confirms that traditional marketing is an impossibility on the Internet; there is quite simply no such thing as functional *online marketing*. Increasingly desperate mass media marketing is pitted against increasingly smarter online communication, which understands and uses the new *participatory dynamics* evolving on the Web.

Syntheism can be described as one long showdown with all the ideologies that are based on *the historical case*. Religion and metaphysics were developed under feudalism from being a cohesive and community-generating world view into becoming a well-honed tool for power and control. The monotheistic religions demand submission; the word is suddenly an order rather than a promise. Sin is basically a revolt against God, a questioning of the divine arbitrariness that is the very foundation of the Abrahamic religions. In practice, the Asian religions accomplish the same thing through making sinful behaviour function as the driver for *desperate reincarnation* rather than invoking *hellish damnation*. However syntheism in no way entails a return to paganism, but instead a dialectical further development. The real return to paganism at the paradigm shift from capitalism to informationalism is instead the bewildering hodgepodge of naive ideas and quasi-religious nonsense that go under the label *New Age*, the phenomenon that, not without reason, syntheologians dismiss as *theological cultural relativism*.

Syntheism however makes use of paganism's community-building properties and its pantheistic search for an existentially transcendental experience. It forms an emotionally engaged relationship with the Universe. Syntheism ought to be compared to *art* instead, which under late capitalism – after previously having investigated everything else in life – was partly reduced to an investigation of itself, a metaphenomenon. Ultimately, art is merely about *pure reflexivity*. Likewise, syntheism is the end of religion's historical voyage where, after having investigated everything else in life and having sought the sacred everywhere except in itself, religion finally finds its home. Syntheism, too, is also an expression of a pure reflexivity. Syntheism is the metareligion, the religion of the philosophers, the religion about and of *religion per se*.

Syntheos is the personification of the world, which gives it its value. Through this value, the dividual and the interactive subcultures get their values. Without a value for the world, the dividual and the interactive subcultures cannot have any values either. Syntheism borrows its fundamental value from the fact that *there is something rather than nothing*, as Martin Heidegger expresses it, and that this something rather than nothing is the basis of life. Syntheism is based on maintaining and maximising the *dynamics* of existence. The place in time–space where dynamics is maximised is called *the event*, and this event is syntheism's metaphysical engine. It takes place all the time and at all levels in the syntheist, indeterminist world view. Every moment in time and every point in space accommodates an enormous number of potential events. Indeterminism also means that no effect is reducible solely to the causes that engender it; the effect might very well be a uniquely situation-dependent *excess* in relation to its causes. We express this as the Universe generating a steady stream of *emergences*.

If history is viewed as a Hegelian dialectics, we see a clear pattern: monotheism is the thesis, individualism is the antithesis and syntheism is the synthesis. That syntheism is the synthesis in this dialectical process is a consequence of the fact that theism and atheism can never meet; they are fundamentally and definitionally incompatible. Syntheism should absolutely not be understood as a compromise between theism and atheism – in Hegelian dialectics, a synthesis is something considerably more sophisticated than just a banal coalescence of thesis and antithesis – rather, it is a necessary continuation of *theism's and atheism's combined dichotomy*, the only possible way out of the paralysing deadlock that arises when theism and atheism are pitted against each other. As the logical synthesis of this pair of opposites (theism versus atheism), syntheism offers a possibility for the atheist to go further and uncompromisingly *deepen atheism*. Thus, in a historical sense syntheism is a radicalised atheist ideology. It is even atheism's logical deepening and elaboration.

Just like all epoch-making ideas, syntheism arrives in history right when philosophy has run aground between a *traditionalism* (in this case theism) and a *cynicism* (in this case atheism). Only through perfecting the individualist paradigm can mankind grasp its terrible consequences, and then, and only then, the door to the syntheist possibility swings open. It is only syntheism that can liberate atheism from its logical curse: its inheritance from theism's negative attitude towards immanent life. Only by going from atheism to syntheism can we open the way for a genuinely sensual and thereby also spiritual understanding of the immanence. Atheism robs the human being of her access to the holy and the divine by first sharing theism's conviction that the holy and the divine must be synonymous with the transcendental, and then murdering the transcendental and thus reducing the human being to a cold and indifferent immanence, which is axiomatic for atheism. What syntheism does is that *it picks up mankind in precisely the immanence where atheism has abandoned him* and makes him *apprehend the immanent as the truly holy and divine* without any nostalgic longing for transcendentalism at all. Through syntheism's deepening of the very premises of atheism, *atheist cynicism* becomes *syntheist affirmation*.

French philosopher Quentin Meillassoux analyses classical atheism's dilemma in his book *Après la finitude*. According to Meillassoux, atheism's problem is that it inherits the tragic remains that are the leftovers from Abrahamic religion when it retires, but does not succeed in building any independent platform of its own. That is, classical atheism retains the Abrahamic idea of the world as destroyed and lost, but without preserving Abrahamism's faith and hope in the possibility and reality of the *utopia*. It is literally just an *a-theism*, a negation without any own content of its own. Classical atheism quite simply bases its world view on a false premise, namely the idea that existence without God must be *mere chance*, when life is in fact a *necessity* if we fully think through physics' basic concept of *contingency*.

Meillassoux argues that the only possible way out of classical atheism's deadlock is to embrace syntheism's idea of a philosophical and immanent divinity rather than a theological and transcendental one in the traditional sense. He advocates the thesis that the constant contingency that characterises existence must be regarded as the logical opening for a possible future God based on the idea of *justice* instead of the idea of *amorality*. Meillassoux's syntheist divinity – he calls his philosophy a *divinology* rather than a theology – lacks the Abrahamic God's bond to the amoral chaos that the logic of moralism demands. Meillassoux thus treats traditional religion's passions in a way that radically differs from classical atheism: *it is the utopia and not the fall of Man in classical religion that must be won back.* And winning back the utopia and turning it into *an immanent divinity* is, with contemporary physics' revolutionary advances, quite plausible. Meillassoux's *God, as a synonym for the utopia*, is of course syntheism's *Syntheos*.

By thinking of God as something created rather than something creating, and thereby as something that only shows itself in the future rather then something that precedes and brings forth existence – that is, Syntheos, the created God – for the first time God can be regarded as internal and not external in relation to the utopia, that is, as *the utopia personified*. This is in contrast to traditional theism's *creating God*, where everything in the world that is created by Him comes down to an indifferent arbitrariness that is perfect for Him, and which therefore cannot have any personal connection whatsoever to the utopia as the dream of another world *unless the illogical fall of Man is introduced through the back door*. For example, Christianity must not just kill *the Son* within the Trinity; it must also sooner or later kill *the Father* in order to rescue its credibility concerning the utopia. Thereby, the God of Christianity is incompatible with the possibility of the utopia. The God of Christianity must die completely for the utopia to be possible.

Meillassoux constructs an alternative that the failed, atheist project in itself cannot produce: existence is eternally contingent and thereby full of potential hope. Classic atheism is namely based on the faulty assumption that existence is controlled by *chance* when in actual fact it is controlled by *contingency*. It is contingency which, through the advances of contemporary physics – in its capacity as *the metaphysical constant of physics* – unites philosophy and religion in a new holy conjunction beyond the narrow horizon of deadlocked atheism. By deepening atheism and developing it to its logical conclusion, we implement the dialectical shift over to syntheism. *Syntheism is radical atheism.*

The syntheist ambition can hardly be formulated more clearly. In the conflict between the traditional roles of *the philosopher* and *the priest* – where Meillassoux of course takes the philosopher's side – the *atheist* is reduced to little more than a deeply irritating, passive observer. Where the atheist lets the priest keep *religion* as his monopoly, Meillassoux responds with the words: *God is much too serious a subject to be left to the priests.* Transcendentalism must be rejected quite unsentimentally in order to leave room for a religion that loves, worships and believes in the immanence and its enormous potential. Only philosophy can carry out this necessary action. For Meillassoux, the demystification of existence, the striving for *deconstruction* – classical atheism's big project – has namely reached the end of the road. Deconstruction appears to be only paralysing for mankind, making him incapable of conceiving of *the utopia*, and thereby also incapable of formulating *the vision*, and in this way cultivating *hope* for the future. Meillassoux turns this upside down and argues that the real blasphemy and idolatry must be to insist on a transcendental god in the contemporary world. According to Meillassoux, God is to be placed in the future and be completely immanent. Like all utopias, Meillassoux's God is virtual rather than potential; neither possible nor impossible, but contingent and thereby beyond any kind of probability calculation.

Here syntheist thinking refers back to Zoroaster's philosophical revolution in the Iranian highlands 3,700 years ago. Meillassoux gets inspiration from Gilles Deleuze, while Deleuze gets inspiration from Henri Bergson. Bergson in turn takes his inspiration from Baruch Spinoza, and Spinoza, for his part, was educated by Moroccan Sufis, who in turn relayed the legacy of Zoroaster's immanent philosophy – the pantheistic branch of *Sufism* should be regarded as Zoroastrian philosophy hidden under the Islamic flag – the original *divinology* if any. Zoroaster's concept of a coming *Saoshyant* denotes a utopian character created by mankind or rather by the future itself, that is, something quite different from Judaism's and Christianity's *Messiah* as a saviour sent by a god who has failed to complete his own creation in a satisfactory way. Since syntheism takes its starting point in Zoroaster, this means that in relation to its precedent Christianity, syntheism must be seen as *historically and logically consummated Christianity*, a kind of monistic and immanent Christianity that accepts both the Father's and the Son's death and which welcomes the divine manifestation through *the Holy Ghost* as their replacement. God springs from the meeting between the faithful and nowhere else. The Holy Ghost, without the Father and the Son, thus becomes merely the name for syntheism's *Syntheos*.

The Abrahamic God is by necessity split. The Slovenian philosopher and psychoanalyst Slavoj Zizek bases his critique of Christianity on this logical necessity: If God really knew everything about us and was never in a state of ignorance at all concerning our thinking and our actions, both we and God would plunge straight down into psychosis. The splitting of God's being is necessary for the cohesiveness of the world view. Without the split between the all-knowing and the naively ignorant, neither God nor the faithful can have any experience of being subjects. This split God is however not the God that appears when the spiritual syntheist bears witness to her religious experience. Here, the Universe as God differs radically from the Abrahamic God. The Universe really knows – and can tell whoever is willing to listen –

everything about the past, but it knows absolutely nothing of its unknown future. And nor does anyone else either.

Nevertheless, the Universe remains totally indifferent to our story. And it is this very indifference that keeps the psychosis at bay. The only thing that would be even worse than the Universe – as is now the case – being all-knowing and at the same time indifferent, would be if the Universe were all-knowing and *actually had an opinion and an intention*. What happens instead in the syntheistic religious experience is that the necessary split does not happen within God, as is the case within Abrahamism and atheist humanism, but rather the necessary split arises between the Universe and one's fellow man, who subsequently take care of their respective metaphysical protagonist roles. *While Pantheos is manifested in the Universe, Syntheos is manifested in one's fellow man.* Syntheism is therefore not just something more than atheism as deepened or *radical atheism*, it is also something more than pantheism as deepened or *radical pantheism*.

In practice, the overwhelmingly enormous Universe cannot form the divine for us – the Universe is divine for us merely through its enormous size, power and stupendous incomprehensibility; *the Universe forces us into submission* – but it is rather the consoling, empathic fellow man, that is, the Zoroastrian *Saoshyant*, who gives God a face and a consciousness. Pantheism is thus just an incomplete form of syntheism. This indisputable fact drives syntheology from pantheism's incomplete utopia *Pantheos* to syntheism's consummate utopia *Syntheos*. Both Zoroaster and Meillassoux thus maintain that the advent of Syntheos is a necessity for the consummation of the utopia and of history. On its own, Pantheism is insufficient foundation for a religion for human beings.

According to syntheism and *syntheist pantheism*, there is no Universe to confess to — you cannot confess to a being, however enormous, if this being lacks both senses and interest — but it is rather the *Saoshyant*, the holy fellow human, who receives your liberating confession, who is converted into *the divinity who does not already know*. Even Zoroaster in his time understands this central distinction within *the divine*: he therefore makes a distinction between God-as-being or *Ahura*, and God-as-thinking-fellow-human or *Mazda*. Zoroaster himself almost always distinguishes between the concepts of Ahura and Mazda in his work *Gathas*. The umbrella term *Ahura Mazda* is only used when his theology for some reason needs a connecting core. And it is Mazda (the mind) and not Ahura (the cosmos) that is prioritised in Zoroastrian theology. This explains why Zoroaster names his remarkably prophetic religion *Mazdayasna*, love of wisdom — the same term as the Greeks 1,200 years later translate as *philosophia* — rather than *Ahurayasna*, love of being. Pantheos is Ahura, but Syntheos is Mazda, and a faithful Zoroastrian — and for that matter a faithful syntheist — is a *Mazdayasni* (a human being who is primarily faithful to the mind) rather than an *Ahurayasni* (a human being who is primarily faithful to being).

Zoroaster wants to see his followers as hedonists and self-affirming *Mazdayasni* with a deep ethics constructed on the basis of their *intentions*, instead of terrified and submissive *Ahurayasni* with their morality constructed on the basis of the *consequences* of their actions. Zoroaster thereby turns his back on primitivism's *consequentialism* and instead develops the first *intentionalism* in the history of ideas; his religion is the first that happens inside the minds of people rather than out there in the endless cosmos. Ironically it is the Arabic neighbour *Islam* that later develops and consummates the opposite idea — of *Ahurayasna* as its own, radically moralist religion (the term Islam itself means *submission* in Arabic).

The difference between Zoroastrianism's intentionalism and Islam's consequentialism is clarified in the syncretistic meeting between them in the Sufi hybrid religion. Instead of a god that does not already know, the Sufi master must step in and assume *the role as the one who does not already know* and who nevertheless still decides everything after the disciple's fetishistic submission. Islam is therefore most clearly and precisely described as the theory of blindly obeying the one who does not already know, if for no other reason than for the exemplary value that Islam attaches to submission itself. This makes Islam the perfect religion for feudalist society, and in this very capacity it is the fastest and most furiously expanding metaphysics thus far in history. This is not to say that Islam is logically coherent. Memetic success has of course nothing to do with either truth or logical coherence, at least not in any other sense than the strictly Darwinian. However, we understand why Sufism, in its capacity as a permanent state of armistice between intentionalism and consequentialism, developed into *the ironic religion par excellence*; a doctrine that can only be expressed through *flowing paradoxical poetry* but which never lends itself – to the great vexation of Islamist fundamentalists; they all hate Sufism – to any kind of solid dogmatic fundamentalism.

The mistake is to believe that it is Allah who must be obeyed. Rather, Islam has always understood that it is Islam's interpreters who must be obeyed, which explains the history of Islam's bitter battles over which interpreter is to be followed, over who represents *the Islamic theocracy*, since Allah can only have a voice through these pretentious spokespeople. The central aspect of the shift from Zoroastrianism's Mazdayasna to Islam's Ahurayasna is that submission is transformed from being the starting point for the religious experience into becoming the objective and meaning of the entire process. The reward for total submission, self-imposed slavery, is of course the fetishist's manifest and immediate enjoyment of freedom from existential loneliness. Islam is *the religion of libidinal enjoyment par ex-*

cellence. Thus, Islam is also the shortest way to numerical success, as a religion without monks, nuns and monastery compounds, where the quest for truth is discarded entirely in favour of *the negative desire for submission.*

Note how Zoroaster's divinity exists independently of the human being and that it does not need her in order to be supplied with its self-glorification. Zoroaster sees no point whatsoever in sitting and romancing narcissistic gods when existence in itself already offers the divine on a silver platter in the form of nature (Pantheos), only to then let the divine be manifested in one's fellow man as *the Saoshyant* (Syntheos). As a consequence of his ambition to make the community the divine, Zoroaster even eschews the construction of reclusive and monastic cultures and other chosen alienation within Zoroastrianism. The community is sacred in its capacity as Mazda's incarnation; according to Zoroaster all people must be accorded a place within the congregation. Zoroaster is quite simply the first thinker for whom fellowship between human beings is more important and above all more divine than the glorious power of *the great Other*, localised in a distant past or above the clouds. Or to take the word religion literally: Zoroaster not only invents the concept of *philosophy* (Mazdayasna) a millennium ahead of his most proximate followers Anaximander and Heraclitus in Greece; he also invents *religion* in its literal sense, as that which restores the intimate ties between people.

This is the core of Zoroaster's revolution within the history of ideas: the advent of Zoroastrianism sounds the death knell for religion's primitivist role as *a placating of narcissistic and psychopathic gods.* For Zoroaster religion is instead a creative and existentialist *attitude* (Entheos) vis-à-vis fellow humans (Syntheos) and the cosmos (Pantheos), sprung from an existential decision about truth (Atheos) that Zoroaster calls *asha.* Following *asha,* the cornerstone of Zoroaster's amoral ethics, is quite simply to make a pragmatic decision to live in harmony with and together with the surrounding world as it actually is. When Zoroaster shifts the focus of theology from Ahura to Mazda, the world stops being primarily *threatening* and instead becomes primarily *engaging*. Without the psychopathic gods, moralism's pathological foundation perishes and the values become *ethical*, that is, grounded in their intentions to attain certain anticipated effects and nothing else.

The Zoroastrian revolution is clearly seen in ancient Iranian architecture. Both sacrificial alters and burial sites disappear when Zoroaster's theological broom sweeps clean across the Central Asian highlands. Because there are no longer any tyrannical gods to placate, and bodies no longer need to be embalmed or in any other way prepared for the afterlife in eternity, but are instead recycled in a natural way, for example, as food for vultures. The Zoroastrians build ascetically bare temples, painted in white, where the community gather around the *atash bahram*, the eternally burning flame in the centre of the temple, the symbol of the infinite expansion and ecstatic intensity of the cosmos. That Zoroastrianism as early as 3,700 years ago was practising such seemingly modern ideas as ecological sustainability, radical gender equality, collective ownership of resources and tolerance of deviant human character traits, is quite consistent if one takes Zoroaster's ideology as a starting point.

Obviously the Zoroastrian revolution is illustrated with perfect clarity in Jesus's reformation of Judaism into that which later became Christianity, where *the law is replaced by the intention* as the driving force in the Judeo-Christian theology and the values shift from the moralising to the ethical perspective (notwithstanding that Paul later frantically tries to drive Christianity back to Judaic moralism.) Just as self-evidently, Paul and St Augustine import the concept of *the Holy Ghost* from Zoroastrianism in order to complete the Trinity of Christian metaphysics. Which in turn explains why the Holy

Ghost is the only component of the Christian Trinity that survives within syntheology (where *Syntheos is the Holy Ghost without the Father and the Son*).

It is from Zoroastrianism that Kant gets the idea that existence is basically a correlation between thinking (Mazda) and being (Ahura), even if Kant sees Mazda and Ahura as eternalised constants instead of the intra-active variables that Zoroaster used in his proto-syntheology. If we use the network-dynamic terminology of the 2000s, we would express this as Kant opening the door to interactivity through his correlationalism, which Nietzsche later consummates through his relativism. But with Zoroaster there is not just one constantly moving activity between different phenomena, but rather *the phenomena are also in constant motion around themselves*. This is why we speak of Zoroaster's building blocks as intra-acting variables in contrast to Kant's and Nietzsche's interactive constants. *Intra-activity* is the historical radicalisation of *interactivity*, and *relationalism* is correspondingly the historical radicalisation of *relativism*.

Syntheism is the Hegelian synthesis of the deadlocked dichotomy between theism and atheism. When we left theism for atheism, we threw the baby out with the bathwater. We became anti-religion rather than anti-theism. But having lived through the atheist paradigm and having come out on the other side, we are ready for the syntheist paradigm with its grasp of the human being's constant and basic need for a functional metaphysics. Syntheism stands out as the only credible metaphysical system for the intellectual human being of the third millennium. Which means that the only alternative to syntheism is to settle for a subconscious and tacit metaphysics, and such a metaphysics can of course be as ill-considered and destructive as anything, since by definition it is not conscious and thus hardly very sensible either. And how intelligent does this alternative, on closer inspection, appear to be?

04
Living religion versus deadly alienation

When Friedrich Nietzsche, as far back as *Thus spoke Zarathustra* and beyond, establishes and announces *the death of God* in the latter half of the 19th century, it also means death to the idea of the availability of objective truth. This is because objective truth as an idea is entirely dependent on a metaphysical constant, *the primary gaze* before which the true object arises. But if this primary gaze does not exist, if the metaphysical god beyond time and space does not exist, the whole foundation for the fixation of the object also falls apart. The phenomena start to dance in increasingly complex patterns of interdependencies, and with the beginning of that dance, the possibility of an objectively attainable, valid truth about the phenomena disappears. There is no longer an authority that issues certificates of authenticity. There is no longer anyone who serves as the object's universal apprehender of truth. All truths become contingent upon *the relative position of the postulator of the truth*, which subsequently means that all truths become *subjective*.

Even before Nietzsche, Kant shows that reality as it is and perceived by no one, *the noumenal*, by definition is inaccessible to the human being, who instead has to put up with the noumenal's reproduction as the object in a world view that consists exclusively of subjectively experienced *phenomena*. Thus the object is subjective, mediated by our unreliable senses, and not the least bit objective *per se*. After Kant, all forms of objectivism are impossible for anyone reflecting philosophically on the matter – the 'objectivists' of the 20th century, such as Ayn Rand, devote themselves exclusively to a kind of autistic vulgar-philosophy without any understanding of the Kantian revolution – and this notion is replaced by various forms of *subjectivism,* and thereby also various forms of *relativism.* Moreover, Nietzsche successfully demonstrates that truths not only must be subjective, they are also influenced by the subject that produces them. By psychologising the observer and thus turning this figure into a mobile body instead of a fixed soul, Nietzsche completes *the Kantian revolution.*

Relativism is already apparent in language. Every concept, every linguistic component, is in a state of constant flux, constantly changes meaning: in time, in space, between and also within those who use spoken sounds or written signs with which to communicate. Seen as a social tool, language can therefore never be objectively valid, and thereby neither can it reflect an enduringly objective truth. According to the French philosopher Alain Badiou there is, however, an exception to this general rule for language, and this is *mathematics*. While mathematics is in essence tautological – what the proposition $2 + 2 = 4$ conveys is of course really that $2 + 2$ is another way of saying 4, the informational value is therefore extraordinarily low – as the optimal *eternalisation* it nonetheless beguiles us with its implicit promises of fixed values located in frozen space–time. Through the natural sciences, mathematics seems to offer a possibility for the human being to establish a truer and more effective contact with objective reality. It beguiles us with the possibility of *objectively establishing qualitative differences* between subjective statements.

German philosopher Jürgen Habermas launches *intersubjectivity* as the highest truth that humans can aspire to after Kant has shifted objective reality to where it is hopelessly out of reach. According to Habermas, the absence of this objectivity can only be confronted and militated against by an extensive plurality of subjective voices. Habermas imagines that intersubjectivity is negotiated between actors on an equal footing in the public sphere, which is both laborious and time-consuming, but which in the end nonetheless yields a satisfactory result, due to lots of subjective positions confronting and interacting with each other. To take one example, the credibility of science is based on the conviction that intersubjective truth can be fished out through the process referred to as *peer review*. No position gains recognition if it is not first sanctioned by a collective consisting of formally educated experts; and contrariwise: if a text contains an abundance of footnotes, it is considered academically true, or at least trustworthy.

Badiou however argues that mathematics modifies Habermas' premises; with the aid of mathematics, we can go beyond intersubjectivity and achieve an objectivity that Kant does not understand. The wide acceptance of the quantum physics paradigm within the sciences – and its subsequent dramatic effects on philosophy, for example through the effect that Niels Bohr's ideas have on Alfred North Whitehead's process philosophy, and vice versa – in spite of its initially highly counter-intuitive claims, proves that this is the case. Badiou argues that thanks to the progress of mathematics, *ontology* can at last leave *representationalism, correlationalism* and even *relativism* behind, only to thereafter take the decisive leap over to *relationalism*. The Kantian paradigm would thus be passé and objectivity would again be possible.

However, the problem is that the phenomenal and indisputable utility of mathematics in the most diverse of contexts has blinded humanity repeatedly throughout history and tricked humans into making the most fatal mistakes. The subconscious attraction in

Plato's dualist philosophy – when it becomes widely accepted in ancient Greece in the 4th century B.C. – probably lies to a large extent in Plato's religious aspirations, and it is of course also these that later make Platonism Judaism's perfect partner when they together constitute the two main ingredients in the aggressively dualist Christianity. Paul is the Greek Jew, the hybrid between Moses and Plato; Pauline Christianity is *ancient Egypt's cosmological dualism,* resurrected through the reunification of its Judaic and Greek branches (comparable to *ancient Iran's cosmological monism* in Zoroaster, represented by Heraclitus among the Greeks).

But it is important to understand Plato's *philosophical temperament.* He constantly and neurotically seeks *exactitude*: the incontrovertible definition. Since life is chaotic and boundless, and since death really is the only thing that is precise, indisputable and definite, the inevitable consequence is that the Platonist is most profoundly a *death worshipper.* If predecessor and rival Heraclitus is *the Iranian Greek who worships life,* Plato is *the Egyptian Greek who worships death.* Heraclitus accepts and embraces the open-ended infinity of existence and of life. Plato, on the other hand, hates both openness and infinity, and it is in mathematics that he finds the magic weapon that will enable him to force the chaotic world, which is impossible to determine and define exhaustively, into one single preordained and limited *totality.*

This means that physical reality, according to Plato, is merely a chimera: a world of shades populated by imitations of secondary quality. The real reality is instead the pure and elevated *world of ideas,* accessible only to those philosophers who think along the lines that Plato himself designates. Here, or course, the chaos and impermanence of the physical world does not prevail; rather, everything is regulated by mathematics' preordained and eternally valid laws. As a predictable consequence of this, Plato also advocates *philosophy's enlightened despotism* as the most desirable form of government. He has no sympathy for the Athenians' democratic and thus *intersubjective* experimental work. Without insight into and understanding of what is true, the ruling collective can only lead the state astray.

Platonism is the first exhaustively formulated *totalism*, and it exercises a powerful escapist pull by stressing a stable, symmetrical and thoroughly regulated alternative to the obviously defective and imperfect life that we live in the everyday. The rising aristocracy thus obtains a brilliantly designed free gift – which it then in turn can pretend to bestow on the cheated and cowed peasants and slaves in feudalist society – namely *eternal life*, the paradisiacal world where a reward for patiently endured poverty and toil awaits the one who has submitted without complaint to every whim and order of those in power. Plato allows himself to be seduced by mathematics' promises of symmetrical perfection and eternal validity. And if mathematics is perfect and eternal, *in the sphere of mathematics existence must also be perfect* and remain perfect forever. The consequence is that if existence in the mathematical sphere is already perfect, it no longer has any reason to allow itself to be changed. A change in something that is characterised by *perfection* can of course only lead in one direction, namely to a deterioration, in the form of *imperfection*. Since time requires change in order to exist – duration is change stacked on top of change – this must mean that *time is an illusion*.

However, the problem with this very thing is that Plato's world view is based on an entirely idiosyncratic and untenable premise. His own autistic neurosis when faced with the shapeless multiplicity of life forces him to devote himself to beautiful reveries of a make-believe world where everything is perfectly ordered (which is easy to effect, since it is only make-believe). But as it turns out, there are plenty of evangelists in the growing feudalist society that are of the same temperament as Plato and who eagerly want to spread his hierarchical ideology. His message is received with joy and appreciation by the Greek and later the Roman aristocracy. By accepting Platonism's false premise and furthermore emphasising the strict logic that later ensues from his imaginary premise, this doctrine is spread with devastating efficiency. Platonism also attracts the great masses with its promise of the perfect paradise that one ought to be able to attain if one only thinks and acts correctly, and it is so incredibly practically arranged that by definition it is out of reach of every form of empirical study.

When Paul later launches *Christianity*, thereby placing Plato's parallel *theory of ideas* beyond death, there is unfortunately no Heraclitus at hand to call his bluff in this bizarre and seemingly endlessly generous promise, which is issued without any risk or cost whatsoever on the issuer's part. Platonism thus wins a crushing victory. And Alain Badiou, unfortunately, makes the same mistake as his predecessor Plato. He is tempted by the aura of perfectionism of mathematics to cultivate an aspiration of being able to discover the eternal laws of physics before the physicists themselves do so. But his view of mathematics' relationship to physics is, unfortunately, both historically and ontologically incorrect. *It is physics that is primary and real, and it does not follow any mathematical laws per se.* Or as Murray Gell-Mann, Nobel laureate in physics, expresses it: "A law of nature is nothing other than a condensed description, assumed and available in advance, of the regularities that an observed phenomenon displays during the period of observation." Therefore the mathematical laws, when they are applied to physics, cannot either be anything other than, in the best case, just approximations; they can never be physically, but only mathematically, and thereby basically tautologically, exact.

On the whole, mathematics is a tautological way for people to tell one and the same *approximatic history* of the world from a host of different perspectives. This is in contrast to an approximate history, which is full of constants, but which for some reason must be regarded as rounded off as a whole, while an approximatic history consists of an infinite series of roundings without any anchoring constant whatsoever, as a stubborn attempt to *eternalise* a world which in reality is entirely *mobilist* (which it of course is). However, mathematics is nothing over and above this. For in all its richness, mathematics never does anything other than tell self-referencing and self-validating stories that in the best case might appear to reflect physical reality, but which *de facto* never can be this reality, and even less so set an example for it, legislate for it or replace it. Therefore, ontologically physics and mathematics must be kept strictly separate. In spite of the fact that many mathematicians and even philosophers have wanted to see mathematics as a *language of God*, this is unfortunately not true. *The Universe is namely an analogue, not a digital, phenomenon.*

The human gaze is so libidinally attracted to symmetrical patterns that it fancies that it finds these in nature, in the same way that the human being tautologically formulates them in mathematics. But however appealing such symmetries may be to the human libido, they are unfortunately not to be found in nature, and above all they are never necessary. Nature does not make it easy for itself, quite simply *because nature does not need to (or cannot) make it easy for itself* in the way that man must (and sometimes even can) maximise his conditions for survival on a planet where the constant lack of food, energy, housing and other resources is a fundamental living condition. The Universe on the whole exists in fact in a state of immeasurable bounty. It is only in *a world characterised by scarcity* that the genetically conditioned search for symmetries that is typical of mankind arises, as if these symmetries were some kind of metaphysical signs of health.

The fact remains that the constant adding of new dimensions and other internal complexity-raising factors to mathematics merely increases the risk of its tautological foundation sinking even deeper into oblivion, and that the mathematician thereby is even more easily fooled into believing that mathematics reflects reality even better. We call this *the tautological trap of mathematism*. The history of Platonism is in principal one big, cautionary tale of this fundamental mistake of perspective. If anything, science is in need of a powerful *demathematisation* to an unparalleled degree. It is one thing to add reasonably relevant external facts to a narrative in order to increase its credibility, but the more internal, complexity-raising factors that are added, the higher the risk, psychologically speaking, of mathematics getting stuck in mathematism's tautological trap.

Like so many Platonists before him, Badiou makes precisely this mistake. He falsely assumes that the *eternalism* that his own perception produces is more real than the *mobilism* that one's perception is constantly confronted with from all directions in one's physical surroundings. Badiou thus thinks in a closed or *anthropocentric* way, rather than in an open and *universocentric* way, when he investigates the ontological status of mathematics. Exactly as Plato did 2,300 years ago, Badiou lets his own neurosis get in the way of his philosophical perspicacity. It is one of syntheism's most important tasks to eliminate the whole idea of *eternal, external laws* with an assumed origin in an eternal, external world to which we have no access. This is superstition rather than science.

So where then does relationalist metaphysics find its historical allies? It is, for example, more correct to say that syntheism strives towards a new *Renaissance* rather than towards a new *Enlightenment*. British philosopher Iain McGilchrist with his tome *The Master and his Emissary* builds a veritably syntheist manifesto around this basic idea. According to McGilchrist, the history of ideas is a struggle between the human being's two cerebral hemispheres for the power and the glory. If the right hemisphere – which is holistically oriented and seeks wholeness in its eternalisations – is allowed to rule, or at least to dominate, it produces mobilist, emotionally driven and culturally explorative epochs such as *the Renaissance* and *Romanticism*. The left hemisphere – which prefers to eternalise the world as if it consisted of a series of isolated components without a context – instead produces totalist, logo-centric and culturally closed epochs such as *the Enlightenment* and *Modernism*.

Even if McGilchrist devotes several chapters to trying to prove the physiological validity in these controversial theories, it is highly dubious. There is quite simply no medical proof for the cerebral hemispheres being as dramatically different as he claims. The interaction between them is intimate and complex. But as *metaphors for different temperaments in collective thinking* McGilchrist's hemispheres are useful. If the left hemisphere, according to this view, is left to its own devices without the right hemisphere's holistic influence, it soon generates a neurotic, inconsistent, and near-autistic world view, which has more in common with the schizophrenic patient's unimaginative closed-mindedness than with contemporary physics' inspiring and expansive geometries.

McGilchrist champions the thesis that when the human being is thinking only with her left hemisphere, and thus immediately breaks everything down into a solid logic of isolated eternalisations, life appears completely meaningless. All that remains is aleatorically joined and basically meaningless *utility functions*, propelled by a folly of *instrumentality*. This, he argues, is because it is only the right hemisphere that can perceive and produce a cohesive meaning between the many eternalisations, give them a metaphysical dimension, while the right hemisphere is *utilitarianism's* worst enemy.

If it is the role of *religion* to have a literally making-whole, a healing, effect on people and societies, to create a functioning unit that is greater than the sum of its constituent parts, then *alienation* is its opposite – an alienation that separates people both from the world around them, from each other, and ultimately even from themselves. The syntheological connection is evident: McGilchrist's holistic right hemisphere is home to religion, while his separatist left hemisphere, consequently, is home to alienation. McGilchrist even goes so far as to claim that various epochs in the history of ideas can be connected without further ado to a kind of hemispherical dialectic: the Renaissance and Romanticism give priority to the right hemisphere and heighten religion rather than alienation, while the Enlightenment and Modernism give priority to the left hemisphere and engender alienation rather than religion. Seen from this perspective, it is with the Renaissance and Romanticism that syntheism – as a dialectical reaction to Modernism – finds its allies and precursors in the history of ideas.

A clear example of an ideology where the left hemisphere runs amok at the expense of the right hemisphere is Auguste Comte's *positivist* nightmare from the mid-19th century. Comte highly arbitrarily divides the history of ideas into three stages: the *theological*, the *metaphysical* and the *scientific* phases. With each stage, the human being becomes increasingly ennobled and perfect, and once she knows how matters actually stand, when she is completely scientific and thus also all-knowing – that is, when the human being becomes Comte himself – it is precisely then that *history* will be complete. Similar to thinkers such as Ludwig Feuerbach and Karl Marx, Comte adheres to *the scientistic conviction*, the blind faith in the unlimited potential of not only rationality but also science.

Evolution is quite simply such a strong and captivating metaphor for many of the 19th century's intellectuals that they very much want to make it the fundamental ethical principle, as if it were the task of the righteous in some bizarre way to speed up a history whose development is of course anyway preordained according to their own determinist conviction. For Marx, the Communist revolution of the proletariat, for example, is a deed that he must command his readers and disciples to carry out, in spite of the fact that, according to his own view, it will take place anyway because of the historical necessity that he himself and Friedrich Engels describe in their writings. In a similar manner, Comte regards his *social evolutionism* as so perfect that strangely enough he wants to turn it into a secular religion. Social evolutionary ideas continue to thrive in Europe up until the mass murders of Nazism and Stalinism around the mid-20th century. Then, if not before, the danger of arguing for a militant ethics based on a vulgar natural determinism and driven by alienation's ressentiment rather than by religion's search for benevolent dialogue with one's fellow man, becomes manifest. In this way the totalitarian ideologies of the 20th century are the dark flip side of the Enlightenment. Rationalism without consciousness of its own fundamental blind faith is, as Habermas' gurus Horkheimer and Adorno show in *Dialectic of Enlightenment*, literally lethal for humanity.

Syntheism is the exact opposite of Comte's *sociology as religion*. In syntheism it is science that gives birth to philosophy and philosophy that gives birth to syntheology. Religion is dependent on and builds on science, not the other way around. But then syntheism is also, if we borrow McGilchrist's metaphors for a while yet, the result of the right cerebral hemisphere's constant search for an applicable *holism*. It is only through setting these eternalisations in motion and in relation to each other, through *remobilising* and thereby making her existence *sacred*, that mankind produces and experiences meaning in life and is able to alleviate alienation. It is only when the human being becomes an *agent* that her life gets a meaning. Adding a holistic perspective to life thus in itself constitutes making the world *religious:* recreating (an idea of) a context, a (basis for) fellowship. Regarding everything that exists as an endless multitude of expressions of and for one and the same substance, *the One*, is syntheism's innermost core.

What happens, historically speaking – if we continue to borrow McGilchrist's cerebral hemisphere metaphors for a little while longer – is that the Enlightenment and the capitalist-industrialist society that it results in, constantly give priority to the left hemisphere over the right one in its increasingly marked and extreme *mathematisation* of existence. By initially delimiting, then separating and measuring everything in the name of science, mankind also subsequently starts to objectify, instrumentalise, conquer, colonise, plunder and consume every thinkable resource in her environment, including himself and her fellow humans. But the mathematisation of existence not only leads to a ruthless and ultimately also self-destructive exploitation of the Earth's finite resources. The exploited identity also generates a particularly trenchant alienation, and with it the lack of a context-creating religion. The right cerebral hemisphere, which experiences wholeness and builds meaning, remained, according to the view that McGilchrist puts forward, underdeveloped for several centuries, which had considerable consequences at all levels in society.

Historically speaking, syntheism returns to McGilchrist's right cerebral hemisphere and its enormous, unexploited potential to build *the new Renaissance* rather than the new Enlightenment. It does this from a conviction that eternalism without mobilism is both misleading and self-destructive. *Eternalism* (the world of rationality) must be subservient for its own sake to *mobilism* (the world of reason); otherwise eternalism results in *totalism*, the blind faith – since the days of Parmenides and Plato – in all motion being illusory, and therefore it is the eternalist reproduction of the mobilist reality that is the only actual reality instead of the other way around. Thus syntheism also includes *entheism*, Taoism's fundamental idea – which was launched by Lao Tzu in Axial Age China in the 7th century B.C. – that *change per se,* and thereby also its by-product *time*, is what is fundamental to existence. According to Lao Tzu, change over time is anything but illusory, and thus mobilism and not eternalism is primary in existence. Taoism's idea of *yin* and *yang* as an ontological foundation is summarised under syntheism's concept of *Entheos*.

If religion *has* functioned as a cohesive force within both man and society, the history of alienation is a converse but closely related history of how man and society are divided over the course of history. Most metaphysical systems are based on the premise that there is an original paradisiacal state and that alienation arises through a dramatic event, for example as a consequence of *the Fall of Man* (according to the Abrahamic religions), or through the deleterious effects of *capital* (according to Marxism). The mission of the faithful is therefore – with or without the help of God or history – to restore the original, paradisiacal state. But the problem is then that these *ideologies of the Fall from grace* are considerably more focused on alienation than on the alleviating utopia, which remains a diffuse mirage on the horizon. It is not what was once good that comes into focus – if anything it is left completely outside the writing of history – but rather the narratives are obsessed with one thing and one thing alone, namely that which has corrupted and devastated all of existence (*sin* in Christianity, *capital* in Marxism, *environmental devastation* in environmentalism, etc.).

It is thus *the dystopia*, not the utopia, which acts as a narrative engine in the ideologies of the Fall from grace. This explains why alienation must be subconsciously stimulated rather than rectified in order for the ideology to be kept alive. Reading between the lines, the sinner must be tacitly stimulated into continuing to sin, capitalism must be spurred on to continue claiming victims with its customary ruthlessness, or else the ideology's very *raison d'etre* will evaporate. The Fall from grace determines the ideology, which without the Fall is pointless. Therefore the ideologies of the Fall from grace constantly produce new moral decrees which thereby keep them alive. For example, Christianity has grown strongest and exercised the most power when it is has preached most aggressively against sin and the sinners, and moreover eagerly added new thoughts and acts to the growing list of sinful crimes. There is, in other words, good reason for the aggressive Church having been the expansive version, rather than the diplomatic version having been so. The aggressive Church is strongly focused on reproducing and promoting the deviations of immorality that legitimise and necessitate the Church in itself as well as its aggressiveness. It is like an old marriage.

Syntheism lacks all forms of nostalgic philosophical theory of a lost paradise and prehistoric world worthy of idealising and bemoaning in general, and it thereby has no reason to stimulate alienation by enticing us with any amount of *libidinal transgression*. Which is quite simply due to the fact that no such original paradise has, nor ever needs to have, existed. Within syntheism, alienation is instead a contingent fact, produced by highly tangible and comprehensible material circumstances, such as the exploding abstraction in increasingly extensive and complex inter-human relations throughout history. This state of affairs is then heightened by internarcissistic thinkers – ruled by their left cerebral hemispheres according to McGilchrist's view – equipped with megaphones that the prevailing power structures officiously supply; thinkers who are enamoured of their own grandiose protagonist roles in totalist ideologies. We must therefore study the history of alienation more closely in order to be able to determine where, in the informationalist society, it actually abides and how syntheism can confront and neutralise it.

Mobilist thinking experiences a veritable golden age in Greece during the early Axial Age. The influence from Zoroastrian Iran is considerable. Heraclitus, Greece's own Zoroaster, lays the foundation for both process philosophy and paradoxism. He gives priority to *sight* (mobilism) over *hearing* (eternalism) among the human senses and direct *experience* over indirect *interpretation*. And while he is at it, Heraclitus also creates *dialectics*; he argues that creativity only can develop and grow where a clear opposition to the prevailing order reigns. Homer's myths and Aeschylus' classic drama revolve around holistically thinking people who live in a monist universe, and these ancient texts bear witness to a protosyntheist world view. It is during this period that Thales, the father of the natural sciences, produces the first syntheist tweet in history: *All things are full of gods.*

But in the 5th century B.C. *totalism* arrives and with it also *alienation* across a broad front in the history of ideas. It is ideas about reality and not physical reality in itself which are the focus for the totalists. The belief in the unlimited possibilities of rationality is proclaimed by Socrates and relayed by his disciple Plato, diligently noting it all down. Deductively reasoning science is everything, and art is worthless or something even worse and must, according to Plato, be expunged from society. Physics is subordinated to mathematics. Pre-Socratic monism ends up under attack. The totalists instead construct a strictly dualist world view. The eternal soul is separated from the corruptible body. The left hemisphere overshadows and dominates the right one, if we once again see the development from McGilchrist's perspective. The human being is no longer associated with either her body or her environment. A human being who has been alienated from the image of her incarnate self, who sees herself as a constantly inflamed, internal hotbed of conflict instead of as a harmonious whole, is easily reshaped from the tribe's incarnation of its members into an isolated peasant slave in the fields and in the pastures of the cattle herds, constantly on the lookout for some kind of abstract healing through hard work. It is important to understand that alienation serves a purpose and that it produces an identity that generates an extensive *enjoyment without pleasure*.

Totalism is driven by *the self-sacrifice myth*, the libidinal connection to self-hatred. What is brilliant about totalism is how for the first time in history it denies the human being's feeling that the whole of her is greater than the sum of her many different constituent parts. Totalism appears with *reductionism* as its faithful side-kick. A whole, according to reductionism, can always be deconstructed into ever smaller components *without the phenomenon's mental weight or value being affected*. Thus, the human body can be reduced to just body parts; the body itself has no value as an emergent phenomenon according to the totalists. Therefore, Plato can contend that *the body is inadequate to define the human being*. He picks out of humans that which arises as an indisputable surplus when the various components are combined, and converts this into a separate magnitude with unique and obviously completely fictitious properties: *the soul*. If the body parts cannot speak or think for themselves, while the body as a whole and as a unit talks and thinks, it must be a matter of a contribution from the outside. It is this soul, added from the outside, not *the emergent body* that talks and thinks. After this manoeuvre, Plato returns to the body. The fact that there even exists a feeling or a thought in conjunction with the whole body's status as – in fact – an entire body only goes to prove, according to this line of argument, *the existence of the soul*.

Reductionism is based on tautological circular reasoning rather than on scientific insight. But its attraction is enormous, and all the way through to the 20th century, totalism's many faithful believers actually persevere in trying to weigh the soul in order to thus establish that it constitutes a physiological surplus which in some essential sense it would be possible to distinguish from the body, for example by throwing dying people onto industrial scales, whereby a few grams of exhaled air disappearing from the lungs at the moment of death are immediately interpreted as scientific evidence of the soul's existence. Reductionism also makes it possible for the totalists to atomise existence, divide it up and sort the world into isolated units, which one naturally does one's best to try to domesticate and control with the aid of constantly ongoing and increasingly far-reaching *moralising*. Totalism has a formidable weapon at hand in this endeavour, namely the most important by-product of written language, *the law*.

When the reductionist outlook on man establishes itself, the totalists return to the human being with the law in their hands and *accuse the soul of not managing to restrain the body*. Because the law requires a division within the accused between *that which obeys the law* and *that which breaks the law*, so that the part which obeys the law can be refined and buffed up in prisons and clinics, while the part which breaks the law can be discarded and hopefully even rectified out of existence. Platonist dualism therefore suits the burgeoning jurisprudence perfectly. The soul is transformed into that which obeys the law, the body is transformed into that which breaks the law. The soul itself is thus never guilty of any criminal act, it is merely guilty of various sins of omission. Consequently, the law condemns the soul because it cannot manage to curb and tame the body in the same successful and convincing way that the law and its owners curb and tame the accused criminal.

With the advent of the law, there is an explosion of what the German philosopher Peter Sloterdijk calls *the anthropotechnics*, that is, attempts by the human being to domesticate not only plants and animals, but also to develop techniques to curb and tame herself. From the arrival of the law and onwards, anthropotechnics and its concomitant *asceticism* dominate human life. In an age obsessed with the successful and wealth-generating domestication of plants and animals in the building of *civilisation*

– made possible by and organised through *written language* – Platonist totalism functions perfectly as the feudalist metaphysics for the masses. As long as reductionism is considered to be natural and beyond all question, totalism maintains its hold on metaphysics. It is not until Leibniz launches his mobilist *monadology* in the 17th century that totalism starts being questioned.

With the arrival of the law, every dialogue between two people gets a third participant. What is said between two people can suddenly be written down and preserved for the future, and this text soon starts to live its own life entirely: it becomes *a third legal person* present in the room, moreover always with the decision in its hand in every type of conflict. The arrival of the law has dramatic effects for all inter-human relations. Suddenly he or she who is adept at exercising and controlling written language also dictates all kinds of rules for how people must conduct themselves in relation to one another, including how transgressions of these rules are to be punished. And not surprisingly this set of rules is constantly adjusted to the advantage of the author of the law himself. The more complex the laws that are written, the more complex societies one can control and regulate by making use of them. And the higher the degree of complexity of the system, the more dependent it becomes on the existence of the law and its assiduous enforcement.

However, the problem here is that the human libido never allows itself to be satisfied. It never gets enough, never lets the human being settle down, satisfied. The libido emanates from desire's constant search for new unsatisfied desires, in its constant postponement of satisfaction in order to keep itself alive. When desire is relegated to anthropotechnics, the libido is therefore shifted from *sexuality* to *asceticism*. Anthropotechnics strengthen desire through constantly postponing or re-locating it. Therefore the human being's self-domestication presupposes a *libidinal castration,* and the Abrahamic religions with their stronger anti-sex moralism fit perfectly for this purpose. The anthropotechnical practitioners get their energy from the dictates of the law, and since according to Sloterdijk the human being constantly strives for *verticality* – a longing to create a connection with the divine, to be able to satisfy *the syntheological imperative* of finding and subordinating herself to a functional metaphysical story – this leads to *the law becoming synonymous with God himself.*

The law's evident and indisputable ability to engender and maintain complex civilizations bestows upon it a holy aura. Since the law is such an excellent instrument for directing culture, and since nature itself also seems to be held together with mathematics' somewhat frightening exactitude, nature too must obey another, even more far-reaching and eternally valid law. This *law of nature* in turn requires an author; quite simply there must be a god behind the law, the god of the law. In other words, *nature obeys the law of God.* This law is so enchantingly powerful that it is soon worshipped as a god in itself. The Abrahamic religions launch the idea that everything else is dependent on and must be subordinate to the law, that this precedes and dictates everything else. "In the beginning was the Word, and the Word was with God, and the Word was God."

Thanks to the arrival of the law, the *Fall of Man* gets a clear narrative, the temporal and therefore supremely human Fall from grace is the absolutely worst imaginable crime against the eternal and therefore divine law. So where is God and wherein lies God's essence, if not in the will to administer justice and enforce submission by means of the law? The law has proven such a powerful metaphor that even after Nietzsche announces *the death of God* in the late 19th century, physics continues its manic search for God's law in nature, as if the law as God was still very much alive. The explanation for this is that the preordained and compelling law has exercised its magic on humans so extensively and for so long that humans can only imagine a Universe without the law's existence with the greatest difficulty. Enjoyment without pleasure drives the determinist world view. Note that this process continues without human law being able to have any equivalent in nature whatsoever. In spite of everything of course, human law functions because the receivers of the decrees, the people, listen to and understand the recited text and shape and calculate their own behaviour based on the current set of rules. People can either allow themselves to be frightened into obeying the decree, integrate it into what Sigmund Freud calls *the superego*, or allow themselves to be tempted into enjoyment occasioned by *a transgression of the decree* – to surrender to the libidinal transgression. In any case, it is man's ability to engage in and become obsessed with the law that makes him its object.

However, no such *legal object* exists in nature. Minerals, plants and animals are, for example, completely unable to assimilate a text which is read to them, just as they lack the wherewithal to allow themselves to be entranced libidinally by the existence of a set of rules. *There are quite simply no laws in nature.* There are only fields, forces and relationships. When and if an event seems to repeat itself in nature before the human observer's attentive gaze, it is merely because the conditions in terms of the forces and relationships in two or more different situations have been equivalent. Therefore, the law is an extremely clumsy and basically misleading metaphor for how nature works. Its popularity as a metaphor is entirely related to the human being's internarcissism; it has no connection with any sort of science. Anthropocentrism, as we know, continually throws a spanner in the works for mankind's understanding of the world around him. We believe that we are observing the world, but we are in fact looking into a mirror manufactured by ourselves, produced out of our self-centred ideas and delusions.

With the arrival of the law, mankind is separated from her internal compass, *the oscillation between desire and the libidinal drive*, and is subordinated to an external set of regulations which immediately attack desire and the libidinal drive in particular and denigrate these as the *vanguard for the Fall of man*. What then happens is that desire moves up in consciousness and internalises the law, making it into its own obsession, its own propulsion engine. Desire becomes a desire to either follow or oppose the law, but primarily a desire to constantly keep the law alive in order to cultivate one's own obsession with it. Thanks to this coalescence with the law, desire receives what the psychoanalyst Jacques Lacan calls an *extimate structure*. The drive is instead displaced into the subconscious, where it churns away and constantly triggers disturbing eruptions of *reality* in consciousness. It is the drive that incessantly reminds the human being that she will never be able to get inside the law, that there is always a residual part of her that shuns the law, that the law is a trespassing alien in her mind. It is this restless residue of the naked drive that constitutes the core of mankind's subjectivity, which drives her longing for a utopian freedom beyond her existential predicament. From a syntheological perspective, we argue that this *obscure core of the subject* is located in Entheos. It is only in the most intense religious experience, in *the infinite now*, that man confronts his innermost being, the coalescence of desire and the libidinal drive in their naked forms.

The law-abiding subject loves to hate itself and longs passionately for its own *domestication*, its own *castration* and finally also its own *extinction* – all under the idealised law which is exalted above all else. Desire no longer oscillates with the drive, but is instead placed above and pitted against it. The good, self-sacrificing soul is separated from the evil, self-absorbed body. Thereby dualist totalism is complete. It promises a future where once and for all man is separated from his filthy desires and drives and with a kind of smug indifference is merged into the law. Therefore its reward in the form of *life after death* is in essence *life in death*. With its cultivation and praise of alienation, dualist totalism is a form of death worship.

The lawless society is presented as a complete nightmare. In the Old Testament, the lawless society – a world where people actually give vent to their desires and drives – goes under the names Sodom and Gomorrah. The citizen in the lawless society is *the evil one* or *the sinner*. To sin is not just to break the law; at a deeper level it is about questioning its authority and thereby undermining the entire good world order. A person who just breaks the law and later confesses, thereby submitting to its authority, can be punished and forgiven after having shown sufficient contrition in word and deed. But the person who cultivates a rebellious attitude vis-à-vis the law, who refuses to accept its imposed alienation, becomes the arch-enemy of the entire order. The Abrahamic religions call this figure *Lucifer*, the angel of light, the figure who ignores the eternal law and uncompromisingly follows his desires and drives, as a temporal and finite being.

However, the law is just a metaphor on which we base blind faith in the pre-eminence of the prevailing order. But the metaphor is so strong that even today it colours not just our view of social relationships, but also feeds our recurring conviction that a society without laws must be a society that is rushing head-long towards its own annihilation. The law is such a powerfully charged metaphor that we cannot even look at nature and the Universe without presuming that these operate according to preordained and eternally valid laws. However there is no proof whatsoever of any such laws, and nor should there be. If we really are serious about our conviction that God is dead, we must also draw the conclusion that *the legislator is dead*. And without the original legislator, the eternal and metaphysical law does not exist either. Were we to carry this line of argument one step further, it would reveal that natural law is to be regarded as an incoherent battery of *anthropocentric chicanery* without foundation in anything whatsoever, and particularly not in nature.

In the situation that thus arises, *metaphysics itself* is the only way to balance the variants of the law. Metaphysics is namely the opposite of the law. Without metaphysics' constant production of hope, visions, utopias and alternative worlds, the human being would never be able to think of any alternative to the law's libidinal security. *A society without metaphysics immediately and without resistance submits to the totalitarian law.* It cannot even imagine any alternative. Consequently, physicists ought to stop talking about laws at all. In relationalist physics there are no longer any eternal laws, but merely a multitude of open and contingent *processes.* The presumed laws can be changed, they even must be changed over time – not least when new emergences suddenly arise, and they constantly do – and then these laws are of course no longer eternal laws that dictate in detail all imaginable events in advance, but are simply probable courses of events in specific, spatio-temporal contexts.

The syntheist utopia therefore entails a longing for a society where the law is no longer recognised and allowed to exercise its libidinal power. It is a society *where religion has replaced alienation.* In the syntheist utopia, bodies identify with their desires and libidinal drives and nothing else. Today's politics might just as well be *liberal-minded pragmatist,* with its sights set constructively on the syntheist utopia by opening up to religion's potential to counteract alienation. Because after all, politics is intimately intertwined with contemporary society and its citizens and material conditions. But *the syntheist utopia* is a completely different phenomenon than liberal-minded pragmatism – to begin with it can, of course, unabashedly take the immensity of the future as its point of departure, instead of, like pragmatism, being forced to stay within the narrow confines of the present

– and therefore professes *theological anarchism* and nothing else.

Because totalism separates the soul from the body, it considers itself able to neutralise the soul and make it independent and *reliable*, disconnected from the body's many chaotic, emotional storms and unpredictable whims. The soul thus becomes a command centre for *pure thought* and it rewards the human being with a kind of chic *essence*. *Rationalism* is thus also an *essentialism*. This essence is of course not just constant throughout life; it also makes the soul immortal. Thereby the rationalists can construct social ideologies without interruption, according to which obedient and subservient slaves are rewarded with a life after death, as free-floating souls without ties to their corruptible and despised bodies.

According to Plato, the soul is allied with the higher world of ideas, while the body must be content with being connected to the lower-tier, corruptible material world. The soul never changes; it is the constant which stands firm at the centre of the body's capricious emotional turbulence. From this dualism, all of human existence is then divided up into the categories *eternal ideas* and *corruptible matter*. This dualist escapism is a perfect fit as the ideology of patriarchy: the man is calm, balanced and constant, just like the soul, while the woman is reduced to an irrational and volatile emotional tempest, just like the body. Power must therefore fall to the man who, by definition, is of course of a higher standing, and the woman must be subordinated to him in order for society not to collapse under the pressure of internal instability, all in accordance with dualism's self-perpetuating, circular reasoning.

Rationalism is based around the idea that the human mind can process information about its surroundings to such an extent that nothing in it need appear the least bit mysterious or inexplicable to the mind. Everything can be experienced, everything can be understood. As long as the human being gets the time needed to process her sensory impressions and organise them logically, everything can be incorporated and appraised, and none of all this that is incorporated and appraised will ever be contradicted by any other conclusions that reason gets to think through to the end. However, the problem is that *rationalism per se* is not grounded in any kind of reason, but instead in a sort of quasi-religious wishful thinking and a blind faith that does not permit any criticism whatsoever. There is not even any reason at all behind the belief that the soul should be able to exist independently of the body. The independence of the soul is rather a product of the agrarian society's need to be able to hold all its members accountable in relation to the rapidly expanding and successively ever-more powerful law.

As long as the soul is kept separate from the body, it can be held morally responsible for any possible transgressions of the body. This explains why totalism is always followed by *moralism,* and with it, the possibility to threaten, persecute, imprison, monitor and terrorise people. If there is anything that totalism is constantly obsessed with, it is the thought of creating *the perfect society,* where the law is always adhered to and need never be changed. The totalist mind is thus obsessed with *stasis* and hates all forms of variability. The variability that can be observed in society and in nature is regarded as a regrettable anomaly which, with some good will and a suitable mix of remedial measures – that is, through criminalising the undesired behaviour that disturbs the statis fantasy – one should be able to wipe out. Totalism is an eternalism that refuses to be part of a dialectics with mobilism. It is, if we use McGilchrist's metaphors again, the left cerebral hemisphere which runs amok devastatingly in the absence of the right hemisphere, and at its expense.

The syntheist response to rationalism does not entail any flight back to the irrational. It instead continues dialectically to *transrationalism*: the idea that reasoning first and foremost must embrace the insight of one's own built-in limitations in relation to one's environment. Man is a highly limited creature in both time and in space, and moreover completely dependent on the strictly limited quantity of sensory impressions he has the time to assimilate from a rapidly expanding universe where much more information is produced every moment than any active participant, let alone any passive observer, ever has the time to process. Existence is literally rushing away from the human being; it does not lie down obediently, neatly packaged in his narcissistic bosom, ripe for consumption.

Just like syntheism, as a whole transrationalism and its basic condition can be viewed as both a *logical deduction* and a *historical conclusion*. There is no rational foundation *per se* for naturally limited human rationality to ever have the capacity to comprehend everything in a constantly expanding universe. Plato's and Kant's variants of rationality get caught in their own trap; they are both *per se* founded on a blind faith and not on any kind of rationality. Humanity has repeatedly surrendered itself to rationalism as a social ideology, but the results are frightening. Sooner or later, rationalism – in spite of considerable achievements in civilisation – invariably degenerates into *totalitarian utilitarianism*. Therefore Plato is quite correct in claiming that a consistently practised rationalism must develop into a *dictatorship*. Anything else is impossible.

Before the arrival of totalism, man apprehends himself as a cohesive whole. There is no need to separate an eternal soul from a corruptible body. Although he is mortal, man is part of a natural cycle where life and death are both natural and necessary, regularly recurring fixed points. Above all, everything hangs together with everything else in a monist universe. Totalism destroys this harmony between mankind and her environment. In conjunction with the mobilist Heraclitus being overshadowed by the totalist Plato as an influential thinker in ancient Greece in the 4th century B.C., we can easily note totalism's ideological victory, at least temporarily, and from this follows also alienation's invasion – as rapid as it is destructive – of man's conception of himself and the world.

Narcissism is alienation's clearest symptom. Narcissism is a *compensatory phenomenon*, it originates in its own radical opposite: the fantasy of the world without the subject. The subject must choose to manage the fantasy of the world outside itself in one of two possible ways. Either all production of value and identity is shifted back to the world – for example by creating and worshipping a *god* – or else the shock of the insight into the subject's fundamental emptiness is internalised by turning this emptiness dialectically into its radical opposite: the castrated subject is transformed into *the omnipotent centre of existence*. The fantasy of the world without the subject is so hard to grasp that the simplest way to manage it – if no divinities are invoked – is to place the subject in the driving seat of existence. But if the subject ends up in the driving seat – where it does not reasonably belong, almost everything that happens to us within our lifetime is really out of our control, even if we believe in the illusion that the subject has the possibility to influence its environment – this immediately triggers a whole series of reactions that only can be described as powerful *compensatory behaviour*, which results in *the narcissist condition*. Thus *the Cartesian fantasy* of the subject as the only unerring fixed point in existence and thereby also its centre, becomes a reality.

A flagrant example of such a compensatory narcissist ideology is the British philosopher Jeremy Bentham's utilitarian vision of a future prison, erected according to the architectural *Panopticon* model, a complete institution built in pie wedges around a single human, all-seeing eye at its centre. Bentham imagines a prison built from a central viewpoint from which a sole actor constantly surveys all other activities within the construction. The panopticon is of course nothing other than a material reflection of Bentham's own self-image and world view, his attempt at *a Napoleonisation of bureaucratic architecture*. The panopticon is quite simply the dark flip side of Bentham's *utilitarianism*, his runaway fantasy of a *hyperrationalist ethics*, which can calculate every individual's wishes in advance, put a price on and determine the value of all people's wishes vis-à-vis each other and then compile how one might be able to maximise these wishes into empirically measurable, maximised total utility.

Even though Bentham himself does not even seem capable of understanding that his bizarre *ultrautilitarianism* is a physical impossibility – what can never be formulated in advance, for example human utility, can of course never be measured in advance either – the Panopticon is an exceptionally interesting metaphor for Bentham's own and his many followers' autistic fantasies about their own castrated and isolated subjects as the self-evident centre of the Universe. It is hard to imagine a clearer example of how *the psychotic reversal from impotence to autocracy* constitutes the necessary dialectics for generating the Cartesian fantasy. What we see is a battle over who is the most autistic out of the two most autistic thinkers in the history of philosophy. Through his utilitarianism, if possible Bentham makes himself even more Cartesian than René Descartes himself. But thereby also even more alienated and *alienating*. The Panopticon exposes utilitarianism's view of humanity, the concept reflects Bentham's total lack of trust in his fellow humans and also in himself. The legacy from Bentham has given us what is possibly alienation's clearest contemporary symbol, the paranoid *surveillance camera*.

Monotheistic fundamentalism is the religious version of the Enlightenment's rationalist fantasy. Note how the sectarian leaders who want to maintain their superiority vis-à-vis the rest of humanity always position themselves as *the enlightened*. Monotheistic fundamentalism is a rash and furious *ratio*, literally founded on an idiotic divinity that lacks a *raison d'être*, where this ratio is frenetically maintained by the practitioner's manic conviction that he himself would disintegrate and be annihilated if he really were to recognise God's non-existence. This explains why the fundamentalist does not care whether he lives or dies (which makes him such a resolute terrorist, frustratingly difficult to defend oneself against). The threat to the fundamentalist's fantasy is not physical death, but the disintegration of blind faith. So what is this, if not *theological rationalism* in its purest form?

It is thus also fully logical that the fundamentalists refuse to listen to and reason with their opponents, but would sooner murder them at the first opportunity. It must be extremely taxing to refute intellectual attacks on a divinity which one does not believe in oneself. Least of all if one has lost all faith in the potential of religion and sees *the elevation of alienation to a religious foundation* as the only possible way out. For it is precisely when one reaches the point *where alienation replaces religion* that one starts to execute those who do not agree with, or who quite simply just deviate from, the pattern of one's own fantasies – without remorse. Hitler's Germany and Stalin's Soviet Union functioned according to these same mechanisms. The actor knows that he is lying, but tries to convince himself that everyone else also must be lying, as if this mutual lying and a contest in murdering each another was the only reasonable response to *hyperalienation*. But as it happens, syntheists refuse to participate in this lying. Their reply to the dead religion of the fundamentalists is *the living religion*.

The living religion that moves away from alienation and towards the resumption of community is the opposite of monotheistic fundamentalism, which moves in the opposite direction and *makes alienation its religion.* For the living religion is, like art, implicit rather than explicit, admits several interpretations rather than being simple-minded, is reasonable rather than rational, open to contingencies and emergences rather than fixed in space-time; and above all, it is always *embodied.* Even before fundamentalism surrenders itself to a near-autistic denial of the fact that the meaning of the words which it professes devotion to are in a constant state of flux, this fundamentalism is tripped up by another and more fundamental premise: since fundamentalism always puts the word before God, it reveals that it uses the word to protect itself against the subconscious realisation that whispers that God in truth is already dead. If the law is the only thing left when God has disappeared from the equation, *the law must be regarded as God.* But a living god does not need the word as protection. A living god stands without any irresolute tottering or any ulterior motives in front of the word instead of anxiously hiding behind it. A living god exists based on the premise that an overwhelmingly large part of all communication between people is non-verbal. Already the well-known words of the Gospel of John "In the beginning was the Word, and the Word was with God, and the Word was God" reveal a religion which has lost faith in God's existence. The only thing left even at this early stage is just *the empty incantation as God's proxy.*

The more acute the alienation, the more powerful the narcissism becomes. In late capitalist society with its *hyperalienation,* the Cartesian fantasy transitions into a *hypernarcissism,* a state characterised by a complete distrust in all intersubjective intentions other than the purely instrumental. Hypernarcissism is internalised as the subject's own instrumentality world view, where other people are reduced to isolated bodies, monitored and controlled by an authority with a far-reaching mandate and with the aid of game theory calculations. This is a subject whose libido is obsessed with strategic planning, conquest, colonisation, plundering and displacement. When the libido tries to adapt itself to hypernarcissism's instrumentality view of humanity, the result is not only a consistent sexualisation of all intimate relationships, but also a powerful fetishisation of sexuality *per se*. The hypernarcissist – whose own sexual activity ironically can be both manic and minimal, often oscillating violently between extremes – sees reproductive organs everywhere and in nearly everything. Culture is filled with them to the extent that it almost becomes parodical. In this paralysed libidinal state, no living fellow humans remain, but only dying bodies drenched in disdain for their lack of Platonic perfection. *The alienation is complete, and the living religion is conspicuous by its tangible absence.*

When hypernarcissism becomes socially burdensome, the result is yet another subject that can act as *an agent of transfer*, another subject with which the hypernarcissistic subject establishes an apparent trade, a kind of psychological "if you scratch my back, I'll scratch yours". When the compensatory self-worship becomes psycho-socially unbearable, it also becomes the object of a transferring exchange between the subjects. One subject worships another subject in exchange for the corresponding worship in return, as if to conceal that the original compensatory act is banal narcissism in itself. Thus hypernarcissism transitions into internarcissism, precisely the state that completely dominates the late capitalist social arena. Syntheism however offers a possible way out of the internarcissistic cul-de-sac. By confronting the trauma from the fantasy of *the world without the subject* and through *seeing the living religion* as the way out of *murderous alienation*, the subject can at last be liberated into something greater than its limited, incarcerated self and become incorporated into the syntheist community, *the manifestation of Syntheos*!

The syntheological pyramid – Atheos, Pantheos, Entheos and Syntheos

The fundamental question within phenomenology is at what point the human being is confronted for the first time with the need to produce a credible *totality* of her chaotic existence. That this doesn't happen already at birth is beyond all doubt. The newborn infant only experiences *world*, but no *self*. The child sees itself as one with the mother; in its fantasy their bodies are still a single whole, as they were when the umbilical cord bound them together, and they were not yet separate entities. Understanding this requires insight into *difference* which means that the child can experience *chaos;* and from this literally chaotic experience, the (somewhat older) child can proceed to first identify and then satisfy its need for a phenomenological totality.

So where in the child's development should one place this onto-phenomenological moment? The psychoanalyst Jacques Lacan maintains that it occurs in connection with what he calls *the mirror* stage. The body develops an imaginary ability to regard fragmented reality as in fact a cohesive reality; perception converts the noumenal chaos into *a phenomenal world.*

The subject then emerges in relation to this surmised and self-produced entirety: the human being's self-image is always a *mirror image* of her world view. Thus, it is not about the moment when the child literally sees her body in a mirror for the first time – not until the 19th century did the classic mirror on the wall become a common item of interior decoration – but rather a first *reflection of the self in the world*. This in turn explains why an altered world view, *a new paradigm*, always is followed by a correlated change in the human ideal and self-image. The latter goes hand in hand with the former.

The reflection of the self in the world is, however, in no way harmonious, observes Lacan, but rather extremely frustrating for the subject, tending to breed aggression. In order to try to resolve the tension in its relationship with the chaotic environment, the subject starts to identify with the *image in the mirror*. This leads to an imaginary feeling of overview and control: the subject apprehends itself as the centre and master of existence. The result is that *the subject deifies itself*, in particular precisely that within itself that it cannot master, that which Lacan calls *the other*. And the other of psychoanalysis is of course just another name for theology's *God*. Since syntheism is the doctrine of how and where we find a pedestal for the other within our own paradigm, it can be viewed as a *Lacanian theology*. The question is not whether we need a Lacanian theology for the Internet age – we will end up constructing such a theology subconsciously and thoughtlessly unless we have first done so consciously and carefully – but rather exactly which Lacanian theology is relevant and credible for the dynamic environment which frames and determines our current existence.

In our eagerness to discern patterns and create meaning, we repeatedly believe that we are able to observe how what was once, in a distant past, a mysterious myth, a fairy tale, is transformed into a tangible and ultimately established technology at a later stage. And sometimes this also happens to be correct. The majestic *gesamtkunstverk* "Koyaanisqatsi" – directed by Godfrey Reggio, produced by Francis Ford Coppola, with music composed by Philip Glass – had its première in cinemas in California in 1982. The film's story is based on a thousand-year-old apocalyptic tale, told by the Hopi Indians in Arizona, of a mastodonic spider that weaves a gigantic web around the world, a web that unites all people and objects in nature and transforms them into *a single emergent phenomenon*. When this phenomenon finally emerges, according to the Hopi Indians' myth, history is complete.

Reggio's own growing up and domicile in California is hardly a coincidence in this context. Because it is precisely in fact during the film's genesis in the 1970s in California that the Hopi Indian myth is actually realised through the birth of the Internet. The Internet is *an eminently emergent phenomenon*, which takes over and reshapes the world entirely on its own terms; a phenomenon that we cannot control but merely try to adapt to as best we can. For what is the Internet at its core if not in fact a global web of threads that binds all human beings and objects together into one single global, organic whole where the web itself is greater and more important than the sum of its many constituent parts? Syntheologically we regard the Internet as *an incarnation of Syntheos*, a divinity which (naturally) has not created Man – which traditional gods previously were considered to have done – but rather a god who in the first instance allows itself to be created by Man only to later, in the next phase, recreate Man by colonising his lifeworld and thereby dictating his new living conditions, thus sparking new characteristics and qualities.

At no point in history has Man been able to or chosen to live without gods. And one is either – in the best case – conscious of this and chooses one's gods with the greatest care, or else one is – in the worst case – ignorant of the fact that this need exists and believes oneself to be historically unique in the respect that only oneself in particular, in precisely the enlightened – in the secular sense – era in which one happens to be living, has succeeded in liberating oneself from this need and therefore can manage just as well, if not better, without it. But Man can never be liberated from religion unless he ceases to be human, because *mankind produces gods* at the same moment that she *prioritises anything at all in existence ahead of something else.*

For mankind surely does prioritise from the moment she is born. Even the new-born infant's very first desperate clambering towards her mother's nipple – the first and most obvious example of Lacan's *objet petit a*, the small object that the human being must use as a cornerstone in constructing a meaningful world view – in the pursuit of security, warmth and nourishment in a cold and uncertain new world, is a crystal-clear *prioritisation*. The breast comes before all else. The mother's breast is thereby the first divinity in the human being's life, the prioritised comfort in existence once the paradise in the womb has been lost and the child hears her own scream express loneliness and vulnerability for the first time, the meeting point between two bodies united in pleasure where the hope and longing for a reunification that can dissolve the self's painful isolation from the world shines most clearly and warms the most.

The production of holy things is thus in full swing even during life's first, explorative promenade across the mother's belly and then continues all the way to the inescapably holiest state of all, *death*. Existential gaps open up and confront Man constantly, and all she can do is fill these *negations* with fantasies, which later prove to be more or less functional. The question is thus not whether gods exist in any deeper sense. They unquestionably do. The subconscious mind can never accept any kind of *atheism*. Syntheism rather poses the question: *which divinity or divinities is/are credible for informationalist* Man? What could and should be *theos* under informationalism? Where do we place the repressed hope of self-dissolution and communion with being, the longing of the subconscious for death which consciousness must repress and transform into the subject experience's fanatical will to live?

After philosophy and science have killed off the Abrahamic gods – a process which, in the mid-19th century, Friedrich Nietzsche sums up in the idea of *the death of God* – syntheism, the metaphysics of the Internet age, poses the question of which potential divinities remain, and which have been added for informationalist Man to tinker with. It is of course the case that where knowledge is *passive*, faith is *active*. At best, knowledge can never be anything other than *the truth about that which has transpired,* while faith understands itself as *the truth about that which is to come.* Reason cannot stand on only one of these two legs, or it will plunge into either *neurotic rationality* or *psychotic obsession*, for both are necessary mainstays in a reason that is functional. As it turns out, there are a host of divinities that the informationalist human being can believe in, or rather already does believe in. Let us start by revisiting Nietzsche's two magnificent predecessors Hegel and Spinoza for inspiration.

Hegel is unique, not least because he remains *de facto* outside the regularly recurring *dichotomy between totalism and mobilism* in the history of philosophy. Instead he concentrates on drawing innovative conclusions from the revolution within the history of ideas that his predecessors have begun – primarily Newton within physics and later Kant within philosophy – by moving philosophy from the external, physical world to the internal world of the mind. There Hegel resolutely builds a complete theory about *how the mind views itself, as a mind.* Thus he makes himself into an eternalist, without, in the manner of a Kant, thereby resorting to totalist fantasies. Hegel's point of departure is that if the noumenal reality that surrounds Man still remains impossible to reach (which Kant maintains), and if it makes itself apparent in a way that, in the best case, can only be measured (which Newton does), philosophers should hand over external reality to the natural sciences and instead concentrate on the most important aspects of what science cannot tell us anything valuable about, namely the human mind's conception of and obsession with itself.

It is important to understand that Hegel is not talking about some kind of *narcissistic self-reflection* – which might be easy to believe if we take contemporary Man's view of the world as a starting point: *narcissism* is fundamentally a misdirected neurotic *compensatory behaviour*; even Hegel knows this, long before his disciple Freud. On the contrary he is talking about a self-centredness which if anything is reluctant, but from a historical perspective highly motivated; a logical consequence of the intense, subconscious search for *self-love*, which drives all metaphysics. It is a phenomenological, not a psychological self-seeking. For Hegel the subject is only found in one place, namely as what tacitly does the asking when the question "Who am I?" is posed. And this *it* asking the question, he deliberately calls *the spirit* – as in *the Zeitgeist* or *the Weltgeist* (*"World Spirit"*) – and not *the soul,* as if it were about some kind of Platonist opposite to the body. For just like Spinoza, Hegel is a *monist,* not a dualist. It is after having read Spinoza that he utters the familiar saying: "You are either a Spinozist or not a philosopher at all."

Hegel ignores Kant's striving to capture the complex relationship between Man and his environment and instead goes directly into *the mind,* where he builds a phenomenology around *the paradoxist subject,* its genesis, structure and future (see *The Global Empire*). His most famous work is consequently entitled *Phenomenology of Spirit.* Hegel regards this voyage as one, long *self-reflection process.* He deduces the consequences of value and meaning being created and existing only within the mind and that this creation of value and meaning fundamentally has the sole function of being Man's existential pastime while waiting for his necessary dissolution and inevitable expiration. For Hegel, for the first time in the West's history of ideas, the concept of *God* is *merely a necessary concept, not a physically material reality*. According to Hegel, like everything else in the mind, God is an internally manufactured product, a necessary component in humanity's historical equation, not an external fact. This does not make him the first *pantheist*, but it does on the other hand make him the first *atheist* philosopher in the West's history of ideas. Hardly surprisingly, this has dramatic consequences.

From the preordained conclusion that, in the final analysis, the mind strives to be able to think itself as itself, Hegel sets in motion one of the most original and most innovative projects in the history of philosophy. How does the mind arrive at *the thought about itself as itself before itself*, if the only possibility to do so is to pass through an endlessly long historical, tautological loop? And correspondingly: If the mind is free to form its own opinion of itself independently of all conceivable external influences, in that case what *religion* – credible to itself – would this mind invent and develop? After an extremely long and roundabout but unremittingly exciting journey, Hegel arrives at his final destination, *Atheos*, the god that does not exist, the god of emptiness. The history of the mind begins in any case with emptiness; non-existence not only predates existence but according to Hegel is also its engine – and then not in any kind of *physical* sense. The Universe starts with a something; there is no nothingness before somethingness in physics, except as always with Hegel in just the *mental* sense. For this reason he lands exactly there.

Hegelian atheism is the perfect complement to *Spinozist pantheism* in what together constitute syntheology's two mainstays. Syntheology thus starts from the Hegelian *Atheos* and the Spinozist *Pantheos*, and since it is relationalist, primarily from *the oscillation between these two poles* – see also the phenomenological *dialectics between eternalism and mobilism* (see *The Global Empire*) – which is later complemented by two further divinological concepts, *Entheos* and *Syntheos*. Together these four concepts form *the syntheological pyramid*, and thereby all the necessary prerequisites for the Internet society's religion are at hand. The four divinities in the syntheological pyramid are, quite simply, the personifications of the four supraphenomena that surround the informationalist human being. Atheos is *the potentiality*, Pantheos is *the actuality*, Entheos is *the transcendence* and Syntheos is *the virtuality*.

These well-considered choices of names are of course open to discussion in this *ironic polytheism* for no end of time; the four syntheological concepts were created in a participatory and intersubjective process in a syntheist online forum and, in good netocratic spirit, lack an original dividual author. The movement has thus agreed as a collective on these names together. But these supraphenomena are highly real and together with Friedrich von Schelling's powerful foundation work and Martin Heidegger's magnificent extension work constitute the groundwork within advanced metaphysics. And both extension and interior design work is still ongoing. American philosopher Robert Corrington, for example, in his book *A Semiotic Theory of Theology and Philosophy*, constructs a system around what he calls the four infinities. Atheos corresponds to *the sustaining infinite* in Corrington's metaphysics, Pantheos is another name for *the actual infinite*, Entheos corresponds to what Corrington calls *the prospective infinite*, and Syntheos is another name for *the open infinite*. The Irish philosopher William Desmond constructs a similar system in his book *God and The Between* around *the three transcendences*: Atheos is here the name of *the interior potentiality (T1)*, Pantheos is the name of *the exterior actuality (T2)* and Entheos is the name of *transcendence as transcendence per se (T3)*. The only reason that Desmond does not use a fourth component in his metaphysics is that he chooses to completely avoid the future as a theme; otherwise Syntheos would be obvious as Desmond's T4.

The syntheological pyramid starts with a relational *interiority* with Atheos at the one end, which shifts to a relational *exteriority* with Pantheos at the other end. In the world of cosmology this even occurs literally: a black hole *absorbs*, it happens interiorly, while the Universe *expands*, it happens exteriorly. Exteriority then continues with Entheos, with its explosions of irreducible differences, multitudes and emergences over time, but shifts back to an interiority with Syntheos, as the utopia, the concentrated point or *God* for all of humanity's dreams of the future. Atheos and Syntheos are primarily introvert or *absorbing* concepts, while Pantheos and Entheos are primarily extrovert or *expansive* concepts. If we express this relation phenomenologically, we say that an eternalism apprehends a mobilism – it is when Atheos is applied to Pantheos that Pantheos emerges as *the One*: a mobilism that is augmented in the next step and then switches back to an eternalism. It is for example when Entheos is applied to Syntheos that *the agent finds its place within the phenomenon* and syntheist activism takes shape as *the truth as an act*.

The syntheological pyramid can be traced back to Zoroaster and his work *Gathas,* which he authored as early as 3,700 years ago. According to Zoroaster, *Ahura* (being personified) is generated by the oscillation between Atheos and Pantheos, while *Mazda* (the mind personified) is generated by the next level, the oscillation between Entheos and Syntheos. If the oscillation between Atheos and Pantheos has a name of its own, it is *Ahura*; if the oscillation between Entheos and Syntheos has a name of its own, it is *Mazda*. When Zoroaster proclaims his universal religion, interestingly enough he calls it *mazdayasna* (love of the mind) and not *ahurayasna* (love of being). This explains why we refer to him as the first *protosyntheist*. Zoroaster prioritises the god that the human being creates, *Mazda*, over the god that creates himself independent of Man, *Ahura*, while also uniting them under the name *Ahura Mazda*, being that includes consciousness. According to Zoroaster, Man is *an internal agent within the Universe as a phenomenon* and not some kind of external, alien accident in relation to the rest of existence, as in the Abrahamic religions and their philosophical offspring.

It is eminently possible to use the French philosopher Gilles Deleuze's concepts to describe the current dialectics between eternalism and mobilism: eternalism is a *territorialisation*, a fixation of a specific phenomenon (which for example occurs when the interiority Atheos is applied to the exteriority Pantheos); and mobilism is a *deterritorialisation*, a shaking-up and setting-in-motion-again of the phenomenon in question (as when the exteriority Entheos is applied to the interiority Syntheos). *Territorialisation* is fundamentally preserving; *deterritorialisation* is fundamentally radicalising. Thus, to take a concrete example from netocracy theory, new information technologies are deterritorialising, while identity production in a society is territorialising. Movement within the syntheological pyramid is thus initiated by a territorialising (a preserving but productive fixation), but is concluded by a deterritorialising (a radical liberation of sundry *expansive potentials* in the direction of *the absorbing utopia*). Syntheism is supremely a *theological Deleuzianism*.

It is important to point out that syntheism sees *the world itself* as fundamentally mobilist, and not as eternalist. Faith in the world itself as eternalist belongs within totalism, the trap that we strive to avoid at all costs. Like interiority and territorialisation, eternalism must be limited to phenomenology. *Atheos, Pantheos, Entheos and Syntheos are creative eternalisations of the void, the cosmos, the difference and the utopia.* It is as fundamental and powerful eternalisations that we use them for constructing a functional, relevant and, in the deepest sense of the word, *credible* metaphysics for the Internet age. Since they are ontological eternalisations, we do not need to look for them and demonstrate their external ontic existence in nature in relation to us humans; the crews of the space stations are never ever going to find our gods above the clouds. All four of them are figments of the brain of some kind, but highly consciously created and creative such.

Atheos, Pantheos, Entheos and Syntheos do not receive their enormous potency as some kind of long-lived giant beings from parallel universes, like antiquity's or Hinduism's worlds of divinities, but as dramatically useful metaphors for the structure of existence (from Atheos to Pantheos) and the place of consciousness and scope for action within this structure (from Entheos to Syntheos). Therefore the syntheist divinities are immanent, finite and mortal, rather than transcendent, eternal and immortal, like traditional gods. Mortal creatures in a finite universe can only create mortal and finite divinities. The immortal god, created by mortal creatures, is an absurdity, a self-contradiction in a Derridean sense. Therefore, in the name of consistency, syntheology stops at mortal gods. Here it is worth recalling Blaise Pascal's pragmatic concept *Deus Absconditus* from the 17th century: it is quite correct to say that syntheism stops at gods that reveal themselves *only to those who seek gods*, but avoids the gaze of all those who would rather avoid gods.

Atheos means *the god that does not exist* in Greek. Atheos is the god of the void or the black hole, the zero position of existence, the existential rather than the physical *nothingness*, and simultaneously the origin of everything and the engine of all identities from which *the subject* arises and gets its driving force. The void is namely an anthropocentric illusion. There is no actual void in the Universe; what appears to be empty space is full of physical activity. So the actual space in the void thus has a substance. However, everything beautiful and meaningful in our existence arises out of mental voids. When we are going to define why we love someone or something, exactly what we *de facto love* in the person or thing in question will invariably evade our description. The reason is that it is precisely *Atheos*, the void, the unknown, the utopian in the person or thing that we love, which we love and which becomes all the more desirable since it never allows itself to be captured or even articulated exhaustively. Atheos is Hegel's god, and the syntheists celebrate him at *midwinter,* which is followed by the *Athea* quarter. Midwinter is the celebration of the Universe's existential necessity, *the celebration of the origin of life and existence.*

Pantheos is the Universe as the divine. Because there is something rather than nothing – there is after all a life, a world – this something is equivalent to God: *the Universe is God.* If God exists, God must be the Universe. It would be pointless for an existing God to be separate from the Universe, since God does not have any need whatsoever to be a soul of any kind, separated from a body. The Universe is in fact characterised by expanding bounty, not by a struggle over insufficient resources, like life on Earth, which means that God never has to be manipulated away from an infirm body of limited durability in order to live on somewhere else, liberated from this body. Consequently God is immanent rather than transcendent, and physics is not some substandard representation or copy of divine mathematics, which totalist thinkers from Plato during antiquity to Alain Badiou in our own era are constantly drawn to believe. *God is physics and physics is God.* Mathematics is merely the human being's approximatic tool for trying to catch up to, describe and thus understand God. Pantheos is infinite multiplicity beyond infinite multiplicity, the multiplicity of multiplicities as *the One.* Pantheos is Spinoza's god, and the syntheists celebrate him at *midsummer,* which is followed by the *Panthea* quarter.

Entheos means *the God from within* in Greek. And our inside is fundamentally split, for we are dividuals and not individuals and thus tangible evidence ourselves of the *irreducible multiplicity* of existence. Therefore Entheos is *the difference as a divinity*, and since difference piled on difference becomes a *duration* of differences, we are also speaking here of *the god of time*. Entheos is quite simply *the historical differentiation* as divinity, simply because the lapse of time is and must be *a constant repetition of ever so small differences* and not an eternal repetition of the same. Aside from being the divinity of difference and duration, Entheos is also the divinity of contingency, oscillation, plurality, transcendence, ecstasy, melancholy, transformation and emergence. Entheos is the borderland between Atheos and Pantheos, that which sets the dialectics between Atheos and Pantheos in motion, the medium through which Atheos and Pantheos communicate with each other. Entheos is the very relation *between* Atheos and Pantheos set in motion, but also the constant, high-octane oscillation *within* both Atheos and Pantheos. Entheos is the syntheist agent's god and the common name for, and oscillation between, Taoism's *yin* and *yang*.

Here it is important to understand that time is probably the most mysterious concept within both philosophy and physics. Even if totalist-oriented philosophers such as Plato and scientists such as Einstein in some strange way were to be proven correct in that *time is an illusion,* they still do not succeed in thinking of the world without a *metatime* within which this illusory time is presumed to exist. Even if Einsteinian mathematics succeeds in magically tinkering with time by turning it into an extra dimension in connection with space, and thereby, for example, forcing it to move backwards as well as forwards, there is no proof whatsoever that any such time as an extra dimension in connection with space actually exists in physical reality. Nobody has yet succeeded in turning the uncompromising *arrow of time,* which inexorably moves from the past into the future through a now which is in constant motion (at the very moment that you speak the word *now* it has been supplanted by yet another now and has therefore advanced to become a *then*). This explains why duration stubbornly bounces back as a metatime every time the Platonists try to convert it into an illusion. It is quite simply impossible to get past time, and already with time as god, *Entheos* thus is necessary in syntheology.

When Einstein proves that time is relative, he also proves that time elapses more quickly or slowly depending on *the local context*, but this does not change the fact that it still and always travels in one and the same direction through the Universe. Within syntheology one is careful to distinguish between *time* as a physical phenomenon and *duration* as the existential experience of the direction of the arrow of time. In any case, Entheos is the divinity of both time and duration, since time and duration present the clearest evidence that the *difference* is the foundation of identity production. We can talk about the arrow of time, duration, history – we find many names for the things we love – but what we are actually talking about is a recurring feedback loop with infinitesimally but – thanks to their identity-dislocating function – extremely significant changes for every cycle that occurs. Entheos is quite simply the name of the constant repetition of the difference itself, that which Nietzsche and Deleuze call *the eternal return of the same*.

Entheos is also the divinity we encounter when we experience what Sigmund Freud calls *the oceanic feeling*. To devote oneself to Entheos is to worship the brain's and the body's ability to carry out mental voyages and to emotionally experience the sacred, to allow oneself to be transcended into a new and qualitatively different subject. Entheos is therefore also *the divinity of the sublime and of art*. Syntheistic transcendence is entirely a subjective experience; it thus has nothing to do with any Platonist dualism or Kantian transcendentalism. Syntheistic transcendence takes place in a completely immanent world, just as the eternalisations of perception are housed within an otherwise completely mobilist world. Entheos is driven by the desire towards immanent *change* and the search for transcendental *intensity*; it is the divinity that we encounter in the psychedelic experience, which personifies the entheogenic worlds. Entheos is not just Nietzsche's and Deleuze's divinity, but also the god of Heraclitus and Lao Tzu, and is celebrated at the spring equinox, which is the syntheist calendar's new year. The Spring equinox represents the celebration of the enormous and irreducible *multiplicity* of life and thereby also the celebration of our own human *dividuality*.

As the roof above the Atheos-Pantheos-Entheos triangle, *Syntheos* binds the other three divinities together and completes *the syntheological pyramid*. From the triangle Atheos, Pantheos and Entheos, three lines strive upwards and are merged in a point that is Syntheos, which thereby holds the entire structure together and gives it its name. Syntheos is the divinity of the collective, humanity, the future, creativity, dreams, aspirations, visions and utopias. All gods that have ever been invented are illustrations of one and the same god, namely the need for a personified, cohesive component in order for the world to appear as *the One*, a meaningful whole. A human being without desires is a dead human being. In the same way, a society without a utopia is a dead society. Syntheism therefore maintains that it is not the content of the utopia but *the utopia in itself* that is the divine. *According to the speculative logic of the syntheist, the need for the divine is divine in itself.* The Greek word for the creating god is *Syntheos*, from which syntheism gets its name. God is no longer a patriarchal creator of worlds from the past or a longed-for saviour on a white steed, but the *de facto* name of *the collective utopia* of the collective itself in the future.

Syntheos is driven by the desire for meaningful fellowship and an idea of the perfection of history. If the Father died with the Word, and if the Son died on the Cross, Syntheos is what is left of Christianity after its ideological collapse. Syntheos is the divinity of theological anarchism, a kind of independent *Holy Ghost without either the Father or the Son*. Syntheos is introduced historically, of course, by the syntheists themselves and is celebrated at the autumn equinox. The autumn equinox is the celebration of the *community* as the manifestation of the divine. The autumn equinox is also the celebration of the return of everything to its origin, of how creativity and destructiveness are two sides of the one coin, of the perfection of all circles, of *death on the horizon as the creator of meaning for every living thing*, and is followed by the *Synthea* quarter.

The movement in the syntheological pyramid goes from *the possible* in Atheos to *the realised* in Pantheos; from *the mutable* in Entheos to *the consummated* in Syntheos. The syntheist calendar is constructed around syntheology's four cornerstones and their quarters: *Enthea* starts at the spring equinox which is the syntheist new year, *Panthea* starts at midsummer, *Synthea* starts at the autumn equinox and *Athea* starts at midwinter. And then everything starts again from the beginning: repetition but with constant displacements. The movement within the syntheological pyramid also goes from the top down. When *Syntheos* is completed, *Entheos* gets a cohesive meaning: the chaotic differences and repetitions get a context since they suddenly appear as creative intensities on top of the stable community that Syntheos constructs. Entheos can be apprehended as the individual human being, *the dividual subject,* divided and fundamentally homeless. Syntheos is *the collective subject*, the holy community which is bigger for the dividual subject than the dividual subject is in relation to itself. We can express this in the following way: Syntheos is the emergent dimension where Entheos finds its home and is realised. Syntheos is the place where Entheos is transformed into the syntheist agent and meets its transience with dignity.

This means that the *cosmos* no longer appears as a cold and indifferent machinery grinding away, but instead as an holistic divinity filled with meaning – *Pantheos*. The arrival of this Pantheos in turn opens the way for a new appreciation of the creativity that emanates from the void of its predecessor, *Atheos*, the non-god, which is the origin of all subjectivity processes. For while Pantheos resides in consciousness, Atheos rules in the subconscious. This is completely in line with what Lacan says: the subject is created in and belongs to the subconscious. Therefore Lacan also speaks of *the barred subject*, that is, the subject's inability to know its own origin, and how this very impossibility is constitutive of the subject itself. It is the uncompromisingly barred Atheos that is the source of the subject. Note how the four concepts in the syntheological pyramid are completely dependent on and include each other. Pantheos, Entheos and Syntheos all reside within Atheos. Atheos, Entheos and Syntheos are all housed within Pantheos. Atheos, Pantheos and Syntheos all reside within Entheos. Atheos, Pantheos and Syntheos are all housed within Syntheos. If Christianity is based on God as a trinity, syntheism is instead based on *God as a quadrinity*.

Syntheism presupposes both a *religious atheism* and a *subjective pantheism*. It is important to distinguish between on the one hand a subjective and on the other hand an objective pantheism. Subjective pantheism is an *active choice* to see the fact that there is something rather than nothing as the foundation for *the holy*. The truth is an act. Through this decision, the Universe and its history are put on a par with the divine. That which exists is made into something holy. However, objective pantheism requires a blind and indisputable conviction that the Universe actually is God. But this position is of no interest to syntheism. In order for *pantheism* to be woven together first with *atheism* and then with *entheism* – in order to lead on to *syntheism* – in fact requires that it is strictly subjective. We find no signs that the Universe regards itself as divine – it displays no signs whatsoever of having a consciousness of its own that can produce a religious conviction similar to that of humans – and if this were the case, the syntheist premise would collapse. The four divinities in the syntheological pyramid are in fact all created by ourselves for ourselves, as named *projections* of existence; they are all *syntheist*, so too are Atheos, Pantheos and Entheos.

There are grounds for declaring that syntheism can and should be regarded as *'New Age' for the thinking man*. The critically thinking Man, one should then add. For with a blind faith built into the core of the construction, syntheism would never hold up logically. The truth is of course that syntheism is anything but 'New Age'. It is a construction *on top of* modern physics and *after* the atheist revolution, without in any way therefore opposing the preceding advances in the natural science and metaphysics – but rather by deepening these further. While New Age at best must be regarded as a kind of postmodern laissez-faire laughing stock, full of folly, an anti-intellectual mishmash of superstition, nonsense and general fear of conflict in sundry variants – as well as a variety of old ideas that are trivialised and commercialised so strongly that they become meaningless, an unsystematic recycling of worthless thinking from times gone by – syntheism is instead the logically deduced metaphysics for a new era. For real.

It is important to distinguish between *classical atheism* and *syntheist atheism*. Classical atheism not only maintains that God does not exist, it also presumes that God cannot exist. Syntheist atheism, on the other hand, maintains that God might well exist, partly as a divinity placed and created in the future (*syn-theos*), partly also as a constantly present productive void (*a-theos*) in space–time that supplies the cosmos (*pan-theos*) and its conscious inhabitants with subjectivity in an indeterministic process of constant change (*en-theos*). The reason for this is that *existence expresses itself unremittingly*, and quite regardless of whether or not there is an internarcissistic, human participant present in the process.

While classic atheism zeroes in on the one god after the other in its dedicated ambition to deconstruct and empty these of content – there is thus no cohesive, classical atheism, which means that classical atheism can only exist in the plural, where every orientation has a specific god in its sights – syntheist atheism is based on something that actually exists already: Atheos, the non-god, or *the void per se*, and it focuses on the enormous productivity of this void – from quantum fluctuations to subjectivity processes. Where classical atheism is merely *reactive* – always awaiting new theist innovations to attack and thus being dependent on the gods it so eagerly denies – syntheist atheism is *active* and thereby offers an existential substance which classical atheism lacks. The syntheistic atheist builds cathedrals to celebrate her conviction and the collectively edified fellowship, while the classical atheist on her part just has to make do with sitting on the side-lines, paralysed by a religion-envy that must be kept secret. Classical atheism is instead the little temperance movement of the territory of spirituality and outlook on life, forever doomed to miss out on all the fun parties.

Faith is always a belief in the impossible being possible. Only a faith without assurances is an authentic faith. That is what the word faith actually means. Therefore syntheistic faith is *the authentic faith par excellence*. Ultimately, all forms of faith up until syntheism have been based on calculations of utility and anticipated rewards. There is no such *speculative appeasement*, no servility and no sucking up to an external fetishized power within syntheism. Atheos gives without taking, Syntheos takes without giving, while Entheos is always being recreated, and Pantheos always is. This means that syntheist ethics is based on the principle that the agent gives in and of pure joy, without expecting any kind of reward in return. Syntheism's *ethos* is a wilful act, an identification with the act, *I am doing this only because I am the one who is to do this*, without the slightest trace of the traditional religion's at times appeasing, at times calculating, ulterior motives. Syntheist ethics is a pure form of *activism* – rather than a passive *reactiv-*

ism – an activism which in turn is founded on *faith*; on a faith which through being activated unleashes a truth, *the truth as an act*, an action that uses the void's vacuum energy as an engine to revolutionise the world, in order to constantly create the world anew in a similarly constant expansion.

Atheos is the *void* that generates the repetitious *drive*. Pantheos is *the cosmos* that generates *desire* that is always on the hunt and never entirely satisfied. Entheos is the transcendence within the immanence, the engine behind all change, difference and diversity. Syntheos is the divine dissolution of the self in the collective, of the self in the cosmos, the sacred meeting between bodies and minds. Syntheos is also the creation of the syntheist religion through the creative coalescence of Atheos, Pantheos, and Entheos as the consummated and healing (whole-making) *syntheology*. Therefore it is also in Syntheos that we find *the ethical imperative* to overcome and become one with something much greater than one's own subject, that is to *become one with Syntheos*. The dance between Atheos, Pantheos, Entheos and Syntheos opens the way for divinities that are finished with their work – divinities that hand us over to ourselves.

All of these four concepts relate to the search for *the sublime* as equivalent to the deepest pursuit of religion. The quest for the religious experience is the quest for a life intensity which is so strong that it bridges the gap from the moment to eternity – what syntheology calls *the infinite now*. Atheos motivates and drives the religious impulse, Entheos is the impulse in itself, Pantheos is its horizon and Syntheos is the moment when the impulse reaches its target and religion is realised as *pure religion*. Metaphors borrowed from the *diachronic* world of quantum physics shed light on the process: Atheos is the wave and Pantheos is the particle. Entheos is the relation between them, the movement between; on the one hand the perfect wave where no particle exists any longer, and on the other hand the perfect particle where no wave exists any longer. Syntheos is this entire complex seen as a cohesive unit, as a single *phenomenon*. It is through the presence and realisation of Syntheos that the phenomenon becomes an active *agent*.

Physicist Stephen Hawking argues that physical reality becomes accessible to us via models that function within our world view, that are relevant for our era and above all are scientifically verifiable. He calls this conviction *model-dependent realism*. We create *history* (Entheos) through our specific participation in it, rather than history creating us. When Hawking's colleague Edward Witten launches the *M-theory* in the mid-1990s, he presents a multiverse theory where all previously relevant explanatory models for physics are brought together under a common mathematical roof. According to M-theory, there are at least 10 to the power of 500 different possible string-theory universes. What M-theory *de facto* does with these multiple, possible universes, means that *existence* can no longer be regarded as a miracle loosely dangling in nothingness, but rather must be seen as a *necessity* with a solid anchoring in somethingness.

According to this, our latest, model-dependent realism the metaphysicists Martin Heidegger and Slavoj Zizek make one and the same mistake when they construct their respective ontologies on the premise that nothingness is just as reasonable an assumption as somethingness. For nothingness has never been a possible or even a conceivable alternative in the world of physics. Zizek thus misinterprets Bohrian quantum physics when he says that *the Universe is a mistake* (even if the statement naturally, as usual for Zizek, works as a funny and thought-provoking provocation). Existence itself is namely the only sufficiently stable state in the physical world. Non-existence, on the other hand, is an extremely unsteady state and it is precisely for this reason an impossibility in a long-term perspective, since existence itself is constantly being offered such an infinite number of possibilities to be brought to life. Nothingness is thus unstable in itself, and with this instability it necessarily follows that a quantity of universes are produced in it at a torrential rate. Something always exists. Nothingness in principle never exists. And to the extent that it does exist, it is always something in any case.

The recurring mistake is Man's constant anthropocentric, internarcissistic projection on the terms of existence: it is the absurdities we experience *in our own existence* that make us regard the Universe as a mysterious coincidence where existence miraculously enough happens to defeat non-existence. This anthropocentrism rests on facts that are irrelevant for the cosmos such as the fact that only one of several million sperm succeeds in fertilising one of millions of eggs in order for ourselves to arise as embryos; or that millions and again millions of possible variants of ourselves die every moment to enable just one of all this infinite number of variants of ourselves to survive, all the way through to all the variants finally perishing when death catches up with everything living within us. But in the world of physics there are no such balances, no trade-offs between *something* and *nothing* as probable, equivalent alternatives. The possibilities of somethingness completely crush the probabilities of nothingness through the entheistic oceans of existence, until somethingness becomes the metaphysical foundation of model-dependent realism.

The human mind is the arena for a constant battle between the extremes *Atheos* (the absorbing subject) and *Pantheos* (the expanding cosmos), where Atheos represents *the drive* while Pantheos represents *the desire* within psychoanalysis. Atheos is the Universe as it apprehends itself, it is the subject's experience of itself as a subject. In the same way that we must regard ourselves as voids where life seeks meaning through an always unsuccessful but nonetheless always repeated struggle to fill the void with content; in the same way Atheos is the idea of what the Universe sees when the Universe observes itself, from the inside. Pantheos is the Universe that we humans observe and to which we ascribe divinity; it is the Universe as object, observed by a subject (the believing dividual or the community). This means that syntheology emanates from a dialectics between Atheos and Pantheos, it is between these two concepts that we are moving – constantly, restlessly – they are our sacred extremes, midwinter and midsummer in the syntheist calendar, where Entheos is their common product, *the fate* that we unconditionally love: *amor fati*.

It is Atheos who drops *the event* as a bombshell into the metauniverse that beforehand appeared to be balanced. The Universe arises as a minimal but decisive quantum deviation in a metauniverse *where something is less than nothing*. It should be pointed out in this context that the void is never empty. A nothing in the classical sense does not exist in physics. In its apparent emptiness, a void is also full of *pure activity* and, as long as the total energy amount is zero, is capable of producing and maintaining any amount of quantitative substance. Existence, life, and consciousness are all examples of magical, incomprehensible, unpredictable *emergences* that Atheos drops into history. Every event of every kind in the Universe is of course actually incredibly unlikely on closer inspection, but occurs nonetheless only according to the principle that *something happens because something must happen sooner or later*. Atheos is the engine in syntheism's Pantheos. What separates Man from other animals is not just that Man is endowed with a consciousness, but that he also has a subconscious. It is *the subconscious* that spurs mankind on in her quest for the truth event. The quest for the truth event is the focus of the death drive. Or as the *a-theist* Hegel would express the matter: *Atheos is constantly on the lookout for itself.*

It is in mathematics rather than in our senses that we find the opening to the new realism, which, while being a model-dependent realism, is nonetheless a realism in the sense that our senses achieve an authentic contact with our environment. In a defence of the mathematical revolution that Georg Cantor initiated, with the launch of transfinite cardinals in 1904 Cantor's colleague Ernst Zermelo proves the existence of an actual but indeterminist infinite. Thereby the door is left wide open to *model-dependent realism*, beyond naive realism, which of course Kant dismisses by insisting on a necessary, radical separation between the phenomenal and the noumenal. In syntheology, the Kantian precipice is replaced by the oscillation between an Entheos in escalating expansion and a Syntheos of creative pleasure that arises in the playing in earnest with a ceremonial quest for understanding in the explosive multiplicity of Entheos. To live in Syntheos is to enjoy the philosophical creation and redesign of models of fleeting reality in a never-ending flow.

Through Cantor's revolution in mathematics and Niels Bohr's in physics, the natural sciences land once and for all in the victory of indeterminism over determinism. But there has always been a cosmological logic that argues for *indeterminism*. And it is based on the ontically necessary presence of *chance*. In a determinist universe absolutely nothing can happen by chance, which every friend of order will realise is tautological; determinism means of course that *everything is predestined* in which case this of course applies without exception, otherwise the position would be untenable, including *predestination itself* too. Determinism thus argues that if we only know the historical conditions and the physical factors that exist and precede each course of events, we can calculate with absolute certainty how every course of events (and in principle the entire history of the world) will unfold.

This requires however that there be only one possible course of events for every set of given premises. *And above all, this requires that the laws of the Universe precede the Universe itself.* Including the necessary law of the law's own existence, that is, *the metalaw*. If we are to take determinism seriously, we are thus mercilessly cast back into the arms of the pre-atheist god: the patriarchal creator, dualistically distinct from the rest of the Universe. And with him also follows his necessary creator, and this creator's creator, backwards in a chain in all infinity. But no such pre-atheist god exists, as we know. The future is thereby not closed and illusory in the way that determinism both suggests and requires. Rather, it is the case that if the Universe were not open to the future, and thus indeterministic, it could never exist either. It is not just a matter of exactly the same premises in physics being able to yield more than one result, as Bohr points out. It is in fact the case that these very premises must be aleatoric in order to even be able to exist as premises at all.

The existence of the Universe *per se* is indeed no accident, but the fact that the Universe is constituted precisely as it is includes considerable and decisive amounts of chance. Determinism collapses at the same moment that we are confronted with the minutest unpredictability in the history of the Universe. But the history of the Universe is filled with chance, or rather filled with widely differing outcomes that are the results of defined *probabilities*. Even our specific universe *per se* represents such an accident. Not aleatorically like existence – that something rather than nothing exists is a necessity rather than an accident – but aleatorically as a detailed phenomenon, that is, *as its own specific history*. Or as the syntheist philosopher Quentin Meillassoux expresses the matter: "The only thing that is necessary in existence is contingency." But contingency is then all the more necessary.

There are only processes in syntheism; everything is *pure movement on top of pure movement*, and only in the antagonism and oscillation between the extreme states of these fields do eternalisable phenomena arise. The world reflected by perception is the scene of the *antagonism between Atheos and Pantheos*. This antagonism between Atheos and Pantheos is the phenomenological engine; the oscillation between them is the arena in which the subject can arise as *the self-image* Atheos, which initially positions itself in relation to and then chooses to project the holy onto the Pantheos *world view*. This fundamental, religious *truth as an act*, the movement from *atheism* to *pantheism*, generates the dividual *entheism*, on which syntheists then choose to build the collective *syntheism*.

The existential experience places the subject in the world of psychology, and psychology is embedded in eternalism and in itself has nothing to do with the mobilist reality outside the mind. The human mind and its peculiarities primarily belong in *empirical psychology* and not in the world of ontology. Syntheism regards them as creative attributes of their divinities, rather than as philosophical foundations. Subjectivity is thus a subconscious by-product of an external movement rather than a conscious construction in a stagnant mind. It is, as the existentialist Martin Heidegger would say, *the activity in the lifeworld and not the passivity in the mind that gives the subject its essence*. The syntheistic agent thus arises in the oscillation between Atheos and Pantheos. Syntheism is thus supremely a proud heir of *existentialism* from its founder Sören Kierkegaard via Nietzsche to Heidegger. The syntheist agent's existential experience is definitely a *Dasein* in the Heideggerian sense.

In the next step of the subjectivity process, the dividual, divided subject takes shapes as *Entheos,* and the collective, assembled subject takes shape as *Syntheos*. Here, it is Entheos that assumes the role of mobilism and Syntheos that takes eternalism's role within the dialectics between mobilism and eternalism. It is, for example, the oscillation between Entheos and Syntheos that vibrates through Deleuze's classic work

Différence et Répétition. Entheos stands for *the differences* and Syntheos stands for *the generalities* in Deleuzian metaphysics. The second oscillation in the syntheological pyramid arises between these two poles. The first oscillation between Atheos and Pantheos revolves around *the One,* which expresses itself as a single cohesive substance with an endless quantity of attributes. The second oscillation between Entheos and Syntheos however lacks *the One* as a cohesive point of departure, since the multiplicity in question which takes its starting point in Entheos is *irreducible.*

In the oscillation between Entheos and Syntheos, there are only completely open pluralities, like the infinities placed on top of each other in Georg Cantor's transfinite mathematics. This means that *the One* is always postponed into the future; here the One is namely equivalent to *the syntheist utopia per se* – a utopia of *imperfect multiplicity* rather than of the Platonist utopia's perfect simplicity – which constantly avoids its own realisation. If Entheos is the division of Pantheos into an endless quantity of multiplicities stacked on top of each other – what the German poet Friedrich Hölderlin in a salute to Heraclitus in the 19th century calls "the only thing that differentiates itself as the basic condition of existence" – Syntheos is its opposite: the attempt of perception to try to connect the irreducible multiplicity into a cohesive, creative, collective identity. *Syntheos is quite simply the name of perception's attempt to convert the chaos of existence into religion.* Syntheism is thus literally *the pure religion,* the netocratic eternalism (see *The Netocrats*), religion as religion in its innermost essence.

This syntheist, primordial eternalisation however is not some deeper truth about existence that suddenly makes its entrance into the arena, but *the necessary contraction of information in the perception of mobilist existence.* Only a minute fraction of all sensory impressions are processed at all by one's consciousness. If the brain really were to catalogue all sensory impressions from a single experienced second, it would take thousands of years to do so, during which one's consciousness consequently would be blocked and paralysed (and thereby unable to apprehend anything, be it important or unimportant, in the next second, and the next after that, and so forth). In other words, perception must be extremely selective in order to process information while it registers changes in the always fleeting present. Eternalisation then becomes the engine in the transcendentalisation of immanent reality. The transcendent is accordingly strictly fixed compared to the inexorable mobility of the immanence, but as such is necessary in order to enable the phenomenon to stand out as precisely a phenomenon.

Kant's idea of the mobilist *noumenon* as primary in relation to the eternalist *phenomenon* is fundamentally an idea of a transcendent *God as a passive observer* rather than an immanent *God as an active participant* in the Universe. Kant quite simply imagines that the noumenon is what God observes when the human being merely sees the phenomenon. But an object can reveal itself in innumerable different guises, of which the phenomenon that human perception generates is only one single phenomenon, and an external, divine observer is not needed either. Instead it is *Niels Bohr's phenomenon*, the compact intertwining of the subject and the object, which is the primary starting point in the dialectics between eternalism and mobilism, rather than some kind of unattainable *Ding an sich* in the Kantian sense. A syntheist *Ding an sich* is quite simply the bringing together of the thousands of varying perspectives that one individual phenomenon invites. For perception does not distort reality, which Kant assumes. Perception merely provides both a necessary and intelligent priority for precisely that which is new and different in the information flow compared to earlier sensory impressions, so that a new and constantly minimally corrected eternalisation can occur in every individual moment (see *The Body Machines*). The evolutionarily developed balance between transcendental eternalisation and immanent mobility is merely a question of optimising survival possibilities. The information selectivity is quite simply an evolutionarily smart and beneficial *phenomenological* strategy. But it really says nothing *ontologically* about existence.

The syntheist world is a world of relations and only relations. Syntheism is a *relationalism*. It is *the syntheological pyramid* which constitutes the ontological foundation for all agents in the relationalist universe. The oscillating relation between *Atheos* and *Pantheos*, followed by the oscillating relation between *Entheos* and *Syntheos*, together form a cohesive, pan-dimensional, vibrating coordinate system: *syntheology as a phenomenon*. The syntheist symbol – which for example adorns the website syntheism.org – shows Pantheos on top of Atheos as a white ellipsis that represents the Universe on top of a black circle that represents the void, with Entheos as the boundary between them and Syntheos as the complete symbol in itself, drawn by people in whose speculative imagination the most essential relations and intensities in existence have been personified. Syntheists are quite simply people who, once again in history, unabashed, and this time also consciously, create gods.

Irreducible multiplicity – syntheism as a process religion

It represented a major and significant step for philosophy when Friedrich Nietzsche prised it halfway away from *correlationism* to *relationalism*; Nietzschean *relativism* entails a radical departure from the Kantian version of correlationism. There is no longer any fixed relationship between a stable subject and a moving object to use as a starting point. There are only a host of diffuse objects – the human being as an animal body rather than as a rational consciousness is one of these – and the relations between these objects are in constant motion. Relativism is a consequence of there being no fixed point of departure in existence. Without a divine centre – and Nietzsche proclaims, as we know, that *God is dead* – the position of the first object in a network is completely dependent on the other object's position, and the second object's position in the network is in turn completely dependent on the third object's position, which in turn is dependent on both the first, the second and a fourth object for its position. And so on *ad infinitum*. Which ultimately involves all objects in the Universe in a kind of massive, abstract, impenetrable spreading out of everything with everything else in constant motion.

If Nietzsche is the godfather of relativism within philosophy, Einstein is relativism's executive producer and the scientist who consummates relativism in the natural sciences. In an absurdly large universe with an absurd quantity of discrete objects, according to Einstein it is ultimately impossible to establish an objectively valid position for any of the objects at all. All positions in space–time are *relative.* But it is still a world that consists of *discrete objects*; their ontological status is not questioned by Nietzsche or Einstein – just the possibility of establishing a valuation. Therefore, the problem with relativism is that it maintains Kant's rigid division between the subject and the object as an ontological foundation. While Kant's static construction is set in motion, it is however *relativized* – everything gets its value *only* from its relative position – but *the correlation between the subject and the object per se* is never questioned. Within the confines of relativism, if anything the relationship between the subject and the object is more or less impossible to define precisely, since it appears to concern a kind of insurmountable problem connected to the measuring itself. But that the correlation is still there, and that it is ontologically essential, is established beyond all doubt.

Nietzsche's ontology opens the way for enormous creativity. It is, for example, a gold mine for Einstein's relativistic physics. According to both Nietzsche and Einstein, the angle from which the subject observes existence determines absolutely everything. Only in this special perspective can a *truth* appear, and that truth is of course, like the subject itself, highly temporary and in practice invalid as soon as the moment in question has passed and the conditions have changed. Therefore we speak of the relativist world view as *subjectivist* rather than objectivist. What remains is only the subject's own highly private and temporary truth, impossible to convey other than in a more or less desperate attempt at communication through art or poetry, always doomed to be twisted and distorted in the process, always doomed to age and be weeded out as constantly new information arrives.

Nietzschean and Einsteinian relativism is still however a *correlationism*. The objects are presumed to correlate to each other as *noumena* rather than as phenomena. Nietzsche still presumes that the objects have a form of *essence*, that they are internally stable. Einstein makes the corresponding observation within physics with his beloved atoms (he refuses to accept the ontological victory of magical quantum physics over classical physics). According to the relativists, the instability is entirely *external*. Even if *the epistemological correlation* between thinking and knowing proposed by Kant is shattered, Nietzsche and Einstein keep *the ontological correlation* between subject and object. They still live in a world over which Kant casts his imposing shadow. Syntheism, on the other hand, moves on from relativism to its dialectical intensification: *relationalism*.

The relationalist philosophers Karen Barad, Ray Brassier and Quentin Meillassoux push through and past relativism when, at the start of the 3rd millennium – inspired by pioneers such as the process philosopher Alfred North Whitehead and the physicist Niels Bohr – they construct a *speculative materialism* that attacks *the entire correlationalist paradigm* and its fixation with an original subject that correlates with an original object as its ontological foundation. They are quite simply searching for a deeper foundation beyond this premise, which has dominated phenomenology ever since Kant's heyday. While relativism settles for stating that the relations between the fixed objects are relative – what we call *an interactive ontology* – the relationalist philosophers maintain that the relations within the phenomena are also mobile in relation to each other – that is, they advocate *an intra-acting ontology*. There are no discrete objects whatsoever in the Universe. Not even at the minutest micro level. Thus, nor are there any Kantian objects in physical reality, not even any noumenal such; what really exists is merely pure *relata*, or *relations without their own inner substance* between and within abstract fields of *irreducible multiplicities*.

If relativism is process philosophy's introductory stage, then relationalism is its consummation. And as process philosophy's theological extension, syntheism is the *process religion par excellence*. Syntheism not only distances itself from dualist totalism; it also rejects the recurring *death worship* that is closely connected with the totalist ideologies, that is, the anthropocentric and internarcissistic deification of the human being's own existential effacement. It is our own mortality that makes us obsessed by *nothingness* and tricks us into regarding it as a reasonable ontological alternative. This is why as widely diverse thinkers as the Buddha, St Augustine and Meister Eckhart are fascinated by *the god of negative theology*. In various ways they are looking for the possibility to deify the moment of human death, *turning death into God*. And out of the reverse perspective, the desire is instead to make life and its intensity into the divine foundation for *positive theology*, whose more or less syntheist proponents include Zoroaster, Heraclitus, Spinoza, Nietzsche, Whitehead and Deleuze.

Desire in consciousness seeks most of all a kind of constantly dislocated *metadesire* – every time it looks as though the desire might be satisfied, it quickly shifts its focus to something completely different – the reward of which is *the will to survive,* since a desire that is never satisfied cannot either ever be content with life as it is, and wants to die. On the other hand, *the drive* in the subconscious deep down wants to die, that is, it stubbornly wants to return to the cosy absorption into the cosmos which means that the subconscious is spared the pressing desires of consciousness, and that no demanding subject need exist any longer. Consciousness is of course, as most people experience on a daily basis, obsessed with survival. But the subconscious is driven (subconsciously) towards death. The subconscious is namely embedded in the nostalgic longing for the preconscious state in the womb, where everything in existence is interconnected as one single thing – the mother, the child and everything else united in a cosmos free from confounding differences – and life is carefree and free from paradoxes, which would mean that *life does need not to be contemplated,* it does not need to be made consciousness with toil and pain. What is the symbol for this permanent matrix state, without any of the trying oscillations of change, if not the Buddha's fragile dream of *nirvana*?

A central component in syntheism is how it takes a stand for positive and consequently rejects negative theology. To start with, the repression of the death drive has a clear function: according to pantheist ethics we live because the Universe seeks its own existence and its own consciousness through us. As conscious beings we are not only part of the Universe; we human beings also together constitute *the Universe's own consciousness of itself.* In syntheological terms, we express this as *Pantheos* emerging into *Syntheos* through our truth as an act. But syntheism supports positive theology also because it sees time or *Entheos* as both a physical and ideological foundation. Death has its place at some point along the arrow of time, but *the time for death is not now.* The present always belongs to survival in consciousness. *Syntheism's activist ethics* can therefore only be constructed out of *survival* as a propelling principle – not from *immortality.* Totalist death-worshipping moralism is fundamentally just a form of reactionary masochism.

Therefore syntheism finds ideological allies among mobilist philosophers such as Lao Tzu, Leibniz, Hume, Hegel, Charles Sanders Peirce, William James, John Dewey, Martin Heidegger, Henri Bergson and George Herbert Mead. All of these thinkers are veritable gold mines for syntheology. To take just one example: Heidegger and Deleuze shift the phenomenological focus to *the oscillation between Pantheos (becoming) and Atheos (being).* Heidegger calls this relational phenomenon *finite transcendence,* while Deleuze discusses the same thing under the concept of *psychic individuation.* And it is precisely finite transcendence and psychic individuation that makes possible the transition from process philosophy to process religion.

What then is process religion in practice, if not the collective name for *immanent spiritual experiences*?

Deleuze advocates a Nietzschean affirmation of *the eternal return of the same* in constantly returning loops of a kind, without substance of their own, with only minute changes for every revolution, which opens the way for the sudden genesis of *emergent novelties*, for example in the process-philosophical, artistic search for the genuine *expression,* or in the process-religious, spiritual search for the genuine *impression*. Therefore, artistic expression and spiritual experience strive towards the syntheist emergence made sacred, through which they can communicate an actual meaning, impart an *existential substance*, to the syntheist agent's existence. The conclusion of this train of thought is that *the credible spirituality* of our time – which is important when syntheism is compared to competing religious and metaphysical alternatives – can only arise within the confines of the immanent process religion. It is not possible to take other religious and metaphysical alternatives seriously as spiritual projects in the Internet age; they cannot be anything other than guilt-driven nostalgia (like holding on to the religion of one's parents in spite of it having become irrelevant) or nonsensical superstition (such as *New Age* and other commercial, exoticised posturing masquerading as spirituality).

While Deleuze finds process-philosophical dynamite in Nietzsche's thoughts on the cosmic *drive,* there is no support for a corresponding syntheist renaissance for Nietzsche's concept of the cosmic *desire,* that which Nietzsche calls *the will to power*, his most famous idea. Nietzsche's analysis of desire is founded in 19th century Romantic mysticism around power, but does not hold water in relationalist physics. His idea of the will to power as a cosmic struggle for finite resources in a finite universe should rather be viewed as relativism's most magnificent phantasm. While the will to power can most certainly be used creatively as a social-psychological explanatory model for human behaviour – since we live in a world filled with acute shortages and murderous competition – it would immediately collapse as an ontological basis for a universe that is always expanding and growing in complexity, without the need for any specific will or power over an unfounded, presumed competition within a limited sphere that actually does not even exist. Since the Universe has of course no competition in its cosmological existence, projections onto the Universe that assume a fundamental scarcity-and-competition situation do not hold water either. The Nietzschean will to power is thus a psychological attribute, but hardly a universal phenomenon.

A logical consequence of the pioneering M-theory within physics, which was launched by Edward Witten in the mid-1990s, is that the Multiverse in which our Universe is anticipated to be situated always spontaneously creates something. A multiverse always makes sure that there is something in some form, always. In contrast to the human being, the Universe is not in any real sense mortal. This means that the Universe both *is* and *does* many different things, but *the Universe wants nothing in itself* since *it does not need to want anything in order to exist* in the way that it does. We must instead regard the will to power as a logical consequence of the state of affairs where that which has been endowed with an installed repression mechanism linked to the death drive – a mechanism which makes this something believe that it wants to exist rather than wants to be dissolved – trumps that which is conscious of its death wish as long as we find ourselves within a limited sphere with finite resources. However, there is no need whatsoever for this kind of will to power globally or universally, which is why the concept cannot shoulder nor receive the role as the ontological foundation for existence as a whole. *The drive belongs in nature, but desire stems from culture.* And it is in nature, not in culture, that we find the ontological foundation for mobilist philosophy. The drive is primary and desire is secondary, as Lacan would have answered his predecessor Nietzsche.

This means that the will to power is not any kind of cosmic drive, as Nietzsche thinks it is, but rather a necessary ethical principle, perfectly adapted to a finite creature on a planet permeated by a struggle for limited resources, a position for *action* and against *reaction* in the ethical collision between them. With the will to power as an ethical principle, syntheism is – as a doctrine created by people for people – for *affirmation* and against *ressentiment*. However, existence operates as an entity as one big oscillation between Atheos (non-existence) and Pantheos (existence) at all levels, with highs and lows of intense oscillations and oscillating intensities. In this Universe, there is only an enormous multiplicity for its own sake, without any need whatsoever of or opening for any particular will or anything to master and thereby have power over. The Universe has no direction whatsoever of the type that the will to power presupposes. Rather, Nietzschean relativism should be regarded as a particularly advanced precursor to the extended relationalism that Whitehead, Deleuze and their successors constructed in the 20th century – for example through adding Leibniz' and Spinoza's more radical protorelationalism to Nietzschean process philosophy – where syntheism quite simply is the name of the process religion that accompanies the Whiteheadian and Deleuzian process philosophy.

Within process philosophy, ontology and epistemology are intimately intertwined in each other. *Being* and *the movement* interact in such a way that the movement can only be transformed into and apprehended as being through an agglutinative *onto-epistemology*. The dialectic between eternalism and mobilism is the onto-epistemology of the Internet age (see *The Global Empire*). Contingent reality must be frozen in space–time in order for it to be apprehended and decoded; it must be *eternalised*. The more factors that interact in such a freezing, the more qualitative the eternalisation becomes. The *internal* eternalisation must then be set in motion anew and is cast back into the *external* mobilist reality, and not – however tempting this may be to *the Platonist impulse* – be misinterpreted as a kind of eternal truth about existence. On the whole syntheist onto-epistemology is not well-served by any eternal truths in a Platonist sense; its utopia is imperfect rather than perfect. On the other hand, it is interested in the enormous intellectual advances that can be achieved when the qualities of truth in precisely the relations between different hypotheses are compared. Truth is not eternal, nor is it relativist – *even truth is relationalist.*

Eternalisations are not just ontologically but also epistemologically explosive if they are understood and used as precisely relationalist phenomena and nothing else. Syntheologically we can describe the dialectic between eternalism and mobilism as the constantly ongoing oscillations along the axes between on the one hand Atheos and Pantheos, and on the other hand Entheos and Syntheos. Eternalism on its own should be regarded as an outright *neurosis*; mobilism on its own should be viewed as an equally outright *psychosis*. The functional balance arises in the dialectic between them where eternalism is also set in motion, is cast back into mobilism, *is mobilised,* in order to be able to steer perception's selection of conceivable deviations from previous eternalisations of the enormous, continuous inflows of information to the sense organs. The sum of eternalism and mobilism can never exceed one hundred percent. The stronger the eternalisation, the weaker the mobility; the higher the mobilisation, the lower the eternality.

There is no external god outside the dialectic between eternalism and mobilism. The syntheological concepts of Atheos, Pantheos, Entheos and Syntheos for example are produced within and not outside the dialectic. The fact that nature itself constantly produces new *emergences* means – as the syntheistic complexity theoretician Stuart Kauffman demonstrates in his book *Reinventing The Sacred* – that no external god is necessary. The deeper we delve into the relationalist onto-epistemology, the more clearly it generates an ethics of its own in stark contrast to Platonist moralism with its condemnation of movement and change in favour of *the eternal being*; the perfect and therefore immutable world which does not exist. But relationalist ethics does not maintain some kind of chaos at the expense of the cosmos. The dialectic between eternalism and mobilism instead generates *entheist ethics*. To open oneself up to variability is to affirm the active *affirmation*. On the other hand, to close oneself off in order to fight variability is to surrender oneself to the reactive *ressentiment*. Lacan picturesquely describes eternalism as the *masculine* and mobilism as the *feminine* pole in the dialectical relation between them. Taoism's founder Lao Tzu, the entheist philosopher *par excellence*, of course calls them *yin* and *yang*.

It should be added that experimental metaphysics from the 1980s onwards actually proves that the syntheist onto-epistemology is not merely a perceptional phenomenon; it is not perception alone that makes eternalisation necessary and possible. *Even physics itself creates eternalisations and mobilisations.* Quantum physics starts from wave motions, and when several monochrome wave movements interact and generate a *superposition*, something near-miraculous appears. The superposition between the wave motions displays clear differences even beyond the obvious interference in each of the individual wave motions; the more monochrome wave motions added to the wave package in question, the more clearly it is localised in space–time. Ultimately, already in physics itself a clear phenomenon becomes apparent: add an infinite number of wave motions and the position is determinised; there are no longer any wavelengths left to speak of, and a particle appears, locked in space. The more fixed the localisation in space, the weaker the wavelength; the stronger the wavelength appears, the more the phenomenon spreads itself out in space. The dialectic between eternalism and mobilism is thereby not merely an onto-epistemological complex; the oscillation evidently has an exact equivalent in *the complementarity between wave and particle* in experimental metaphysics.

The current superpositions in quantum physics cause classical physics to break down. The superpositions are namely in clear opposition to the dogmas of classical physics. The difference between the individual substances of *atomic physics* on the one hand – which coolly interact in isolation – and the wave motions of *relationalist physics'* on the other hand – which are literally subsumed in each other in superpositions, as entangled phenomena – is tangible and has dramatic consequences. Not even Werner Heisenberg's otherwise much discussed *epistemic uncertainty principle* captures the magnitude of the current revolution. To embrace the depth of the quantum physics revolution requires instead Niels Bohr's genuinely pioneering *ontic principle of indeterminacy*. It is not some kind of built-in uncertainty as one would find in a measurement instrument that is most fundamental and revolutionary for this world view, but rather Bohr's dazzling proof that we live in *an indeterministic universe*.

Quantum physics thereby opens the way for a whole new metaphysics, a radical monism connected to *an irreducible multiplicity*. Kant's humanist phenomenology no longer has any validity. Starting with Hegel, the way is instead opened for a new phenomenology where the observer always must be included as an actor in every *event-constellation*, in every individual, fundamental *phenomenon*. After Hegel's phenomenological revolution, the Hegelian view of the observer in relation to the observed is fundamental to the field of process philosophy. Thus, Kantian representationalism and its naive atheism are gradually wiped out in three steps: in the first step by Hegel, in the second step by Nietzsche and in the third step by Bohr. It is with Bohr and his relationalism that we land at the arrival of the Internet age. Ontology, epistemology and even phenomenology are merged into a common relationalist complex. We see how *syntheist metaphysics* is solidly founded in contemporary physics.

An interesting observation is that the last person who actually defends atomic physics against the devastating attacks of quantum physics is none other than Albert Einstein. He does so in a document authored with his physicist colleagues Boris Podolsky and Nathan Rosen in 1935. Bohr answers Einstein and his friends six weeks later. The clash between Einstein and Bohr revolves around Einstein and his colleagues insisting that physics must be based on the idea of solid and discrete objects as the foundation of the discipline. "If physics cannot be occupied with calmly observing, studying, and then formulating eternally valid truths about these objects, what then should physics be doing?", Einstein, Podolsky and Rosen wonder disconcertedly. It is clear that these gentlemen cannot imagine any physics whatsoever beyond *physics' elevated isolation* above the examined elements.

Bohr is both surprised and somewhat distressed by this line of argument: suddenly it is clear to him that his highly esteemed colleagues and friends actually do not understand what quantum physics has to tell the world and what this in turn means. Because for Bohr, as early as 1935, it is a given that the physical world's primary building blocks are not objects, but that the world is instead made up of *entanglements*: intra-acting, fundamentally plural *phenomena*, rather than isolated, discrete objects. All the measuring instruments and observers in the world must be regarded as integral components in these phenomena and they must be discounted in every type of calculation and prediction. The independent and separate observer is a dangerous and misleading illusion, argues Bohr. What Einstein and his friends fail to see, and what Bohr's colleague Erwin Schrödinger discovers, is that one can have full knowledge of a system without necessarily having full knowledge of all the components of the system.

The great quantum physicists have parted from the classical physicists of the older generation precisely through their ability to go straight to the big picture of what they are studying, and also keep the big picture – conceptually and empirically – in focus all the way through their study, without getting stuck on trying to isolate the components. It is not the difficulties connected with measuring objects within quantum physics – which for example Heisenberg maintains with the epistemic uncertainty principle – that is the most important lesson. No, the really revolutionary lesson – for which Bohr finds inspiration in Whitehead and then formulates it as *the ontic indeterminacy principle* – is to understand that it is the relations, not the objects within the phenomena that give them their substance and that therefore must be regarded as *primary* in existence. This in turn has far-reaching consequences for all the emergences that are based on the underlying quantum physical reality. For example, French philosopher Bruno Latour formulates a pioneering *actor-network theory* for the social sciences in the 1980s – which among other things presupposes a radical equality between what were previously superior humans and subordinate technological complexes in their surroundings – based on the insight that everything constantly acts *performatively* in relation to everything else in existence, that is, everything is fundamentally interconnected and influences everything else, everywhere and always. This is quite simply what the quantum physical world looks like, and thus, argues Latour, the higher levels in the hierarchy – first classical physics and then the social arena – must also be subordinate to this conception of reality.

The historical problem of philosophy is that it has focused strongly on direct connections between phenomena, and thereby has been forced into extreme theoretical constructs about either direct connections or no connections at all, when the overwhelming majority of all connections in actual fact are *indirect*. It is through this ubiquitous indirectness that everything is interconnected with everything else. It can be difficult to apprehend quantum physical phenomena in the macro-domains that we usually associate with classical physics, but the phenomena repeat themselves there nonetheless, if you only observe them attentively enough. All physics is thus in the final analysis essentially quantum physics, which means that even metaphysics must be concordant with quantum physics. If this constant *complementarity* is not taken into account, we can say goodbye to both intellectual respectability and the contact with physical reality for good. If, on the other hand, complementarity is factored into the calculation, an objectively speaking far more correct world view opens up, more so than anything humanity has ever experienced before. This doesn't exactly lend itself to reducing credibility.

Based solely on its enormous usage in thousands and thousands of experiments, quantum mechanics is the most stable and reliable theoretical construct that has ever been tested and used in the history of the sciences. And the relationalist physics that follows in its wake emphatically invalidates Platonian and Newtonian determinism. The American philosopher Charles Sanders Peirce predicts the coming kiss of death to determinism already a few decades before quantum physics becomes widely accepted when he launches the principle of *tychism* (from the Greek *tyché* = chance) in the 1890s. Peirce maintains that spontaneity is an inescapable fact of the Universe. After quantum physics becomes widely accepted, philosopher of science Karl Popper points out that Peirce paves the way philosophically for quantum physics' indeterminism with his *pragmatism*. The militant indeterminist Daniel Dennett develops Peirce's tychism in his book *Freedom Evolves*. Dennett, also inspired by Leibniz and Hume, argues that while the future is open and the world is indeterminist, everything can still have one necessary cause, since a necessary cause is not tied to just one possible effect. According to Dennett, the fact that all events have a cause is not *per se* a valid argument for determinism.

In Karen Barad's radically universocentric onto-epistemology, we abandon the dividual identity and shift our focus to the Universe itself. Inspired by Whitehead's process philosophy and in particular with support from Bohr's quantum physics, Barad completely pulverises transcendental *correlationism* which had dominated Western thinking since Kant. By pitting Bohr's ontic principle of determinism against Heisenberg's epistemic uncertainty principle, Barad opens the way for *agential realism*, a relationalist philosophy driven by a radical pathos for a completely new kind of potential objectivity. As for Bohr before her, the renowned waves and particles of quantum physics are only abstractions for Barad. The most important thing is not that the waves and particles are contradictory but that they are complementary. This is what is called Niels Bohr's *complementarity principle*. Phenomenologically we express this by saying that *the wave is a mobilist phenomenon*, while *the particle is an eternalist phenomenon*.

Barad argues that, thanks to the principle of complementarity, Bohr succeeds in eliminating the Cartesian subject once and for all. There is never any detached subject that does not at the same time participate in the indeterministic process with openness to the future. There is, according to Bohr, no neutral observer outside the phenomenal processes. And if the observer is always located within the phenomenon, this means that this observer must be regarded as objectively accessible, although not in the classical objectivist sense. Rather, *agential realism* is concerned with a new kind of objectivity liberated from classical subjectivity, since the theory disqualifies all notions of an external subject as a spectator and neutral measurer of the phenomenon. All equipment for measuring the phenomenon is thus part of the phenomenon itself. The apparatus is itself an *agent* that intra-actively produces *fictives* within the phenomena's floating boundaries. This means that we can forget the old phenomenological pair of antonyms, subject and object. The new objective reality is made possible because objectivity refers to possible agential separabilities and not to an impossible, absolute exteriority. This is why Barad uses the term *agential realism*.

Barad's role-models Michel Foucault and Judith Butler also take a thrashing as she constructs her universocentric onto-epistemology. As post-structuralists, Foucault and Butler are, in Barad's eyes, still too anthropocentric. Post-structuralism is wedged between Einstein's Cartesian representationalism and Bohr's agential realism: it has not gone the whole hog and left Cartesian representationalism behind. Kant's ghost lives on. Post-structuralism has, to use Barad's own wording, still not transported itself from *antihumanism* to *posthumanism*. Therefore, post-structuralism still in fact dances around the Cartesian subject that it both claims to and believes it has dissolved. Barad does go all the way however and leaves post-structuralism's antihumanism behind. The Hegelian dialectic between *humanism* (personified by Descartes) and *antihumanism* (personified by Nietzsche) is consummated in Barad's appeal for *posthumanism*; a parallel movement to the dialectic between *theism* and *atheism*, which dissolves into *syntheism*. It is not just objective reality that returns in a surprising new guise through agential realism. The same thing also applies to theological truth, which returns with full force as *syntheist process religion*.

The shift from the human to the universal centre is the necessary and correct manoeuvre. In the oscillation between Pantheos and Entheos, Barad finds the new divinity that replaces the human being that had been declared dead by her predecessor Foucault, namely *the universal subject* as a kind of Bohrian supraphenomenon. It is important to point out that the purpose of Barad's *anti-anthropocentrism* is not to eliminate the human being from all equations. Instead, it is concerned with giving the human being as agent her onto-epistemologically correct place in the greater phenomena that existence is comprised of, and this occurs only when the Universe is held up as primary and the human subject is reduced to something secondary. The Universe is not some transcendental category in Man's orientation through existence, which Kant imagines in his autistic phenomenology. The Universe is instead real and expresses itself in and through the many billions of human subjects that it produces among other things, rather than the other way around. *The Universe lives, thinks, speaks, creates, feels pleasure and multiplies through us.* Nor is this all: through us the Universe dies and leaves room for constantly new phenomena. All this taken together is supreme motivation for naming Barad's book *Meeting The Universe Halfway* a syntheist manifesto.

Baradian phenomenology is based on a constantly ongoing *intra-activity* within phenomena rather than an *inter-activity* between various distinct subjects and objects. Every individual phenomenon is both a fundamental building block in existence and concurrently intra-acting, filled with internal activity in all directions. Barad wants to kill off Kantian representationalism and its fixation with the patriarchal *reflection*. Representationalism is an obvious by-product of Cartesianism. Representations have constantly been prioritised at the expense of what they are presupposed to represent. By instead building first from Foucault's and later also Latour's and Butler's post-structuralist ideas of *performativism*, we open the way for a philosophy that shifts its focus to direct engagement in material reality. All phenomena are constantly affected by the performativity of their environment. Large quantitative differences in performativity create phenomena with radically different properties.

But it is not just Foucault and his successors that inspire Barad. From another of her predecessors, Donna Haraway, she borrows the idea that the *diffraction* of wave motions is a better metaphor for thinking than *reflection*. Ontology, epistemology, phenomenology and ethics are all influenced radically and fundamentally by the new universocentric perspective. They all interact in the new onto-epistemology around agential realism. Quantum physics radically breaks away space–time from Newtonian determinism. With this shift it is also necessary to abandon the idea of *geometry* giving us an authentic picture of reality. It is with the aid of *topology* rather than through geometry that we can do syntheist metaphysics justice, Barad argues. Neither time nor space exist *a priori* as transcendental, determined givens, before or outside any phenomena, which is of course what Kant imagines. Time is not a thread of patiently lined-up and evenly dispersed intervals, and space is not an empty container in which matter can be gathered. The role of the engine of metaphysics is shouldered by non-linear *network dynamics*, which drives the equally non-linear *event*, rather than the old linear *history*, which is supposed to drive the equally linear *progress*. Entheist duration is thus also a dynamic, not a linear, phenomenon.

According to Barad, *the phenomena* arise as intra-acting and agential entanglements. Instrumental measurements expand rather than see through collapsing entanglements. This means that quantum mechanics is really about non-separability, not non-locality. *Quantum physical non-locality* is not necessarily the same thing as *physical non-locality*. Agential separability is quite simply an exteriority within and not outside the phenomena. Phenomena are the basic units of both ontology and epistemology, but at the same time intra-acting and above all fundamentally *plural*. They are *irreducible multiplicities* which thus do not allow themselves to be reduced to isolated units. Not because this inspires some charming philosophy to contemplate in splendid isolation, *but because physics actually functions precisely in this way*. Here Barad resembles other philosophers with a strong involvement in the new physics, such as Ian Hacking and Joseph Rouse. Bohr's realism and objectivism constitute a solid ground on which to build further, since it is solely about factual, material embodiments of theoretical concepts. It is the Universe that speaks through us rather than the other way around in Bohr's life's work as a physicist and philosopher. *Niels Bohr is the syntheist agent par excellence. And Karen Barad is his prophet.*

Cause and effect arise *through intra-activity within the phenomena*. According to Bohr, cause and effect are not deterministic, nor do they perform in any absolute freedom. Cause and effect operate with varying degrees of probability in openness to the future. Exclusions in every intra-acting movement close the possibility of all forms of determinism and keep the future open. Agential realism is thus radically indeterministic, but does not on that account permit any *free will* in the classical sense. Free will namely presumes that everything desirable is possible, but this is of course never the case since every individual process comprises an infinite number of exclusions and takes place in a situation which is defined precisely by its limitations. Thus all the fancy talk about *free will* is pointless. All the more since no Cartesian *cogito* exists that might be able to exercise this free will, if it were to exist in spite of everything. However, *free choice* is a credible and extremely interesting concept for syntheist ethics; however free choice is an entirely different concept to free will.

Barad's *agential realism* may to good effect be pitted against Lacan's and Zizek's psychoanalytic version of *the transcendental subject*; syntheologically it would correspond to Barad's Pantheos being pitted against Lacan's and Zizek's Atheos. It is historically necessary for Barad to act as a radical mobilist in order to once and for all divest herself of Kantian representationalism and think her way fully through the consequences of the quantum physics revolution. Rather, she therefore operates as *a personified oscillation between Pantheos and Entheos*. No thinker succeeded in taking mobilism to its furthest extremity before Barad – not even radical mobilists such as Whitehead and Deleuze – in order thereby to create the necessary opposite to eternalist thinking which together enable the syntheological consummation. Thus, Barad thus does not operate in any kind of opposition to Atheos' two prophets Lacan and Zizek. Rather, she fills the tragically large intellectual void that is the necessary antithesis to their own highly intellectualised void within the syntheological pyramid.

Deleuze's metaphysics otherwise constitutes an excellent transition between Baradian relationalism and Lacanian psychoanalysis. Deleuze places the difference before the identity: according to him identity is generated out of the difference, rather than the other way around. Deleuze thereby precedes Barad's relationalism. At the same time, Deleuze devotes considerable amounts of work to constructing a new concept of the subject in the wake of the Lacanian revolution within psychoanalysis. He seeks a kind of downright ecstatic but still immanent state which he calls *transcendent* rather than transcendental. This leads him to the invention of the *dividual*, the schizoid subject, which has since become the human ideal of the attentionalist netocracy in the Internet age (quite irrespective of whether it was Deleuze's intention or not in the 1970s to create such a future instrument of power).

The Lacanian Zizek often finds himself in dialogue with Deleuze in his books, for example in *Organs Without Bodies* (where Zizek also pursues an extensive dialogue with – in his opinion – the Deleuzian philosophers Bard and Söderqvist). A perfect example of a Deleuzian hybrid concept is *the dark predecessor*, which plays a central part in the construction of Deleuze's dividual subject. The dark predecessor is most simply described as ontology's own Higgs field. *The real* is that which prevents the world view from ever becoming coherent or complete. It is because we never can grasp objectivity that subjectivity arises. The subject is born in the same moment as we are confronted with disturbances and questions in relation to our world view and it is these recurring disturbances that keep the subject alive.

Deleuze prophetically sees how the onrushing Internet age – which he consistently refers to as *capitalism with schizophrenia* in his key works *Anti-Oedipus* and *Mille plateaux*, authored with Felix Guattari – rules out the classical *majoritarian* claims to power. Baradian relationalism goes a couple of steps further in the same direction. There are no secure majoritarian identities left when we start to apprehend the extent of the quantum physics revolution. All remaining identities, except the Universe itself, are quite simply *minoritarian* with Barad. In order to produce an identity other than that of the Universe, there needs to be a clear *minoritarian difference*, which is why only the strongest minoritarian identity can generate what Lacan's and Zizek's predecessor Hegel calls *the universal singularity*.

The unifying narrative can only be told by *the subservient agent* with which all other agents can identify. When the Deleuzian dividual is placed before the enormity of Pantheos, *capitulation* is the only logical response. But it is then not a question of just any old capitulation. Because it is about a kind of Spinozist capitulation, which in turn enables a dialectical continuation in the shadow of Pantheos through the establishment of Syntheos in conjunction with the other particularities of the universal subject. Therefore Zizek and Deleuze are united in their passionate search for *the Internet age's revolutionary utopia*, where it is Deleuze in his capacity as *the voice of Entheos* – in relation to Zizek as *the voice of Atheos'* and Barad as *the voice of Pantheos* – who is closest to the realisation of *Syntheos* within the syntheological pyramid.

For in the same way that the axis between Atheos and Pantheos vibrates in the syntheological pyramid, the axis between Entheos and Syntheos vibrates. Entheos represents immanent becoming and difference; Syntheos represents utopian being and identity. As Deleuze points out: *Entheos always precedes Syntheos.* First Entheos generates the Deleuzian dividual; thereafter Syntheos generates the revolutionary utopia. What is important is that syntheology places transcendence in becoming and not in being. There is no transcendental being within syntheism, which is a radical point of departure from all dualist religions. Transcendental becoming is instead consolidated in a radically monist and relationalist universe. Becoming is primary, *but wills itself into being* and does this time after time through perception's creative eternalisations. This will from becoming to being is the movement from Entheos to Syntheos.

The Universe obviously needs no preceding divinity in order to exist. There is no need for any religion whatsoever when existence is in a state of constant expansion. However, the moment we move from becoming to being, the theological perspective becomes necessary. The dialectic between eternalism and mobilism requires a syntheological accompaniment. The eternalisation of the mobilist chaos in itself gives rise to the metaphysical impulse. We express this by maintaining that *being requires God*. We see this movement with Hegel when he transports himself from Atheos to Pantheos and sees *the World Spirit (Welt Geist)* being born out of this movement. But the same thing also occurs with Deleuze when he moves from Entheos towards Syntheos and sees *the plane of immanence* being born out of this movement. The eternalisation of the mobilist chaos is in itself the original sacralisation of existence, the birth of metaphysics. Through the process of eternalisation, chaotic existence is transformed into a single coherent substance, what the mobilist philosophers call *the One*. And the One is of course the name of immanence philosophy and process theology for *God*.

But inside the syntheological pyramid, there is also movement from Syntheos in the direction of Atheos. Therefore it is interesting to introduce and study a rigidly atheistic nihilist as an interlocutor to Deleuze's and Barad's relationalist metaphysics. The exceptionally learned and colourful Scottish philosopher Ray Brassier in his book *Nihil Unbound* champions the thesis that Nietzsche and Deleuze guilty of a kind of wishful thinking mistake when they place *existential ecstasy* before *existential anxiety*. Like the Buddha, Brassier instead sees anxiety as primary for existence – pain always surpasses pleasure – and he constructs a kind of *Freudian cosmology* out of the conviction that the empty, blindly repetitious drive is the engine of existence. The focus of Brassier's negative theology lies in *the Universe's future self-obliteration,* which according to him must govern all values and valuations until then. Here he takes his starting point in the human being's *will to nothingness* which emerges from the increasingly leaky subconscious and constantly makes itself felt as a theme among the rapidly growing subcultures of the Internet age.

From a relationalist perspective, Brassier however makes three mistakes in his reasoning. First of all, there is nothing that says that ethics must be governed by, or in any way be connected with, how nature works. If that were the case, in principle one would never have needed to question 19th century social Darwinism, and the concept of *civilisation* would be uninteresting in this context. Brassier's ethics really don't deviate on any important point from social Darwinism's bizarre quest to reduce the human being to a creature whose only task it is to *put Darwinian evolution on the right track,* so to speak, as if history – paradoxically enough thus both deterministic and indeterministic at the same time – just like evolution for some obscure reason would need speeding up and to be guided towards its own, explicitly inevitable fulfilment. Brassier is here guilty of a kind of naturalist masochism, an existential resignation in the face of the human being's possibilities of finding her own identity-creating ethics that is independent of her environment's presumed historical direction. Therefore, his ethics comes down to an ambition to given in to and copy what nature is presupposed to tell us through its blind fickleness, and an edict to perceive these ruthless and highly arbitrary culling processes as commendable.

Against the idea of the human being as a malleable creature subject to a fate which is paradoxically both unavoidable and his duty to create, syntheism puts forth the ideals of Zoroaster, Heraclitus,

Spinoza, Nietzsche, Whitehead and Deleuze: the human being as an affirmative activist battling against all that which
she apprehends as nature's – or for that matter even culture's
– systematic arbitrariness in the form of imposed rules of play.
Rather, according to syntheist ethics it is precisely in the protest against the' given conditions of existence and in the human
being's civilizational redirections of history that she makes his
imprint as an ethical creature. It is Man's concrete actions in
the battle against nature's givens which subsequently generates
ethical substance, which thus has nothing to do with any personal suitability for subservience. The same obviously applies
for every thought of an indeterministic world where the task of
ethics would be to call on the human being, against his better
judgement, to behave as though he were deterministic after all;
a position that can be exemplified by the vulgar and stupid imperative "Follow your nature!". If existence indeed were deterministic, which it certainly isn't, this call would be completely
superfluous, since there are no alternatives. Nor any ethical
problems to contemplate either.

Secondly, Brassier confuses quantity with quality. Even if
quantitatively speaking pain were more prevalent than pleasure
in existence – which definitely can be questioned: pain and
pleasure are, to start with, often each other's complements in
various multidimensional experiences rather than each other's
opposites – it does not mean that the pain is qualitatively more
important and thereby more identity-generating than pleasure.
Here syntheism contributes something that Brassier overlooks
in his philosophy, namely *the spiritual experience*. What characterises the spiritual experience is above all its production of infinity in the present, which means that it transcends the quantitative, places quality before quantity, and thereby enables the
existential and thereby ethical prioritisation of life and pleasure
over death and pain. *The infinite now* defeats drawn-out and
maybe even life-long suffering, not just in the moment when
it is experienced concretely, but even more as *the identity-pro-*

ducing memory which generates *ethical substance*; something that arises only afterwards in the processing and *integration of the event* into the life fantasy, where it lives on as a constantly identity-generating abstraction.

A few really profound spiritual experiences may suffice, or even just one, in order to motivate a syntheist believer to endure and soldier on in a life replete with toil and set-backs. The syntheist philosopher Robert Corrington sets up this qualitative spiritual ideal as *intense ecstasy* against its opposite, *drawn-out melancholy*, in his book *A Semiotic Theory of Theology and Philosophy*. Here the memory function of consciousness plays a central role. We need not return to life's greatest intensities all the time in order to recall them, but thanks to memory we can return to, and in this way reuse, life's greatest and most valuable intensities as creators of existential meaning. And it is of course precisely in the form of memories, and not as direct experiences, that emotional intensities give life its meaning. As experiences *per se* the most powerful intensities are almost unbearable in their extension; constantly being in an ecstatic climax must be regarded as a form of psychotic madness rather than perfect pleasure of life.

It is instead the memory of ecstasy that frames existence, and it is this framing in itself that generates experiences of meaning, value, identity and ethical substance. Here, syntheist ethics breaks not only with Brassier's neuronal quantity fixation, but also with utilitarianism's autistic overconfidence in statistical utility functions on the whole; the most important things in life might not always be free, but they are definitely not measurable, nor are they thereby objectively comparable between people. That which cannot be measured cannot be treated as something measurable with one's intellectual credibility still intact. Even less so can an entire ethical system be based on such impossible and childish quantitative comparing. In the same way that utilitarianism must fail to grasp *the central role of the transcending experience* in the syntheist agent's lifeworld – utilitarians are evidently themselves both emotionally and spiritually handicapped – syntheism is definitely not some kind of utilitarianism.

Thirdly, Brassier follows in the post-structuralist Jean-Francois Lyotard's footsteps and is obsessed with the future death of the stars as a horizon for ethics. But this is based on a misunderstanding of what physics tells us. According to M-theory, universa are incessantly generated in a multiverse that has no limits whatsoever for its possible expansion. Regardless of whether our current universe eventually levels out into an endless and cold, black goo, or if its accelerating expansion is dramatically turned into a compressing contraction – or in any other way is suddenly transformed into a new round of accelerating expansion, as the physicist Roger Penrose suggests in his book *Cycles of Time: An Extraordinary New View of the Universe* – there are no obstacles to the rise of new universa both within and outside our own universe. Physics supplies no such obstacles, and once we have got past the spatial and temporal limitations – which in our intuition we find it so infinitely hard to think ourselves past – the death of the stars disappears as a necessary or even conceivable horizon for ethics.

Brassier has a hard time concealing his contempt for Henri Bergson's classical *vitalism.* And physics of course provides no support for life having any kind of peculiar nature or special position in the Universe. Life arises under specific material circumstances, which does not mean that this in itself is some sort of great mystery. What is fascinating is thus not life itself, as classical vitalism maintains, but the enormous complexity and constant generating of even more complexity of existence, as Deleuze assumes in his *revised vitalism.* Instead of, in the manner of Bergson, anthropocentrically preaching vitalism as a life-affirming religion – with the motto that the more life forms that arise, the better – from the perspective of process theology it is more correct to speak of *the enormous and expanding complexity of physics per se*. Vitalism can only survive if it is expanded into a universocentric, general doctrine of multiplicity. If we are to speak of a credible vitalism in the wake of the advent of M-theory, then this vitalism must already regard quantum fluctuations in the great void as a kind of life form. And why not?

Beyond value philosophy's traditional pair of opposites *vitalism* (Bergson) and *antivitalism* (Brassier), syntheism instead is based on the concept of *pure complexity*. It is about a complexity which, like Deleuze's other differences, precedes the production of identity. It is the pure complexity in network dynamics that gives the agents and phenomena their value, not the other way around. For life is, regarded as just life, really not much of a life to speak of. It is mostly lots of death. Life is always based on an act of *self-sacrifice* and must therefore be regarded as an isolating breaking off from life itself. As such life is doomed to obsessive repetition of its own act of death. Vitalism only hits the right note when it ceases to deify life as higher in standing than non-life, and instead views life as large-scale, duplicate non-life, as yet another in a long line of pure complexities. For what is life other than a cloned, discrete feedback loop that happens to be able to multiply itself?

We see clearly how the sacrificial act itself as a condition for life expresses itself as *the collective sacrifice* throughout history. Sacrifice was developed by nomadic society as a response to *nature's devastating power over mankind*. The sacrifice was the tribe's way of trying to buy independence and room to manoeuvre from the gods. However, all organisms invariably sacrifice part of themselves for the sake of their own survival. Only through such an act of sacrifice can the being attain independence from its environment. Independence per definition means of course *a cloning of what is independent* from precisely the bigger phenomenon from which it now stands independent. The great *trauma* is of course what remains after the self-sacrifice; it is *the perceptional protection* against an overabundance of stimuli; it is the foundation for *the new self in what is independent*. It is thanks to the trauma that the being becomes functional, manages to exploit its environment for its own survival, and thereby also assures itself of resources for its future reproduction.

Brassier calls this repetitive complexity machine an *organon of extinction*. However, the advent of syntheism means that the role of the victim in culture fades away. To begin with, syntheists try not to appease any gods in order to keep them at distance. On the contrary, syntheists create the new gods for a new era and above all for the future. And they seek contact with the gods, see their genesis as the realisations of humanity's dreams and utopias. Thus, there is no need for sacrifice in syntheism, what is demanded is rather the direct opposite of sacrifice: the syntheist rituals about coalescence and entanglement; partly between people, partly between the human being and her environment. The worship of the network as an event naturally also relates to *the realisation of the network as an event*, that is, absorption into *the holy intimacy* as the happy ending to the tragic history of alienation.

Just like Nietzsche's creative affirmation, the syntheist conviction is primarily *an attitude*. Syntheism starts with a will to act rather than with knowledge. It is based on the idea of life as something infinitely valuable. A life that uses itself through constant, creative reshaping and valuing of everything and everybody in the environment cannot even contemplate putting a value on itself. Thus, life in relation to life itself must be infinitely valuable. But the infinite value of life in relation to life itself does not automatically mean that this applies to other life forms as well. The collective debt is fed from the assumption that a life that cannot be saved in turn generates even more collective guilt, for example. This not only drives the collective fantasy – and thereby explains why history is constantly filled with myths of the great Fall of Man and the accompanying calls for salvation – but sooner or later pushes the collective identity towards its self-inflicted extinction.

The Nietzschean reaction to this collective fantasy of extinction is of course *amor fati*, that is, not just the acceptance of, but also the unconditional *love of fate*. Goodness and evil meet in the present where fate breaks them down and joins them in a neutral history substance that the Nietzschean *übermensch* loves because it is to be loved as being *the only thing that exists* in history. Only based on the unconditional acceptance of everything in world history up until now – where one's own experience as a subject is included to the highest degree – can the syntheist agent create a radically different *utopian future beyond the present*. For what is *the religious impulse* and its search for *the spiritual experience* if not a reason where the human being concentrates herself on herself and her innermost emotional needs and lets intuition lead her past all of life's excuses that claim that the impossible really is impossible? For this is of course not true: it is precisely when reason takes over from rationality that the impossible becomes possible and Syntheos arrives in the future. *It is there and then that the human being can realise his wildest dreams and create God.*

Intensities and phenomena in a relationalist universe

The history of correlationism is introduced with Immanuel Kant's onto-epistemological project in the 18th century. According to Kant, we can only know what arises in the *correlation between thinking and being*. But with Kant, and also later with the phenomenologist Edmund Husserl for example, there is still a conviction that a *factiality* exists, that the process includes a *thing in itself* to relate to. This notion goes by the designation *weak correlationism*. Later Kant is followed by thinkers such as Hegel, Nietzsche, Heidegger and Wittgenstein, who all ignore this conjectured thing in itself. The Kantian *principle of factiality* is thus replaced by these authors with the Hegelian, absolute, *principle of correlation*. This notion is called *relativism* or *strong correlationism*.

The decisive break with Kantian correlationism comes with *relationalism* in Niels Bohr's physics and philosophy of science in the 1930s. Relationalist ontology is in fact not just *interactive,* like relativism, but definitely also *intra-acting*. According to relationalism, every phenomenon in the Universe is unique, since both its external and its internal coordinates are completely unique for every position in space–time. Symmetries exist only in mathematical models, never in physical reality. This means, among other things, that no scientific experiments can ever be repeated in exactly the same way twice. It is hardly surprising that in the 1930s old friends Niels Bohr and Albert Einstein engage in a correspondence that is often frustrating on both sides. Their letters attest to the dramatic scientific paradigm shift from *Einsteinian relativism* to *Bohrian relationalism*.

There are of course no *de facto* predetermined sets of rules whatsoever in the Universe that precede the phenomena which they, if that were the case, would be designed to regulate, that is, if they existed (which they do not, for in that case their existence would precede existence itself). What in hindsight we may apprehend as *laws of nature* are nothing but analogous repetitions within one and the same system, given the temporarily prevailing, constantly slightly varying circumstances within the complex in question. Admittedly, there is a universal *metalaw* which says that there is always an explanation for every given event – an ontological prerequisite that mobilists from the German philosopher Gottfried Wilhelm Leibniz in the 17th century to the American pragmatist Charles Sanders Peirce in the 19th century investigate thoroughly – but no *eternal laws per se* are required in order for any of the virtualities within the phenomenon to be actualised. Like so many times before in the history of science, nature does not care about our human, all too human, metaphors. *Physics quite simply does not obey laws in the way that the slave is expected to obey the rules his master dictates.*

The problem is that correlationism requires that everything else around the correlation is constant, as if what happens always happens in an isolated and sealed laboratory or on an – aside from the observed phenomenon – unchanging theatrical stage. According to the correlationists, what is relative only limits itself to the relation between the phenomena. Existence is seen as passive rather than active, and without further ado is divided into independent, isolated units without any relevant relationship to each other whatsoever. Correlationism's isolationist view must however yield to the pressure from modern physics, where everything incessantly more or less influences, and is in a state of constant flux in relation to, everything else, *including itself*. The behaviour of physics is thus neither predetermined, necessary nor eternal; the patterns that the phenomena form in a larger perspective – no matter how beautiful and impressive they might seem – could be completely different from what is actually the case, and they might very well change in the future when the conditions have changed.

Kant is thus right about *factiality*, things might be completely different from how things stand for the moment. But Kant's *rationalism* – his blind faith that everything that occurs is subordinate to a divine wisdom, and that his own human *ratio* is fully sufficient to embrace everything that happens given time – results in his never developing this factiality fully and not drawing the inevitable conclusion. It is thus Kant's unfounded rationalism which forces him into *determinism*, not the other way around. Therefore the relationalists must also leave Kant behind and seek other allies in the history of philosophy. The syntheist Quentin Meillassoux finds such an allied thinker in the empiricist David Hume – one of Kant's strongest rivals in the 18th century – not least for the reason that Hume provides support for the conviction that one and the same material and existential vantage point can give rise to an infinite number of different outcomes. Existence outside the correlation in question is neither stable nor fixed and therefore philosophy cannot in all honesty pretend that this is the case. Hume and Meillassoux are thereby joined in *a strong factiality*, from which Meillassoux constructs the philosophical school that goes under the name *speculative materialism*.

Hume and Meillassoux depart from Kant's troublesome, incorrect determinism and opens up philosophy to the empirically established *indeterminism* in Bohrian quantum physics. It should be noted here that Leibniz presages relationalism even before Hume does so with his *principle of sufficient reason*. Leibniz was not only one of the most significant and most original predecessors among the philosophers, but also an innovative and brilliant mathematician. He built a *Monadology*, a kind of early variant of the dialectics between eternalism and mobilism, which precedes Kantian Platonism. Above all, with his credibility within the natural sciences, Leibniz created the most clearly defined mobilist alternative to the contemporaneously developed Newtonian totalism. The metaphysical antagonism between Leibniz and Newton presages the struggle within our own contemporary physics between on the one hand *relationalism* and its *cosmological Darwinism*, with a universe that is constantly becoming more and more complex; and on the other hand *relativism* and its fixation with the second law of thermodynamics, with a universe that is constantly becoming more and more simplified as it expands and disperses.

The relationalist argument is that although the second law of thermodynamics is applicable within isolated subsystems in the Universe, this does not necessarily mean in turn that it covers the Universe as a coherent whole. Rather it appears to be the other way around: the Universe as a whole exhibits a history with an ever-increasing degree of complexity over time, with a steadily growing amount of information, where the total growing amount of information correlates with the total growing amount of entropy. This means that entropy can increase locally at the expense of information, at the same time as information increases globally at the expense of entropy. And that is *de facto* what our Universe looks like today. If theory and empirical data do not agree on essential points, it might be a good idea to first of all revise and modify the theory.

The foundation for philosophical relationalism is laid by the American pragmatists at the end of the 19th century, clearly exemplified by Peirce's familiar quotation "law is *par excellence* the thing that wants a reason.". He argues that the laws of nature ought reasonably to be subject to evolution in the same degree as everything else in existence and that therefore they can never be predetermined. It is simply a matter of the cause of the effect preceding the effect, and this does not in itself require an eternal law. Peirce actually goes so far as to say that if we presume that time is an actual constant, *the behavioural patterns of nature by necessity must sooner or later change over time*. After Peirce's revolutionary contributions, philosophical relationalism is clearly placed within pragmatist metaphysics. And it is also within pragmatism that it is developed in full when the British-American philosopher Alfred North Whitehead, in parallel with the Bohrian revolution in physics, publishes his manifesto *Process and Reality* in 1929.

The American philosopher Michael Epperson shows in *Quantum Mechanics and the Philosophy of Alfred North Whitehead* how Whitehead – a favourite disciple of William James, American pragmatism's other father figure besides Peirce – single-handedly constructs a relationalist rather than a relativist metaphysics in parallel with, and completely independent of, the quantum physics revolution which began to pick up pace during the 1920s. According to Whitehead – whose name was revered among physicists after the publication of his mathematics tome *Principia Mathematica* in 1913, co-authored with his disciple Bertrand Russell – existence in essence consists of *current events* and not of atomistic objects. History is thus an endless quantity of events stacked on each other, where an intense and concrete series of mobilist events always precedes the permanent and abstractly eternalised object. Whitehead's *experience events* can be described as a kind of Leibnizian *monad* – but not without windows, as Leibniz imagines the monads, but rather with hosts of windows that are constantly wide-open to the surrounding world.

What makes Whitehead the first fully-fledged relationalist among the mobilist thinkers, and particularly interesting from a syntheological perspective, is of course that he does not understand the obsession with *killing the idea of God* which occurs in many of his contemporary philosopher colleagues (in particular Russell, who after a strict upbringing in the High Church British aristocracy hated everything that he associated with religion). According to Whitehead, *creativity* is namely existence's innermost essence, and this creativity – which he calls in fact *God* – permeates every single one of the myriad of current events that unfold throughout the course of history in the Whiteheadian universe. According to Whitehead, to not then use the elastic, cogent and extremely functional concept of God in order to encompass this fundamental creativity – thereby formulating a *process theology* as much as a process philosophy – would be tantamount to throwing out the baby with the bathwater for no reason and to no good use whatsoever.

According to Whitehead, God is quite simply not particularly dead, but rather is just *dramatically altered* by – in turn – dramatically changed conditions. There is no hateful desire in him to slash God's throat, when the concept actually appears more useful than ever, but in that case precisely as a *syntheist tool* and nothing else. The parallel with the syntheological formulation of Entheos as the name of the oscillation between Atheos and Pantheos is striking. For what is Whitehead's obsession with creativity as the driving force of existence, if not in fact a deification of the entheist production of difference? *Process and Reality* is so radically relationalist and theologically creative that the work – in which the origin as *Atheos* and the events as *Pantheos* are brought together with creativity as *Entheos,* and where the result is today's Universe – deserves to be regarded as *the syntheist manifesto par excellence.* That the term *process theology* is coined and used for the first time by one of Whitehead's disciples, the American theologian Charles Hartshorne, is not the least bit surprising.

When in 1992 the relationalist physicist Lee Smolin launches the idea that the Universe operates according to cosmological Darwinism – where the maximisation of black holes in a universe is linked to the maximisation of possibilities for the genesis of life – he refers to Peirce's and Whitehead's revolutionary pragmatism. With a simple manoeuvre, Smolin disposes of the recurring problem that haunts the competing physical models, namely that all these models presuppose coordinates for the Universe which means that it is constantly balancing on a kind of existential pinhead in order to be able to exist. With a multitude of possible universa over time, as in Smolin's model, our Universe's specific coordinates do not seem particularly remarkable any longer. Of course they appear extremely well-adapted for the genesis of life and the existence of our own species, but then this must reasonably be the case in at least one of the many universa that are presumed to exist, and in that case the one is just a logical consequence of the other. Irrespective of whether Smolin's speculative cosmological theory of evolution is correct or not, time or *Entheos* has returned with full force as the bedrock of physics. Peirce, James, Whitehead and the other pragmatists could hardly be more satisfied.

The renaissance of time within physics opens up possibilities of, for example, *shape dynamics* – a theory that solves many of the old problems of *quantum gravity* – where time in fact plays the role of the decisive constant. By counting on what are called *observable objectives*, the shape dynamicists consider themselves able to calculate *global time,* liberated from the local restrictions of space. It should be added here that even if Einstein proves that time runs at different speeds at various places in the Universe – that *time is relative* in relation to local conditions – it continues, at least within practical physics rather than within theoretical mathematics, always in one and the same direction: from then via now towards the next now in the future. Einstein's conception that time can go backwards as well as forwards quite simply does not fit with what we can observe in actual reality; this idea increasingly appears to be a *Platonist fantasy* without relevance outside *mathematism's tautological trap*. Global time is in fact more than just a dimension on top of the three spatial dimensions in space–time; it is above all compatible with *relationalism*.

Shape dynamics thereby exist in the same sort of duality in relation to the Einsteinian relativity theories as the wave does in relation to the particle. This means that we can say goodbye all at once to the predetermined, the timeless and the eternal space–time in Newton's and Einstein's Platonist universe. For what is this four-dimensional *block universe* if not just yet another failed attempt to recreate *the ideal world* of Plato – this time not as an opposition between *God* and *Creation*, or between *the soul* and *the body*, or between *the representation* and *the represented*, but instead as an opposition between *eternity* and *time*? Einstein's block universe, with a space–time that moves both backwards and forwards, is yet another flagrant example of a Platonist fantasy which, without any empirical footing at all, acquires a social status as if it were an established physical truth.

It looks seductively elegant in mathematics when time is added to the three space dimensions and *space–time* arises. However, there is no scientific proof outside mathematics that time is some kind of space; rather it is strictly speaking only the mathematical elegance that makes it tempting to believe that this is the case. Even if a phenomenon actually can be registered in space, and even if space can be mathematically expanded by a temporal dimension – which attractively enough enables the construction of a more complex geometry in order to describe various phenomena in even greater detail – there is still nothing that indicates that time really is a fourth dimension of space, ontologically rather than just mathematically. For example, we can travel both up and down and forwards and backwards in space (in relation to an arbitrarily chosen or imagined point). But even if we are travelling forwards in time at various speeds at various places in space, which Einstein proves that we can do, we are invariably still only moving in one single direction along the arrow of time. There is no evidence that anything anywhere in the Universe actually can travel backwards in time. Varying speeds do not automatically imply different directions.

We quite simply must disregard all these beautiful speculations and accept that *time* is a radically different phenomenon from *space*. Mathematics shows no regard for empirical reality in this case. That time travels backwards with the same ease as forwards *in the world of mathematics* only proves one thing; namely that mathematics is constructed by Platonists who are more interested in a theory of an immutable idea than in empirical evidence that speaks of a mutable world. If mathematics were correct about time, time would then of course, by logical necessity, be an illusion. Both Newton and Einstein are swept along by the elegance of mathematism's tautological trap and allow themselves to be really convinced about precisely this, that *time is an illusion*. They do this in spite of the fact that their faith in mathematics' scientific robustness lacks empirical support. They open the door to what we call *Newtonian-Einsteinian mysticism*.

The arrow of time acts as an emergent phenomenon of its very own. Outside of mathematics' tautologies, time and space do not need to have anything whatsoever to do with each other; they are distinctly different phenomena and an honest ontology also treats them in that way: as essentially different. Liberated from eternity, time returns with full force as physics' most remarkable player, as *Zurvan* or the personification of the mysterious duration of the ancient Iranians, as *Cronus* or the irrevocable fate of the Ancient Greeks, or as *Entheos*, the multiplicity of events that stream out of the oscillation between Atheos and Pantheos in the syntheological pyramid. Time is the uniting constant of existence. There is nothing outside duration. Plato, Newton and Einstein have quite simply got it wrong: there is no *timelessness* in physical reality, no more than there is any actual *void*. Because of the return of time in the history of ideas, the post-structural obsession with *non-linearity* also finds itself under great pressure. Linearity returns as a strong cultural metaphor, but in a new and deeper variant, as a *deep linearity* which relates to global rather than local duration.

In the world of physics, the concept of *eternalism* is used as a designation for the conviction that all points on the line of time are ontologically as real as each other. All moments that have ever existed or ever will exist are regarded as radically equal from an ontological perspective. The opposite view, that only the present is real, is called *presentism*. Note how the concepts correlate with the phenomenological pair of opposites eternalism and mobilism (see *The Global Empire*). *Physical eternalism* is the conviction we end up in if we allow *phenomenological eternalism* – with its radically equal *fictives*, since no fixation of the chaos of existence can be more fixed than any other – to run amok because we have forgotten to place it ontologically within mobilism. These radically equal, frozen fictives in space–time are mistaken for being reality itself instead of the chaos of existence from which we produce them. Obviously, Plato, Newton and Einstein are all physical eternalists, and they are such for the very reason that they overestimate the possibilities that phenomenological eternalism offers in what actually is an ontologically mobilist universe.

Physical *presentism*, however, is a phenomenological eternalism placed *within* the mobilist conception of reality; a *transrationalist eternalism* with factually motivated limitations. It is based on the conviction that the past is fixed, while the future is open and nebulous, and only the present is ontologically real. But the presentist position is only correct with the caveat that *the present* must be regarded as an *eternalisation of an ontic flow* which thereby is not an abstract thing but rather *a concrete field*. For example, the present as an event is already shifted to the past, as a *fictive*, in every contemplative moment. Phenomenological eternalism is merely an ontological, perceptional necessity, but not an ontic, physical truth about existence outside the mind. This applies to presentism just as much as to physical eternalism. The present is real, but it is only real as a *relationalist phenomenal field* rather than as a *relativist noumenal thing*. Just like the experience of the object's exactitude as a substantial particle, the experience of the present's exactitude as an infinitesimal moment is nothing other than an *eternalist illusion*. The experience in itself does not constitute ontological proof of anything at all. Thus, the correct *transrationalist presentism* should not be confused with the incorrect classical presentism.

According to the myth that we live in a block universe, which follows from the Einsteinian revolution, *the Universe* and *history* are regarded as united in eternally frozen four-dimensional space–time. Time must be an illusion then, in its capacity as an ontic flow, if it is regarded as the fourth space dimension. There is no evidence whatsoever for this view of time being physically correct, yet it is precisely this that Einstein maintains when the idea of *time as illusion* becomes widely accepted in conjunction with his theories of relativity gaining adherents. That time is made into a kind of fourth spatial dimension – and thereby is transformed into a kind of mathematically, and doubtlessly also existentially, tempting expansion of existence – seems historically speaking not to have any deeper cause than a purely subjective arbitrariness. It mainly revolves around physics suddenly becoming a little more playful as a mathematical exercise in model construction. The thing is though, that if time in principle is regarded as a kind of space, there is not much difference between the ticking of a clock and a measuring tape placed on a stretch of road. The ticking of the clock becomes a smooth way of measuring the distance between two points, which according to the accompanying physical eternalism fittingly enough is ontologically just as real.

The idea that all of existence and its history is reduced in this way to a limited and handy little box, a *block universe*, must have enchanted the physicists. This is understandable. And philosophically speaking, the myth that we live in a block universe is of course an expression of the phenomenological eternalism without the necessary dialectic with mobilism, if possible an even more radicalised version of Plato's dualism – where Einstein actually advocates a *totalist monism* rather than Plato's totalist dualism. But surely it must be the case that not just the arrow of time but all the motion and changes in the history of the Universe must be illusory in Einstein's block universe. Duration is of course the very foundation for all motion and change *per se* – which explains why Entheos is the divinity of time, motion, difference and creativity in syntheology. But Einstein really does everything in his power to revive Parmenides' absurd conception from Ancient Greece that there is no real change in physical reality, that everything is one and the same and that difference and change therefore have no *ontological validity*.

Syntheologically, we express this as Einstein in practice doing everything he can to kill off Entheos, the divinity of process theology, and he must then in the name of consistency also try to kill off Atheos and Syntheos while he is at it. But Einstein never succeeds anywhere in proving any phenomenon in existence that moves backwards in time. However relativist time is, the arrow of time survives the block universe's mythological attack and strengthens in fact its Zurvanite and Chronist magic. Time has still only one direction: forwards. Entheos keeps the syntheological pyramid in motion and is travelling with determination onwards to Syntheos. Physical eternalism and the Einsteinian block universe are, in fact, impossible to combine with quantum physics' most basic axiom: Niels Bohr's *principle of indeterminacy*. A block universe requires a compact determinism – without real time there is no real change – the future is by necessity as fixed in advance as the past is frozen in history. However, this is an absolute impossibility according to

Bohr and his relationalist followers, *since physics according to the principle of indeterminacy is incomplete*, and that fact in itself is incompatible with a block universe where everything, without the least exception, invariably *has already happened.*

The pragmatist philosopher of science and friend of Einstein Karl Popper says to him anxiously in his autobiography: "If men, or other organisms, could experience change and genuine succession in time, then this was real. It could not be explained away by a theory of the successive rising into our consciousness of time slices which in some sense coexist; for this kind of "rising into consciousness" would have precisely the same character as that succession of changes which the theory tries to explain away. The evolution of life, and the way organisms behave, especially higher animals, cannot really be understood on the basis of any theory which interprets time as if it were something like another (anisotropic) space coordinate. After all, we do not experience space coordinates. And this is because they are simply non-existent: we must beware of hypostatizing them; they are constructions which are almost wholly arbitrary."

Popper undoubtedly hits the nail on the head with his ruthless, pragmatist criticism of Einsteinian Platonism. And even so he has not even mentioned that the Darwinian theory of evolution with *the principle of natural selection*, to take one illuminating example, is an impossibility without real time. But then, of course, Darwinism has never been very popular within physics and cosmology. That is, not until now. With the relationalist seizure of power even within the natural sciences, the door is now wide open to duration-bound theories such as *cosmological Darwinism, loop quantum gravity* and *shape dynamics.*

We return to the decisive difference between Einsteinian *relativism* and Bohrian *relationalism.* Einstein convincingly proves in his special theory of relativity that classical time is in fact relativist. Clocks with similar properties run at varying speeds in various places in the Universe depending on the varying local circumstances. However, this does not mean that time somewhere in the Universe suddenly runs backwards. *Above all it does not mean that time is slower in one place than in another place per se*, since such a comparison requires a kind of divine external timekeeping to which both clocks are compared, and any divinely external timekeeping of this kind does not exist anywhere else than possibly in our anthropocentric, inter-narcissistic fantasies. Moreover, the theory of relativity will not allow this either, which means that even Einstein himself momentarily seems to have had difficulty in drawing the correct conclusions from his own model.

With the advent of relationalist physics – for example in the form of loop quantum gravity and shape dynamics – we gain access to a new concept that is a logical consequence of all local times moving in the same direction, but this does not make it possible for us to compare them via divinely external meta-timekeeping. This is *global time,* which is best described as the aggregate internal duration for the Universe as a whole, without any external observer. Global time indeed comprises everything and everybody in the Universe, but without it ever being able to be localised, and thereby without it ever being measurable, since any kind of measuring of something that cannot be located requires some kind of mysteriously arisen observer position *outside the Universe* (one cannot be both inside and outside the Universe at once, not without being some kind of Platonist, dualist magician). The specific conditions that influence global time do of course by definition only exist globally when our whole entangled Universe without exception is included in the temporal equation, and never locally in any distinct region of, or even less so, outside the Universe. Global time thereby differs radically from classical metatime as a concept. It is *both a universal and at the same time monist duration*; a *meme*, quite plausible to physics, but which seems to pass by the otherwise so revolutionarily inclined Einstein, without leaving any deep impression.

However, within relationalist physics it is a central insight that the behavioural patterns of the Universe can look completely different at a global or local level. The point is thus that all the clocks in Einstein's thought experiment only display local time. What Einstein therefore misses – since he has no concept of the deepening that a shift from relativism to relationalism entails – is that beyond his beloved, local clocks global time is still both possible and plausible. The problem for Einstein is that if global time really exists, it immediately kills his most beloved fetish: his determinist block universe. Moreover, all this occurs without us catching the slightest glimpse of any global clock since such a cosmological and quantum physical, relationalist timekeeping cannot exist outside the Universe whose time it is supposed to measure. Presumably it is precisely here that laboratory-fixated Einstein loses the plot. Without his beloved *measuring instruments,* as he despondently confesses to Bohr, he is of course completely at a loss in the face of quantum physics, which is bewildering to him. *According to relationalist physics, the Universe itself has a duration of its own,* which for that very reason cannot be measured by an external, extra-universal observer, which is exactly what an ordinary, classic clock would be. So it is about *time without a clock,* an ontic flow without any measuring instrument. And it is exactly here that Einstein pigheadedly says thanks and goodbye to Bohr and refuses to be involved any longer.

The Bohrian revolution means that it is time and not space that is the really fundamental mystery within physics. Thus, we would do well to ignore Einstein's *spatiocentrism* in order to instead move on with Peirce's and Smolin's proposal to construct *a tempocentric world view.* A more interesting alternative to Einstein's failed attempt to domesticate time and convert it into a kind of extra dimension of space would be to do precisely the opposite: to *regard space as three extra dimensions on top of time.* Loop quantum gravity does exactly this when it quantifies Einstein's general theory of relativity. According to the theory of loop quantum gravity, space is no longer void or fixed, but must rather be regarded as *an elastic phenomenon subject to network dynamics.* The new metaphors of informationalism are quite simply so powerful that even physics goes through a fundamental change with the starting point in the idea of network dynamics. In the new relationalist physics even the Universe itself is a phenomenon of network dynamics.

A consequence of this is that space might have had completely different characteristics in previous historical stages than it has today. For example, it might have had many times more dimensions than today's three under the extreme heat that prevailed during the Universe's very earliest phase of genesis. This opens the way for the idea that both the expansion of cosmic space and today's three dimensions of space can be regarded as by-products of a dramatic cooling down of initially incredibly hot, compressed, network-dynamical primordial space. Such a network-dynamics way of viewing the genesis of the Universe is called *geometrogenesis.* In its initial phase, multidimensional space is a maximally entangled *pure geometry* (it is pure in the sense that its nodes completely lack substance). But for every phase transition ever-more entanglements are dissolved, which means that space expands and is gradually cooled down. As a kind of compensation for the incrementally decreasing interconnections with each other in an expanding and cooled universe, the nodes receive the *substance* we associate with them today, and space thereby acquires its *weight.*

Global time already exists when all nodes in the Universe are connected to each other; a condition that interestingly enough admits the existence of a global time within the Universe but at the same time admits a lack of any vestige of space and thereby also all forms of local time. The clocks would stand still if they had anywhere to be and if there was anyone who could read them. An energy loss causes the nodes to start letting go of each other, and *the Big Bang* is a fact. What is interesting here is how a radically relationalist idea such as geometrogenesis requires global time as an axiom to be able to exist. Local times in Einsteinian relativism arise only when geometrogenesis kicks in; when the nodes loosen their grip on each other and the Universe has cooled; this is when space arises and expands. And with the expansion of space, a speed limit within the Universe also arises, namely at *the speed of light* – note that we are dealing with yet another law that only applies within our present Universe; cosmic space as a whole needs no upper speed limit: *the cosmic inflation* in the Universe's childhood, which both the standard model and geometrogenesis require, expands much faster than light for example – which in turn gives rise to the local subsystems that characterise the universe that Einstein analyses in our time. And what does Einstein find in these local subsystems, if not those beloved clocks of his?

If geometrogenesis proves to be the best theory for describing the origin of the Universe, then it is likely to have no less than dramatic consequences, to put it mildly, for philosophy, too. To start with, the Universe can no longer be a kind of Heideggerian accident in a metaphysical sense; the theory does not provide scope for any *cosmological accidentalism* of the type that the static theories of the Universe's origin *de facto* assume. All forms of accidentalism are of course inevitably based on myths of stasis, equilibrium and isolation as normal states. But this is not what physical reality looks like. It is, as so often the case in history, the metaphor of *death* that plays too large a part in the collective fantasies of human beings for us to be able to understand how physical reality is constructed. From the Garden of Eden to the great silence before, for example, the genesis of physics, life or consciousness: again and again the fantasising returns to the same eternal worship of stasis, equilibrium and isolation, a fantasising that ultimately can result in only one thing: a suddenly emergent, vital chaos that disturbs and interrupts the mortal order, that is, *the decisive anomaly that means that the dreamed-of paradise is lost.* However, cosmological accidentalism seldom or never has any relevance whatsoever in physical reality. The Universe is not human. In fact, the normal state of the Universe is *vitality* and *intensity*, not death and extinction.

The difference between correlationism and relationalism is there already in the difference between the concepts *relation* and *relationality*. A relation is always fixed, a correlation is even a fixation between two fixed points, primarily a subject and an object. A relationality on the other hand is a state where no fixed objects whatsoever exist, where differences on top of other differences create relations between the differences without any fixed objects ever arising other than in an eternalising observer's perception process. In correlationism, the relation is *external and not in the singular* in relation to the fixed objects that, for simplicity's sake, we assume (not least Kant's *thing in itself*). In relationalism however, there are only relations on top of other relations, which in the absence of fixed objects are *external and in the plural* in relation to what Bohr calls a *field* and what Whitehead calls a *process*. Historically speaking, Kant's correlationism is replaced by Nietzsche's relativism, after which the development continues to, and is completed by, Bohr's and Whitehead's *relationalism*, where the object is also not consciously ignored any longer, which was the case with Hegel, but is literally dissolved in the mobilist process.

The physicist and philosopher Karen Barad champions the radical thesis that all philosophy that is produced prior to the advent of relationalism is all too anthropocentric and thereby misleading. The only way out of this fatalist cul-de-sac is to construct a completely new ontology with the existence of the Universe and not the human being as primary. Phantasmic *anthropocentrism* must be replaced by realistic *universocentrism*. The shift from anthropocentric to universocentric metaphysics is equivalent to the shift from *Man* to *the network* as a metaphysical centre. God is thus not in fact dead, it is just the human God who could only live under very special circumstances that has left us. The literally inhuman God lives and thrives and is at last being discovered and analysed by us humans. The inhuman God, the Universe as a glittering network, lives and thrives at the centre of the syntheological pyramid: *God is a network.*

Barad dismantles and disposes of Kant's noumenon, and thereby she also extremely effectively puts an end to *the correlationist paradigm*. Her Bohrian phenomenology, based on relations on top of relations and probabilities on top of probabilities, with varying intensities rather than essences at the centre and without fixed physical boundaries, has no need whatsoever of any Kantian noumenon. Barad comes from the world of quantum physics, which of course is governed by concepts such as complementarity, entanglement, chance and non-locality. The principle of precedence disposes of all ideas of eternally valid laws that precede physical reality. Barad's phenomenon is therefore instead *the phenomenon per se* described based on physics' own conditions, rather than from Kant's blind faith in rationality's conception of reality being sufficiently exhaustive. And it is precisely therefore that her *universocentric* rather than anthropocentric ontology is a *realism*. Every Baradian phenomenon, every *assemblage of intensities*, has its own *genetics* and its own *memetics* as her predecessor Gilles Deleuze would express the matter. It is the current set of genes and memes that we familiarise ourselves with when we get to know the phenomenon. The world cannot be more *real* than it is with Barad.

At the dawn of the Internet age, hardly surprisingly, we were inundated by innovative relationalist philosophy. The culture critic

Steven Shaviro is inspired by Whitehead's pragmatic world of prehensions and nexi in his book *Without Criteria: Kant, Whitehead, Deleuze and Aesthetics*. He does not refrain from also investigating such philosophically controversial concepts as vitalism, animism and panpsychism in his work. In her book *Vibrant Matter* the Deleuzian eco-philosopher Jane Bennett champions the argument that it is time once and for all to abandon the anthropomorphic fixation with the axiomatic special status that *life* constantly has in the world of philosophy, and instead replace vitalism connected to life with a vitalism based on *intensity* in physics as a unifying factor. Bennett constructs a world of constantly vibrating *bodies* rather than isolated things as the eternalised forms of processes, but her bodies are both human and non-human, living and non-living, where it is precisely the *vitality* of the bodies and nothing else that is allowed to take centre stage.

Correlationism's critics often return to the question of *ancestrality,* where they focus on the subject and the object not being historically equal, if they even exist as entities of their own. Human consciousness or *the mind* has only existed for a few seconds of planet Earth's 24-hour history. Existence evidently needs no subjects or consciousnesses in order to exist as a complete existence, and might well be thought to exist without any present subject even in the future. But if correlationism is to be criticised in the right way, it must be from *inside* its philosophical advances and not from the outside, so that we do not relapse into classical realism. It is then clear that the fundamental problem with correlationism is that Kant does not seem to understand *why* the thing in itself is unattainable for the human being. Kant imagines that the thing is out of reach of human perception and consciousness since our senses are not sufficiently expanded and flexible to be able to assimilate the thing in its entirety. The senses therefore create a world of representations only.

Kant still speaks of a kind of clearly delimited thing, what he calls a *noumenon*. The phenomenon is, according to Kant, merely a bad approximation of the – for the Platonist Kant – even more real noumenon. The fact that this noumenon is unattainable is not grounded in the limitations of the senses however, as Kant imagines, but in the fact that all things are in constant motion and change, both intra-actively and interactively, and thereby by definition are not possible to fixate. Kant is the instructive example *par excellence* of an isolated observer within physics who does not understand that his own entanglement with the thing, which he imagines himself to be observing from the outside, also influences the thing itself. He cannot imagine that his external and neutral observer position is a physical impossibility, and that it is this and nothing else that makes the thing in itself something that is unattainable. Kant is quite simply the Newtonian-Einsteinian mystic who does not quite understand the quantum physical revolution. He does not realise that the observing subject also is *world*. For what else could it be? If it exists, it is world.

The thing in itself cannot be experienced as an object, since it is *de facto* not an object, but merely a highly arbitrary eternalisation. It is not the thing in itself but the *eternalisation of the thing* that must be regarded as the real conjuring trick in Kantian correlationism. Once we understand this, we need no longer accept the Kantian axioms. A new kind of ontological realism at once becomes possible, what Barad calls *agential realism* and Stephen Hawking names *model-dependent realism*. The relationalist response to Kant is that the phenomena are fields rather than particles. The fields consist of intensities and probabilities and in fact never have any clear boundaries. For physics *per se* has no use whatsoever for clear boundaries. The clear boundaries must rather be viewed as an expression of narcissistic wishful thinking in an anthropocentric world view which is wrestling with its lack of processing capacity in relation to the inexhaustible oceans of information in existence. Every time we are forced to hear the clichés about quantum physics being obscure, mysterious and startling – or see how it is accused of being some kind of shallow forgery of reality, a mirage which clearly hides a more intuition-friendly and therefore more real reality, hidden behind some kind of cosmic, mysterious veil – it is Kant's voice within us and in the prevailing culture that is speaking.

However, it is exactly the other way around: However counter-intuitive quantum physics may appear at first glance, it is *de facto* real reality, or more correctly, as close as we can ever get to a scientifically verified as well as perceptionally accessible reality. Quantum physics even opens the way to *ontological realism* – both the agential and the model-dependent – that is, precisely the onto-epistemological accessibility to the surrounding world that Kant believes that he dismisses once and for all through his almost autistic separation of the subject and the object. In fact, reality is the subject and the object entangled into one indivisible *phenomenon*, without any real separation. Whoever most smoothly manages to upgrade their world view by calibrating their *intuition* in accordance with this insight also has the most to gain in conjunction with the paradigm shift in question from correlationism to relationalism. And this applies of course to a high degree in the areas of metaphysics and religion.

The eternalist world view exists because the human being needs it: physics on the other hand manages splendidly without eternalism in our mobilist Universe. The perception process transforms the mobilist field into an eternalised thing. The abstract thing thus does not exist in an ontic sense, it must instead be understood as a kind of *concrete field*. Evolution has conveniently developed perception into a highly efficient *information prioritisation mechanism*, rather than into the ontological truth producer that Kantian rationalism in its superstitiousness desires it to be. It is thus the perception that freezes the concrete field in space–time and decodes it as a delimited *fictive*. The key word here is *intensity*. A phenomenon is mainly a kind of noumenal intensity. The higher the activity and complexity within a concrete field, the higher the intensity. The physicists Julian Barbour and Lee Smolin have defined complexity in a physical sense as *multiplicity*. The greater the difference within a subsystem, the greater the variation. Self-organised systems organise energy flows as *feedback loops*, for both positive and negative feedback. Thereafter it is simply a case of multiplying *the variation* by *the activity* in order to be able to calculated *the intensity* of the phenomenon in question.

The correlationists do not seem to understand that *stability* as a property is independent of all requirements for *necessity*. Oddly enough Zoroaster realises this difference already in ancient Iran about 1,700 years B.C. when he formulates the concept of *haurvatat*, a state that contains a kind of sacred perfection and at the same time is constantly in motion and dynamic; *haurvatat* may well be regarded as a synonym for the syntheist idea of *the infinite now*. Zoroaster's genius lies in that he places holiness in *the mutable* and not in *the immutable*, which is in total contrast to Platonism and the Abrahamic religions. What brings Zoroaster and the relationalist physicists together is that they all maintain that relatively stable states can arise more or less regularly in an otherwise completely contingent universe. The symmetry that is so passionately desired – from Kant to Einstein, both within philosophy and within physics – is actually the opposite of contingency. *Symmetry is eternalist* and *contingency is mobilist*.

There is of course an ongoing oscillating dialectics between eternalism and mobilism *in the human mind*, but the truth and reality beyond Man's perceptional fantasy world is fundamentally mobilist. The Universe is thus contingent and not symmetrical. Stability and necessity have nothing whatsoever to do with each other: connecting them logically is to let oneself be hypnotised by an eternalist illusion. That existence on a fundamental level is *transfinite* does not mean that it cannot produce temporarily stable states. Quite the opposite: temporary stabilities in complex systems can be every bit as common as explosive changes. They are however, just like the explosions, always temporary. Since everything influences everything else in a mobile and contingent universe, everything will sooner or later change and transition into completely new emergent states. And what is this if not the physical realisation of Zoroaster's ethical ideal of *haurvatat*?

We can therefore completely refrain from building even more constructions using the isolated objects that Kant uses as building blocks in his outdated metaphysics. But this does not mean that we are relativists. For relativism does not move sufficiently far away from individualism and atomism; it should rather be regarded as an inconsistent half-measure in the development from an understanding of existence as an *atomist* world full of discrete objects to the understanding of existence as a *relationalist* world consisting of irreducible multiplicities and endless relations. Even relativism must be dialectically developed into relationalism. There are no things whatsoever to relate between, which relativism requires; there are only *relata* that in turn always are relata to other relata, and so on *ad infinitum*.

According to syntheist metaphysics, relations therefore must be what is ontologically primary. This also means that the *ontology* in a fundamental sense precedes the *phenomenology*, since external existence, among other things according to the principle of ancestrality, always precedes the internal observation. The *intra-acting* phenomena are in themselves as relational as the *interactive* relations between them. Objects do not arise independently only to be later evaluated in relation to other objects, which is what post-Kantian relativism claims. Syntheist phenomena are not stable objects at all filled with heavy essences, but extremely mobile and fluid *phenomena* in constant interaction both within themselves and with everything else in their environment, and often also far away from this environment, such as in the case of *quantum teleportation*.

In his book *Time Reborn* Lee Smolin draws attention to the recurring dilemma, that scientists constantly assume that ontologically speaking existence is both mobilist and eternalist. But as we have seen that is not at all the case. *Existence per se is only mobilist.* Eternalism is something that our senses and our consciousness produces, but it has nothing to do with the world outside our senses and our consciousness; crassly speaking eternalism is just a phenomenological by-product. This relationalist position results in *the wave* (mobilism) having priority over *the particle* (eternalism); they are thus not ontologically equal in merit, for the wave is *primary* in relation to the particle, which is *secondary*. And yet science is constantly tempted to fall into the trap which entails assuming there is an eternalist background to the Universe, either through the mistake of mixing eternalism into mobilist physics, or, which is even worse, *through assuming that eternalism is the real reality*, while our mobilist Universe in that case must be a chimera. Both Newton and Einstein are Platonists who get stuck in this trap, and the same goes, for example, for the majority of contemporary string theoreticians.

However, it is the eternalistic background that is the real chimera in this context. To take one example, there are of course lots of *local subsystems* but no *isolated systems* anywhere in the Universe. This means that all the theories that require the existence of isolated systems collapse sooner or later. As a consequence of this, it is pointless to go further into physics with theory building that is not *background-independent*, because if they are the least dependent on a fixed eternalised background, these theories do not hold up to closer scrutiny. In fact, the Universe displays no need whatsoever for fixed backgrounds. The eternalist background is merely a fiction, the last remnant of the Abrahamic and Platonist fantasy of the God that precedes the Creation. But such a God of course does not exist, as we know. He died. The Universe does not need the eternalist background any more than it needs God the creator. Whitehead, Bohr, Barad and Smolin understand this, and their predecessor Leibniz understands it much earlier, but it turns out that this is something so extremely hard to accept for Einstein, who both idolises and is intoxicated by mathematics, which explains why from the point of view of the philosophy of science he clings onto *relativism* and is not able to move on to *relationalism*.

What disturbs the Platonists about relationalism is that the mobilist world view sooner or later must yield to *the principle of explanatory closure*. The ontic flow must be eternalised in order for it to be converted into words and numbers. The principle of explanatory closure means that eternalisation is unavoidable, but the trick is of course partly to freeze eternalisation where it captures mobilist reality as well as possible, partly to most humbly realise that every eternalisation is only a clumsy digital rounding-off of a much more complex, analogous phenomenon in expansive motion. Process philosophy, and in the case of syntheism *process theology,* is therefore the best vaccine against *the taxonomic deification of the object*. Only a consistently executed process philosophy can immunise us against totalism's tempting, simplifying superstitions. Syntheologically we express this as *Entheos' presence* preventing us from getting stuck in Atheos or Pantheos *per se*, and instead continuing to direct our attention towards the real oscillation between them.

We can express this as though the relation between on the one hand Entheos and on the other hand the oscillation between Atheos and Pantheos links back to Spinoza's classical division between *natura naturans* (active nature) and *natura naturata* (passive nature) in the monist universe, which is a productive division within *the One,* the pantheistic deity. Entheos is quite simply the name of nature's own built-in activism, its constant quest for change, its enormous production of differences and multitudes; while Pantheos is the name of nature as a gigantic and historically speaking passive object where the differences and the multitudes dwell *before Entheos' gaze* (with Atheos as the hidden but necessary underside of Pantheos). The Spinozist relation between *natura naturans* and *natura naturata* thus has a syntheological equivalent in *the relation between Pantheos and Entheos.*

In his book *Charles Sanders Peirce and a Religious Metaphysics of Nature* the syntheist philosopher Leon Niemoczynski constructs what he calls a speculative naturalism which takes its starting point in the idea that nature generously enough offers us lots of possibilities for insight into its infinitely productive, vibrating foundation, which he identifies as *natura naturans*. Niemoczynski brings back Peirce's own favourites from times gone by, Spinoza and Schelling, to American pragmatism, and then flavours the hybrid with the 3rd millennium's European anti-correlationism into one of the sharpest contributions so far to syntheist discourse. In the oscillation between Schelling's Atheos and Spinoza's Pantheos, what Niemoczynski himself describes as a naturalist *panentheism* arises, which is immediately recognizable from the foundation of the syntheological pyramid.

At the same moment that the eternalisation is carried out, as Heraclitus points out, existence has already changed and moved somewhere else in history. The Platonists are of course disturbed by the epistemological impossibility of *de facto* knowing and discerning a mobilist world when their evidently clumsy eternalisations are the only way to gain contact with physical reality. They flock around *the fetishistic dream* of gaining direct access to an existence that constantly eludes them. When the relationalists then claim that existence is radically contingent, that the future is open, that all apparently durable laws can be altered at any time; then we can of course, and unfortunately, write off all attempts to achieve a sustainable universal theory of everything for physics. For it is precisely this fetish that the relationalist deprives the Platonist of; *the desire to experience and rule the world as it is* can never be fulfilled in any way. It is both physically and in principle impossible to *catch the world* in a constantly expanding universe with the magical *arrow of time* as a given constant. This is the meaning of the principle of explanatory closure.

Eternalist hypotheses are characterised by simplicity and purity, and it is for this reason that they are aesthetically pleasing to a constantly eternalising mind that is continuously wrestling with the complexity of existence. In the best case, that this is so can indicate *intuition*, but in the worst case it is more likely an example of autistic wishful thinking. A clear example of the physicists' unfortunate attraction to Platonism is the constantly recurring idea that the discovery of *the simple, the pure, and the aesthetically pleasing* is a sign that physics is getting closer to the truth. The aesthetic eye is attracted to symmetries and, to take one example, the most efficient routes between the different nodes in complex systems. The banal reason that aesthetics leads us to arrive at precisely this fixation is that it is based what the human eye desires, but this eye is not some metaphysical truth agent *per se,* merely the constructionally dubious by-product of millions of years of Darwinian struggle for limited resources. In complex systems characterised by *scarcity,* efficiency is something extremely valuable. Thus the human eye appreciates and prefers what seems *efficient.* And what is more efficient in complex systems than the simple and pure, what takes the shortest route between the nodes, what keeps to the straight and clear without any tiring and time-consuming convolutions?

The problem is just that the conditions of scarcity that the human being has endured on planet Earth for several million years have no equivalent in the Universe whatsoever. *The Universe is one gigantic expansion, where there is no scarcity of resources of any kind.* The Universe is 93 billion light years wide. And it is finite but limitless. An eye that over innumerable generations has been evolutionarily honed for hunting, gathering and reproduction has no benefit whatsoever from its natural, intuitive aesthetics when it comes to understanding the Universe, which may be regarded as a latter-day occupation. Here the eye is groping in a cosmic darkness which it really does not understand. Thereby, the whole idea that aesthetics, which has finite resources as its starting point would have any applicability whatsoever to a cosmos that is characterised by enormous bounty, falls down. Rather, time after time, throughout history, physics has proven to be even more confusing, even more complex, even more bizarre, than the human being with her narrow, anthropocentric imagination has been able to even begin to imagine in advance. On further reflection, Plato's neurotic minimalism is to be regarded as the worst possible guide through modern physics.

After all, we live in a mobilist Universe, and thus relationalism is the only possible way forward towards a deeper understanding of existence, however difficult and complicated that path may seem. Pantheos offers no incentive whatsoever in terms of making it simple for us in the way that rationalism in all its forms would like to believe. No incentives whatsoever can exist in a state of bounty, since an incentive by definition requires a scarcity. Rather, physics only becomes more and more complex the more deeply we delve into it. And why would Pantheos want to have it any other way? God apparently loves to play hide-and-seek. The only theory of everything that stands the test of time is therefore *the relationalist metalaw* which says that eternally valid theories of everything are in principle impossible. When the physicists' megalomaniac boyhood dreams of *the great unified theory of everything* thus collapses in the face of the ruthless principle of explanatory closure, this is where the syntheists take over and enthusiastically pick up the only reasonable ethical imperative that remains: *Go with the flow*!

From semiotics via memetics to the collapse of militant atheism

We live in a relationalist universe. It is not relativist, and it is definitely not dualist, in either a Platonist or in any other sense. Which leads to complications when we humans, with our limited perspective – for understandable reasons, a strictly anthropocentric one – and our expedient but extremely selective and elucidating perception apparatus, are going to form a picture of the world and everything that transpires in our environment. What we see and apprehend is a world filled with clearly delimited things: chairs, tables, and pots and pans that are either standing on the stove or inside cupboards, if they are not lying around somewhere cluttering up where they really have no place being. But these clear delimitations constitute a mixture of wishful thinking and simplifications that are dictated by functionality. We must be able to orient ourselves and act in order to survive. In reality, the world consists of more or less impermanent and fuzzily delimited phenomena, where it is the system's organisation that determines their function and properties to an infinitely greater extent than the phenomena in themselves. These systems are changing all the time and are in incessant and infinitely complex interaction with all other systems, which also keep changing all the time. This means that the constant conflict between form and matter is illusory. Form is matter, matter is form. There is no conflict between the one and the other. The world is a whole thing, but it never stays the same from one moment to the next.

The principle of explanatory closure is based on the insight that at the end of the day the Universe is a gigantic, unmanageable *ontic flow* that is expanding at a tremendously high rate. The Universe did not create itself in some kind of unique moment of self-genesis – in the manner that the traditional religions, and up until recently the natural sciences as well, imagined the whole process to have taken place. Rather, it creates and recreates itself all the time in a constantly ongoing process. But all explanatory models of everything require an arbitrarily chosen but nevertheless necessary freeze of this flow, an *eternalisation*, in order to be possible, or even conceivable. The reason is quite simply that as soon as some individual explanation has been formulated, the world with all its mutable and interacting systems of atoms has already rushed onwards in all directions from the eternalisation in space–time that the explanation requires and claims to interpret and clarify. The Universe thereby constantly evades all of Man's pathetic attempts at explanatory candour. Everything of this nature by definition lies outside our human capabilities. This means that the only intellectually honest attitude to the Universe is to accept it as a constantly mutable entity that continuously evades us, pantheism's *the One* as God, the explanatory closure *par excellence*.

But we are also living in an informationalist world – no longer in a world of just written language or oral communication – where the total quantity of information is expanding at such tremendous speed that the world around us is becoming increasingly difficult to grasp and more and more incomprehensible to us. We see how the ontic deluge in the Universe gets an *ontological* equivalent in the gigantic, rapidly expanding and thereby incalculable flow of words, thoughts and ideas that confront us in our immediate environment. This ontological rather than ontic flow of impulses gushes – with the same torrential force as our expanding Universe – through the interlinked, interacting and therefore in practice convergent media that shape and dictate the conditions of our socio-cultural biotopes, which puts a lot of pressure on our brains and senses. We cannot possibly not be part of it, but instead live very much within – always and only within – the ontic as well as ontological flows of existence. This means that the principle of explanatory closure, at least under informationalism, also must include ourselves and our communications with each other and the world around us.

The concept of information stress is not particularly old, but with the advent of informationalism we have been forced to relate to this phenomenon and create strategies for managing it to some extent and preserving at least an illusion of overview and control. This means that our only possibility of embracing the world as a whole under informationalism arises if we complement the ontic *relationalism* for the natural sciences with ontological *social relationalism* for the social sciences. We are now being forced to realise that we are not only constantly forced to *eternalise* the mobilist world around us in order to make it understandable and manageable (see *The Global Empire*), but that in addition our new eternalisations on top of our earlier eternalisations – because of the explosive expansion of the Universe and the sheer quantity of information – are constantly being moved further and further away from the fundamental mobilist *ontics* of existence. This insight means that we are reduced to trying to manage our relations with both the surrounding world and ourselves, our own identity as ethical creatures, through *transrationalism* – and with the starting point in a conception of existence as an open entirety, not through *rationalism* based on a conception of existence as a closed logical construction in all its constituent parts.

We are forced to abandon the old *Cartesian internarcissism* in order to construct a *universocentric interdependism* instead. And based on a universocentric interdependism, society or *the social* must be a primary emergence, that is, we apply *the One* in a Spinozist sense to the social under the name Syntheos, in the same way that we already apply *the One* to the universal under the name Pantheos. What is essential here is that the social as a whole thereby precedes the Kantian relation between the subject and the object instead of the other way around, just as the Universe on the whole precedes all kinds of atomist constructions within physics. In addition, interdependism must be relationalist and not relativist; the mutual dependence of the agents applies at all levels in the hierarchy, and thus also within the phenomena themselves.

This has the consequence that syntheist ethics cannot be based on anything other than a kind of constantly variable *existentialist adaptation* to the irrefutably overwhelming ontic and ontological flows of existence, a pragmatist as well as spiritual *subordination* in relation to the expanding, mobilist enormity. For us as temporal creatures, this existentialist adaptation must take the form of *amor fati,* the unconditional acceptance of and love for the past as the basis for syntheist ethics. Once we have accepted the past as one long line of always equally unlikely but nevertheless real *actualities* in an endless ocean of never realised *potentialities* – just think of how many millions of sperm nature wasted in order for just one sperm to penetrate the only egg at your own genesis – we turn *amor fati* towards the future, a future that is open, indeterminist and full of potentialities that can all be brought to life. In this future, the utopia may be highly unlikely and yet fully possible, and this fact becomes the target of our syntheist faith. *Amor fati* is consummated as a *truth as an act* in a fixed direction towards the utopia; an act from which everything else of importance in our lives subsequently gets its ethical substance.

Syntheist ethics is thus sociorelationalist and not cultural relativist, based on the original Zoroastrian understanding that intention, decision and interaction sooner or later coincide and together form the only possible ethical substance of both the individual human being and the collective civilisation. This means that the principle of explanatory closure not only kills Kant's rationalist idea that Man is born with the natural ability to understand rather than simply subordinate himself to the world in its entirety; even Kant's rationalist idea of Man being able to understand himself as a being within his own lifeworld is dead. The solid, closed and primary *individual* is replaced by the divided, open and secondary *dividual* as the human ideal. This means that the conceited idea that our thoughts and words belong to ourselves, that we can identify ourselves with what we think and say without connecting this to body, action and environment – as though what we are thinking and saying were originally created by and exclusive to ourselves – is dead. We will never have any sustainable identity as the inventors of these ideas, but on the other hand as their potential thoroughfares and interim receptacles.

This in turn means that we need a new, informationalist explanatory model for how words, thoughts and ideas arise and are formed, and above all for how they are interpreted and altered over time; how communication between bodies and media occur and above all what consequences this process has for our new, dividual identity. Precisely such a de-personified explanatory model has also emerged in parallel with digital technology, which is the foundation of the ongoing paradigm shift, and it is called *memetics*. We have already written extensively about this research field numerous times from many different angles (see *The Futurica Trilogy*). Memetic theory – which explains how words, thoughts, ideas and cultural components of various kinds multiply and are modified according to the same Darwinian selection principles that also regulate how genes multiply and are modified within biological systems – was launched in an essay by Ted Cloak in 1975 and popularised in exhaustive detail by Richard Dawkins in the book *The Selfish Gene* one year later. It was also Dawkins who coined the term *meme* for this *replicator* which is active within the sociocultural biotope and which is selfish in the same sense that the selfish gene is selfish, that is, its primary interest, if we allow ourselves to reason with the aid of an anthropomorphic image, is to multiply itself through dissemination to the greatest possible extent. It wants to infect the world.

Memetics simply strives to construct an evolutionary model not just for natural but also for cultural information transfer. A meme is quite simply the cultural gene, a package of information, a kind of cultural unit – for example an idea, a technology, a belief or a pattern of behaviour – which is lodged in a mind or a medium and which cannot reproduce itself through producing copies of itself and transferring itself between different minds and media. The meme's reproductive success is conditional upon people's ability and desire to imitate each other and thus pick up new thoughts and behaviour. This means that we no longer regard communication as primarily something that concerns an individual who is trying to influence another individual in a certain direction, but instead as a flow of selfish memes that reproduce themselves to the best of their abilities by travelling from mind to mind via various accessible media and making themselves at home the moment they find a receptive environment in the form of a brain furnished with various sets of compatible meme clusters, called *memeplexes*.

An interesting aspect in this context is that memetics pays no heed to whether any particular meme proves to be true or false, useful or useless, from some arbitrarily chosen perspective. What is decisive is that the memes which are best suited to the prevailing conditions will survive and be disseminated. Meme X either fits with the patterns formed by the dominant memeplexes in an environment, which might just as well be a dividual brain as a collective community, or else it doesn't – an environment that this meme then contributes to modifying by adding to the existing patterns, even if only the tiniest little bit. The decisive factor for a meme's success is thus how it matches already existing memeplexes in the host body in question and whether it appears useful or in any other way appealing in the life situation in which this body finds itself. This means that the more effectively the meme offers *infotainment* to the intended host organism, the greater the chance that this host will spread the meme further by inspiring imitation in other potential hosts.

The American philosopher Daniel Dennett connects memetics to a more extensive *theory of mind* in his book *Consciousness Explained* from 1991. According to Dennett, the majority of our memes are undisturbed and inactive in our brain, and only when the brain experiences a concrete change in its lifeworld does it react by accepting new or modifying old memes, in order to then spread them further. The mind, according to Dennett, consists of memes and only memes that have taken control of the brain and that think the thoughts of the host, and it can also be described in precisely this way. Thus, there is no longer any need for an individual in the Cartesian sense. Even the *I-experience* as such is a meme in itself and nothing else, albeit unprecedented in its success. It constitutes a phenomenon that we, with a clear reference to the father of individualism, call *the Cartesian meme*.

The British psychologist Susan Blackmore, author of the influential and controversial book *The Meme Machine*, defines memes as all things that allow themselves to be copied from one human being to another: habits, fashion trends, knowledge, songs, jokes and all other forms of packaged information. Memes are disseminated horizontally through imitation, learning and other methods. The point is that the copies are never one hundred per cent identical to the original; in the same way as genes, memes are also copied with extensive variation. Most mutations are completely unviable, while some exceptions constitute a competitive improvement in the interplay with the conditions that happen to prevail. Since the memes are often spread considerably faster than genes – mutations occur at every interaction, so too within the brains and media where the memes are located – the speed of mutation within memetics is extremely high in comparison with biological systems, where the spread occurs exclusively vertically. And just like genes, memes can be said to compete for a limited space where they are located, and thereby also fight for the chance to survive, be copied and spread further. The critical factor here is people's attention – a very strictly limited resource.

But while Dawkins has a markedly *reductionist* attitude towards memetics – all human expressions can be broken down into their smallest components, individual memes – Blackmore is the first proponent of a *relationalist* memetics. She points out that a cluster of memes often undergoes an emergence and together these memes form in fact a *memeplex*, a phenomenon that *de facto* constitutes something more than just its smallest constituent parts (the various memes). Thereby Blackmore succeeds in doing something which Dawkins and Dennett failed to do: namely, to explain how a society, a culture, a civilisation – the outermost forms of memeplexes – arise, survive and even propagate, based on a strictly memetic explanatory model. Thus, as a memeplex of its own, memetics must be regarded as a memetic replication of *semiotics*, a discipline in the borderland between philosophy and science whose roots go back to John Locke's vision of a *science of signs* which he formulates in *An Essay Concerning Human Understanding* as early as the end of the 17th century.

Semiotics deals with the investigation and interpretation of signs within all sorts of communication: firstly, the relationship of signs to what they are intended to represent (*semantics*); secondly the relationship of signs to each other (*syntactics*) and thirdly the relationship of signs to their users (*pragmatics*). The American pragmatist Charles Sanders Peirce and the Swiss linguist Ferdinand de Saussure are usually regarded as the two philosophical giants of semiotics. From the mid-19th century up until the early 20th century, quite independently of each other, they both constructed extensive systems that were later used as platforms for all subsequent forms of working with semiotics. Peirce launches the idea of a *triad of signs* and, as early as a century before Dawkins, is inspired by Charles Darwin into describing the signs as *replicators*, while de Saussure – who for the sake of clarity calls his theory *semiology* rather than semiotics – focuses primarily on the binary relationship between *the word* in itself and *the concept* behind the word within language.

The transition from semiotics to memetics – that is, the transition from the sign to the meme as the smallest component of information and communication – is partly about a broadening of what it actually is that is transferred between minds and media when information is communicated to one or more recipients – a broadening that semiotics itself deals a lot with after Peirce and de Saussure (when the semiotics of the 21st century uses the term *sign*, this is more or less synonymous with the term *meme* in memetics) – but above all it is about a deeper understanding of how mobile and mutable information is, and how this influences our philosophical understanding of subjectivity and social identity.

Semiotics is primarily pragmatic rather than syntactic, not least since Peirce is a *relativist* and not yet a *relationalist*. Thus it is still in the individualist paradigm. Semiotics is namely focused on what the sign is presumed to represent – according to Peirce the sign would not be a sign if it did not correspond to and translate some external *object* into language – while memetics chooses to act regardless of typically Kantian concerns, such as whether external, objective or intersubjective truths really exist, and if so in what way. This means that semiotics presumes that the interpretation of signs in a prevailing society – the discipline that is called *hermeneutics* within philosophy and *exegesis* within theology – can be carried out by an independent, external observer: the *hermeneuticist*. But nothing could be further from the truth. The hermeneuticist is of course also steeped in the prevailing paradigm, and therefore must be primarily regarded as a technological as well as ideological by-product of the same, and not, in some exceedingly diffuse and mysterious way, as its neutral and distanced interpreter. There are indeed no neutral and distanced interpreters, either within physics or sociology; such a position is quite simply both physically and socially impossible.

A meme survives and multiplies by making copies of itself, and thanks to its ability to blend in and appear useful or entertaining for a certain subject in a given situation at a certain point in time. Once again: it has nothing to do with what is true or false. This distinguishes the meme from the sign as a concept. Memetics quite simply constitutes a relationalist radicalisation of semiotics in the same way that Whitehead's process philosophy is a relationalist radicalisation of Peirce's and William James' relativist pragmatism. Through memetics – in particular through the introduction of emergent memeplexes – we shift towards a network-dynamics understanding of culture's relationship to nature. The individual is no longer needed and has no function in this analysis. The dividual of network dynamics (see *The Netocrats*) takes over, and as a result of this paradigm shift, Man is taken from the centre of science to a peripheral seat in the grandstand, where he must be content with acting as the passive spectator and at the same time being seized as a storage and transportation vessel subservient to the extremely dynamic evolution of memes. All the work is done by the memes. The anthropocentric impulse and Man's pride thus gets yet another flick on the nose, which in turn opens the way for *universocentric interdependence*, which is attendant on network dynamics.

This does not have to mean that the role of semiotics as a scientific discipline is passé – quite the contrary. The focus of modern semiotics is in fact no longer on producing a theory of signs, and not of memes either, nor how these relate to each other – it is nowadays memetics rather than semiotics that is fulfilling Locke's original vision of a science of signs – but on a theory of how the signs are interpreted by, and both mentally and physiologically *de facto* influence, their hosts: a pragmatic phenomenon that is called *semiosis*. What is really interesting arises and shows itself when we remove ourselves from the mental to the physiological, since we can then just as easily study the spread of signs between animals and plants as between humans, not to mention the communication across the boundaries between the various categories of biology. Accordingly, semiotics comes down to the study of biological *signalling systems*, while memetics pursues the construction of explanatory models for the genesis and the disintegration of cultural *paradigms*.

This explains why *biosemiotics* (the study of the relations between signs and the biology of the senders, receivers and users of the signs) is a rapidly growing area, while an equivalent area does not exist within memetics. Consequently it is a biosemioticist, Thomas Seboek who, in his book *A Semiotic Perspective on The Sciences* from 1984, independently of Dawkins and Dennett claims that not only can we exchange metaphors to advantage between nature and culture, but also that the very division between the natural and the social sciences, from a biosemiotic perspective, must be regarded as both fundamentally arbitrary and extremely unfortunate. But while Seboek's ideas get a very limited spread among semioticians, the ideas of Dawkins and Dennett successfully spread across a considerably broader philosophical and scientific field. Ironically, memetically speaking memetics becomes more successful than its predecessor semiotics.

If we conceive of a relationalist version of semiotics and memetics, in the same way as a relationalist version of the natural sciences, it must be based on a deep understanding of the largest unit and then build downwards towards the smallest, instead of the classical reductionist obsession of semiotics and memetics with the little sign or the little meme, which is presumed to explain everything that goes on higher up in the hierarchy. According to the writing of the history from the point of view of information technology, the necessary point of departure is that *Man is the constant and technology is the variable*. For Man, this means that technology drives a *paradigm* (see *The Futurica Trilogy*), a plane that sooner or later has its structure studied and explained by a *metaphysics* that is already initially logically built-in but tacit, and is only formulated and engineered after the fact. Metaphysics then shapes the conditions for the *ideology* that is tied to the paradigm, the sign-interpreting narrative that prepares you for choosing, the narrative about why things necessarily are the way they are. The ideology in turn consists of large, sluggish blocks called *fictions* – consciously created narratives about current people and their relationships to the world around them, in contrast to the necessarily subconscious ideology – where the nimble and smallest components of fictions are called *fictives* (see *The Global Empire*), a kind of network-dynamics cousin to the signs of semiotics and the memes of memetics, and accordingly also the fundamental component in the paradigm hierarchy.

Note how the relationships between each step, just like when it comes to all forms of relationalist hierarchies, must be understood of course as *emergent* rather than reductionist. The fiction is not built into the fictives beforehand; it seems to always deliver something extra over and above the fictives in themselves. In the same way, the ideology is not built into the fictions in advance; it always appears as something more and extremely attractive over and above the fictions. And it is precisely these emergent qualities that keep us adamantly embedded in the ideological memeplex in question – every new level adds yet another layer of a kind of compact mysticism to the growing *metanarrative*, not least in the big step from the seemingly open and therefore creative fictions to the obviously concealed ideology, which brings us to a standstill – which explains why our relationship to the outermost framework of memeplexes, *the metaphysical*, can never be anything but *humbly subservient*. Even our relationship to a created syntheist god – a deliberately named projection surface vis-à-vis an indisputably real phenomenon in the surrounding world that we must relate to, that is, *fiction par excellence* – must subordinate itself to this premise. This is precisely because no memes exist outside memetics, just as no signs exist outside semiotics. Nor are there any fictives – and in turn fictions constructed from these, and in turn ideologies constructed from these – nor are there in turn any credible metaphysical systems deduced from these ideologies that stand *outside* the current information technology paradigm.

This means that the medium is not only the message, as the Canadian literary historian Marshall McLuhan clear-sightedly proclaims as early as the 1960s, but that the medium also creates the actor herself, rather than the other way around. *We are literally the media with which we communicate.* The netocrat of the information age therefore has a sober view of herself as an affirmative by-product of the interactive technologies that she is using in order to interact with her environment, rather than the other way around. And it is precisely because of the superiority of interactivity vis-à-vis the preceding one-directional communicating technologies – given the choice between on the one hand interactivity, with its equality at all levels, and on the other hand one-directional communication from the top down, from those in power to the masses, the current actors always choose interactivity – that ultimately the *netocracy* vanquish the *bourgeoisie* of the industrial age and take over society's central functions. Since the ideas are fictives – concealed within ideologically coloured fictions, which move according to a certain metaphysical structure – according to the syntheist view, the ideas can never be said to be owned by any individual actor or any group of actors in any real sense.

Not surprisingly, the memeplexes of the powers that be and religion throughout history tend to be entangled and therefore also mutually reinforcing. Religion legitimises power, which protects and enriches religion. In many cases, over time the collaboration became so intimate that it was no longer possible to distinguish the one from the other. But this in itself does not constitute a particularly elucidating answer to the question of why these winners in the cultural evolutionary process in particular have developed the way they have done, and why these memeplexes in particular have been as tenacious as they actually have been and have wiped out all the losers. Why God in particular? Why the Bible in particular (for example)? There has hardly been a lack of alternatives, to put it mildly. But the great majority of these were weeded out, ruthlessly. This is, of course, a topic that has not given memetics any peace; it is close to being a whole science in itself.

The problem could be presented in this way: If religion happens to be the answer, which it apparently has been in every type of society that we know of throughout all of human history up until today – what then is the question? What is it that makes the religious memeplex in particular so attractive and successful in the cultural evolutionary process?

To start with, we cannot help but note that the human brain has been shaped by natural selection to eagerly welcome religious memes and become a believer brain. Being part of the religious community is thus something that in one way or another feels satisfying for the individual member of the congregation, while the religious collective gains competitive advantages in relation to other groups because of their special form of cohesion and mutual understanding which creates trust, impetus and efficiency to an extent that is hard to top. Moreover, at least in the transition from the nomadic existence of hunters and gatherers to a settled agricultural one, religious memes are blessed with dedicated propagandists and watchdogs, who regard it as their mission in life to spread these memes in particular further, and to protect them from dangerous competitors in the struggle for survival.

So what is it then that religion has to offer and that makes up for the small and big sacrifices that have always been connected with the practice of religion? First of all, we must start by bearing in mind that this question would be entirely incomprehensible to our forefathers on the savannah and in the first permanent settlements. For these people, religion was a completely unknown concept. What we call "religion" today was for them quite simply everyday thoughts and actions, conditioned by a surrounding world that, for obvious reasons, could appear to be controlled by supernatural forces in many respects. That which we see as the "religious" element in their lives would be impossible for them to distinguish from everything else in an existence that crying out loudly for theories intended to clarify obscure causative links, real or illusory. Old Hebrew is one example of a language that lacks a word for "religion". There was nothing that was not religion, and against which such a concept could be contrasted in a meaningful way.

But the crass and simple answer to the question of what value religion – or what we call religion today – had and still has to offer its practitioners, is survival. Man is a flock animal and can only cope with the hard struggle for survival to the extent that he can create well-functioning groups. A lone individual is easy prey on the savannah. In order to achieve a well-functioning group, at least two things are required: effective communication, and mutual trust which functions best when in it based on common values. And it is precisely that you share the values and feelings of the collective which the devoted practice of religion signals to the world around you. You show that you can be trusted, that your loyalties are the right ones, and that you are a worthy member of the community.

Therefore, there are also invariably costs involved in the practice of religion: through paying what it costs to demonstrate your commitment and loyalty to the continued existence of the group you signal that you are prepared to set aside self-interest. A religion, argues the anthropologist William Irons, is basically a control system where the loyalty and devotion of the members of the congregation is monitored by examining the zeal with which they carry out the mandated and preferably also costly rituals.

In this way, you lay the foundation for the necessary trust within the group, and also lay the foundation for the body of regulations that has the task of governing the actions of its individual members, which in turn creates order and security within the system. Accordingly, the selfish deviant is provided with strong incentives to align herself with the group and subordinate herself to its values and set of beliefs. Or at least act as if subservience were the obvious choice. The alternative would be ostracisation or some other powerful sanction. And considering that our hunting and gathering forefathers in principle were constantly at war with other groups of species kinsfolk, who constituted their determined and dangerous competitors in the daily struggle for crucial resources, the cohesion of the collective has always been of the greatest importance. With time Man develops such an intense dependence on the chemicals serotonin and oxytocin, which are released in a torrential stream right at the point when feelings of belonging to the collective are felt, that this dependence in itself appears to be an equally strong foundation for Man's special status as language or consciousness are.

Warfare necessitates collaboration, in both people and ants, as the science journalist Nicholas Wade observes in his perceptive book *The Faith Instinct*. For both these species, it is necessary to be able to reliably identify group membership.

The ants handle this exclusively with the aid of chemical signals and therefore, in contrast to humans, have no need for religious symbolism. In this context and from this point of view, the fear of the wrath of all-seeing divinities is a good thing: it increases the precision of the signalling system. People believe that selfish behaviour is punished and therefore submit to the given rules. The stronger this fear, the stronger the fabric that binds the society together will be. And the stronger this fabric, the more powerfully the chemical-hormonal reward system that the human being partly shares with the ant will be strengthened. This explains why soldiers who return from the most brutal conflicts often long to be back on the battlefield so intensely that they find it completely impossible to adapt to the peaceful environment at home. They quite simply lack the intense fellowship in the trenches and the chemical-hormonal rewards this sense of belonging is associated with – an experience whose strength only war and religion have succeeded in matching throughout history. With this fact in mind, it is not particularly easy for pacifist atheists to find satisfaction in life.

Islam originally means precisely *submission* and every faithful Muslim submits to a strictly circumscribed way of life filled with more or less arduous duties in the form of daily prayers, fasts, pilgrimages, etc. The believer thus becomes a small but significant cog in an infinitely much greater machinery. In key respects, religion is precisely this: a liberation from the petty perspective of one's own ego and the limited possibilities for asserting oneself in the world, which leads to a merging into a collective organism with everything that this means in terms of the feelings of expansion and ecstasy associated with coordinated behaviour, that is, participation in a socio-cultural emergence process. Singing, dancing, speaking in tongues: through various types of liturgical rites, religion binds the collective together emotionally and creates at least one convincing illusion of access to the transcendental. Personal antipathies and conflicts are lessened or disappear in the rhythmically synchronised intoxication of the community.

When the material conditions of a society then change, the function of religion is also changed. The hierarchical complexity that grew in the settled agrarian society demands other and more controlled forms for how the community is manifested. Gradually the music and dancing are regulated. The direct channel to the supernatural is abandoned and is increasingly taken over by a specially educated clergy, while the focus in this communication with the worshipped god is gradually shifted from good fortune in hunting and bountiful harvests here on Earth to eternal happiness among the angels in the afterlife. For a long time, it is the individual and her salvation that is the core activity of religion. The questions change, and therefore religion's answers also change. The primary task of the church pews is by no means to make the visitors to the service comfortable – and they are not particularly comfortable either anywhere – but quite simply to prevent dancing.

This functionalised and utility-centred view of religion stems to a large extent from the theories of the French sociologist Emile Durkheim. Interestingly enough, it is self-evident for Durkheim that capitalist ideologies such as nationalism and individualism must be regarded as religion's latest forms of revelation. Ironically enough, two of memetics' prominent figures – Daniel Dennett and Richard Dawkins – who are also two of militant, scientific atheism's pioneering mouthpieces, speak for a diametrically opposed point of view. If the atheist Freud regards religion as an illusion determined by existential anxiety and feelings of defencelessness vis-à-vis the overwhelming and inexplicable forces of Nature, Dennett and Dawkins argue that the memeplexes of religion should be regarded as a dangerous virus that, without invitation and without offering any advantages whatsoever, penetrates people's brains and devastates their cognitive abilities. Accordingly, religion's role vis-à-vis mankind would be purely parasitical and not symbiotic in any respect.

If we stay with Christianity, it is of course indisputable that it must be regarded as an unprecedented success from a crassly Darwinian perspective. The Catholic Church's brand has held up remarkably well through the centuries in spite of considerable difficulties connected with doctrinal oddities and clerical misbehaviour of various kinds. At the same time, the Bible must arguably be the most successful text in history if one looks at the number of copies that are spread across the world. It exists in countless variants everywhere, in more than 2,000 languages and in many of these languages in several translations. As the theologian Hugh S. Pyper writes in his essay *The Selfish Text: The Bible and Memetics*, the Bible must be a strong candidate for the title of best-suited of all texts ever if the concept *survival of the fittest* has any plausibility whatsoever. It colours Western culture to an extent that is impossible to overestimate; regardless of how much the Reformation, to take just one example, damaged the Church, it involved a powerful push out into the world for the Bible, whose text preaches explicity and repeatedly that it wants to be copied and spread. In this way it builds "survival machines" in the form of brains that pay attention to and relay its message. Pyper points out the ironic aspect of the energetic Bible opponent Dawkins himself having allowed his own presentation to become heavily influenced by the Bible in fact, to which he constantly refers, which makes even Dawkins himself one of many survival machines of the Bible that is so harshly criticised.

And so the question is: At the deepest level, is this about symbiosis or parasitism? Does the memeplex of religion mean that the odds of the host organism surviving are bettered or worsened? In his book *Breaking the Spell,* Dennett recounts the story of the little ant in the meadow that laboriously climbs up a straw of grass, only to fall to the ground and then immediately resume its climb, over and over again. The reason for this behaviour is not that the ant is striving to survey its surroundings in order to improve its chances of finding food, but that its little brain has been taken over by a microscopically small parasite which is called the lancet liver fluke (*dicrocoelium dendriticum*) and which necessarily must get to a sheep or cow stomach in order to procreate. Therefore, the parasite manipulates the ant to position itself in a way that favours its own survival but which grossly disadvantages the ant's survival. This is Dennett's graphic image of how religion manipulates human beings, who, he claims, have died in great numbers in their misdirected eagerness to defend and conquer holy sites or texts. That religion might be able to be of some reproductive use to us is not a theory that is closely examined by Dennett.

In his essay *Viruses of the Mind,* Dawkins assumes the role of spokesperson for the defenceless little children, who are said to be particularly vulnerable to attacks from the dangerous parasite of religion. In his view, the human child is designed by evolution such that it willingly lets itself be brainwashed, since it is precisely during childhood that the human being assimilates the culture of his environment and the foundation for all the knowledge he needs in order to survive and procreate, something that the cunning parasite of religion exploits in other words. The small child's gullibility is programmed into him and makes her utterly vulnerable to evil nuns and others that are already infected by this virus and who are therefore programmed to promote its propagation to the innocent brains they are educating. The result of all this is that various absurd and meaningless types of behaviour are reproduced in yet another generation: one bows in the direction of Mecca, nods rhythmically towards a wall, shakes uncontrollably ("like a lunatic"), speaks in tongues, and so on.

This enumeration of various sorts of nonsensical behaviour caused by the religion memes leads our thoughts to the superstition among pigeons that was documented by the behaviourist psychologist B. F. Skinner. A group of pigeons were "rewarded" with food at arbitrary points in time completely unrelated to what the pigeons happened to be doing or not doing, and soon enough one could observe how these pigeons started to perform complicated dances which, according to Dennett, proves that superstition and self-suggestion can cause amusing miracles even in small and unremarkable brains. The dynamics that drive bizarre effects of this kind do not require any conscious reflection, merely amplification. In brains that are designed to discern intentions and causes everywhere, the effects become all the more spectacular.

Dawkins emphasises the memeplex of religion's kinship with the computer virus: its success is partly dependent on it being difficult for the victim to discover the infection, at least until it is too late. The person who is actually a victim of such a virus probably does not know it and would anyway energetically deny the infection. How does one then ascertain that the evil parasite has taken hold of a brain? The first indication that Dawkins mentions is that the patient usually is inspired by a deep, inner conviction that the one thing or the other actually is true; a conviction that in no way is related to any proof or any reasonable argumentation, but that nevertheless feels entirely convincing to the infected person. And here it gets interesting in a way that Dawkins probably has not intended. In his aggressive attacks on religious faith, in fact he makes an extremely accurate diagnosis of himself.

If it had been the case that religion really had been parasitic on mankind and had impaired the chances of survival and procreation of religious people and other groups, one might argue whether this state of affairs deserved a categorical condemnation from any other point of view than the strictly anthropocentric. For the planet as a whole, it might even be something positive if people did not multiply as vigorously and if religion therefore to some extent held back the population explosion. There are scarcely any scientific reasons to moralise over what the little parasite is doing to the ant, any more than there is reason to moralise about what the sheep is doing to the grass (and thereby also the ant), or about what the wolf or any other predator does to the sheep if an opportunity presents itself. It is quite simply nature taking its course; every attempt at moralising is as misdirected as it is irrelevant. And the same must probably also apply to an attack on religion for the reason that it impairs people's survival chances by occasioning cost without handing out any rewards to the host organism, that is, it is at the very least misdirected and irrelevant from a Darwinian perspective. So if our brains happen to be the survival machines of religion, this is simply the way it is.

But that's not all. It is also the case that the notion that religion would impair people's chances of survival quite simply is not correct. Conversely, there has long been very convincing evidence to the contrary: religious people and groups unequivocally demonstrate that they enjoy reproductive advantages, which has been proven a number of times, among others in an essay by the religious studies researcher Michael Blume which is entitled in fact *The Reproductive Advantage of Religion* and which has been noted by Susan Blackmore, among others. Statistics unequivocally show that religious peoples have more babies. This applies across the board in all countries. Dawkins, Dennett and the other true-believer atheists are incapable of including this uncontroversial data in their argumentation that is strongly critical of religion, and is one of the cornerstones of their faith in science, and they therefore choose to turn a blind eye to it. But this, as Blackmore points out, is not the way that science is meant to function. If indisputable facts contradict theory, one simply has to shred one's theory and produce a new one that is in line with the knowledge in the area that actually exists. But living up to this strict ideal is not easy, particularly not when one happens to be a believer oneself, and particularly not when one is completely ignorant of the fact that one is in fact a believer either. In that case, the temptation to devote oneself instead to one's deep inner conviction and close one's eyes to awkward facts that point in a completely different direction is virtually irresistible. It is faith and nothing else that gives one the strength to soldier on.

With the advent of syntheism, we witness the death of the Cartesian theatre – and thereby also the individual. The wide acceptance of memetics gives us a superior alternative to faith in the atomised *individual* as the centre of existence. We are talking here of *a syntheist agent* which, in contrast to a Cartesian subject, never imagines that she is a little isolated figure, a sort of tenant who temporarily resides in the body; a passive observer behind the eyes who sometimes reluctantly, sometimes neutrally ontologically speaking, anticipates the surrounding world with which it then communicates via the lips and hands. An agent is instead an actor in various combinations and situations; partly an arbitrarily and temporarily delimited dividual, partly an arbitrarily delimited body, but also a body in collaboration with other bodies and phenomena in her environment. And it is as such an actor, mobile at all levels, in the midst of, and not in any mysterious way preceding *the intra-acting* – which in every moment is eternalised – that syntheist *agentiality* can arise as a *self-experience*.

However counter-intuitive this may sound for the syntheist agent, she can only regard herself as a by-product of the ideology coming from the future, and in this Hegelian sense act in a revelatory role and as a supervisor vis-à-vis the now prevailing but rapidly eroding ideology. For it is only in the collision between the ideological paradigms – the history of ideas time after time shows how philosophy virtually explodes with creativity as a direct consequence of a socio-cultural paradigm shift, with Axial Age Greece and India and early Industrialism's Western Europe and North America as illuminating examples – that speculative philosophy can see through and reveal the illusory qualities of the prevailing ideologies. And there we are at this moment, in informationalism's infancy, in the midst of a cascade of information flows exploding in all directions, where syntheism is slowly but surely growing as the paradigm's built-in and necessary metaphysical Higgs field.

From this insight concerning the logical terms and creative possibilities of the metalevel, we can formulate syntheism's revolutionary ambition – its sabre thrust straight into the *solar plexus* of the old individualism – with the battle cry that is devastating for capitalism: *Ideas want to be free, ideas cannot be owned!* In fact, ideas do not belong to any of us; it is we who belong to them, and we cannot do anything other than obey them. Without owning one's ideas, which never even belonged to the individual except in her own imagination – which was not either the individual's own to command, in accordance with the free will that she has never owned either – the individual is completely castrated. And it is precisely in this manner that the netocratic dividual wants to regard the bourgeois individual. Therefore the question of who owns the ideas – not to mention the question of who, practically speaking, can own them – is the greatest, most important and controversial question of the current, burgeoning paradigm shift. Power's memeplex has been set in motion and the world is trembling. Welcome to the informationalist class struggle!

The syntheist agent and her desires and drives

As physics migrates to *informationalism* and thereby becoming *relationalist*, a new view of humanity and a new world view are becoming apparent. Metaphysical *individualism* is dead; it disappears along with physical *atomism*, since these constitute two sides of the same outdated coin. Both stem from Kant's onto-epistemology from the second half of the 18th century, which in turn is based on Descartes' classic proposition "Cogito, ergo sum", where the subjective experience is the only indisputable thing in existence and therefore constitutes the point of departure for all assertions about anything at all. This axiomatic subject then relates to other objects, which in the same way as the subject and its Cartesian theatrical stage is construed first as noumenal and then as phenomenal, indivisible entities with solid substances, that is, as *individuals* and *atoms*.

But since syntheism, when it investigates the world, finds neither individuals nor atoms, it becomes necessary to break with the individualist-atomist paradigm in order to connect instead to the metaphysical alternative that actually has support in the sciences' observations of the world, that is, *network dynamics* and its attendant *social relationalism.* Just like in relationalist physics, there are only relations on top of other relations and probabilities on top of other probabilities even within psychology and sociology, and these relations and probabilities do not stop at the externally *interactive*: they are very much also internally *intra-acting.* First there is the network, then there is the node and only thereafter does the subjective experience arise. What applies here is thus an inverted procedure compared to Descartes' and Kant's narcissistic fantasy of the genesis of the subject and its position in the Universe: "I am, therefore I think." Man himself is a phenomenon of network dynamics, localised within other network-dynamical phenomena. But when she also becomes conscious of this, he can start to act as something far more than merely a relationalist subject, namely as *the syntheist agent,* syntheism's ethical human ideal.

The human being's self-experience is of course as relationalist as everything else in existence. According to relationalist phenomenology, the human subject arises, if anything, as a kind of *minoritarian* by-product of a larger *majoritarian* phenomenon, where the majoritarian phenomenon that transcends the subject's self-experience is its *agent.* It is thus not the case that separate souls sit and wait to be mounted inside shiny new bodies in some kind of creation factory – which Descartes' and Kant's dualism requires – but the self-experience is instead a highly efficient but nevertheless illusory by-product of the body's many other doings – the borrowed component, taken out of empty nothingness, which means that the human equation suddenly seems to achieve an acceptable solution for itself. The self-experience is quite simply the logical end point where the subject process ties together for itself. Thus it does not come first, as Descartes and Kant presume, but rather last, so that the void that ties together all divided components within the dividual so that it can experience itself as a phantasmic unit and as a whole. All this thus takes place within *the agent,* the transient subject that cannot in any way precede or exist outside the basic *agency*. The body, the congregation and the society can all be agents, but without an agent that houses this subjectivity, it cannot exist at all.

Thus, the conditions for the development of consciousness are not either in any way universal, but rather highly contingent and bound to a very specific, spatio-temporal situation. The Kantian transcendental subject must be replaced by *the syntheist immanent subject*. And the syntheist immanent subject has no need whatsoever of any kind of correlationalism, in either the weak Kantian or the strong relativist sense. In a radically relationalist universe the need for correlationalism disappears. Thus, the syntheist immanent subject does not arise in opposition to the phenomenon but instead is an integral part of the same. The subject is best described as the phenomenon's agentiality.

The syntheist agent does not seek contact with the outside world from any kind of passive observer position. Instead she lives as an intra-acting phenomenon, participating interactively, at the centre of the world. Quite simply, no original individuation arises that can be regarded or used as the cornerstone of existence. There is no individuation whatsoever. What arises is a *dividuation*, and it is a by-product of the current region's many relations and not the other way around. Syntheism does focus at all on the subject, which it decentralises, but takes the *inversion* of the Cartesian *cogito ergo sum* very seriously and therefore shifts the existential focus to agentiality as a phenomenon, an intra-acting concentration of intensities, which is an irreducible multiplicity of identities within a diffuse and mobile field. These identities gather around *a truth as an act*, namely the subjective experience as the impoverished void *Atheos* within the rich multiplicity *Entheos*, located in overwhelming existence *Pantheos*. The subject's illusoriness is not externalised however, as relativist critics of Descartes and Kant such as Nietzsche, Kierkegaard, Heidegger and Derrida imagine – these philosophers are quite simply not radical enough in their break with Kantian correlationism –they are instead *internalised* right from the very beginning. The illusory aspect of the subject, its self-experienced substancelessness, is included as a fundamental and integral part of the subjective experience as such.

Among the old authorities, it is the godfather of German Romanticism Hegel who really displays an understanding of the genesis of the subject, which is apparent when he becomes the first to construct a subject theory using the concept of *Atheos* as his point of departure. According to Hegel, the subject is not just fundamentally empty and developed as a kind of tragic response to unanswered existential questions – it is moreover a highly temporary and local eternalisation complex without any relevance whatsoever outside of itself. There is, to express the matter in Kantian terms, nothing universal outside the subject that it can transcend into. If, for example, we were to amuse ourselves by condensing the Hegelian and relationalist subject experience into three words, then the concepts *emptiness, diminutiveness and transience* fit just perfectly.

However, this basic illusoriness should be understood as something extremely productive: a limitation of external stimuli is a fundamental prerequisite for the flowering of inner creativity. The less information that is added to the syntheist agent's mind, the more richly she can fantasise about and expand her subjective experience. The Hegelian philosopher Slavoj Zizek develops the idea of *illusoriness* as basic to the subjective experience. He argues that, seen at its most profound, the subject must be regarded as *the excluded* in the subjective experience, as the subjective experience's *excrement*, the piece of the puzzle that does not fit in, that which constantly fails and never succeeds in hitting home, that within the subject that the subject itself tries to push away and hide from itself and from the surrounding world. We call this *the abjective subject.* Or as Zizek himself expresses the matter: "I am my own lack, I am my own excrement." This restricted subject is maintained through a pronounced internal distance. And the distance is existentially necessary; if it is nullified, the subject collapses.

The Zizekian abjective subject is fundamentally internally divided. The split within the subject precedes and is also the prerequisite for the ensuing distinction between the subject and the object. The subject is thus a reaction against its own cause; its *modus operandi* is to constantly rework the constant failure of being its own substance. The subject is quite simply the product of its own failures. Above all it is a product of the failure of the mystery. Only through insight into this state of affairs – let us say obtained through the syntheist *schizoanalysis* (see *The Body Machines*) – is the subject's understanding of and functional relation to the real enabled. In the schizoanalytical process, the syntheist agent gets the chance to construct an infinite number of credible dividual identities within one and the same body. But that which ties all these identities together into one big circle – and makes them one single cohesive *agential phenomenon* for itself – this is the gaping void in the middle of the circle, Zizek's abjective subject, *Atheos*.

Individualism's misleading *anthropomorphisation* of consciousness leads straight towards an impossible dead end. But it is not merely Kantian correlationism that must be discarded in conjunction with the necessary massive clean-out associated with the transition to relationalism. This also applies, to take one example, to all Eastern or New Age-related ideas of some kind of *cosmic consciousness*. The Universe not only lacks a brain to be conscious with: *the Universe has de facto no incentive to acquire a consciousness*, since consciousness is only produced in order to cover up the failings that are specific to the life situations of human beings. Not only is Man the only animal that talks – and thereby also thinks in the abstract – he is also the only animal who develops this ability in order to be able to survive at all. Language is developed as a

Darwinian response to the human being's evolutionary short-comings. To speak and think is just the human being's way of compensating for her own physical weakness and the evolutionary advantages of other animal species.

It is fully understandable that language acquires a magical aura, since it is a devastatingly effective weapon *for Man* against competing species in the struggle for limited resources. If mankind lacked these communication-technology advantages, these rivals would, without further ado, have killed mankind and relegated him to the long list of losers wiped out by the evolutionary process. However, language has no other function over and above this contingent and emergent role, and this of course also applies to the thoughts and consciousness which it in turn produces. The primary aspect of Man is his existence and enjoyment in this existence, that is, the *nature* she shares with, and not the *culture* that separates him from, all other animals. The secondary capacities of language and thought have arisen in order to enable the development and enjoyment of existence, not the other way around.

However, the Universe has no need whatsoever of or interest in language or thoughts or any kind of consciousness. While consciousness might be extremely valuable and remarkable for the human being in her self-absorption, it is completely meaningless for all other significant entities in the Universe. *There really was not even the slightest trace of words in the beginning.* The Word can only be placed at the beginning of Creation when the uniquely talkative Man uses language in order to try and comprehend that which is difficult to comprehend, locked in a consciousness that is furnished and wallpapered with language. Language and thereby also thinking and consciousness has actually been around for 200,000 years at most. And what do a mere 200,000 years of gossiping and reflecting within one single species of animal on just one single planet matter in a 14 billion-year-old, gigantic and moreover constantly expanding Universe? The question is of course rhetorical and the answer is nought. We have an endearing tendency to mistake what appears important to ourselves for what is important in an overarching perspective.

When it comes to the historically necessary *decentralisation of consciousness*, syntheism differs radically from *objective pantheism* in all its variants, such as Buddhism, Hinduism, Sufism and New Age. Searching for a cosmic consciousness outside Man, as these ideologies are doing, is nothing other than a childishly misdirected projection of anthropocentric, internarcissistic fantasies onto something that is particularly ill-suited for this. The truth is that the Universe, with its enormous creative potential, is far too fantastic to need a consciousness. Narrowly limited human beings on the other hand are – probably – the only consciousness in the Universe, since consciousness has arisen solely as a means of damage control, precisely because of Man's existential limitations. Syntheism therefore only professes itself an adherent to *subjective pantheism* and not to the objective variant. We choose to project divinity onto existence as a whole – subjective pantheism is instead *truth as an act par excellence* – instead of believing that the cosmos imposes its divinity on us through a variety of dubious and self-appointed messengers. Syntheologically, we locate consciousness between *Entheos* (the dividual subject) and *Syntheos* (the collective subject), dancing on top of *Atheos* (the engine of the subject). But it is extremely important to keep it as far away as possible from *Pantheos* and all other superstitions regarding a cosmic consciousness.

The French philosopher Gilles Deleuze devoted a lot of work to the art of managing the chaos that occurs in the world before Man appears. He goes back to humanity's nomadic roots and calls this deeper picture of the human being the *dividual* (the divisible human being), in contrast to the capitalist *individual* (the indivisible human being). Deleuze's post-humanist dividual in turn happens to fit perfectly as an ideal for the rising netocracy under informationalism (see *The Netocrats*). Deleuze argues that the dividual is *autoimmune*. To be autoimmune is to see both good and bad sides in oneself as necessary. To be autoimmune is to acknowledge that one is finite and constantly divided in every moment, driven by internal *desires* and *drives*, which in the encounter with an incessant flow of external *memes* unite around the nomadic, dividual identity. To be autoimmune is to give full expression to our pathological sorrow and fear of death. The dividual is of course always conscious of the fact that the Universe has both the right and the capacity to crush her at any moment. Life is very fragile for real; this is not just some maudlin, sentimental phrase.

In contrast to the fixed individual, the nomadic dividual is just as playfully divisible inwardly as he is flexibly inconstant outwardly. In addition, the dividual is not the least bit interested in acting as some kind of centre of existence on individualism's ramshackle, theatrical stage. In contrast to the Cartesian individual's existential *self-absorption* – what else could we expect from a starting point that says "the only thing I am aware of is that I myself exist" – the dividual sees and understands herself as a kind of auto-suggested spectre of the mind, an emergent by-product from a specific evolutionary process, a highly peripheral creature in a monstrous Universe, who only gets a value for itself through creative interaction with other dividuals, who also themselves in the same way are always mutable. The dividual is not merely the historical and philosophical replacement of the individual, but also the consequence of the dismantling and decentralisation of the individual. *Because it is not the dividual but the network that is syntheism's metaphysical core.*

This means that syntheism liberates Man from *anthropocentrism* and *internarcissism*. That the individual human being is freed from the responsibility of being an individual and instead is being encouraged to be a dividual is something that syntheism regards as a kind of existential salvation. *Dividualism* colours every fibre of the syntheist agent. Man is not the centre of existence any more than the *ego* could be the centre of Man (since it does not exist – see *The Body Machines*). Obviously, humanity and its attributes have no primary status in the Universe. Civilisations have arisen as an emergent phenomenon on a planet after aeons of history without any people at all. They have also perished without the Universe taking the slightest bit of notice. Humanity is a phenomenon that has sprung from other intra-acting phenomena. Nor is any human being created by other humans. Biological parents do not create their offspring – despite the fact that they would like to believe that this is the case – but are rather tools for the Universe's constant production of new organisms furnished with bodies, language, ideas, consciousnesses and subconsciousnesses.

In this context it is extremely important to distinguish between psychotherapy's utilitarian search for happiness in life and *psychoanalysis' existentialist search for the truth about existence*. Psychotherapy is a product of psychology, which is a social science. Psychoanalysis, on the other hand, is a product of philosophy, which means that at its deepest level it is an art form. Psychotherapy is an *anthropotechnical project* – developed by the capitalist power structure and its nation states and large corporations – which is dedicated to defining *patients*, that is, deviants from the momentarily prevailing societal norm. The scientists supply these patients with functional *diagnoses*, filled with an expanding flora of *pathologies*, which must be treated in order to promote the societal body's well-being. Historically speaking, and possibly with a measure of cynicism, we can regard the psychotherapist as *the capitalist tamer of individuals* – a professionalised and commercialised replacement for the shoved-aside, good-old, good friend – whose task it is to adapt the citizen to a closed life-cycle of work, consumption and sleep, by robbing her of all forms of authentic intimacy with other people.

Psychoanalysis, on the other hand, starts from the vantage point that all people are and must be fundamentally pathological creatures; the human being is, and has never been anything but, *homo pathologicus*. The very fact that the human being believes that she exists as a subject and that she will live and not die attests to a pathological foundation for consciousness that is as powerful as it is necessary. The pathological subject exists in a dialectical tension between the two contracting parties *desire* and *drive*. Western philosophy reflects this dialectic as *the history of desire* from Spinoza and onwards (materialism), pitted against *the history of the drive* from Hegel and onwards (idealism). The dialectic is essential for both of these forces to be able to survive. Desire is ultimately an attempt to flee from the drive, and the drive is viewed at the most profound level as an attempt to flee from desire.

Syntheism regards *the antagonism between desire and drive* as equivalent to the existential experience itself, and its syntheological equivalent is of course *the oscillation between Pantheos and Atheos*. Riding the intensity at the centre of the oscillation is to be merged with *Entheos*; building utopias of other worlds in other times with other human beings based on the current position is to create *Syntheos*. Here, it is important to understand that *desire* is specific to Man and her consciousness. Desire is a by-product of language and belongs to culture. *The drive*, on the other hand, belongs to nature and literally *drives* everything outside of Man's consciousness. Although *the subconscious* is structured so that it really wants to die, and although the subconscious is therefore an engine of *the death drive*, consciousness fights to the end for *survival* in the struggle with irrevocable death.

Syntheist ethics is based on this state of affairs. At the same time that the syntheist agent understands the terror of *eternal life*, right up until the moment of death she still seeks the continued dividuation in survival as desire's conscious response to the drive's subconscious longing for dissolution in constantly new phenomena. Therefore – as the syntheist philosopher Martin Hägglund shows in his book *Radical Atheism* – survival is the cornerstone in syntheist ethics, while *immortality*, because of its infantile premises, does not belong in the syntheist utopia at all. There is a logic in wanting to live longer, deeper and more intensely. But there is no logic whatsoever in trying to prolong something forever, since immortality robs that which is to be prolonged of all its meaning. To wish for immortality is the same as wishing away desire, and without desire the whole point of wanting to exist as a human being disappears. And then there is not either any reason to survive. We express this as *the death drive being the compulsion to return to the inorganic* – which expresses itself as a constant striving to minimise, avoid and defer life's intensity – while *desire is the will to prolong and maximise the expression of the organic* in the infinite now.

The cosmological *drive* is without a doubt considerably more complex than any anthropocentric projection can ever do justice to. Above all, it *wants* nothing in advance. It is not a hunter who fells its prey in order to try to impress a partner in conjunction with an approaching tribal mating dance. And it does not seek any kind of *power*, since it does not find anything that it must control in order to serve a specific purpose. Honestly, it does not matter if we ourselves exist; in the universocentric world view the main thing is that the Universe – this *something* without a doubt, rather than *nothing* – manifests itself for itself through us. If we only leave our own subjective experience of the surrounding world and consider that the Universe is *the world before the world itself*, then we ourselves are not wiped out by death either, since existence continues beyond death. Existence in fact never ceases to exist; dying is to return to the enormous dimensions of existence from which we come. Death is nothing other than the termination of the momentary, marginal fluctuation in the vast history that we, from our twisted perspective, call *our existence*, the Universe's minimal and local game with itself. Birth is the loan and death is the just and reasonable payment. The Universe always wins in the end, just as the house always wins at the casino. And we are and always will be participants in the Universe.

The oscillation between Pantheos and Atheos vibrates in the subconscious, and it is there that we find the starting point for Man's self-image: the subject lives in and is construed from the subconscious. However, the subject lacks an essence of its own. It is the *extimacy* in the subjective experience that carries the subject. Quite simply it arises through extimacy, and not through intimacy. As compensation for the strenuous extimacy in relation to itself, the dividual seeks *intimacy in the other*. The driving force is that intimacy with the other should soothe the existential angst that arises from the necessary, inner extimacy.

In the intimate relation with the other, *ethical* and *moral* values arise, respectively (see *The Body Machines*). The concepts *ethics* and *morality* originally had the same meaning: ethics comes from the Greek word *ethos* and morality comes from the Latin word *morales*, and both these terms can be translated as *customs*. But after Spinoza's philosophical divide between ethics on the one hand and morality on the other in the 17th century, the concepts have come to have completely different meanings. Ethics thus concerns an *attitude* connected to an *identity*, confronted with a choice between different anticipated constructive or destructive effects of the contemplated intervention in a surmised course of events. Being an ethical being is to go through life with the right, and in all respects reasonable, intentions. Ethics thus concerns the right or wrong choice in relation to the actor herself. It is an internalised evaluation process. *Being an ethical agent is to identify oneself with the intentions of the decisions one makes.*

Morality instead concerns a displayed attitude to the arbitrariness of a powerful external judge who might be, for example, God, the nation, the State, the leader, or the law *per se*, that is, the phantasmic figure that is called *the great Other* within psychoanalysis. The subject is forced to take a stand in the struggle between *good* (pleasing the judge) and *evil* (rebelling against the judge). Morality is thereby an *externalised* evaluation process. This is on the assumption that the subject who acts needs to be castigated, tamed and made subservient to the powers that be, rather than acting freely from a will of its own. Being moral thus primarily concerns *following laws* without questioning them. Moralising is attempting to impose one's own values, in the form of laws or quasi-laws, on others, for example through laws or other regulations. This is in contrast to being ethical, which can best be described as intentions and actions *following an inner conviction* for the purpose of becoming one with this conviction, without taking account of, for example, prevailing social norms. The purpose of the ethical agent is not to placate any external judge, but to give oneself an ever-so-momentary *existential substance*, internally for oneself.

Morality implies a gloomy seriousness, while ethics implies a playful abundance. Note how the pair of opposites *good versus evil* implies *moral decadence*, which must be rectified by being offered a reward, or the threat of punishment. On the other hand, the ethical pair of opposites *right versus wrong* implies a search for and strengthening of *the inner identity*, quite irrespective of the outcome of the course of events in question. Note that we are speaking of an inner ethical identity that is created through *the intention* and is strengthened through *action*: it is definitely not about some kind of essence that is already at hand in the way that Descartes and Kant imagine the moral subject. The syntheist agent thus does not see ethics as arising from any kind of individual identity, but as *a truth as an act* that provides the tangible void in the centre of the subject with a sincerely longed-for *attribute*, however short-lived.

Morality also has a rationality, but it is produced from an external subject that is *irrational* in itself. This dark origin of morality can be summed up under the term *the crazy dictator syndrome*. In order to be able to maintain the requisite claim on universal validity, morality namely requires as its foundation *an abundant libidinal power*, that which the Abrahamic religions refer to as *the divine omnipotence*. The problem is just that power in abundance must logically be viewed as irrational. The dictator in question cannot make himself subservient to any external power, and every form of logic assumed in advance would be precisely such an external power. He must therefore be illogical and irrational, that is, in fact crazy, in order to be able to autocratically dictate the laws and rules of morality. As law, morality thus must apply to everything and everybody, without exception, *except precisely the one who creates the morals*. God, the nation, the State and the leader – that is, *the great Other* – need not follow the law. The creator of morality must not in fact follow the law, but must be fundamentally amoral and thereby evil in order for morality to be coherent. The price for morality's apparent external consistency is thus that it is entirely subject to a single internal amoral source, namely *the crazy dictator's capricious libido*.

One way of clarifying the difference between ethics and morality is to study a typical borderline case. Kant creates his transcendental philosophy in the 18th century in the borderland between monotheistic Christianity and atheistic individualism. On account of the growing German and French bourgeoisie, he carries out the self-imposed task of calculating how *Man* could replace *God* as the metaphysical centre of existence. Kant borrows the answer from Descartes and maintains that Man is the Master of existence for the simple reason that he can think. But existence can of course only be experienced by Man, the reason being that it requires a consciousness in order to be able to experience it and only Man thinks consciously. He is thus master of a house that he inhabits all by himself.

Since ethics is a more or less free choice between various alternatives – the more freedom that exists in a context, the more ethics is required – and since Kant has made the subject and object of ethics into one and the same thing, he is forced to reduce his ethics to a *tautology*. When asked the question why it is right to do the right thing, Kant answers laconically that every action should be carried out as if it were universally valid. In other words, it is right to do what is right for the simple and pointless reason that it is right to do the right thing. And then we have not even touched upon the question of exactly what this automatically executed *right thing* actually is. The only reasonable reaction to Kant's tautological imperative comes from his successor Nietzsche, who realises that all notions that value philosophy is able to formulate as *the right thing* in advance must be rejected. Instead he recasts value philosophy as an anthropological project occupied with what *Man is anyway already doing* and why. The prescriptive value philosophy of Kant is answered commendably by Nietzsche with a descriptive and interactive enlightenment project. Thereby Kant is reduced to a banal moralist, while Nietzsche stands out as the real ethicist.

The point here is that in the Kantian borderland between two value paradigms, interestingly enough Man has neither the amoral God's freedom to behave as he pleases, nor any judge left to appease in order to get his points registered in his quest for an anticipated reward in eternity. The consequence is that when Kant desperately tries to build a new ethics on top of the old morality – without any foothold in an amoral god – he reduces his phenomenologically divine human being to an ethically paralysed robot. Thereby moralism returns with full force, but this time as a self-referencing feedback loop, where moralism itself has become its own external judge. Understandably enough it is precisely Kant's peculiar moral philosophy that the succeeding ethicists Hegel and Nietzsche direct their sharpest criticism towards when it comes to Kantianism; in their eyes Kant is nothing other than a naive nihilist, distressingly unaware of the *theocide* he has just committed. For this reason, both Hegel and Nietzsche pit their pantheist predecessor Spinoza against the deist Kant, and thereby open the way for *affirmative nihilism* (see *The Global Empire*), the creative generation of value out of *Atheos*.

Ethics is an intention founded in an identity in relation to the anticipated result of a cause and an effect. It is the anticipated effect of the action that gives it its ethical weight. The German philosopher Jürgen Habermas thinks of ethics as an internal, intersubjective process without any requirements whatsoever on external, objective truths. Various conceivable intentions are weighed against various conceivable chains of cause and effect in a kind of civilised dialogue. Regardless of whether we apply ethics to a dividual or a collective, ethics is founded on an *attitude*. Nietzsche argues that this attitude is either active or reactive. The active attitude seeks an impression, an impact on existence, a confirmation of the agent's interaction with its surroundings, in order to attain existential affirmation, a realisation of its own substance. Nietzsche calls this attitude *the will to power*. Against the will to power stands *the reactive attitude*, the will to submission, obliteration, a production of identity through identification with *the victim* rather than with *the hero*. This reactive attitude creates a bitterness towards existence, it produces and is driven by *ressentiment*, a perverted pleasure – rather than authentic pleasure – based on an escalating narcissistic self-loathing.

The active attitude produces a steady stream of identities, it seeks creative novelty in an active engagement with its environment, it builds an emergent *event* emanating from *the oscillating phenomenon* that includes *the syntheist agent*. On the other hand, the reactive attitude thrives on maintaining distance, through a *narcissism* turned away from reality, where the energy is used to stimulate *ressentiment* for the purpose of repudiating the surrounding world, so that the subject can cultivate the belief in itself as an abandoned and isolated object, floating in a state of *permanent masochistic enjoyment*. Since *the slave mentality* – dissected by Nietzsche – constantly seeks a minimisation of its own living throughout life in order to be as close to extinction as possible (what Freud calls *the death drive*), it also seeks submission in relation to other agents, because it flees from *authentic intimacy* for fear of losing the masochistic enjoyment where it has found its existential sense of security. The slave mentality prefers safe totalist suffering over unsafe mobilist pleasure.

This deep-seated and serious mental masochism should of course not be confused with playful sexual sadomasochism, which has nothing at all to do with any kind of ressentiment. However, there is in all masochism a desire to engage in play-acting, to pretend intimacy when the sadomasochistic act in reality aims to maximise and maintain *the distance to the other*, which, for example, explains the strong connection between sexual sadomasochism and polyamorousness. This play-acting in the public sphere becomes an (often fully conscious) protection against intimacy in the private sphere in the same way that the connection to many in practice is the same as the connection to no one at all. To the extent syntheism is *a doctrine of salvation*, it is thus about salvation from this masochistic enjoyment and towards the affirmation of authentic intimacy, completely independent of sexual practices. It is about making *the syntheist agent and her desires and drives* into an existential hero instead of a pathetic victim. In other words, the syntheist agent is identical with *the Nietzschean übermensch*.

Nietzsche's idea-archaeology project leads to a powerful recognition of nature's enormous rather than Man's minimal power over both the elements and the mind. With Nietzsche, Nature has of course not only the last word about itself, it is also Nature that acts through Man regardless of what this subject, as with Kant, imagines about itself. What would the subject be otherwise, if not in fact a portion of Nature? This means that Nietzsche transposes ethics into an open issue of what culture is possible on top of such a dominating and framing Nature. It is thus in *culture* that we find the affirmative in Nietzsche's affirmative nihilism: a cultural concept that Nietzsche transforms, in a pioneering way, from Nature's opposite into an *emergent phenomenon* arising out of otherwise indifferent Nature. According to Nietzsche, culture is nothing other than an engaged extension of Nature – or as we express the matter in *The Futurica Trilogy*: Culture is *Nature 2.0*. Only by bravely attempting to build *culture on top of Nature*, rather than to just yield to Nature, can Man procure an ethical substance.

In *Ecce Homo* Nietzsche tells of how he allows himself to be inspired to develop the idea of ethics as the agential identity of Zoroaster, history's first great ethicist. Through recasting the Iranian author of *Gathas* as the protagonist in *Thus Spoke Zarathustra,* Nietzsche reconnects with the pagan, non-linear circle rather than with the monotheistic linear road to doomsday as the foundation of ethics – all in accordance with Zoroaster's words of wisdom "I am my thoughts, my thoughts govern my words, I am my words, my words govern my actions, I am my actions, and my actions govern my thoughts". Where the radical aspect lies of course is in the minimal *contingency* that is added for every new revolution in the ethical feedback loop, the minimal *difference* that every morning makes the world a completely new world that is expanding along the arrow of time. Zoroaster's and Nietzsche's syntheological divinity is of course called *Entheos*.

The ethical consequence of the Nietzschean revolution is that the subject – which hovers in the minimal space between the current event and the next thought – must contemplate the ongoing identity-producing cycle, which *de facto* is *the subject's engine*, in order to be able to shape the next thought as *a free choice,* a choice whose freedom means that the accomplishment of the intention rewards the subject with ethical substance. Nietzsche's ethics is thus founded on a syntheist contemplation, which is followed by concrete action that is consistent with the contemplation. It is precisely this human being, she who consistently completes the necessary cycle of ethics to its inexorable end, that Nietzsche terms the *übermensch*, and it in on her that he pins his hopes when it comes to culture. It is hard to get further away from Kant's morality robot paralysed in value philosophy than this.

The subject arises as an emergent phenomenon when perception is forced to prioritise in the overwhelming flow of information from the sensory organs – that which the pragmatist Charles Sanders Peirce dubs *semiosis* – in order to give the enormous amount of data an actual utility. It is in this freezing and regulating of the perceptual flow that *dividuation* occurs; it is then and there that the subject arises as a necessary eternalisation of the body's mobilist chaos, as an organised *contraction* rather than a galloping inflation in the mind. The reward for dividuation is that a tangible and manageable world view is immediately produced, with the contentless subject as its fictitious centre. When the subject then contemplates itself as objectively being before itself, it becomes conscious of itself as the empty subject, *Atheos*.

Just like all other eternalisations, dividuation is based on deviations and asymmetries in the perceptual flow. The mind has no reason whatsoever to make an effort or to be switched on when a phenomenon repeats itself identically or follows predictable symmetries. It is only when a clear departure from the pattern appears that the mind switches on *the subconscious*. And it is only if the deviation evokes strong emotions – at the same level as earlier dramatic peaks in life have done – that the information processing makes the effort to shift itself from the subconscious to *the conscious* and thereby plays along with or against the current self-image and world view. This also applies very much to the subjective experience. The subject slumbers comfortably until its perception process imposes a change upon it. Then and only then does the subject experience itself as a subject.

The existential experience is thus fundamentally conditioned by *change* in the semiotic flow. Thereby the subject *per se* is in *a mobilist process*, provided that its products are eternalist. The eternalist subject is thus never eternalist *per se*; it becomes eternalist, it gets its name, precisely *through being eternalised by itself into its own object*. In the syntheological pyramid, we place consciousness with Entheos. At the most fundamental level, thinking is of course an ongoing organising of differences. The syntheist subject arises as a consequence of provocations from differences in intensities. Without a preceding problem of some kind, there would be no thinking; and without dividuation, which arises when thinking shuts down the semiotic flow, there would be no subject. Since the task of perception is to transform chaos into order, to eternalise the mobilist environment, thinking is first and foremost thinking's reduction of itself into a *dividuation*. The subject is neither more nor less than a necessary by-product of thinking as a process.

The discrepancy between Man's *external* and *internal being*, the difference between the human, physical brain and Man's mental image of his own thinking, has always been a fascinating topic for philosophers; in modern times often dealt with within the borderland between philosophy and neuroscience that is called *theory of mind*. When we make comparisons, the brain has often drawn the short straw and been considered a relatively simple organ, while the mind has been presumed to be incredibly complex and therefore has often been made into something much greater than the brain, into an external phenomenon, a *soul* that in some mysterious way transcends the obviously limited body. Research concludes however that the human brain has a degree of complexity that is not far behind the rest of our enormous universe. The brain is actually by far the most complex phenomenon that we have so far found in the Universe. A mere fraction of the brain's capacity is needed for the mind to work satisfactorily. And what we call the soul, that is, the illusory and fundamentally contradictory feeling of owning and being a soul, is very much just a small internal aspect, rather than a great external agent within this greater phenomenon. On the contrary, it is our thinking that is limited and historically speaking a relatively recent acquisition in this context. The difference between the philosophical phenomena the *human being* (the creature *with a mind*) and the *animal* (the creature without a mind) is actually minimal.

We break down the mind into two divisions: *consciousness* and *the subconscious*. To start with, consciousness can be neither understood nor surveyed by consciousness itself. And in actual fact there is no compelling reason for consciousness to devote valuable resources to acquiring an insight into itself in real time, which means that consciousness itself is located in its own dead angle. Consciousness must instead devote itself to tracking itself only after the fact, and then only through its effects. The reason that we use the newer concept of *the subconscious* instead of the older concept of *the unconscious* is that there is no clear boundary between our consciousness and that which influences our thought processes without us being aware of it. A large part of the subconscious fluctuates from one moment to the other between consciousness and the unconscious. Quite simply, there is an ongoing information exchange between consciousness and the subconscious; the border between them is highly arbitrary from one moment to the next and in every moment is fleeting, indeterminable. We therefore replace the relativist concept of the unconscious with the relationalist concept of the subconscious in our work.

The subconscious thus not only includes the unconscious in Sigmund Freud's classical sense, but also the information that consciousness half-consciously, half-unconsciously uses in its intuitive speculation. Neither the externally observed brain, nor the internally experienced mind uses any red or green lights in order to direct incoming information flows. The brain is not a computer. The information is not transported around within the brain in tiny, fixed, compact packages. The brain is namely *analogue* rather than *digital*, it is influenced and changes continuously. The human mind is very much a *relationalist phenomenon*, and the really remarkable aspect of this lies not in its unique position in existence, but rather in its typical *materiality* in fact. It is matter that is much more complex, active and, if one so wishes, *spiritual* than we have previously believed. *The brain* and its by-product *the mind* should therefore be regarded as typical rather than special material phenomena, even if this insight disturbs our internarcissism.

The subconscious is driven by *desire* and the *drive*. Desire is given shelter by Pantheos, the drive comes out of Atheos. Desire is fundamentally always a desire for itself, therefore it constantly tries to postpone or displace its own satisfaction in order to be able to keep going and avoid its own self-inflicted annihilation. Desire is thus fundamentally a *metadesire*. The drive, on the other hand, is a repetitious will, a stubborn quest to return to the inorganic. It is best described as a compulsive repetition of the same, revolving around *a fundamental, compact trauma* that the mind lacks any control over. This formative, existential experience is called *the great trauma* and occurs already when the child is cast out at birth and separated from the safety of the womb. Here there is thus a kind of death that transpires even before birth. Therefore we call this moment *the aboriginal death*, since it is a kind of death that both precedes death as the end of life, but also constitutes the phantasmic backdrop onto which the living human being projects all of her fantasies of life versus death.

It is *de facto* the case that the closest we have been to death during life is precisely the state in which we found ourselves just before we were born. The aboriginal death is in turn the fundamental requirement for *organic dividuation*. At the aboriginal death, the great trauma moves downwards into and then steers from the subconscious. The great trauma quite simply becomes the engine of the drive. The trauma can be described as a vestige, but it is a vestige of something that might very well be something fabricated rather than something that has actually taken place. This is typical of the living organism, which must constantly sacrifice something of itself in order to be able to manage the enormous semiotic flow with which it is constantly inundated. The trauma thus plays a central role in the perception and consciousness system, since the process of dealing with superfluous information is much more important for survival than the receiving of new information, which is something that we definitely do not suffer from any shortage of.

So if desire is based in the organism's existential pleasure, in what Nietzsche calls *the will to power*, then the drive at the deepest level according to Freud is *the death drive*, the longing for the extinction of painful life and merging into the non-organic. The Freudian drive can be linked to the metaphorical usage of the cerebral hemispheres' roles in human psychology, a psychology which, according to Nietzsche, shapes all human thought. There is no external philosophy outside Man's own world; all philosophy is created by and for Man. Thus, philosophy is always very much influenced by psychology. Both the philosopher and the philosopher's readers participate in the philosophising with their emotions fully switched on. There is no philosophy without emotions, without a strong psychological component.

If we use Iain McGilchrist's division between the role of the cerebral hemispheres in *The Divided Brain* metaphorically, the left hemisphere thus constitutes a centre of eternalism, subjectification, objectification, mathematisation, individuality, hierarchisation and logical cogency. If left to its own devices, or if allowed to dominate too much, it leans towards *neurosis*, and remains *at a distance* and acts *indirectly* vis-à-vis the surrounding world. The right hemisphere, on the other hand, is the centre of mobilism, motion, change, holism, dividuality, diversity and intuition. If left alone or allowed to dominate, it leans towards *psychosis*, and it remains *engaged* and acts *directly* vis-à-vis the surrounding world. The left hemisphere is thus the centre of *the death drive*, and its transcendental philosophers champion *immortality* as a principle, which means that the present life that we are actually living should be ignored and should just be gone through and stoically endured, since its intensity can be postponed in all eternity anyway. Correspondingly, the right hemisphere is the centre of the *libido*, and its immanent philosophers fight for *survival* as a principle, where the actual life that we are actually living is to be lived with the greatest possible passion and intensity, since it gets its subliminal quality precisely from its *transience*.

Free will is a dualist myth, which has been produced in order for us to be able to hold the soul responsible for the weak and dissolute body, which it is of course set to battle with in the eternal duel of dualism (see *The Body Machines*). On the other hand, we can speak of *free choice* in a contingently monist universe, with the quantity of different choices that are offered the body in every given situation. However, there is no such thing as a will that is free in the midst of this choosing, nor is there any agency of will where this illusory will could be given shelter and exercised. The will is nothing other than the status of the moment in the current tug-of-war between the desire and the drive, and since these dwell in the subconscious it is not possible to achieve any conscious balancing between them. There is thus no individual free will, but rather an endless plurality of wills, which hardly become fewer because the current situation offers so many different choices.

There is an infinite number of agents at an infinite number of levels. According to the mobilist Spinoza, the consequence is that it is the prime task of ethics to maximise *potentia agendi*, every current agent's potential. Here memetics comes into the picture and provides us with an excellent, non-linear alternative to Cartesianism's linear world view. Instead of a subject that is manifested as an individual through giving full expression to its ideas, we get a *memeplex that materialises as an agent by invading and occupying a body*. It is and has always been our thoughts that control us, instead of the other way around. There is no subject beyond or behind the mental activity that is driven by memes. What is amazing is not that there is a little subject somewhere inside the brain – in the form of a man or woman staring at his or her own cinema screen, on which the incoming stimuli from his or her perception apparatuses are projected, and who then makes and executes decisions based upon the received information (which thus is a fiction manufactured by himself or herself) – but that the brain is so clever that it produces *the illusion of a subject* which the body harbours for its own survival's sake.

Descartes is thus correct in one sense, at least to some degree, but not in the way he himself thinks: there is really a subject, but it is a fundamentally illusory such. *The subject experience* is impossible to deny or even regulate or avoid once one is clear about its illusory nature. It exists only in our own heads, yet exists to the highest degree. The subject is a constantly recurring element of disturbance in the flow of being which precisely therefore succeeds in tying together being into a being that appears as something that can be taken in and is at least manageable in patches. Since first and foremost this subject is the necessary first eternalisation of the mobilist chaos of existence, we call it *the eternalist subject*. But the subject should in no way be regarded as a 'managing director' of consciousness. As the psychoanalyst Jacques Lacan points out, the subject is instead harboured in the subconscious. However, it is not synonymous with the subconscious. Rather, the subject is synonymous with *the struggle between consciousness and the sub-*

conscious, in precisely the subconscious, and survives since this antagonism never reaches or can achieve any permanent solution. The fact that we cannot imagine the subject as a completed project, that we cannot see ourselves as complete human beings, is the very prerequisite for the subjective experience. The change in our essence and inadequacy drives us towards the change.

It is Hegel who digs the Cartesian subject's grave. His logic is a redoubled contingency. His rationality is a redoubled irrationality. Hegel's most brilliant insight lies in that thinking starts and ends with *paradox* and *inconsistency*. Thinking is nothing other than a production of problems; it is only activated at all when it is confronted with enigmas. Hegel's stroke of genius is the insight that knowledge reaches its absolute limit, is transformed into what Hegel dramatically calls *absolute knowledge*, just when it understands and acknowledges its own built-in limitations. Hegel thereby pokes holes in *rationalism*; the blind faith in the scope of human logic as the foundation for epistemology, which his predecessors Spinoza and Kant cultivate and celebrate. Hegel instead opens the door to *transrationalism*, the idea that Man's thinking is founded on his conditions for survival and based on an extremely narrow perspective, as a contingent phenomenon without any chance of being able to embrace and comprehend in advance the enormity of existence.

According to Hegel, absolute knowledge is nothing other than the fundamental and historically necessary insight that reason is always relegated to a framework within which it must be limited. For Hegel, absolute knowledge is a *metaknowledge*, an historical consummation of epistemology, which comes down to a humble insight into its necessary built-in limitations. Transrationalism leads to *paradoxism*, which gets its clearest expression in the Hegelian subject's insight into its own illusory foundation. *The paradoxist subject* appears before itself as the starting point and centre of existence, but at the same time is a gaping empty hole; an illusion that arises as a by-product of language and the small child's need to *eternalise*, to divide itself and its surrounding world into delimited, cohesive phenomena.

Hegel's role as a magnificently emergent phenomenon in the history of philosophy all of his own is difficult to overestimate. He realises that it is in the oscillation between the experience of an intense being and being convinced of one's own non-existence that the paradoxist subject resides. Hegel's transrationalist understanding of the existential experience sounds the death knell for the jewel in rationalism's crown, *the Cartesian subject*. Hegel bases his transrationalism on an epistemological necessity: no truth is ever complete in a contingent universe. The stronger an emotional truth experience is, the more clearly it is revealed that it is based upon a kind of mystical, hidden core of *epistemic incompleteness* that the truth experience intensely tries to conceal precisely through a desperate *overemotionality* (compare with the fervour of the newly-saved sect member).

The future is always open and multiple. History never rests, but always hurries on. Truth and totality remain incompatible. This means that Hegel's notorious and idiosyncratic *totalism* – his seemingly megalomaniacal conviction about the historical arrival of absolute knowledge through his own philosophy – is completely correct if we place it and maintain it at the *metalevel*. But he does not actually plead for totalism *per se*. Hegel is definitely not a Platonist; rather, he buries totalism at the metalevel, beyond the eternalist subject's everyday obligations, but as an abrupt historical conclusion to its vain, narcissistic push for omnipotence. Hegel does not care at all about the *individual*, Descarte's and Kant's divine linchpin down there on the system's basement. Hegel's God is named *Atheos*, the holy void, and nothing else.
The syntheist agent stands out even more clearly with Hegel's

successor Martin Heidegger. He mistrusts Buddhism's idea of *enlightenment* as a possible and desirable consciousness beyond the subject, and argues that the subject is located in and expands from its formative illusion. With Heidegger, the illusion is the subject's engine – that is, identical with syntheology's *Atheos* – and not a problem for the existential experience. It is instead the illusory quality that gives the subject its – for Heidegger decisive – *presence*. Heidegger here stands considerably closer to syntheism than Buddhism. The syntheist agent's character traits present themselves most clearly in her relation to her own transience. This is the engine of culture: our mortality and the mystery of death. Death is characterised first and foremost by its *anonymity*; the subject is dissolved at death into a pre-dividual anonymous dimension. To die is to be dissolved into the Universe, to become part of that which is universal, which already within the subject is greater than the particular subject *per se*. That which dies in death is *dividuation* and nothing else. According to Gilles Deleuze, the death instinct should primarily be understood as a lack of imagination in relation to the existential experience. A lack of imagination which the syntheist culture is more than happy to remedy, and where the point of departure is given: *Be your desire, be your drive, ignore everything else so that you may live life to the full!*

The free and open Internet versus the ecological apocalypse

Everything is religion, but everything is also politics. And politics is religion, and religion is to a high degree politics. Without utopias there are no visions, and without visions there is no collective and organised hope of a better life in a society that has undergone desirable changes. In a society without utopias, *cynical isolationism* reigns supreme in the public arena. For this reason, such a society is the most dangerous society of all. Each and every person at the most cares about herself and her loved ones, but displays a programmatic disinterest in how everyone else fares. This lack of social cohesion sooner or later leads to societal collapse within all key areas. The opposite of utopia is, as we know, *dystopia*. The approaching ecological apocalypse has emerged as our time's great and dominant dystopia. The fateful question that will be decisive for the 21st century is how the approaching ecological apocalypse is to be prevented or at least tackled in order to ameliorate or postpone it if possible.

We thus live in an age that lacks a credible utopia, but that at the same time is coloured by a doomsday narrative that is every bit as powerful as it is threatening in the political discourse.

Environmental issues are constantly on the agenda, as is the collective guilty conscience because these issues are constantly being down-prioritised by politicians who instead give priority to short-term measures on hip-pocket issues, measures that might perhaps yield the odd job opportunity but that also damage or preclude the necessary improvements in the environment. The growing *plurarchy* in a society where everyone talks at cross purposes, and increasingly vociferously focuses on pseudo-issues, evokes a paralysing state of *hypercynicism* (see *The Netocrats)*. At the same time it is at precisely chaotic points in history of this type that new metaphysical systems are established – with *Pauline Christianity* in the crumbling Roman Empire and *Kantian individualism* in conjunction with the French Revolution as two very clear examples – and there is no reason to believe that our age should be any different in this respect.

The hypercynical state is namely due to the fact that the prevailing ideological paradigm is no longer in step with its surrounding material reality. Rather, the lack of utopianism and the abundance of dystopianism is the final proof of the prevailing paradigm having reached the end of the road and lost all remaining remnants of relevance. The central dilemma is quite simply not the surrounding material reality – even if it constantly produces a never-ending stream of problems to manage – but the prevailing ideological drought. What is needed is a new metaphysical story that is more relevant for the new age than the old one, where the dystopia is replaced by a credible utopia that includes the prevention of the dystopia becoming a reality. It is in fact not enough to just paint a picture of a powerful dystopia and moralise about all who are making it real with their opinions and behaviours. Because in the subconscious, the human being is ultimately driven by *the death drive* and the masochistic enjoyment of arranging one's own extinction. According to this logic, *eco-moralism* is accelerating and affirming the ecological dystopia rather than preventing or mitigating against it, which eco-moralism believes and claims that it wants to do. The dystopia must instead be used as a lever in order to achieve an open and contingent landscape of creativity and intensity, directed towards the future and *the syntheist utopia*.

All political ideologies under the capitalist paradigm are fundamentally *individualistic*. *Conservatism* maintains that the authentic individual has existed, but that she has unfortunately been lost and must be restored by a return to the past. *Anarchism* maintains that the individual is the purpose and meaning of existence and that the influence of politics must be minimised in order to liberate the individual's spontaneous and innate capacity for self-realisation. *Liberalism* is anarchism's older and more pragmatic relative, and it differs from anarchism by maintaining that the individual's self-realisation is metaphysically connected to *ownership of the Kantian object*. The liberal fantasy thus distinguishes itself from the anarchist fantasy through its special fixation on requiring that all assets must be owned by one or a few specific individuals in order to be ennobled into ever-more complex *atoms* and reduce liberalism's metaphysical reward, *growth*. Therefore, in contrast to the anarchist, the liberal maintains that the law and the State are needed in order to protect all the belongings that are the object of individuals' fetishism. *Socialism* also claims to fight for the individual's self-realisation, but it sees the conservative class system as the obstacle to this utopia, where the upper class's control over society's most important resources and its refusal to share power and wealth must be rectified. What distinguishes *democratic socialism* from *the revolutionary variety* is how one answers the question of what is the most efficient and at the same time most ethically correct route to the common objective: that the working class lay their hands on the abundance of the upper class, which in turn means that one achieves the classless society. This is the objective that socialists of all stripes share: the individual's self-realisation and liberation from the shackles of the class system through the ultimate triumph of *communism*.

This means that if syntheism is to be successful in establishing itself as the metaphysics of the Internet age, it must be constructed on the foundation of an entirely new utopia; an idea that in contrast to individualism in all its forms has credibility in the network society, where the individual is reduced to a curious remnant from a distant past. It must create the hope of the impossible being possible, even for informationalism's people. Naturally syntheism has no chance of accomplishing this if it were to start from a capitalist perspective, since individualism is just as dead within philosophy as atomism is dead within physics. Syntheism's utopia must instead be formulated as *the consummate network dynamics.* And how could a network be consummate, if it were not free and open to the surrounding world and the future in a contingent and relationalist universe?

In the same way that cosmologists and quantum physicists strive for agreement on a theory of everything in physics, syntheologists are working towards constructing a *social theory of everything* for informationalism. What is striking about the syntheist utopia is that it cannot be formulated beforehand – since it is located in a contingent and indeterministic universe – which means that instead it must be practised before it is articulated. Therefore it is of central importance for both syntheist ethics and creative development that the ideas in a society are not kept locked away behind virtual firewalls or towers of legal papers, but that they can be exchanged in complete freedom between the active dividuals on the Internet. The syntheist utopia is thus first and foremost a society where *ideas are free and are not owned by anybody,* where the memes form memeplexes that wander freely from human to human, from network to network, and are transformed during these movements without being met with any resistance whatsoever anywhere, apart from the lack of attention that sifts out all memetic losers. Therefore, the digital integrity movement receives the syntheist movement's full support as the necessary path to this state, which we consequently call *utopian memetics.*

The healing potential of the syntheist faith shines most brightly when strangers are randomly brought together around their common humanity in the temporary utopia, such as at the spontaneous meetings that occur on the playa at the Burning Man Festival in Nevada, possibly the largest remaining meeting place in the world where an exchange of calling cards would be regarded as vulgar and sacrilegious. It is there and then that the syntheist dream of the religious *intersubject* is realised. A *you* and an *I* become an emergent *we* that is tangibly far greater than the sum of its parts, and the proof that this is the case is that, if anything, the *we* is strengthened by the spontaneous meeting's participants going their separate ways. The *you* and the I don't just become the *we*, they also become directly interchangeable with each other; *agentiality within the phenomenon* is set in motion, reshaped and radicalised, and expands.

The sudden *synchronisation* between the subjects in the temporary utopia is strengthened rather than weakened over time, since *the memory of the infinite now* in the loving meeting between strangers in an environment from which instrumentality has been removed just grows and grows. And it is precisely in this memory of an ecstasy directly linked to *the religious belonging* that the syntheist intersubject is born and grows. When all other social factors are eliminated, it is in this, the most random of all meetings – without any other binding connections between people than *the syntheist faith* – that the manifestation of Syntheos shines the brightest. So what are our age's local eco-villages and global participatory festivals (Burning Man, Going Nowhere, The Borderland, etc.) if not in fact experimental, temporary utopias that point forward towards and provide a tangible notion of the permanent utopia?

Outside the temporary utopia, however, we live in an age where the collective world view is crumbling due to the sheer infirmity of old age. History is beyond our control. The only thing that remains when plurarchy becomes widely accepted is the virtual subculture's fractionalised planet. Human life on the planet can only be saved by an initial, and subsequently gradually increasing, physical *monastisation*. Therefore a specific subculture is required that sees saving the planet as a whole for human life as its mission, and which realises that this work, in order to have a chance of succeeding, must start with a radical distancing from *the individualist paradigm* and its programmatic *atomism*, *capitalism* and *expansionism*. Out of this necessary negation rises the utopian idea of *theological anarchism*: the dream of a sustainable society beyond the nation state and capitalist expansionism. However, in the same way that Karl Marx defines socialism as the necessary path to communism, we must assume that there is an experimental *practice*, oriented towards utopia on the road to theological anarchism. As a spontaneously arisen movement from spontaneously arisen needs in the shadow of spontaneously arisen technological complexes, syntheism is precisely such a practice. Suddenly the movement is simply there: as the emergent answer to the new era's strongest human needs it is realised through an innovative use of new, disruptive technologies. All that is needed is that the syntheist memeplex, in as refined a form as possible, drops into the new communication-technology reality and spreads itself.

Political ideology in the Internet age has two metaphysical starting points. First of all, there is the enormous expansion of the Internet and takeover of power that opens the arena for an antagonism between the rising netocracy – which with the aid of its ever-more powerful networks wants to liberate information flows – and the marginalised bourgeoisie, which with its nation states and major corporations wants to fence in and control information flows. And, secondly, there is the approaching ecological apocalypse, which absolutely must be averted if humanity is to survive at all. The syntheist politician is therefore first and foremost an *environmentalist netocrat*. But in order for syntheism to succeed in realising its ambition of opening the door to theological anarchism, it is being forced to take on the conflict with the old capitalist power structure, which consists of the nation states and the big global corporations.

In order for syntheism to be able to defeat the statist-corporatist establishment and its dysfunctional, apocalyptic and hypercynical metaphysics, syntheists – as the American philosopher Terence McKenna prophetically claims in a speech at the University of California in Berkeley as early as 1984, eight years before the World Wide Web saw the light of day – must have free and unlimited access to its keenest weapon, *the free and open Internet.* McKenna argues that the free and open Internet quite simply is humanity's only chance to save the planet for human life by enabling a longed-for and long-needed counterweight to *the eschatological drive* which is built into capitalism. For this reason, the first action of the syntheist theory of everything is to unite late capitalism's two new political mass movements, *environmentalism* and *the digital integrity movement,* under one and the same roof. It is hardly a coincidence that these two movements are arising in the same places in the world – namely in Northern Europe and along the coasts of North American – since it is in these places that the expansion of the Internet is most powerful, psychedelic experimentation most extensive, and thus the insight into the planet's vulnerability is being disseminated most rapidly and is gaining first a foothold. These two movements are, quite simply, two sides of the same metaphysical coin, and *it is syntheism that is the coin itself.*

The key issue when we are talking about a free and open Internet is of course how much *transparency* a society should and can handle. It is then important to understand that the problem with transparency is never the transparency itself – to confess, to lay bare one's heart of hearts for one's fellow sisters and brothers in the community, is also a holy act within syntheism – but how it affects the network pyramid in question, that is, who lays himself bare for whom and thereby risks, at least in the short-term, a possible loss of power first? Does the current *transparentisation* strengthen the top, middle or bottom of the prevailing power structure in the society? Is the power structure levelled out in the direction of the syntheist utopia's *radical equality*, or is the prevailing power structure reinforced in such a way that social inequality is preserved?

We seek the answers to these questions for example in the French philosopher Michael Foucault's pragmatist ethics: If the transparentisation begins from *the top down* – that is, if it is the rulers who have all of their secrets exposed first – it can be implemented painlessly throughout the entire power structure from the top and all the way down. On the other hand, if the transparentisation begins from the bottom up, the consequence will no doubt be a *capitalist police state*, and thereby – apart from all the other misery that such a development would entail – the ecological apocalypse would soon be unavoidable. It is the citizens who must first know everything about the activities of the nation state and the major corporations rather than the statist-corporatist establishment being allowed to bug and register the citizens' opinions and preferences.

Therefore, according to syntheism the battle of WikiLeaks and other whistle-blower organisations to disclose cover-ups of the activities of people in power is a *sacred project*, while conversely the attempts of the nation states and the major corporations to bug and register the views of citizens represent a flagrant violation of universal, human rights. Transparentisation in an increasingly transparent society must quite simply spread from the top down *by being switched on from the bottom up*. The order must be the following: first the person in power bares himself, then the citizen bares herself. And it is precisely here that the antagonism between the new syntheist netocracy and the old statist-corporatist power structure becomes most apparent.

The netocracy regards the Internet as *a relationalist phenomenon*: to be a netocrat is to identify with the network itself, to act as the Internet's agent. The bourgeoisie, on the other hand, regard the Internet as *a correlationist object*, alien to and hostile towards the individualist subject and therefore a troubling object that must be tamed and controlled, by force if necessary.

This explains why it is the netocracy that is driving the transparentisation of the old power structure by defending the free and open Internet – and as a consequence is seeing old nation states and major corporations lose their unmotivated and ethically objectionable upper hand in terms of power – while the old bourgeoisie moralise against the freedom and equality on the Internet and frenetically try to control and domesticate the Net in order to be able to thereby defend their own positions of power with the aid of their information advantage. This is the 3rd millennium's great political conflict, and as the Internet age's built-in metaphysics there is hardly any doubt about which side syntheism chooses to stand on. The world needs more, not fewer, whistleblowers, and the frenzy with which they are hounded, bad-mouthed and punished is a clear indication of the statist-corporatist establishment's understanding of the value of what is at stake.

From the 1960s onwards, *individualism* and its ally atomism are put under enormous pressure from a new supra-ideology: *relationalism* and its partner *network dynamics*. The capitalist patriarchy – from Napoleon onwards, probably the most evident individualist power structure – is attacked by *feminism*, which puts forth demands for equality between the sexes, and thereafter by *the queer movement*, with its requirements of equality between people of different sexual orientations and identities. The feminists represent female individuals' interests, and the queer movement is fighting for sexually divergent individuals' civil rights. This means, of course, that both these movements are still fundamentally individualist. The criticism against the patriarchy thus has come from *inside* the individualist paradigm. But the argumentation contains numerous *network-dynamical arguments*, for example that the woman's freedom is also the man's freedom from patriarchy, and that the liberation of homo- and transsexuals also entails the liberation of heterosexuals from narrow and repressive heteronormativity. The dividualist criticism thus begins from inside individualism – through informationalism liberating new desires and drives in the collective subconscious and thereby exposing the shortcomings of individualism – in order to slowly but surely establish a new, independent paradigm where the old individual is dead.

However, the first relationalist attack on the individualist paradigm comes from *environmentalism* in the form of its aggressive demands that capitalism's environmental destruction and ruthless plundering of resources must cease. Environmentalism is clearly based on a network dynamics theory without any focus whatsoever on isolated individuals or atoms. Here, the planet is regarded as a more or less closed system, which must be treated as just such a system, since all individual agents and nodes are completely subservient to the overarching network. Therefore environmentalism gives priority to the network over the individual; for the first time in these contexts Man is reduced from an individual to a dividual. And thereby clear ethical boundaries are set for what the human being can and cannot do in relation to the dynamic network's interests. Environmentalism is a *globalism*, since a national environmental policy is in principle meaningless, and it must by necessity fight for the global solidarity which, in a network-dynamics theory, includes not just people but also plants, animals and natural diversity in itself. Quite logically, environmentalism begins to replace socialism as the seat of radicalism.

But if environmentalism is the most powerful reaction directed towards the old paradigm's destructive death drive, it is only with the fight for the free and open Internet that we observe the growth of a political ideology that is grounded in the new paradigm's utopian possibilities rather than in the old paradigm's dystopian variants. In its capacity as a negation of capitalism, environmentalism is a parallel to *atheism* in the history of metaphysics. The digital integrity movement on the other hand is *a dialectic negation of the negation*, and is thereby to be regarded as a parallel movement to *syntheism*. Rick Falkvinge, the founder of the Pirate Party and one of the digital integrity movement's foremost pioneers, pinpoints the relationships of the movements to each other in his book *Swarmwise*. Environmentalism is driven by the conviction that nature's resources are finite rather than inexhaustible, which capitalist mythology constantly assumes. At the same time, argues Falkvinge, the Pirate movement is based on the axiom that culture and knowledge that is shared without friction between people in a society where information sharing no longer incurs any surplus cost, is an infinite rather than a finite resource for the future.

The dystopia concerns itself with the finite, utopianism focuses on the infinite. Accordingly, the fight for the free and open Internet is the answer to what must be done; it is the engine that drives the new utopia rather than the brake that hinders the old dystopia. What we are talking about here is far more than just parallel phenomena in the market for the shaping public opinion: syntheism is *de facto* the name of the digital integrity movement's underlying metaphysics. This explains why the fight for the free and open Internet is the central political struggle in the 21st century. All other important political conflicts that play out during, and contribute to giving colour to, informationalism's growth, are completely dependent on how this conflict unfolds. It concerns far more than the growing *netocracy's* striving to ignore the ruling *bourgeoisie*, which has controlled the world since the paradigm of the printing press gained broad acceptance. Beyond the fight for the free and open Internet, the approaching ecological apocalypse is rearing its ugly head: a potential catastrophe that capitalism is responsible for and at the same time evidently lacks the ability to prevent.

There is a risk of planet Earth becoming uninhabitable for human beings within a few generations – many of the various deleterious effects for which humans are responsible are already irreparable – unless this development leading towards the ecological apocalypse is halted and steered in an environmentally friendly direction. We already know how the capitalist society governed from the top-down, with individualism as the State religion, is managing the ecological apocalypse; this insidious catastrophe has of course been created by this system, which has subsequently shown that it is unable to rectify the damage. On the other hand, the growing and aspiring netocracy has a burning interest in saving the Earth for human life – and moreover access to a considerable arsenal of new *communications tools* with which to do this – in contrast to the cynical and resigned bourgeoisie. The free and open Internet is therefore a necessary milestone in order for ecological salvation to be possible at all.

In October 2013, it was revealed that the US intelligence organisation NSA had bugged, among many others, the Chancellor of Germany, Angela Merkel, continuously for five years without the knowledge of the US President Barack Obama. It is difficult to think of a clearer illustration of how the democratic system *de facto* has collapsed under late capitalism and has now definitively morphed into a chaotic *plurarchy*. If an intelligence agency can grab the power from elected representatives, the word *democracy* loses all meaning. This is no longer about a democracy but about a massive, paranoid bureaucracy that does not need to take into account at all any form of democratic or even judicial influence over how certain State agencies operate. Late capitalism's obsession with *security*, which is constantly mistaken for *safety*, could hardly have been exposed any more clearly. Therefore the capitalist power complex of nation states and major corporations has only one priority for the future: commandeering and controlling the Internet.

The statist-corporatist establishment understands the Internet as a disagreeable and unruly *hydra* – moreover extremely difficult to handle when it comes to exploiting information flows and making money (see *The Netocrats*) – that constantly disrupts and is gradually eroding the foundations of the patriarchal fantasies of omnipotence of politicians and business leaders. Jacques Lacan's psychoanalytical concept of *the real* could hardly be more fitting than when it comes to describing the digital hydra that is creeping up on the old patriarch and threatening to expose the latter's mental nakedness. For the rapidly growing netocracy however, the Internet is a sacred phenomenon, both for the netocracy *per se* and for its desire to save the planet for the survival of humanity. The truth is of course that the more time passes, the more alternative contingency plans collapse; and accordingly the closer humanity comes to the ecological apocalypse, the more clearly the free and open Internet emerges as the only tool with which the planet can be saved for human life. In an information, communication and network society, ecological salvation must occur through information, communication and networking in order to have a chance of succeeding. There are no other options. Therefore the insight that the free and open Internet is the only conceivable ecological saviour is growing steadily ever-stronger.

What is striking in the information-technology writing of history is how Man hardly changes at all over time. Our genes are largely identical with our ancestors' genes from 50,000 years ago. It is our technological environment that has undergone an incredibly dramatic change over the past 5,000 years, while we ourselves must be content with the same cognitive and intellectual equipment that people had back then. Five thousand years is quite simply an all too short time period: it spans an all too small number of generations for any dramatically significant mutations in our genetic make-up to be able to arise. In addition, during the last few decades technological development has undergone an unprecedented acceleration, not least when it comes to information technologies. This means that *Man is the constant and technology is the variable* in the information-technology writing of history.

The capitalism writing of history, on the other hand, is based on an axiom that is called *meliorism*. Meliorism argues that there is an objective development over time, that objectively speaking civilisation moves forwards and upwards. It is not just technology that is developed by becoming increasingly complex and with an increasing capacity to solve ever-greater problems ever-more adroitly and cheaply. According to meliorism, the syntheist constant *Man* is also developing over time and is moving forwards and upwards. Consequently, there should be *some kind of ongoing mystical ennobling even of Man himself* throughout history. Thanks to meliorism's widespread popularity, we are saddled with *generationism*, the idea that every new generation is intellectually superior to the preceding one. Generationism is not as widely questioned and attacked in contemporary political discourse as *misogyny*, *racism* or *homophobia*. But it is just as widespread and superstitious, and at least as socially destructive.

One of the problems is that the innocent victims of generationism are absent and cannot speak for themselves when they are attacked, since they are either too old to make much of a fuss, or have already passed away. But generationism's negative consequences for its adherents remain, and the idea of the innate and unquestioned excellence of one's own generation is one of the most dangerous and destructive ideas throughout history; it both precedes and augments virtually all great social crises. What is so unpleasant is that the generationist myth has never been made so invisible and at the same time, and in part precisely for that very reason, has never before been so powerful either, as in our time. The problem is that the person who believes himself to be superior to previous generations also believes that he has nothing to learn from them and is thereby doomed to repeat their mistakes.

It is important to understand that humanism, including all of its political ideologies such as liberalism and socialism, takes meliorism for granted as a basic axiom. However, it is sufficient to study human genetics throughout history in order to be able to determine that empirically meliorism is entirely a myth – a kind of failed post-Christian *self-salvation doctrine* for humanity – which among other things must be held accountable for all kinds of eugenic *human betterment miseries* under capitalism. The problem here is that liberal heroism is an impossibility. The liberal can never be a hero, at least not in her capacity as a liberal. This is for the simple reason that liberalism includes rather than excludes the totalitarian tendency in its incessant, utilitarian calculating – if nothing else works to defend its position of power, liberalism *de facto* has no built-in barriers against the totalitarian ambition within itself – which in turn means that it lacks a functioning immune system against outbursts of totalitarianism.

Time after time throughout history it has been shown that, as soon as they find themselves under the slightest external pressure, liberal societies rapidly transform into totalitarian power apparatuses that shy away from both public accountability and democratically elected control. This applies not least to the country that, more than any other, has acted as the emblem of liberal democracy, the USA. This once proud defender of universal freedom – in pace with an increasing number of hysterical narratives of fabricated external threats having been put forward – has been reduced to a lobby-controlled plurarchy in the hands of religious extremists and intelligence bureaucrats that operate in secret, backed up by interests that represent an enormous and thus depleting drain on resources (such as the NSA). It has gone so far that it is no longer the dream of individual *freedom* that is the engine in the American identity, but instead the collective *paranoia*. To be an American is no longer about being a citizen in the land of the free and the home of the brave on Earth, but is nowadays equivalent to an overindulgence in paranoid conspiracy theories.

Liberal multiculturalism and religious fundamentalism are consistently described as being each other's opposites. In reality, they are two sides of the same dysfunctional coin: *cynical isolationism.* At the same time, the lack of religiosity within liberal multiculturalism means that it is unable to understand and refute the onslaught of religious fundamentalism from inside its own ideology. In the eyes of the fundamentalist, liberalism is dead and only religion can offer a utopian hope. This means that only syntheism – or for that matter any other system of ideas with built-in room for *transcendental ecstasy* and the dissolution of the ego that is its desired effect – can refute fundamentalism and constitute a solid foundation for an alternative, genuinely emancipatory politics.

The dark underside explains why, on closer inspection, liberal democracy lacks incentives to defend the free and open Internet, and why if anything it is developing into netocracy's most aggressive enemy. Because one of liberalism's basic tenets is, in fact, that individual people – liberalism likes to call them *individuals*, and not without good reason – are so different from each other that every material form of mutual sympathy is precluded by definition. This is in spite of psychoanalysis teaching that the differences within *the divided subject* are greater than the differences between people. This has the consequence that if the mythology of liberalism is to be taken seriously, *self-love* is an impossibility. And without genuine self-love, there is no *heroism* either. Quite logically and consistently, syntheism's monist and holistic dividual is therefore the radical opposite of liberalism's dualist and divided individual.

The catastrophic meliorist utopias of the 20th century – Fascism, Nazism, Stalinism and Maoism – finally force the philosophers to wake up and realise meliorism's responsibility for the totalitarian delusions about human nature and its possibilities. From the Frankfurt School in the 1930s onwards, criticism is first of all voiced against the myth of progress and thereafter ever more strongly against the entire, worshipped project of the Enlightenment, from Kant and onwards. Syntheist metaphysics consistently breaks with the meliorist fantasy. *Progress* as a driving notion is a capitalist myth just as much as *eternity* as a driving notion is a feudal myth. According to the syntheist approach, no objectively valid progress exists. Objectively speaking, there is only change for change's own sake and, from the beginnings of permanent settlements and onwards, history is mainly to be regarded as a contingent, growing information-technology complex and nothing else. The number of memes that surround us has indeed exploded and reached a scale that is impossible to survey, just as their speed of circulation has escalated beyond all limits and our own ideation in most cases, but our genes in principle have not changed at all. The differences in Man's lifeworld are thus only *external* and *quantitative*, rather than *internal* and *qualitative*, as the progress myth claims.

Statism, faith in the nation state's necessary supremacy and monopoly on violence, is capitalism's political *supra-ideology*. Under statism's banner, *conservatism* emerges as a protector of the establishment and its interests; *liberalism* constitutes a faith in the individual as a rational accumulator of resources in a market governed by a mystical hand which is invisible to the naked eye; while *socialism* is a blind faith in the political party as a substitute for God. Obviously, the advent of informationalism puts all these ideologies into deep crisis, since it attacks the very foundation for statism by undermining the drawing of borders in an increasingly irrelevant geography, which makes accessible alternative and infinitely much more tempting possibilities in terms of identity creation. In this process, not only is meliorism exposed as a banal myth, it also loses all its power of attraction; the netocratic dividual would much rather experience herself as a constantly ongoing and dynamic *event* throughout life than as a representative of any kind of slowly developed and predetermined *progress*. The old ideologies are quite simply plagued by statism's deterministic view of history, which no longer has any credibility in an indeterministic universe. Therefore the ideological work must be done anew, and in that case all the way up from *the theological foundation*.

The progress myth is closely linked to *expansionism*, the banal faith that phenomena such as capital accumulation can expand in all eternity without any negative side-effects for itself. But all network-dynamical systems that are driven by the myth of their own growth do of course collapse sooner or later – which the American brain researcher Jeff Stibel shows in his book *Breakpoint* – under pressure from the consequences arising from a quantitative expansion without qualitative consideration. This is because the network *per se* does not contain any critical stop function that militates against its own quantitative expansion, but instead it is driven by the *deification* of the same, that is, by *the progress myth*. What environmentalism tries to do is to install such a crucial stop function within global capitalism before it destroys its own fundamental conditions: the existence of a planet that is suitable for human survival at all. And thereby everything else as well.

In an age obsessed with syntheist network dynamics, history cannot credibly strive for either feudalist eternities or capitalist progress. Above all, the human being has of course not changed much during the course of history, at least not into something objectively better than she has been previously. For example, we use a smaller part of our brain today than we did 10,000 years ago, mainly due to the fact that more and more of the calculations and considerations essential for our lives are today outsourced to external technology instead of being managed by the brain in-house. This fact kills meliorism. Syntheist utopianism instead focuses on planning for the definitive *event*, informationalism's fundamental metaphysical idea. For this reason syntheists are fighting for both *the free and open Internet* with its anarchist information flows and against *the ecological apocalypse* in order to save the fundamental prerequisite for human survival, the planet itself. That in addition social policy must be pursued based on the principle of minimisation of harm – not with banal, knee-jerk moralism as its guiding light – is a foregone conclusion based on these two positions. The free and open Internet is also of course driving *chemical liberation* – one of our three dramatic revolutions at the start of the Internet age – and we cannot take care of our planet in a constructive way if we do not also take care of each other in a constructive and preferably also a loving way. *Syntheism is the social theory of everything that merges these three ideological projects.*

When the banknote establishes itself as the dominant form of communication between people and societies in the 17th century, it generates an accelerating technological development and increased prosperity to an extent that the world has never seen before. It is easy to be blinded by this efficiency and progress; liberalism is a particularly popular ideology, entirely based on this blindness, spurred on by capital's formidable historical successes. But capital liberates all this human creativity and makes possible all this specialisation at a very high cost. Within the capitalist system the good, the service and the banknote are namely all disconnected from their interacting agents, which results in these agents being *cynically isolated* from and insensitive to each other. Both capital's own isolation of its interacting entities – you have no idea who owned your banknote before you, and you have no idea of where it will end up after it has left you – and its accelerating production of new human pathologies – a constant stream of new shortcomings in relation to a projected normality and an ever-increasing number of frustrations to be compensated for by a constant stream of new goods and services – makes capital the strongest *alienation generator* in all of human history.

Among other things this is why the American political scientist Francis Fukuyama shoots himself in the foot when, with a great hullabaloo, he proclaims the death of history in the early 1990s. It is namely not history as such that has died – not even in some kind of metaphorical sense of any interest whatsoever: it is merely a kind of writing of history that has reached its conclusion, namely Fukuyama's personal favourite narrative of the individual and the atom in *liberal democracy's linear history*. However, *metahistory*, the history of the writing of history *per se*, teaches us that when a certain narrative has reached the end of the road, this immediately opens the door to a completely new kind of narrative. This applies in particular at a paradigm shift, when one type of writing of history loses its social relevance only to be immediately replaced by another. Metahistory is quite simply a relay race that never ends.

History starts anew so to speak, and with this manoeuvre, even the past receives a new interior design that conveys completely new meanings. Since all identity is founded in an understanding of history – a subject always sees itself as a conceived history from an original birth onwards to the current moment – the growth of a new and dominant social identity requires a *rewriting* of all of history. This is necessary because the new writing of history obviously has the ambition of – and can only serve its clearly formulated purpose in the new paradigm through – depicting entirely different metaphysically driven prioritisations than what the old narrative did in the abandoned paradigm. We know today, for example, that concepts such as the Stone

Age, the Bronze Age and the Iron Age were created in Europe during the 19th century for a highly specialised purpose, namely to serve capitalism's need for a writing of history that is fixated on the industrial domestication of physical materials, one after the other. Therefore history is written as a long series of incremental and purposeful shifts in a direction towards the consummation of this history: *the modernist factory.*

The industrialist writing of history however is completely irrelevant for people in the age of informationalism, since they neither own, nor work in, nor relate to heavy-duty factories, and have much greater use for a history retold from the vantage point of various information technology paradigms. Spoken language, written language and the printing press replace stone, bronze and iron as prefixes to the epoch divisions that are construed as relevant. The writing of history in terms of information technology (see *The Netocrats*) has only just begun, and it also inevitably has the narratives of relationalism, attentionalism and dividualism in tow. Syntheism is the name of the metaphysical system, the social theory of everything and its ideological network, which ties all these narratives together and gives them their relationalist *substance.* Thus, informationalism's netocrats at last get a narrative that gives them a cohesive social identity. Through *the intersubjective identification* with *the writing of history in terms of information technology,* they get the strength and self-confidence to take power.

The current rewriting of history enables the individualist epoch to be viewed with new, more critical eyes. For example, capitalism is exposed as the tyranny of numerical slavery *par excellence.* The deeper we delve into its exploitative nature, both ideologically and historically, the more clearly capitalism's obsessive fixation with finally being able to *mathematise* all human thoughts and activities into a sum of dollars, a number of votes or a series of orgasms, emerges. No one illustrates this better than the American economist and Nobel Prize Laureate Gary Becker, who in his work reduces all human activities to a kind of constantly ongoing rational calculation of utility. His work is about a consummate capitalist logic that takes Becker all the way into people's bedrooms and places of worship – according to him, even an act of sexual intercourse is nothing other than a calculated, selfish utilitarian venture worked out in advance. What Becker thereby reveals about the seat of his own ideology is how rationalism, individualism, utilitarianism and – in all cases calculating and profit-maximising – capitalism really are one and the same ideology. Becker quite simply takes the Kantian paradigm and its isolated, compulsively colonising, patriarchal subject to the end of the road. And there he finds nothing other than an eternally empty *calculator*, grinding away.

This means that capitalism must be organised in such a way that it constantly excludes the glaring void at its own centre, all in accordance with the principle that something must be subtracted from or added to perceived reality in order for it to be ideologised, where this hidden something returns as *the ideology's demonic universal*. After capitalism's tyrannical pillaging throughout all of society's nooks and crannies – there is hardly anything left to exploit that has not yet been converted into an open market, just as there is hardly any human effort left to exercise that has not been converted into a taxed professional category – there remains only one single subject area where an opportunity to author an alternative, cohesive, universal story for humanity is still offered. To the disappointment of many philosophers this will not occur within art – even art has long ago been transformed into an entertaining and somewhat piquant euphemism for money, whatever art and its vociferous supporters may claim – but here we are talking about the underestimated theological arena. For it is in theology's meeting with the revolutionary trio of interactivity, quantum physics and chemical liberation that there arises a genuine possibility of creating the necessary metanarrative of the Internet age: *syntheology*.

Capitalism, on the other hand, drives Man away from *religion* and straight into the arms of *alienation*. The dislocation occurs even within the hypercapitalist religious sects that are rapidly expanding in the confused beginning of the Internet age. This means religions arranged like department stores and entertainment arenas, philosophies of life built on progress mythologies, but without any annoying *religiosity* whatsoever. Typical examples are the hyperindividualist self-help theologies in primarily the United States, such as Charismatic Christianity, Mormonism, Jehovah's Witnesses, Scientology, New Age and Californian Zen, as well as their various branches and equivalents in Asia, South America and Eastern Europe. Here there is a lack that capitalism creates in order to subsequently and fundamentally worsen it, a lack that it never deals with, since a rectification would kill capitalism itself. We are talking about the gradually increasing acute lack of *empathy*. Capitalism strives to minimise empathy in order to thus be able to maximise alienation, which increases emotionally compensating consumption and thereby also even production additionally – as we know, capitalism is driven by the growth maximisation principle – while syntheism conversely strives to maximise empathy, and in order to do this it must fight alienation through actively minimising the influence of capital inside the syntheist temporary utopia.

This means that syntheism is capitalism's antithesis. It is not superficially and merely formally anti-capitalist, such as the capitalist ideologies *socialism* and *conservatism* with their saccharine dreams of a controlled, top-down market – as though a pragmatic domestication of capital really would be able to affect alienation; rather, historical experience says that it is the other way around. No, syntheist anti-capitalism is deeply and genuinely radical on account of its being seated in *theological anarchism*. The syntheist reply to capitalism's pillaging is not to start an anti-capitalist, bloody revolution with dramatic riots on the streets – after which the system would in any case soon re-emerge, insignificantly modified, since it *de facto* emanates in an emergent way from our age's specific information technology structure. Such an ambition is indefensibly naive and belongs more in the Enlightenment's patriarchal rationalism than in *syntheism's relationalist renaissance*. The logically consequential, syntheist response to late capitalism and its hyperalienation is – as the syntheist philosopher Simon Critchley writes in *The Faith of The Faithless* – not the pretentious *revolution*, but instead the discrete *subtraction*.

According to *the principle of necessary subtraction*, the only right and reasonable thing for the radically convinced person on many historical occasions is to simply withdraw from the system – to refuse to participate in the social game, to quite simply leave the system in order to build up parallel, temporary utopias, whose objectives with time are made permanent – and to do this together with dedicated syntheist brothers and sisters. What is right and reasonable is not just to shoot at a hydra that in any case cannot be felled, since new heads constantly sprout where the old ones recently were, but to live out *truth as an act* and thereby rob the hydra of its oxygen. To think is namely not to understand the world. Thinking is not separated from the world in such a way that this is even possible. *To think is instead to act*. The syntheist agent is a human being who acts without necessarily being able to articulate a full understanding of exactly why. She lets *intuition* guide her. It is first on the basis of her actions that the syntheist agent can work out the necessary meaning, in order to retroactively give her action this meaning. It is in any case in this way that consciousness and intuitive action relate to each other: the former explains and legitimises the latter by creating an appealing narrative that matches the pattern in the surroundings with which one identifies.

Syntheism is thus a revolutionary *subtractionism*. To subtract is to withdraw from the contemporary chaos in order to be able to formulate an accurate truth of the future that can then be given full expression. Both Critchley and the French philosopher Alain Badiou claim that the genuine utopia is based on subtraction and not destruction. But it is not a pause from reality such as during a capitalist holiday in the sunshine that we are talking about here. Critchley is even an aggressive opponent of the Marxist John Gray's ideas of subtraction as a rational and tranquil oasis in an irrational and chaotic reality, something which he contemptuously considers to be a kind of *passive nihilism*. He rejects Gray's external and objective shift within physical geography and replaces this with a genuinely syntheist subtraction, which is an internal and subjective experience that entails a shift in the mental landscape and makes possible truth as an act. Critchley calls this truth as an act *mystical anarchism*.

It is only through something important being eliminated from the fantasy of reality that *the real* can break through and remind us of reality as a false fantasy and thereby awaken *utopianism* within us. However, it is important not to try to annihilate *the symptom*. The symptom is namely the best tool within socioanalysis for reaching *the real* behind the contemporary façade and understanding its relation to the current fantasy of reality. We trace the symptom by analysing the numerous microscopic breakthroughs in fantasy that the real does in everyday life in the form of our *sinthomes*, the small, bizarre and apparently illogical thoughts, the words and the deeds that suddenly disturb the predictable pattern in our everyday lives. *The sinthome is the symbol of the symptom.* Without access to and an understanding of the symptom, we can never understand our era. And nor can we generate our own religio-political pathos.

Syntheist subtractionism must be understood from the actual paradigm shift's historical possibilities and impossibilities. Paradigm shifts always entail giving the production of the new metaphysics the highest priority, since the one who formulates the new metaphysics also becomes the new paradigm's truth producer and thereby also one of its most important rulers (such as *the clergy* under feudalism and *the university professors* under capitalism). The great new religions and the metaphysical systems are always launched in the transition phases that arise at paradigm shifts. Political activism must therefore often *wait for the right point in time* in order to have any chance whatsoever of taking off. Critchley's logic is based on the premise that theology precedes philosophy; it is primary where philosophy is secondary. And philosophy precedes politics; it is secondary and politics tertiary. Theology delves deeper than philosophy, since it engages Man more thoroughly than philosophy can ever do. And philosophy lies deeper than politics, since philosophy is the well from which political activism gets its nourishment. This means that however much we long for a new cohesive *political ideology for the Internet age*, the creation of the new theological metaphysics and its religious practice must precede the articulation of the corresponding political ideology and activism. Syntheism stands ready when the present system breaks down. But the only possible way forward is to first build a living religion, while waiting for the time to the right for being able to establish and launch the new political ideology.

The first person to take the mighty march of attentionalism seriously is the French sociologist Pierre Bourdieu when he distinguishes between *economic capital* and *cultural capital*. The metaphor cultural capital proves effective and quickly becomes widely spread, but it is nonetheless unfortunate and leads one's thoughts astray, since cultural capital *is not a form of capital at all*. As opposed to economic capital, cultural capital cannot be saved or stored externally, it cannot be swapped or exchanged discreetly without friction, nor can it be used as a means of social communication, which are of course precisely the qualities of economic capital that give it world dominion under capitalism. Describing attention as cultural capital is thus just as misleading as describing food production under feudalism as *agricultural capital*. The metaphor is historically illogical and with time becomes more and more grotesquely misleading.

Attention has of course in reality few or no links at all to *capital,* aside from the fact that they have both been power-generating during different historical epochs. Attention is, for example, not a structural lubricant, even if it both creates and changes power structures to a dramatic extent. Its power instead arises as a response to the Internet's enormous information offering and *the plurarchical chaos* which this abundance creates. The need for *curatorship,* qualified information processing, is growing explosively, and *the sorting* of information is much more important and more valuable than *the production* of the same. At the very moment that information sorting becomes more important than information production, power over the society shifts from the producers of goods and services, *the capitalists,* to information sorting and its practitioners, *the netocratic curators.* We go through the paradigm shift from *capitalism* to *attentionalism.* With the advent of attentionalism, the focus of ethics shifts over from the individual's self-realisation, the capitalist ideal, to the network-dynamical utopia, or what is termed *the ethics of interactivity.* What is important in existence are the nodes in the network and how these nodes can be merged as often and as much as possible in order to maximise agential existence. The power in this hectic network-building ends up with those who succeed in combining *plausibility* and *attention* in the virtual world. And even if this attention can be measured – according to the brilliantly simple but correct formula *credibility multiplied by awareness yields attention* – it cannot be substituted or in any other way used in transactions in the same way as capital and capitalism's other valuable assets.

Attention is in essence a completely unique kind of value, a historically emergent phenomenon, arisen out of the acute lack of overview in the informationalist society. And it acts *de facto* without connection to any form of capital. The driving ambition of the attentionalist society, hardly surprisingly, is *imploitation* rather than capitalism's exploitation. That which is constantly desired is a value that can be saved for the few and thereby is maximised – rather than being spread to the many, which would mean that it would thus be diluted and minimised – an option that surfaces as a historically emergent effect of attentionalism's victory over capitalism. This explains why the netocrats are obsessed with the search for *authenticity*, the metaphysical reward promised by imploitation, while the informationalist underclass, *the consumtariat*, is characterised by its very search for *exploitation* and its desire to let itself be exploited, totally oblivious of the constantly ongoing but incomprehensibly symbol-laden netocractic imploitation that is transpiring in parallel, but all the while out of reach and out of sight.

Capitalism and its nation-state and corporativist bureaucracies optimise themselves, not by solving problems, but by creating more problems for themselves to solve, at the same time as more and more goods and services are demanded in order to satisfy a continuous stream of newly-produced needs. Therefore new laws are constantly being produced, new crime classifications, new pathologies, new defects, new failures to rectify, new problems to investigate, which one can later expand on even further, rather than rectify them. Postmodern society offers no *catharsis* and lacks a narrative of how the capitalist tragedy is to be brought to an end. Capitalism quite simply lacks an *exit strategy*. Liberal democracy's dilemma is not primarily that it is based on obsolete individualism – liberalism is individualism's political ideology *par excellence* – but rather that it is based on the myth of *the invisible hand's mystical self-regulation*. But such a hand does not exist, an unregulated market always moves towards sundry variants of corrupt monopolies or oligopolies as their terminuses. The invisible hand cannot do anything itself to stop this; that can only be done by visible hands. Pragmatism defeats liberalism every day of the week in actual politics. Contingent disruptive technologies, when such emerge, and an innovative regulation of the market are, in the long term, much more important and healthier than any invisible hand.

The most persistent myth is that, with the right external measures, the economy can attain a constant – and for all the involved parties' optimum – *equilibrium*. But long-lasting equilibria are unattainable in information-complex systems such as meteorology, ecology and economics. Every time an equilibrium seems to have been reached, one or more agents within the system will introduce a speculative behaviour with the purpose of exploiting the suddenly arisen stability, which thereby is destroyed. Game-theory models of an equilibrium never cope with a rendezvous with reality in the form of experimental tests. Sooner or later, a speculation bubble always arises somewhere in the economy, fuelled by both investors who believe themselves to be smart enough to be able to bail out before the bubble bursts – and who try to make pure speculation profits from the bubble, fully conscious that it is in fact a bubble – and by investors who naively believe that just this particular bubble will behave differently from previous bubbles – not seldom prompted by venerated governors of central banks who sincerely assert precisely this: that this time it is not a question of a bubble at all – and who therefore keep their investments in the conviction that it is safe and will grow. Precisely here, in speculation's rational irrationality, lies the problem. There are to be sure good reasons to fuel bubbles since it is possible to earn large sums of money from them if one only sells one's shares in time. And the longer the speculation bubble is kept alive through media hype as well as artificially cheap credit, the larger it will become, and the harder and more devastating the final and inevitable crash will be.

The American economist Hyman Minsky describes these processes with great accuracy. As the first relationalist economist, he turns to *network dynamics* in order to find an answer to how bubbles should be managed. Minsky's answer is that speculation bubbles *de facto* cannot be or even should be avoided. His advice is rather that many small bubbles that burst often are better to have than just a few that burst seldom but then all the more dramatically and devastatingly. Naturally the dream of an economic equilibrium is yet another variant of the same old Platonist death worship that constantly recurs in the worlds of philosophy, physics and social science. However, the truth is that the economy is also a network-dynamical phenomenon that must be regarded not just as relativist, but relationalist. And it is at the transition from relativism to relationalism that the economy starts to include ecology and all the other factors that sooner or later will influence and interact with everything else of value within the economy. *Relationalist economics* does not preclude anything that influences dividual or social value creation, particularly factors such as clean air, clean water and the sustainable management of nature's resources.

There is seldom or never any social change without *articulation*. Under capitalism, the new literate nation state replaces the old illiterate Church as the common arena, and the statist articulation says that *society is a body*. But the body metaphor – which statism obviously borrows from the ecclesiastical articulation that says that *the congregation is a body* – must be exposed. For society as a body never generates any narrative for increased cohesiveness, as Michel Foucault points out, but instead functions as *a latent threat to the deviant person* in the nation state. It is perfectly possible to be an individual, but it is only acceptable to be exactly the individual who maximises her own frustration, alienation and consumption, and who pays for all this by maximising her production for the capitalist power structure, moreover in the shadow of the prevailing phantasmic behavioural imperative: *Whatever you do, blend in!*

Syntheism's *community*, on the other hand, is open and therefore radically different from the concept of the society. It encourages the creation of living narratives, which the syntheist community can gather around; narratives that bring together many disparate groups and create a powerful hegemonisation. This hegemonisation is the articulation of a common vision for disparate groups and identities. The name of a community is of central value, and the name must include, rather than exclude *the outsider*. For it is only with the outsider inside the community's walls that *the particular* can give life to *the universal* and the universal can give life to *the syntheist utopia*. It is to the outsider that the syntheist agent reaches out on the free and open Internet, and it is together with the outsider that the syntheist agent can save the planet from ecological apocalypse. Only thus. It is in the communication and cooperation between outsiders that the Internet displays its historically completely unique potential. On the Internet, we can demonstrate to each other in action that we believe in the same thing and in this way build rock-solid trust, which opens up completely undreamt of possibilities for us to play new, complex non-zero-sum games with in fact outsiders. When push comes to shove, the free and open Internet is a brilliant deification of *Syntheos*, the created God. The logical conclusion is therefore a given: *What happens if the Internet is God?* We decide the answer together.

Syntheism as a radicalisation of atheism – and its dialectical dissolution

Syntheism is the third wave – or if one so wishes the second coming – in a series of culturally radical epochs that starts with the *Renaissance* as the first wave from the 14th century onwards, followed by *Romanticism* as the second wave from the end of the 18th century onwards. The Renaissance is confronted by the *Enlightenment*, after which one can view Romanticism as partly a defence of the Renaissance. Romanticism is then confronted by *Modernism*, after which syntheism, according to the same argument, comes to the defence of Romanticism. Syntheism is thus in some respects a rebirth of both the Renaissance and Romanticism. What unites these three culturally radical epochs is their common quest for a basic *framework* vis-à-vis existence. They put more faith in *intuitive reason* than in *logical rationality*, and they prioritise *the will to mobilism* over a *striving for totalism*.

This historical kinship with the Renaissance and Romanticism should not however be misconstrued as syntheism preferring opacity and musings over logic and precision – quite the opposite. To begin with, syntheism is of course a *scientistic pragmatism*. It even regards the scientific exercise *per se* as a holy act (one of the Syntheist Movement's first known manoeuvres was to declare the research facility CERN in Switzerland sacred ground). Or to express the matter syntheologically: *To do science is to play hide-and-seek with God.* However, all verbal and literary statements and standpoints throughout history must be treated sceptically based on a *fallibilism* where every statement, no matter how convincingly it is considered to be proven at any particular point in time, remains always open for revision in the future. This is also the essence of science and the only attitude that is productive: a constant re-evaluation and modification of accepted explanatory models. What was true yesterday may be an obvious delusion today, which becomes clear when new facts are on the table. Fallibilism is the pragmatist conviction that even innumerable verifications of a certain standpoint are no guarantee that a future falsification is impossible. As a consequence of this, it is not a given that previously accepted knowledge takes precedence over culture when the two seem to collide. One must namely keep in mind that culture lies deeper in Man than knowledge. We express this by saying that culture embraces knowledge, while knowledge is completely dependent on culture.

The foundation for this *transrationalism* – the conviction that rationality only functions within those areas where it is possible, and that critical thinking must be fully conscious of and discount this limitation in its world view – is laid with the Renaissance and Romanticism to then be consummated with syntheism. This means that syntheism's connection to its previous sister epochs is *cultural* rather than epistemological. In addition, there is a strongly pragmatist connection: We humans are our actions just as much as we are our thoughts. To be a syntheist is to act based on one's richest knowledge of the state of existence, but it is above all to always dare to act, and then draw valuable conclusions from this truth as an act. Or to personify syntheist activism: its heart does not get its nourishment from

Jean-Jacques Rousseau's *rationalist idealism*, but from Friedrich Nietzsche's *Romantic pragmatism*. We act with an open, contingent and indeterministic future as the backdrop; a backdrop that we can know a lot about, but never everything, before we act. And in this situation, we honestly have no more reliable resource to use than *intuitive reason*, the ideal of the Renaissance and Romanticism.

The problem with both the Enlightenment and Modernism is their common overconfidence in their own scientific and artistic potential. The near-autistic conventionality in both their logical and their aesthetic premises – always this love of mathematics, minimalism and formalism – lead to both an overconfidence in their own rationality and, sooner or later (which as we know applies to all kinds of Platonism), to a *totalitarianism* and an overconfidence in (seemingly logical) *authorities*. With a belief in there being only one eternal truth about our complex existence, and that this truth is attainable for the rationally reasoning person, it is horribly likely for someone to feel called upon to invoke this truth and appoint himself its guardian and interpreter. Dictators consequently tend to have a predilection for invoking the Enlightenment and/or Modernism in particular as the raison d'être for their own positions of power. While sound pragmatic scepticism, that is, *empiricism*, comes from Romanticism's reaction against the Enlightenment, from David Hume via Hegel to Nietzsche – it is hardly the Enlightenment's own product. And if there was a need for intelligent Romanticism in order to parry inflated Enlightenment in the 19th century, there remains the same need at the transition from statist Modernism to globalist syntheism in our time.

When nation states construct heavy barriers along their borders and waste enormous sums of money on gigantic, impregnable and corrupt intelligence bureaucracies – with the stated or implicit aim that *the free and open Internet* must be brought to nothing –

this is done with the rationalist arguments and concomitant demands for silence and obedience of the Enlightenment and Modernism. But it is once again a logic grounded in a blind paranoia and not in any scientific approach (the logic is occasionally dazzling, it is just that the foundation poor). The similarity with the axiomatic self-glorification of the Enlightenment and Modernism is striking. The only decent reply is syntheism's requirement of a global opening of borders and free communication without either state or corporatist control and supervision: *the libertarian truth as an act par excellence*. Not because this response is a *logically rational reaction*, but because it is in fact an *intuitively Romantic action*; it is the only possible way out of suffocating alienation to the living religion. The dialectical transition from paralysing *atheism* to revitalising *syntheism* of course runs in parallel with this phase shift. Atheism's hopeless dilemma is that it is the child of the Enlightenment and Modernism and, just like its parents, unaware of its own built-in, paralysing limitations. Syntheism is a radical response that also resolves this dilemma.

There are people who admit that they *believe*, and there are people that insist that they do not believe in anything at all, but that they definitely *know* and base all their decision-making on this knowing about which they are sure beyond all doubt. The problem for those that claim to *know* is that they seldom or never doubt their own existence, in spite of neuroscience teaching us that *the ego is an illusion*, generated by the brain in order to economise with precious resources and make sense of existence from a composed and artificial but functionally integrated perspective. What takes place within those who know with such certainty is evidently not at all as certain as the knowing itself would have us believe. And without the one, the other of course falls down. This position is called *epistemological naivism*. The truth is that all people, whether they admit it or not, by necessity are *believers*. Stubbornly maintaining the fictitious ego is in no way intellectually more honest than, for example, maintaining the existence of a god or a Santa Claus, but something that is taken out of thin air to exactly the same degree, regardless of how much (in this case unreasonable) intuition the believer invokes.

The same thing of course applies to *the network*, informationalism's fundamental metaphysical idea, which does not either exist in any physical sense. The concept does not acquire weight as a consequence of any tangibly physical existence, but as the node that connects the dominant memes of the moment together into a cohesive world view, where this cohesive world view then in turn subsequently accords the node its weight. Naturally this *social relationalism* is analogous with how phenomena in relationalist physics acquire weight from the network in question and not the other way around. Without a fictive but nonetheless highly functional node such as God, the ego or the network, the world view does not hang together. And if the world view does not hang together, nothing in existence acquires any meaning or context. Thus we must first of all believe and act in accordance with this faith of ours in order to then be able to know, in exactly the same way that within physics we must first of all weave together a network in order to then be able to give its nodes substance. *Relations generate the substance and not the other way around.* And even the most fanatical atheists are thus true believers. They just think that they are not.

By reason of this, the existentially necessary *metaphysics* seems rather to be disengaged from the *physics* that is every bit as inevitable. Without thereby succumbing to any kind of dualism, even in a monist world we are reduced to this *duality*, but it is our human senses and their phenomenological information processing that compels this, not some external, ontological property of existence. This means that there is *a transrational wisdom* in this metaphysical madness. To put it plainly, it is actually impossible to think ourselves past the ego experience. A world without subjects is a logical impossibility, since however illusory or artificial the ego is in the equation of life, the ego remains the basis for the entire existential experience. It is simply necessary for Man to be a pathological creature, to so to speak consciously fool himself, in order to be able to achieve the existential experience at all. And when we finally do choose to accept the ego that we have just revealed to be an illusory trick, we also get access to all the dazzling metaphysics. We believe consciously against our better judgement, and this we do wisely.

It quite simply does not matter that we know that Atheos is just the name of the void. We still perceive a substance behind *the name* Atheos, it is quite simply how we are programmed to perceive our environment, and moreover this substance is extraordinarily productive and functional for our senses. Towards the end of the 18th century, Johann Wolfgang von Goethe, the great German classicist, argues that it is part of the nature of the subject to maintain an *obscurity* for itself. The subject must experience itself as incredibly small when it is brought face to face with *the immensity* of existence. And it is precisely this terrifying insignificance in the face of the immensity of existence that generates precisely the psychotic *compensatory reaction* within the young subject which is subsequently its engine throughout life, its *constitutional lie,* as Slavoj Zizek expresses the matter. So if anyone manages to capture the syntheist credo of the subject's relation to the surrounding world, it is Goethe. *Atheos lives, thrives and produces subjectivity in this obscurity.*

This means that the ensuing intellectualisation of the preceding emotional experience of necessity must be constructed from an illusion. In fact, there must always be *something there* inside the actual experience; something that is, in the experience, that which d*e facto* experiences that it experiences it. And, according to an intuitive reasoning that follows closely on the heels of Descartes, this something is *the ego*. Thus, it is quite reasonable to ask ourselves why people today are afraid of, uncomfortable with, or become quite frankly embarrassed by talking about the idea of *God*, when they should be every bit as afraid of, or uncomfortable with, or embarrassed by talking about the ego and its existence. Consequently, syntheism also entails a successful resuscitation attempt on the newly pronounced dead ego; it lives on, redefined, and proves useful on the same terms as apply to the idea of God.

Syntheism takes the logic connected to the subject's pathological origin to its utmost limit. For if it is a pathological necessity for us to consider ourselves as subjects in order to be able to understand ourselves as *agents*, we must also admit our pathological need to establish phenomenal objects in existence in relation to this subjectivity – our respective subjects as fellow humans are of course each other's objects to start with – and the optimal object has of course historically speaking always been *God*. There is thus nothing wrong with or even particularly remarkable about talking about God as an actual phenomenon; not as long as we regard God as a borrowed illusion in the existential equation in the same way and with the same importance as we talk about the ego. *God is neither more nor less than the name of the empty backdrop against which the equally empty ego constructs its more or less functional fantasy world filled with fabricated meaning.* This is ultimately the way in which we create meaning: we invent it, we create fictions around which we weave meaningful stories, which then form the basis for all human values. There is thus no deeper human activity than *play*. Even the best science is based on a playful attitude to the mysteries of existence rather than some kind of strict logic. Here we return to transrationalism: *Logic follows strictly on from play, not the other way around.*

When we say that *the network is informationalism's fundamental metaphysical idea*, this means in fact that we are theologising God's most recent reincarnation in the form of the network. We are saying that *the Internet is God.* And when a sufficient number of people adhere to this view it becomes a fact: a truth. It was in precisely this way that the 18th century Enlightenment philosophers turned *the individual into God.* Neither more nor less. Syntheism quite simply addresses itself to conscious believers who have understood *the conditions of the existential theatre* and who want to live affirming and complete lives within this credible *and* intellectually honest framework. We may then, in the best democratic spirit, leave those of our fellow humans who do not understand or do not want to understand the beauty in this project to their superstition, free in peace and quiet to spend their time consuming entertainment and empty enjoyment from the broad and varied offering that is directed precisely at the consumtarian masses. Syntheism is *not*, nor can it ever be, a religion that forces anyone to do anything. And quite honestly this is connected to the fact that this sort of thought control is almost impossible to administrate in *the informationalist plurarchy.*

Regardless of whether we introduce divinities or not in syntheist metaphysics, the actual process is finally about taking advantage of metaphysics' unique opportunity to imagine existence to its utmost limit. To convert metaphysics into theology, *to think about God,* is thus not a matter of some kind of shallow fantasising about an Old Testament father figure who sits above the clouds and observes his children playing on the face of the Earth with tender or irascible eyes. Instead, theologising metaphysics is thinking one's way forth to the outermost horizon of the time in which one is living and based on the knowledge and spiritual experiences that one has access to. And then not merely in a physical sense, with God as the concept for the beginning, middle and end of the Universe – in that case we might just as well settle for classical *pantheism* and not need to develop its completion *syntheism* – but even more so with God as the name of the surface on which to project the meaning and purpose of everything. In that sense, the concept of *God* is fundamentally not just *the Universe*

(Pantheos), but also *the utopia* (Syntheos), the imagined backdrop located in the future – a backdrop that nourishes all of humanity's dreams and aspirations.

Syntheism is radical and evolved atheism, a philosophical concept that captures the inexhaustible and unattainable in existence that philosophy and theology sooner or later must confront. Not least theology, since traditionally utopianism belongs in the world of theology rather than philosophy. More often than not it has been a matter of a longed-for reconstruction of a lost paradise. *Syntheology* thus takes theology back from its dull life among the traditional religions and gives it a renewed relevance historically. By leaving its traditional hermeneutic search for a meaning that is *externally* produced in advance, theology instead gains the central role as the intellectual engine for Man's *internal* production of credible and functional utopias. For it can no longer pretend to be occupied with silent and inaccessible gods that do not exist. But theology can aid in building longed-for and credible gods centred in, for example, physics, psychoanalysis and utopianism. Syntheology forces theology to give up its historical fondness for *transcendence* to instead give structure to the new and growing religious *immanence*. Classical theology shifts over to syntheology, and when all is said and done, syntheology is a *utopology*. The question of whether any particular god exists or not syntheologically speaking is completely irrelevant. Such a question of course assumes that we are intimately acquainted with some kind of god who does not exist anyway nor has ever existed, and beforehand at that. The correctly posed syntheological question is instead which god might come to exist, and the answer to this question is always synonymous with the core of the vision that is driving the paradigm in question. The syntheological response runs as follows: *Tell me your utopia, and I will tell you what god you are seeking and following.*

Syntheism is about deriving and describing new and more relevant explanatory models for existence. This means that it regards the sciences as very much a *theological exercise* – while the syntheist *religion* serves as a collective term for the emotionally engaged, social practices that follow from this search. God is the name of the engine behind *utopianism*, which drives human creativity and adventurousness. This means that if, for some prejudiced reason, we are to deny ourselves the option of including the idea of God in our equations, it also means that we deprive ourselves of the option of producing utopias. We castrate utopianism for no reason whatsoever. Without utopias, no visions, and without visions, no hope. For what reason should we accept such a meagre *atheist asceticism*?

This question brings us to the dramatic difference between classical atheism and syntheism. We repeat time after time in our work the dialectical necessity – personally as well as socially and historically – of removing oneself from traditional religion *via the atheist baptism of fire* in order to only then be able to arrive at *the syntheist position*. Syntheism is thus not a reaction against atheism, but instead its logical conclusion, its historical and intellectual deepening (the philosophical concept of *radical atheism* as it is used by the philosopher Martin Hägglund among others is synonymous with *syntheism*). Syntheism is eternally grateful to atheism for a cultural act of cleansing that was as grandiose as it was necessary. But classical atheism has an obvious weakness, and it is not particularly surprising that it is from this very vulnerability that the syntheist impulse arises. Atheism is of course reactive in nature and a pure negation; it has no content in itself, and at the full extent of its creativity it can only represent one of the four basic concepts within syntheology, namely *Atheos*. But that is all there is.

Philosophically, classical atheism lacks a logical conclusion and fears instead its necessary extinction; the point where atheism becomes so strongly radical that, in the best spirit of fallibilism, it can finally leave the arena to give way to syntheism. And while the rumblings that herald the syntheist revolution grows stronger, a considerable proportion of atheism's militant proponents hide away in an ill-considered, conceptually confused and blind contempt for religion; a kind of autoimmune defensive reaction against its own flagrant meaninglessness. The reason for this behaviour hides behind classical atheism's Achilles heel: atheism in itself lacks an understanding of Man's highly justified *sense of wonder at existence*. It does not see that Man only exists as a being in the midst of a world from which she gets her substance. It does not understand that the psychological tension in the relation between Man and the world is existentially fundamental. Thus, classical atheism has no qualifications for being anything other than *a temporary springboard between two religious paradigms*.

When classical atheism is placed alongside holistic syntheism, the latter suddenly stands out as a conservative, autistic perpetual loop that has got stuck and just repeats phrases that are increasingly pointless. While syntheism represents what Nietzsche calls and celebrates as *the Dionysian drive*, atheism gets stuck in its retrospective opposite, *the Apollonian drive*. This is not to say that the Apollonian drive is illegitimate: it is no more illegitimate than the left hemisphere (if we once again allow ourselves to borrow metaphorically the human cerebral hemispheres' apparent peculiarities). But it cannot act unimpeded without a fatal imbalance arising. Atheos must be placed in relation to *Entheos, Pantheos* and above all *Syntheos*. The Apollonian drive that Atheos displays in isolation must be made subservient to the Dionysian drive in the other parts of the syntheological pyramid. In the same way that the eternalising left cerebral hemisphere, which divides up and freezes events in separate fragments, must interact with the mobilising right cerebral hemisphere and its holistic perspective in order for the human being's self-image and world view to be complete.

In spite of the fact that all metaphysics begins, revolves around and ends with Man's wonder at existence – or if you prefer:

nature's own wonder, embodied by and in Man, at itself – this constantly recurring complexity of emotions remains a mystery to many militant atheists. They stubbornly cling to their own, fragile, subjective experiences – many somewhat fetchingly refer to themselves as *humanists*, as if they themselves were able to serve God's utopian purpose with their pious belief in reason – without understanding that all subjective experiences, even their own, merely consist of *emotions*. Which is not the worst thing in this world, but this fact must be acknowledged and analysed. The relevant response is of course to ask how emotions could have become a historical problem for such an emotional being as Man. They are after all as genuine and real as any other physical phenomena. And they are indisputably inevitable. So why not instead capitulate to these emotions, in order to later investigate what great exploits such an acceptance can inspire?

While the atheists stay with their positions and protest against all other illusions than their own, to which they are blind, while they ironically enough wonder why nobody wants to engage emotionally in their noble cause – except with a limited but intense envy directed at something one lacks and never believes oneself capable of achieving, namely *a living faith* – the affirmative post-atheist syntheists decide *to engage and integrate emotional life directly into their world view*. By moving through four concepts rather than just one; by leaving the categorical cold in *Atheos* and letting in the emotional warmth of *Entheos* in the appreciation of *Pantheos*, a formidable religious experience springs to life. It is this indisputably *religious emotion*, this strong mystical experience, that sets the syntheist agent in motion towards the utopia, towards the syntheological pyramid's consummation, since the experience generates a desire to make the impossible possible. Here the desire to create *Syntheos* is awakened. Or to express the matter poetically: *Syntheism is the light that lets itself be sensed at the end of atheism's dark tunnel.* Sooner or later we are confronted by the enormity of existence.

To start with, there are enormous distances between us and the things that surround us in everyday life on the one hand; and the smallest components of existence – the vibrating, geometrically multidimensional figures that bind together to form space, time, vacuum and matter – on the other hand. But there are also enormous distances between the small things that surround us and the gigantic multitudes of galaxies in cosmology, the enormous, vibrating voids between them, not to mention the infinite number of possible universes besides our own in a fully conceivable multiverse. The result is the syntheists' fundamental appreciation of the immensity, intensity and productivity of existence, the theological conviction that the syntheist philosopher Robert Corrington – in his radical reading of the father of pragmatism Charles Sanders Peirce in his book *A Semiotic Theory of Theology and Philosophy* – calls *ecstatic naturalism*.

Between these extremes we find people in alternating states of confusion and wonder where everything, including ourselves, exists in *ecstatic intensities*. What classical atheism does not seem to understand is that it is precisely in this existential confusion and wonder that religion has its origin, not in any quasi-scientific, more or less lame logic. Religion comes out of mysticism's handling of the immensity of existence, and that immensity has neither shrunk physically nor become any less fantastic as a result of the last century's overwhelming scientific advances – from quantum physics to cosmology. *Logically, we ought to be considerably more religious now than ever before.* The miracle of *reality* is constantly becoming ever more fascinating. From our wonder at the immensity of existence (*Pantheos*) we continue to our wonder at our fellow human being's difference in relation to ourselves (*Entheos*) and to reconnection between people as an empathic collective (*Syntheos*). For where the Universe meets us with indifference, we meet the potential for love in our fellow humans. It is when we build further from pantheism to syntheism that love comes into the picture. By definition love cannot expect love in return as a condition. Then it is not love, but merely internarcissistic manipulation (what follows from this manipulation is then the individualistic idea that *the other* is to be conquered and owned as a kind of colonised possession).

The romantic elevation of a single other human being to *the only other*, followed by a shutting out of the rest of the world as if it were hierarchically inferior to this only other is bizarre enough. That this deification is then mistaken for love is even more absurd. But if nothing else, the dark underbelly of this symbiosis-seeking manipulation is revealed by its ethical consequences. What characterises *authentic ethics* is namely that it is merely carried out, without a single iota of calculating ulterior motive, as an identity-reflecting truth as an act. Only then does the action become ethical: if not, the act can only be regarded as a cynical manipulation, a banal attempt to harness another person's body and mind for short-sighted, egotistical purposes. Authentic love may indeed be an emotion, but the ethics that it must be based on are considerably more robust; it is a love that does not wait and see, that actually and most profoundly defies death. Syntheologically we express this by saying that love reveals itself in *Entheos* with its sights set on *Syntheos*, as a truth as an act originating in *Atheos*, carried out in *Pantheos*. But in order to understand how this complicated process works in practice, we must divide love into several dialectical steps.

In Ancient Greece, three different concepts of love are used: metaphysical love (*agape*), erotic love (*eros*) and friendship love (*philia*). The definitive test for love is *attraction to the radically other*, and this can only arise as *agape*. In this way, the three loves form not just a triangle but also an inclined plane, sloping from *agape* down towards the pair *philia* and *eros*. In the 17th century, Baruch Spinoza added a fourth concept of love: *amor dei intellectualis*, the intellectual love of God, a love sprung from an intellectual conviction and recognition of the actual conditions of things, above all in relation to his monist universe where *God and Nature* are two names for one and the same thing, *Deus sive Natura*. Spinoza's *amor dei intellectualis* is first and foremost a radical act of will, which makes it *truth as an act par excellence*. For he maintains that the ethically desired attraction to the radically other does not start with the emotions we normally associate with love, but as a logically and cogently performed act of duty.

An authentic attraction must be about loving the radically other passionately without hopes of any love whatsoever in return. Otherwise it is not a case of authentic attraction, but merely a case of hypocritical and banal bartering which we call *internarcissism*. This explains why Spinoza argues that *amor dei intellectualis* must come first, before *agape*, *philia* and *eros*, quite simply so that authentic love can gain a foothold at all in the Greek inclined triangle. Syntheologically, Spinoza's idea of the fundamental value of intellectual love has the consequence that neither the empty subject (*Atheos*) nor existence on the whole (*Pantheos*) leaves room for any emotional opinion of them; instead these are to be loved without reservation, since they can neither be added nor dropped. All of life's other experiences are then based on Atheos and Pantheos, including everything else that is loved, hated or in any way at all related to emotionally. *Amor dei intellectualis* is this dutiful, logically cogent and fundamental attraction. An authentic *agape*, an authentic *eros* and an authentic *philia* with their strong emotions can only arise as a consequence of *amor dei intellectualis* first offering a necessary platform. Syntheologically, we express this as we must first submit to Atheos, in order to subsequently be able to abandon ourselves to Pantheos and Entheos on the way to the ethical objective, the authentic love of the radically other, where *Syntheos* arises.

Spinoza's concept *amor dei intellectualis* is a predecessor to Nietzsche's complementary term *amor fati*, which was coined 200 years later. It is enough to add *duration* to Spinoza's love which is dependent on logical dutifulness to the *Universe* in order to get Nietzsche's love which is dependent on logical dutifulness to *fate*. In both cases it is about the same attraction as a truth as an act, where the identity-reflecting decision precedes the emotion. Syntheologically of course we place the universe-fixated Spinoza with *Pantheos* and the time-fixated Nietzsche with *Entheos*. That Nietzsche adds the arrow of time to the ethical equation results in *amor dei intellectualis* and *agape* being merged as the basis for *amor fati*. His own world view is of course based on the Abrahamic God's death, and since it also heralds the death of the individual, the Nietzschean *übermensch* ends up in a deadlock where everything in history up until now must be loved – both dutifully and without reservation – since no external salvation or other mental relief whatsoever exists. This means that an accepting attitude is not enough: Nietzsche unreasonably maintains that in fact *a transcendent love* is required for a possible reconciliation with fate. Since the love of fate is logically deduced, a necessity for the ethical substance rather than some kind of freely chosen emotion, only metaphysical love, *agape*, is suitable for this task. Fate arises and must be loved as truth as an act where the events are fixed in history. Therefore we place *amor fati* in the oscillation between Pantheos and Entheos in the syntheological pyramid.

The most intimate of relations remind us that everything essential in life starts with two and not one. One is nothing: the attraction always starts with two. And as the definitive truth event, attraction is in focus for mysticism. Zoroaster already understood and talked of this already with his concept *asha* in ancient Iran, followed by Heraclitus, who consummates the idea with his concept *anchibasie* in ancient Greece. Interestingly enough, both concepts are ambiguous: they can be translated as both *to be present* and *to be close to being* (not to be confused with late capitalism's obsession with all kinds of pseudo-Buddhist *mindfulness*). Because two is the minimum in syntheist ontology – nothing can ever be just a one, other than *the One*, the Universe as a whole itself – a closer association with the object cannot either be a point of departure for the ontology. Instead this must be based on the actual relation between at least two, from the existential being in the division between them. Thereby *asha* and *anchibasie*, brilliantly, have not just ontological and epistemological but also ethical consequences. To live, understand and act correctly is to constantly remain as close to the states *asha* or *anchibasie* as possible.

This is abundantly clear to the protosyntheists Zoroaster, Heraclitus and their Chinese counterpart Lao Tzu as early as a few thousand years before their devoted successors Nietzsche and Heidegger complete their thinking. And as for Heidegger, he of course constructs his entire *ethics of presence* from *anchibasie* – this concept is the very key to his existentialist objective, *Gelassenheit*, or spiritual liberation. For syntheism *asha* and *anchibasie* are not just inspiring concepts from the infancy of philosophy but also the basis for its *existentialism*. The search for closeness to the truth and the will to presence in the truth's inner division – caused by its constant oscillation and the impossibility of ever being eternalised outside the fantasy world of Man – means that the core of syntheistic mysticism already existed with Zoroaster and Heraclitus. *Asha* and *anchibasie* are not just the fundamentals of syntheist onto-epistemology – we cannot in any way make use of the dialectic between eternalism and mobilism without assuming them – but are also the ethical substance in syntheist mysticism.

We arrive at *asha* and *anchibasie* at the same moment that we let their meaning pass from *being-external observing* to *being-internal participation*. From this point of departure in syntheist mysticism, of necessity we land in fact in *relationalist ethics*. No other philosopher either before or after Heraclitus – with the possible exception of its predecessor and source of inspiration Zoroaster – has been so close to defining metaphysical truth with such precision. For it is precisely in its intense closeness to the truth event – rather than in some kind of absorption into the event – that the metaphysical truth is manifested, in its constantly failing yet necessary attempt to unite the *at least two* at the core of the ontology. We express this by saying that through all the thousands and thousands of truths we constantly produce, we find *the primordial eternalisation* as the defining truth as an act for our existential substance, as the primal act for us as creative *truth machines*.

The consequence of this is that, if we try to avoid *asha* or *anchibasie* as an onto-epistemological foundation, it becomes necessary to deny all forms of motion at all. This means that all motion without exception must be regarded as illusory. Parmenides is the Greek philosopher who draws this logically necessary conclusion, and with Parmenides the revolt against Heraclitus' pioneering, counter-intuitive, but nevertheless logical insights is born. Parmenides' ambition is fulfilled by the physicists Isaac Newton and Albert Einstein when they create a world view where all motion is illusory in a Platonist *block universe*, where the various forms of laws and determinism in a frozen space–time precede everything else. The problem is however that mathematics does not precede physics. Existence is not primarily mathematical (ideal) and secondarily physical (actual), as Plato claims. It is merely physical. We quite simply do not live in some form of Einsteinian block universe, however tidy this might look on the drawing board; we live *de facto* in a considerably more complicated Bohrian *network universe*.

Mathematics is actually just advanced, idealistic addition. If you take something and then add something else to this thing, all in all the whole obviously expands. It becomes something more. From this unavoidable fact, the first mathematicians draw the conclusion that 1 plus 1 might possibly be 2, and then go on to build the entire science of mathematics from this axiomatic assumption. The problem is however that this line of reasoning only works in theory, which means that it is only applicable to mathematics itself. And why is that? *Because in nature the second 1 is never identical to the first 1.* In nature there are never two absolutely identical objects to symmetrically add or exchange for each other. Nature is not only *analogue* but also fundamentally *asymmetrical* in all directions. There are never two of anything at all – phenomena in existence not only have fluid boundaries but are also completely unique, which has the consequence that all our generalisations, however epistemologically necessary they might be, can never be more exact than arbitrary approximations. Syntheologically we express this as Entheos being ontologically in the same class with Atheos and Pantheos – or to express the matter more poetically: *two is the first sum for the fundamental difference within the One,* and it is in the capacity of this scientific axiom that *multiplicity is the foundation of ontology.*

Thereafter we only have to reverse the addition to get *subtraction*, the temporarily negative addition – neither more nor less. In the next step, we build further with *multiplication* and *division* as shortcuts to increasingly complex additions and subtractions. And so on, and so forth. But we never leave eternalism within mathematics, which of course ultimately is *applied eternalism par excellence.* Mobilist existence outside mathematical construction does not take any notice of this however; it is not the least bit more mathematical than it is eternalist. All such things are merely illusory conceptions that are nourished by our inadequate albeit functional aids for navigating the turmoil of existence. It is important to note here that mathematics does not distinguish itself from physics as some kind of latter-day *emergence* – no such suddenly arisen mystical degree of complexity is needed – rather, this separation actually occurs right at the same moment that mathematics starts to come into use at all. The structured fantasy sets off in one direction, the chaotic reality in another. We live in a radically relationalist universe – not in a mathematical one. We must not follow the autistic Plato and mistake mathematics' tempting simplifications and fancy symmetries for endlessly complex reality *per se*. Mathematics is merely our eternalised way of trying to understand a mobilist environment that constantly evades our descriptions of it, and at the end of the day this must also apply to mathematical formulas *per se*, which become tangible within Georg Cantor's transfinite mathematics. According to the British philosopher and mathematician Bertrand Russell, one of Whitehead's most prominent disciples, Cantor succeeds in creating *a science of infinity*. Syntheism can only agree and if nothing else say thank you for the inspiring metaphors.

According to relationalism, as the Swedish philosopher of religion Matz Hammarström claims, an intra-acting interdependence between Man and his environment always prevails. Or to put the matter phenomenologically: there is no real boundary between Man's *near-world* and his *surrounding world*. All phenomena that Man is confronted with already include himself ontologically. Then even epistemology, and ultimately also ethics, must submit to this fact. Knowledge of one's surrounding world cannot be attained without the human being herself being an integral part of the object of this knowledge, the relationalist phenomenon, whose participation must be constantly discounted in every eternalised calculation. It is here that Plato and his mathematics depart radically from mobilist thinking. For Plato, the duality that mathematics offers is a fundamental given for ontology, but existence contains no such dualities outside the world of mathematics. Phenomena can be *diachronic* in relation to each other, but that in itself does not mean that they are *dual*, which mathematics beguiles us to believe. Two phenomena can arise concurrently or in the same area, but never both at the same time. And conversely: if two things occur either at different points in time or in different places, they are thereby automatically always different phenomena.

Heraclitus is the first person in history who seriously both realises and formulates this. His universe is vertical and sees *context* as primary. Parmenides responds with a universe that is horizontal and sees *sequences* as primary. It is not the degree of truth of these statements themselves that determines which of these branches dominates the philosophical arena, but how well they match and adapt to the prevailing power structures. It is thus nothing other than the usefulness of Parmenides' world view to the feudalist and capitalist elites that gives it its dominant status, right up until Whitehead's and Bohr's *relationalism* arrives when, after all this time, Heraclitus is proven right – at least for the time being. The Enlightenment's three celebrated civilisational mainstays – *the individual, the atom* and *capital* – and the primordial forms of Kant's subject and object, have their roots with Parmenides. At the same time as the network-dynamical revolution pulls the rug out from under the feet of *individualism and atomism* as well as *capitalism*, and thereby from Parmenides' entire legacy.

Syntheism embraces an *ethics of survival* as a counterweight to *immortality's moralism*, which is characteristic of the dualist philosophies' outlooks on life. The Platonist obsession with immortality and perfection attests to its hostility vis-à-vis existence and life, a phobia of change that at its deepest level is a death worship. From syntheism's Nietzschean perspective, Plato and his dualist heirs therefore stand out as the prophets of the death wish. Syntheism instead celebrates the eternalisation of the decisive moment, the manifestation of *the One* in the irreducible multiplicity, as *the infinite now*. All values and valuations must then be based on *the infinite now* as the event horizon. Eternity in time and infinity in space are not extensions of some kind in Platonist space–time of some kind, but poetically titled compact concentrations of passionate *presence*, as Heideggerian-inspired nodes in Corrington's *ecstatic naturalism*. Eternity in time and infinity in space can only meet in *the infinite now*, in temporality's minimised freezing, rather than in some kind of maximised extension. We are thus not eternal creatures because we are immortal, but because *we can think and experience eternity* as a logical as well as an emotional representation of the infinite, focused to the current moment.

Which in turn means that *the syntheist transcendence* is localised inside rather than outside the immanence.

Love and mysticism in *the infinite now* constitute the very nucleus of *the ethics of survival*. Here, an alternative to all forms of moralism based on the preconceived state of things appears. That valuations that are loosely founded in the state of things being able to motivate a kind of "the future should be more of the same as now" as an ethical beacon, is not something that has any logical robustness. That nature appears to act in a certain way in a certain given situation of course does not mean that Man must have nature's mechanisms as an ethical beacon. While *amor fati* is a dutiful love to the closed past, the imperative does not include the open future; rather, it implies a contradictory encouragement to break with everything that has been, that is, *to expand rather than minimise the spatio-temporal multiplicity*, as the arch-Nietzschean Gilles Deleuze would express the matter. Thus to act ethically is at least as often about violating nature, *participating in and driving the cultural and civilisational process*, as it is about following it. Nature is not any kind of Abrahamic god and neither is truth an ethical guiding principle.

Even relationalist philosophers can fall into the trap of wanting to convert Nature's behaviour into precisely such an ethical beacon. In his *Nihil Unbound,* Ray Brassier depicts a kind of fascinating Freudian cosmology with the Universe as an entropic giant, dazzled and on his way towards his own extinction – what he calls *an organon of extinction.* Brassier's point of departure is that culture has done everything it can to eschew *the trauma of extinction.* His ambition is instead to construct meaning based on the inevitable *annihilation* of existence. This Brassier does by attacking both the phenomenological and the hermeneutic branches of Continental philosophy, but also Deleuzian vitalism, which he argues tries to inject all sorts of meaning into existence, as a kind of failed and fundamentally ineffective invocation against the trauma of extinction. Brassier instead bases his ideas on thinkers such as Alain Badiou, François Laruelle, Paul Churchland and Thomas Metzinger when he makes his appeal for his radical *ultranihilism*. He points out that the Universe comes out of nothing (syntheism's *Atheos*), and his idea of the organon of extinction as a philosophical point of departure – the fact that life can only be experienced against the backdrop of its own inevitable annihilation – according to Brassier is also the condition for thinking existing at all. Syntheologically, we express this by saying that he regards *Pantheos* and *Entheos* as merely subordinated aspects of the thoroughly dominating *Atheos*, where any form of *Syntheos* is nowhere to be seen at all.

Brassier's dramatic achievements are that he attacks Kantian correlationism based on the assumption that thinking does not exist in relation to being, as Kant claims, but *in relation to non-being*. Only there does the possibility open up for a philosophical way forward, and it is relationalist. But even if his cosmology were to be physically correct – syntheist physicists such as Lee Smolin and Roger Penrose definitely do not agree with him – this does not entail that conscious people themselves need to behave as repetitive organons of some kind, replete with naked death drives (even if the elder Jacques Lacan toys with the same idea). Expressed in a Lacanian manner, Brassier thus constructs a kind of *theology of the subconscious* as an ethical guiding principle, but he attaches it to the same shaky place as 19th century socio-biologists did – when they lay the foundations for, among other things, 20th century Nazism – namely in the masochistic will *to submit to, follow and amplify nature* in exactly the same way that, on scientifically extremely shaky grounds, it is already assumed to be.

The syntheist response to Brassier's radical nihilism is of course that it gets stuck half way in syntheist dialectics, in a kind of *permanent masochistic enjoyment under Atheos*, without completing the pyramidal thought movement via Pantheos to *the affirmative oscillation* between Entheos and Syntheos, where the four corners of the syntheological pyramid are radically equal. Brassier's role model Nietzsche of course never based his affirmative nihilism in his otherwise beautifully failed concept of *the will to power*. Nietzsche's affirmativeness can instead only be achieved through a fully conscious *existential act of truth*, where the act produces the truth, which in turn produces the *Übermensch*. There is thus considerably more of Nietzsche's postnihilist affirmativeness in his role model Badiou's existentialism than Brassier seems to understand. It is also therefore that Brassier's otherwise impressive nihilist reasoning – except that it is based on a probably incorrect although particularly interesting reading of modern cosmology – lands only half way in syntheist dialectics.

But if nature does not actively provide us as passive receivers with any valuations whatsoever, a possible future extinction of the Universe does not do so either, since the annihilation most definitely also is part of the nature that, according to Brassier, is silent. Syntheism is therefore based on an even more radical nihilism than that of Brassier, since its emptiness is even deeper and above all lacks Brassier's wishful-thinking foothold along one of Atheos' slippery verges. Within syntheology *per se*, the existential experience – regardless of whether it has the trauma of extinction as a backdrop or not – offers no possible values. The insight that reaches us when we take atheism to its utmost limit is instead that valuations really must be created *strictly ex nihilo*. This is *radical atheism*, the dialectical turning point where the fully reasoned nihilism, as a notorious extinguisher of all historical values and valuations, is converted into *affirmative syntheism*.

Instead of Brassier's organon of extinction, syntheist ethics is based on Zoroaster's classic axiom: Man's ethical substance is his thoughts, his words and his actions, and in precisely that order. It is only on the basis of a radical identity creation that ethics finds its mark. And what is this ethical principle founded on if not self-love's being or non-being? Only the creature who loves herself as she is, from a crassly logical and ethical acceptance of herself, rather than based on any kind of sentimental and unreliable emotional passion, can act in an ethically correct way. And then *survival* is the ethical beacon, based on *the principle of maximisation of existential pleasure* – most clearly manifested in the religious ecstatic state that syntheologists call *the infinite now* – rather than any kind of premature mimicking of an alleged future universal annihilation.

Nietzsche, the father of European nihilism, interestingly enough goes in the opposite direction compared to Brassier and instead argues for an ethics based on resistance to nature's doings. He pits culture against nature and finds the heart of the *übermensch* in a kind of *aesthetics of resistance* – but not without first confronting Man with his deep animalistic nature – an ethical turnaround that is investigated and applied to perfection by his French successor Georges Bataille among others who, with his extensive *atheological project* in the 1950s in turn is one of Lacan's and obviously also syntheism's foremost sources of inspiration. According to Nietzsche and Bataille, it is precisely by opposing the natural – by surviving rather than conforming – that Man gets his own ethical substance. So if the Universe really is on the road to a final death and extinction, a Nietzschean response to this state of affairs might be to defend *survival* against extinction as a norm through every thought, every word, every act. Thereby Nietzsche with his wealth of tragic heroes is *the ethicist of survival par excellence*. He pits *the principle of maximisation of existential pleasure* against Brassier's ambition to speed up and put into effect *the death-wishing masochism of the subconscious*.

Brassier's philosophy is indeed firmly anchored in syntheology's cornerstones Atheos, Entheos and Pantheos (what he misses is the affirmative launching to Syntheos). He is right in saying that this nihilist fundament must be understood as a great historical achievement, a kind of collective intellectual maturation, and not as a regrettable spiritual emergency. But since Brassier's world is nothing but sublime physics – and he does not, in contrast to Alain Badiou for example, take into consideration Man's ability to create *the truth through an act* – he also opens the way for the counter-question of whether his own nihilism means the end of history. And there Brassier has no unequivocal answer. His Freudian cosmology is not even verified within physics. It is sufficient – in the manner of Niels Bohr – to regard *time as physics' real constant,* in an indeterministic rather than deterministic universe, in order for Brassier's drawn-out apocalypse to collapse.

What syntheology adds to Brassier's ultranihilism is that it draws lines from the base constructed around the three basic concepts, up towards the top of the syntheological pyramid. Thereby it adds Man's emotions and creativity to the world view; and it ironically enough includes Brassier's own highly libidinous philosophising *per se,* whose driving force Brassier can never explain based on his limited atheological model. It is about emotions and creativity that a seemingly depressed or malicious Brassier does not experience or attempts to ignore. *Syntheos* is Man's highly conscious creation of God, her sense of wonder and confidence vis-à-vis the fundamental triangle of the syntheological pyramid, which she builds on with a *logical faith.* It is about Man's vision of a new and different future, *the utopia,* in relation to her present existential situation, and is constructed on top of her established knowledge of the fundamental nature of existence.

Brassier does in fact understand *the trauma of extinction,* but he is evidently wrestling with *the shock of affirmation* which follows from the insight of one's own mortality. Therefore *Nihil Unbound* gets stuck in the category *protosyntheism*. This otherwise so impressive philosophical work, this consummate *atheology*, remains at a standstill in one of the three bottom corners in the syntheological pyramid, unable to rise towards the top. Brassier claims, which is entirely reasonable, that Atheos is the Universe's own formidable engine, but he has not started the engine himself nor allowed himself be carried away by the journey within the syntheological pyramid. And the explanation is, as is so often the case concerning philosophical fallacies, psychological. In his quest to stand outside the relationalist universe as a neutral observer, Brassier misses the point that such a psychological alienation for the philosopher is just as impossible as the corresponding physiological alienation for the physicist. Brassier's inadequacy is that he lacks *the oceanic feeling*, which is the reward for a genuinely participatory philosophy. Consequently *the spiritual work of syntheists* strives to attain and then maintain this *oceanity*.

The utopia is the God called *Syntheos*, and the core of Syntheos is the existential experience of ego-dissolution and uniting with *the One*, the unit of existence. Here syntheism leaves classical philosophy and steps into the world of theology. For the step from an illusory existential dividuality to a considerably more credible existential oceanity requires that one leaves *philosophy* as a transcendental totalism in order to proceed to *theology* as immanent mobilism. Therefore Brassier's role model François Laruelle describes the speculative totalism of Hegel as the pinnacle of the history of philosophy, since totalism – which Hegel first completes and then also turns around dialectically – at its core is *the essence of the philosophical exercise*. If this is the case, mobilist thinking must use theology as a weapon in order to change the course of philosophy away from its fixation on extinction. Since it evidently requires a theological dialectical reversal to reintroduce Man's emotions as the decisive factor – or syntheologically expressed: Syntheos must be added to the metaphysical triangle Atheos–Entheos-Pantheos – mobilist thinking must claim that *theology is deeper than philosophy*. Thereby syntheology can begin to act as the necessary metamorphosis that saves philosophy from totalism's wearisome and destructive death wish.

Mobilist thinking has always factored in the emotions of beings; totalist thinking is instead based on a picture of beings as frozen objects. It is only when we consider Man as a disengaged external observer of existence, Kant's fantasy, or as a disengaged isolated near-world without an authentic relationship to the surrounding world, Hegel's fantasy, that we can accept that totalism displays any intellectual honesty whatsoever. On the other hand, for example Heidegger's and Ludwig Wittgenstein's emotionally motivated and theological search for *an engaged presence* requires a correct overall picture of Man's lifeworld, syntheology's saving and concluding addition. Through the addition of Syntheos the syntheological pyramid is *humanised*. Only in this way can philosophy save its integrity from Laruelle's anti-philosophical attacks and win a separate role from the otherwise all-embracing physics. Thanks to the constantly emotionally engaged human being's actual presence, both in the world and in philosophy, syntheology's last step is historically necessary. Oceanity is not just a wonderfully liberating feeling, a sweeping emotional experience, it is also the necessary antithesis of cynical isolationism, the necessary logical antithesis of individualism, the only way for thinking to dissolve and once and for all leave the philosophical prison of the dishonest Cartesian theatre.

Heidegger attempts to change transcendence from within. He argues that transcendence acquires a new, credible role if it can be understood as an internal human *activity* and not as an external separate domain that Man tries to achieve and conquer, that is, as a *transcendental psychology* rather than a Kantian phenomenology. Heidegger's search can be compared with *the dialectics between eternalism and mobilism* (see *The Global Empire*). Without eternalism, perception would end up in a complete *psychosis*. While without mobilism we would end up in an equally complete *neurosis*, since everything would then be transformed into a single gigantic, incalculable mess without any distinction or limitation whatsoever. Eternalism is the expression of transcendence, mobilism is the expression of immanence, in a Heideggerian sense. And both are just as necessary, and moreover in a dialectical relationship to each other, in order for Man to be able to construct a functional world view to be *de facto* present in.

Eternalism distinguishes itself from totalism inasmuch as it does not adduce any kind of ontological status or pretend to be primary and external in relation to mobilist reality. Instead it is strictly *phenomenological*. The father of pragmatism Peirce emphasises mobilism's primary ontological status precisely by calling it *firstness*; consequently he confers a status on eternalism denoted as *secondness* and in closing refers to the dialectic between them (that is, when phenomenology returns to mobilism after a digression via eternalism) as *thirdness*. Thus as *secondness*, eternalism has no Platonist ambitions at all. It instead apprehends itself as a brilliant, perceptive response to the massive semiotic flow from an immanent and contingent universe (Peirce is not very surprisingly also the father of *semiotics*). Eternalism is thereby very much in fact a transcendence as an activity, exactly what Heidegger would like to see, and as such it manages all of totalism's hobbyhorses excellently without totalism being able to sneak in the back door and once again try to attack mobilist ontology.

The original dividuation arises through an organic contraction. We can call this condition *primitive subjectivity*, in contrast to the organism's primitive objectification of its environment. From primitive subjectivity, the organisms later develop into the thinking and feeling human being of our time with his language and his consciousness. The ideas are dialectical in nature, the intensities are aesthetic in nature. The existential experience is best described as an oscillation between these two poles. The more eternalist the syntheist agent is, the more mobilist the phenomenon becomes, and vice versa. The subject is produced by the perception in order to give the semiotic flow its context and meaning. But if the subject were not there, if it were not produced, both we ourselves and existence would remain irreducible multiplicities piled on top of each other without context or meaning. But without any form of *personification*, no unit arises. Without personification, a chaos can never be understood as a cosmos. Whether one later, like the classical mystics, claims that God ought to remain nameless in order to maintain God's illusory personification, or as the syntheists say that the illusoriness should be affirmed openly, so that personifications can be infinitely produced as long as they are creatively and explanatorily motivated – syntheology starts with four, deeply rooted in the history of metaphysics – is rather a matter of preference. However the syntheists are happy to let this issue be decided in a future comparison of *the creative effect* of these positions. Up until then, the transrationalist question to the believer is: What standpoint do you choose to identify with and follow as your *truth as an act* in particular?

For it is Man's emotional engagement that is needed in philosophy and theology, not his internarcissistic and anthropocentric projections on his environment. But neither the void, *Atheos*, nor nature, *Pantheos*, offers us any safe haven. We do relate to and allow ourselves to be fascinated by the void and nature, but we do not on that account have to follow their contingent whims at all. We can only create our religious home together with other dedicated believers through an affirmative cultural expression rather than through an ingratiating imitation of nature. For life is not a long drawn-out destructive death; life is instead *a passionate, creative dying*. Only through its mortality can the subject, Atheos, be experienced in its fundamental, creative emptiness. To live is therefore to live in the direction of death and the subject is that within the agent that is constantly dying. Life is a becoming: only death supplies the being. Syntheologically, we express this by saying that *only through dying can God become God for God's self.* By reconnecting Man to this historical origin, this meta-theological fundamental prerequisite, syntheism brings Man back to his rightful place in existence, and in the safest possible company, surrounded by his own most beautiful invention: *the created and therefore by definition mortal God's religion.*

Truth as an act
– the road to the fourth singularity

Rational thinking perceives intuition as *magic*. That which seemingly functions intuitively is regarded by rationality as something magical and fundamentally incomprehensible. Since religion respects and is partly based on intuition, religion cannot either be regarded as anything other than magic by narrowly limited rationality. Rationalism's standard accusation against *transrationalism* is therefore to dismiss it as a bag of magical tricks – or quite simply as pure superstition. But what was magic yesterday is technological reality today. It is sufficient to study the four epoch-making information-technology paradigm shifts in history in order to conclude that this is the case. So while it is cynical to wish, on the other hand longing is a utopian act. And seen historically, longing for the utopia that today appears magically unrealistic is more of an expression of highly sensible forward planning.

If *spoken language* constituted the first dimension in the complex universe of language, *written language* must have appeared as pure magic when it gained a foothold as the second dimension and in a heartbeat enabled the building of the first civilisations and empires in history. And it is exactly thus – as (dangerous) magic – that

Plato portrays writing in the dialogue *Faidros*. It is sufficient to imagine how impressive the first agricultural temples must have appeared in comparison with nomadism's unassuming, temporary earthen floors for rain dancing which preceded them. With the arrival of the printing press, humanity entered the third *mass medial* dimension in the universe of language. Now it was accessibility – written texts suddenly became much cheaper – and the speed of the production of text that impressed to such a degree that the entire activity suddenly shone with a magical glow.

What was previously unattainable for almost everybody – the precious and sacred text with its information, knowledge, wisdom and magical narrative – was suddenly within reach of anyone who made the effort to learn to read, which before the printing press had been fairly pointless, since all laboriously hand-copied text manuscripts were unattainable for all except society's richest and most privileged. Thus, in their capacity as readers and writers, people also quickly became accessible to each other to an extent never before seen. Thereby the general public was also widened to an unparalleled extent, and suddenly there was a considerably greater collective than the tribe or the village community – namely *the nation* – which provided the collective identity.

The *Internet* is of course the fourth dimension in the universe of language. If we had asked someone a hundred years ago how that person would perceive a world where billions of people and trillions of machines are intimately, communicatively, entangled with each other at every moment, constantly communicating, this fourth dimension of language would hardly have been called anything other than magic. The Internet has such dramatic consequences and thereby entails such a radical revolution that we must also regard this phenomenon as a fourth dimension in relation to three-dimensional physical space. Global geography is being rocked to its foundations because of the radically truncated distances on the planet – this applies both to human and mechanical players – that the Internet entails. And every time this magic appears, it means that a new hope is born. It does not require any unrealistic superfluity of historical insight to understand the human need for utopias. For without utopias, there are of course no visions, no ideals in common to strive for; and without visions there is of course no hope, at least not in the form of any concrete formulation that can constitute an objective for how society should be organised. To *long for the utopia* is therefore not to wish for the impossible; it is rather to understand the importance of *thinking the magical*, that which today seems completely impossible, as something that is tomorrow's most necessary, beautiful and actually most reasonable possibility. So what then does *the road to the utopia* look like?

In relationalist physics *emergences* play a central role. Emergences appear when a more simple system for some reason or other attains a higher degree of complexity to such a great extent that it changes shape and transforms into a completely new phenomenon with completely new properties. An example might be that biology is regarded as an emergent phenomenon in relation to chemistry, in the same way that chemistry in turn is an emergent phenomenon in relation to physics. And if emergences play a central role within the sciences, there is no fundamental reason to exclude the possibility that the metaphysical equivalent to these emergences could play as important a role in social theories. There is thus good reason to regard the metaphysical *event* as the social equivalent to the physical *emergence*.

Relativist metaphysics attacks the classical idea of truth. There is nothing strange about that. Throughout history we see time after time how yesterday's established truth is phased out to be replaced by a new and soon equally established, alternative truth. The intensity in this process increases when the new elite takes over a society in conjunction with a paradigm shift and prioritises completely different ideals from those of the displaced elite. Relativist philosophers such as Friedrich Nietzsche and Michael Foucault confront these historical shifts with a pragmatist attitude to truth production: truths are produced first and foremost by the prevailing power structure for the purpose of confirming and consolidating the power of the powerful. Nor is there anything strange in that; the opposite would be extremely remarkable. A truth can only become and remain a truth as long as it stays within the sociocultural paradigm that is embraced by society, which means that various and conflicting truths are pitted against each other during every transitional phase. The truths are therefore always relative. They should and must be able to endure constant criticism. When they no longer hold their own against this criticism in the light of new information, they must be phased out and replaced.

However, *relationalist metaphysics* takes this Nietzschean and Foucauldian critical thinking about truth production one step further. Quite simply, according to relationalism, relativism does not go far enough in its criticism of an antiquated and useless idea of truth. A new *metatruth* is required for the Internet age. It is correct that the prevailing power structure strives to produce the truth that confirms and solidifies its position. But regardless of this, a new truth may have a higher informational content and a stronger empirical demonstrability than an old one, that is, aside from its greater relevance and usability for a new power structure. According to this view, it may thus climb higher in a hierarchy of produced truth and *de facto* be closer to an imagined, but in fact in terms of its formulation, inaccessible reality well-founded in physically indisputable facts, by constituting an *emergence* in relation to the old version of truth.

A new, emergent version of truth is born out of the old truth, but takes the whole issue to a completely new level, and at this higher level the new version of truth has a whole new acceptance and all new consequences for the collective world view compared with the truth that was previously generally embraced. The new truth is *intersubjectively* rather than objectively *truer* than the old one, both nominally and relatively. For example, when from a contemporary perspective we dissect capitalism's and industrialism's writing of history and dismiss the idea that the events that transpired in Paris during a few years after the initial shot that was fired in 1789 really constituted a *revolution* in any interesting sense, and instead classify it as *a symptom of a real revolution* that had taken place long before – where the actual revolution we are then referring to obviously is that the printing press starts to produce reading material that is accessible to the general public in Germany in the mid-15th century – it means that we upgrade the printing press to a predecessor of the Internet revolution of our own age, where the genesis of the Internet is *the emergent phenomenon that compels us to rewrite all of history* in order for us to understand both ourselves and the events that have created us in an intersubjectively deeper way than was previously possible.

Through this new, information-technology writing of history, we receive not just a more relevant and more power-generating world view for the burgeoning netocracy – thus far a relativist historian would agree – but we also receive, through the Internet's status as an historical *emergence*, also a *de facto* truer, and from an intersubjective perspective more realistic, view of history as such. The emergence quite simply helps us to see *a greater depth in the past* that has previously evaded us, as Hegel would express the matter. And the emergence changes the historical playing field once and for all, not just directly in contemporary time and in the future, but even indirectly, projected onto the past. For this reason an emergence is not just a completely new phenomenon that appears in conjunction with a higher degree of complexity in the underlying structure. An emergence is also a truer phenomenon than the preceding phenomena further down in the hierarchy to the extent that the emergence *per se* enables a deeper understanding of the hierarchy as a whole.

This applies to social emergences just as much as physical emergences. Biology brings something new to *chemistry as such*, which in turn brings something new to *physics as such*. In the same way that the Internet brings something new to the mass media from precisely a mass medial perspective, which in turn adds something to written language as such. How could the *potentialities* of physics or written language be apparent to us today without their subsequent and amplifying historical actualisations? This becomes even clearer when one brings into the argument the fact that there are no laws that make these emergences necessary in advance in our contingent universe. As Hegel very correctly points out, the actualisations only appear as necessary afterwards for us constant rewriters of history. The reason for this is that the emergences – in contrast to, for example, the phase transitions in physics – are not preprogrammed within the phenomena that are located in the hierarchy's lower tier. *The emergences are completely contingent phenomena.* They thus arise *ex nihilo* at a certain, arbitrary moment, without, as is the case with the phase transitions, having been built into the lower tiers from the start.

Since relationalism drives the new physics, it is hardly surprising that the metaphysics of the Internet age – from Jacques Derrida and Gilles Deleuze via Alain Badiou to Slavoj Zizek – revolves around and is driven by the notion of the emergent event. Interactivity produces a class structure with *the netocracy* as the upper class and the *consumtariat* as the lower class. While the consumtariat is relatively uniform – consumtarians are of course defined by what they are not rather than what they actually are – the netocracy can be divided into three distinct categories. The first of these is the netocratic *pioneers*; the second category is the netocratic *aspirationists* who copy the pioneers at an early stage and successfully, and if possible milk an even greater surplus value out of their creativity than the pioneers do: *imitation* is the mother of survival. The third category of netocrats is the *experimentalists*, who, while they initially fail in copying the pioneers and who are rather too late to copy the aspirationists, for precisely this reason they are forced to and subsequently succeed in inventing their own original solutions, which motivate their position within the netocracy. The consumtarians meanwhile have their plate full passively chewing the nonsensical content, the calming and soporific *entertainment* that is produced in various trashy networks with no status whatsoever.

The individual was constructed by the Enlightenment philosophers in the 18th century, both to give the growing bourgeoisie a new human ideal – there has scarcely been any stronger individual than the 19th century Napoleonic industrialist – and to get the literate workers in capitalism's factories and the nation states' armies to obey orders and work hard without being able to complain about or protest against the state of things. Therefore the gospel of progress was connected to faith in the individual. *The progress mythology* is the conviction that as a reward for their toil every generation of workers and civil servants will be better off than the previous generation, thanks to the increased productivity that bestows an increased affluence on the entire national community, which quite simply points towards the workers' offspring one day, in a distant future beyond the horizon, at last being fully-fledged individuals.

But when the individual no longer functions in a society built on networks, the Internet age's netocracy seeks a new human ideal. One does this while the consumtariat also desperately seeks a new potential identity other than the tragic state of being *the last individual.* The new, attentionalist human ideal that appears is the *dividual,* the divisible rather than indivisible Man (see *The Body Machines*), a body experiencing pleasure, involved in constant networking with all interesting humans and machines in its surroundings. The dividual is a protean creature, powerfully coloured by *schizoid creativity.* If we study the netocratic categories more closely, we see how the concepts *dividual* and *event* interact in a clear quest to capture and strengthen the new attentionalist human ideal.

The netocratic pioneers build and lead the netocratic networks. In contrast to capitalist leadership, they lead from below and not from above. This means that they work purposefully with liberating the joy and creativity of other netocrats, and when this happens the event arises as confirmation and reward, for and within the network. The copying aspirationists follow the pioneers' templates and set up the networks that in turn raise the status of the pioneers' networks in the network pyramid as a whole. The Internetified physical world is already full of these obvious spinoffs, from the *TEDx conferences* (small-scale versions of the TED conferences in California and Canada) to *regional burns* (small-scale versions of the participatory Burning Man festival in Nevada), and then these various examples are nothing at all in comparison with the powerful network pyramids that are growing online with *the Syntheist Movement* – who are already practising what we are building a theory about in this book – as a striking example.

But the netocracy would not be the formidable power elite of the Internet age if it did not concurrently comprise the third category: the experimentalists who fail to, or for various reasons quite simply neglect to, copy the netocratic leaders and therefore find their own ways towards attentional success. These netocrats build a dividuality which is so attractive for the established networks that these seek out and incorporate them in their agendas rather than the other way around, and it is in the meeting between these headstrong *outliers* and the most potent networks that new events arise all the time. There is thus a third possibility outside the seemingly cynical or busily copying strategies to become part of the netocracy, and it goes via *pure creativity*, exposed vis-à-vis the networks as *an eventist dividuality*. But the third category, the experimentalists, must not be mistaken for an expression or an updated variety of the discarded *individuality*. Because in the network society individuality no longer has any value at all. It is merely offensive, and it is only when the dividual is connected with the netocracy that the dividual gets her agential value. *It is the network that gives the agent her value in the relationalist society and not the other way around.*

An *event* is a spectacular occurrence, a *revolution* is a spectacular event, and a *singularity* is a spectacular revolution. Events of various importance take place several times per year, genuine revolutions only once or twice per millennium. Singularities are easily counted, from an anthropocentric perspective we can only be said to have gone through three singularities: the commencement of the Universe, the genesis of life and the birth of consciousness. The question is whether we can imagine such a fourth singularity. For syntheism however the answer is clear. *The fourth singularity must be God's entry into history.* For whatever it is that would be able to match the weight of the emergent genesis of existence, of life and of consciousness earlier in history, for the people of today it must have the same weight as if God suddenly appeared. *Whatever it is that is hiding beyond the fourth dimension, its right and only name is God.* Thereby the interesting question is what the arrival of God might be and what forms it might assume.

The French philosopher Alain Badiou, one of Jacques Lacan's most well-known successors, starting with his work *Being and Event*, constructs a complete philosophical system based on the informationalist *event* as the deepest *truth* about Man's existence. The biological, mental, and social structures that characterise Man are empirically verifiable *generalities*, and as such are of course contingent. The truths we produce and know of are dependent on this contingency, which summarises them all. Being is not everything to Man, as the totalist philosophers imagine. Thinking can very well be constructed with its starting point in *ontology's constant inconsistency* instead of using the fictive being as the basis. However, Badiou argues that *the universal is independent on the contingency.* Every singularity in itself consists of an infinitely internal chaos, but through the singularity's internalisation of this chaos, a kind of encircling stability is created around the chaos which makes the universal's identity possible. From a geometric perspective, we can express this by saying that it is the stable ring around what is transient and chaotic that is the actual singularity; a stable universe around chaotic matter, a stable life around a chaotic biology, a stable consciousness around a chaotic hodgepodge of thoughts, followed by God as a kind of stable ring around a chaotic future.

Badiou assumes that thinking is universality's true element. In the same way that the event arises as a result of the circumstances that prevail where it materialises – not in the capacity of *the event per se* – the universal stands above and free from the chaotic contingency. A truth is derived from the set of circumstances under which it is produced – regardless of whether these circumstances are social, psychological, or cognitive – but only the truth that satisfies Badiou's specific criteria for *an authentic truth* can be regarded as a universal. It is here that Badiou uses the concept *singularity.* The authentic truth is characterised by the fact that it is in fact a singularity; it cannot in itself be subordinated to any particular previous particularity, group or identity. And it arises through an act, through an *intervention,* which establishes a subject/object relation within a specific, larger phenomenon. Waves become particles, chaos becomes cosmos, mobility is eternalised, and so on. Thereby a genuine truth can be established, after which there is no way back whatsoever.

A central theological idea for Badiou is *that the singular in the universal has no name.* Badiou therefore calls this truth substance *the unnamable.* It is thus the unnamable at the innermost core of truth that makes it *axiomatic*. The unnamable for Badiou is of course merely another name for the fundamental syntheological concept of *Atheos*. Badiou argues that there can be no love or loyalty towards anything unless this love and loyalty first *goes via Atheos as its productive engine*. Only by devoting oneself to the void as precisely a void can truth be produced and set in motion. Even if Badiou calls Atheos the unnamable, it is not about a destructive but rather a highly productive void. This contrasts with how Slavoj Zizek, another prominent Lacanian, describes Atheos as *the excremental remainder* that is the subject's and thereby the truth's foundation. Zizek may by all means ascribe whatever attributes he wishes to Atheos; at any rate this attribution says more about the philosopher's emotional fetishes than about the actual nature of Atheos. But the fact remains: the effect of Atheos – and it is the effect and not the character that is interesting – is an enormous productivity, both in the external world of physics and in Man's internal world.

According to Badiou *every universal is born in an event*, an event that is impossible to predict in advance, and which therefore first of all occurs in *the subconscious*. Furthermore, a universal is characterised by being based on a sudden decision, where it gives value to something that was worthless before the decision. The universal creates meaning; it implies an ethical approach, and thereby also a specific course of action from all those who are involved in its genesis. The universal can, at least initially, only have one meaning for those most closely involved. The universal is a *univocality*. It gets its value from an unswerving loyalty to the consequences of its truth – not through long, drawn-out interpretation of its meaning. This means that Badiou is strongly critical of post-structuralism's obsession with *interpretation*, which has received enthusiastic support within the academic world. He despises *the postmodern paralysation*, which he traces to what we call *the hyperhermeneutic condition*.

The academic establishment's *monopoly on critical thinking* – which is already regrettable in itself, since it effectively shuts out life-giving impulses from outside – has placed thinking in a vicious circle of interpretations of interpretations: a collective, somnambulist movement towards *a vegetative passivity* without any critical questioning whatsoever or any social activism directed towards *the statist-corporatist complex* that controls late capitalist society as a whole. This relationship is illustrated by *the fact that research is conducted on* old philosophy rather than any new critical thinking being created. The question we must ask ourselves is why, under late capitalism, the academic world should be better at thinking critically – critical of precisely the system that, by definition, it is an integral and moreover fundamental part of – than other old and in the same sense corrupt institutions in history. This would be like us expecting the Catholic Church during the 18th century to create the Enlightenment and kill God. One does not tend to bite the hand that feeds one, at least not deliberately and consistently.

Since an outwardly directed criticism would imperil today's comfortable *status quo* and force undesirable changes, all energy is instead directed inwardly. Research takes over philosophy. And one thing we learn from history is that corrupt, clerical elites in every era have devoted considerable resources to the interpreting of signs and numerology. In the light of this, our age's academic obsession with hermeneutics appears to be completely according to the programme and logical in terms of self-interest. Therefore the new netocratic elite must establish new and independent institutions – filled with knowledgeable and innovative netocratic thinkers or *eternalists* (see *The Netocrats*), without connections to nation states or big capitalist corporations – in order to get informationalist truth production started. This must occur unconditionally outside of the academic world, which cannot very well welcome and promote these new and free institutions without condemning itself.

Here Badiou has an important point: *hermeneutics is the opium of the academic world.* Against the cultural relativist curse of hermeneutics he pits *mathematics* as an opposite pole and as corrective: only through mathematics does he see contact with *the real* as possible; only through mathematics can Man *think being.* Badiou's obsession with the possibilities of mathematics is a direct consequence of the fact that his master Jacques Lacan insists that language must be regarded as an ontological network that can only lie above, and thus both excludes and acts independently of, the real. Where language is based on an eternal stacking of vague abstractions, mathematics is instead concrete and exact. Not least thanks to its enormous accuracy within quantum physics, mathematics has proven its credibility in the role as a bearer of *philosophical realism.* Idea and flow are merged in mathematics; the difference between eternalism and mobilism is prised up, the vision of an eternalism that is more than just a temporary freezing in perception is realised, and a *model-dependent realism* becomes possible.

In his work, Badiou in particular discusses the *theological revolution* that is introduced with *Georg Cantor's transfinite mathematics.* The reason why Cantor's calculations are called transfinite is that with them he proves that a greater cardinality (a measure of the size of a quantity) is always possible. *Mathematics can very well provide a number for the totality, but never totalise the number per se.* Cantor quite simply proves that mathematics is always open, and then, according to Badiou, there is no reason that physics also could be open either. Cantor's transfinite mathematics thereby pulls the rug out from under the totalist tradition within philosophy and theology, and at the same time, it confirms the mobilist tradition's sudden upper hand under informationalism. Zoroaster and Heraclitus all at once appear considerably more contemporary and clear-sighted than Paul and Plato.

The theological consequence of Cantor's transfinite number series is that they confirm and formalise the dogma of negative theology: *God is the nothingness!* Beyond all multiplicities there lies a solid and overwhelming emptiness. And what name does this Badiouian, ontological emptiness go under if not *Atheos*, the engine of the multiplicities and existence within syntheology? Whether one then like Badiou decides to regard Cantor's mathematical revolution as the final proof that the Abrahamic God does not exist, as atheism thought through to its ultimate conclusion; or like Cantor himself one throws *Entheos* into the game and chooses as a point of departure that *the transfinitude in itself is God* – a thought that gets strong support from the American syntheist Leon Niemoczynski for example – in the syntheological, always pragmatist sense, it does not matter at all. What is important, according to both Badiou and Niemoczynski, is to accept and to act based on the ethical decision through *the power from the unnamable,* which is the foundation of and constitutes the decision itself as such. The foundation is always called Atheos, as F W J Schelling would express it.

Badiou defends the mobilist position with the relationalist argument that *the pure multiplicity* must be the ethical starting point. Syntheologically, this means that Badiou converts *the unnamable* into *Pantheos*. The Lithuanian-Jewish philosopher Emmanuel Levinas – another of Cantor's most famous philosophical interpreters, and the one who probably lies closest to Cantor's own persuasion concerning the theological consequences of transfinite mathematics – defends the eternalist position in a radically inverse way with the relativist argument that *the One* must be the starting point. Thereby Levinas chooses to follow the opposite path, seemingly on a direct collision course with Badiou, and converts *Pantheos* into *the unnamable.* And it is precisely here, in the dramatic meeting between Badiou and Levinas on ethics' tautly strung tightrope, that syntheism appears most clearly as *the social theory of everything par excellence.* Since syntheism comprises the entire syntheological pyramid – and therefore understands the origins and supports the pathos of both Badiou and Levinas – it maintains of course that *both alternatives are correct.* The ethical act in this context is to choose any of these alternatives and then *faithfully act in accordance with this decision.*

Never before has the ethical imperative of *the truth as an act* been clearer. What then follows in a Badiouian scenario is that the activism that emanates from *the three unnamable names Atheos, Entheos and Pantheos* builds the stable foundation for *Syntheos*, the formalisation and realisation of the utopia. Since syntheism's mobilist universe is both contingent and indeterministic, obviously Syntheos cannot be realised through the historical objective's mystical, eschatological arrival, in keeping with what Marxism and the Abrahamic religions so imaginatively preach. Syntheos is instead realised through a focused but nomadic, creative activism in a capricious, contingent universe, driven by the hope of the impossible suddenly appearing and being realised as *the fourth singularity* – an idea which is consummated by being *theologised* by Badiou's declared syntheist disciple Quentin Meillassoux. The lesson from both Badiou and Levinas is that life-long devotion to truth as an act is *the innermost existentialist substance of metaphysics.*

The concept *truth as an act* is central in understanding syntheist utopianism's refusal to be either optimistic or pessimistic. It is possible, not to say likely, that the great majority of people will always turn with sparkling eyes towards the charismatic authority up on one stage or another and demand an answer as to whether she is an optimist or pessimist in terms of the future, but even to formulate this question in a reasonable way requires so many nuances and so much clarification that a meaningful reply for mass consumption is impossible to imagine at all. The syntheist who protects her integrity and values a serious discussion about the future naturally declines, in a friendly but firm way, to express an opinion. This is where epistemology is replaced by ethics. It is here that we must refer to *faith* and its possibilities and to reject the demand for certain knowledge.

First of all syntheism assumes that time is real in a contingent universe. This makes all predictions extremely uncertain, at least in the long-term, just like within meteorology or ecology. But there is also a built-in paralysis in the faith in some kind of generally positive or predominantly negative development. Whether the expectations tip this way or that way basically does not matter; merely the fact that the expectations tip in any direction whatsoever weakens *the will to act.* If the driving existentialist principle in syntheist ethics is that *truth is an act* – you are everything if you act, you are nothing if you do not act and are content to react – it has the consequence that if the actor is to maximise his or her opportunities for power and influence, all predictions concerning the future must start from *an absolute neutral position.* The future is not better or worse in any objective sense: meliorism is fundamentally mendacious, the mythology of doom likewise, *the future is merely open*, full stop. It is from this prediction-neutral starting point that the syntheist ethical imperatives can be formulated. *The impossible is possible – if you want to be associated with truth: act!*

Badiou maintains that every universal singularly is open vis-à-vis the future and remains constantly unfinished. It is not concerned with our mortality or general fragility. He sums up universality as *the faithful construction of an infinite, generic multiplicity* where the multiplicity must be primary since *the One* is merely a verbal illusion (that is, *the One is the eternalised fictive par excellence,* if we use a syntheological vocabulary). Multiplicity is merely a linguistic singular; any singular outside the irreducible plurality does not exist. Every universality is exceptional, has its origin in a single emergence, is assembled step by step, is the consequence of an existential decision, generates an ethical subject and is based on a becoming in an active truth and not on any specific knowledge. Badiou argues that philosophy obviously comprises the art of analysing, but above all is *the art of articulating universalities*. The truth event arises, according to him, *ex nihilio*. To begin with, this event is invisible rather than obviously identifiable where and when it occurs. It is not possible to predict or trace based on the circumstances around the situation where it occurs. Instead the truth event gets its status from *the faithful* subsequently, and its general acceptance is determined by the strength and perseverance of the faithful, their *loyalty*. It is quite simply the faithful who must make the event true; it can only get its status as a singularity by means of an *aesthetic retrospectivity*.

The singularity is defined by the fact that it overthrows the prevailing rules of the game, it begins a new era, it sends out a powerful shock wave through the ethical subject, which is changed so radically that we must speak of a kind of *rebirth*. Note that *the truth event is always internal, it occurs from the inside out* rather than from the outside in. It can thus not be forced by some external power that invades the phenomenon in some mysterious way. This means that, for example, military interventions and incoming meteorites are never events in this specific sense. This is where *Badiou's ethical imperative* breaks radically with *Kant's moral imperative*. According to Kant, Man becomes an authentic individual by carrying out his duty. According to Badiou, it is instead a necessity to oppose the external norm, vis-à-vis the accepted duty. *According to Badiou, it is this opposition to the norm and not the fulfilment of duty that is the condition for living subjectivity.* The singularity is a cultural and not a natural phenomenon. Badiou's ethical imperative entails that Man becomes *an authentic dividual* by opposing the prevailing norm and fighting for a new world order with an eye to *the syntheist utopia*.

If the truth is an act that generates an event, the genuine event creates a new truth. The truth event is followed by a decision that is followed by a loyalty vis-à-vis the decision about the truth. Aside from this there is no truth beyond the event. Here Badiou breaks radically with Karl Popper's obsession with *verification* as the guarantor of truth. Badiou argues that verifications take decades to construct and that the proponents of truth wisely enough never wait for the verification before they act on the basis of the truth. He thus defends *an active truth concept* vis-à-vis Popper's extremely reactive truth concept. He then divides up the development of the truth event into four phases which we go through, both as dividual truth actors and as an historical collective.

1. The revelation of the truth event.
2. The denial of the event as the truth.
3. The repression of the event as truth.
4. The resurrection the truth as the event.

But what happens to rationalism's idea of truth as the correct assertion about existence? Like all other forms of *transrationalism* from Hegel onwards, syntheism does not deny that such a deepest truth about existence actually exists. But the enormous complexity in such a deepest truth, and the insufficiency of language and thought when it comes to even getting close to it, makes it unattainable. However not in the Kantian sense – where the noumenal object ends up outside our horizon because the phenomenal object gets in the way – but instead as a considerably more radical consequence of *transfinite mathematics*.

The truth about existence is so deep, so complex, so multifaceted, that it is impossible to reach, since it lies infinitely far from the outermost limit of Man's perception and the power of mankind's imagination (designed by the process of evolution for functional orientation in our environment, not for revealing the truth), on the other side of the border to *psychosis*. This means that quite irrespective of whether Man likes it or not, he is forced to outsource the deepest truth to *theological mysticism*. For what is the concept of God seen at the deepest level, if not the ultimate truth about existence which Man, with his mental limitations, never can reach? We therefore place the deepest truth with *Syntheos*, the God that we create based on the insight into our mental limitations, and we place it in the open-ended future, while at the same time we generate both scientific and existential truths through our actions. *The truth as an act is not just the most important principle within ethics; according to transrationalism it is also the only possible truth within epistemology.*

To philosophise is to metathink, and what Jacques Lacan calls *the real* and what Badiou calls *the unnamable* is philosophy's eternal variability, its own built-in impossibility, its genesis that consistently avoids transitioning into a becoming. Here Badiou stubbornly opposes Gilles Deleuze's process philosophical foundation: where Deleuze in following Spinoza states that multiplicity is identical with *the One*, that multiplicity is *univocal*, Badiou argues that multiplicity is undefinable. He accuses Deleuze of building a lovely constructivism that relies entirely on intuition, while he himself relies only on the stringency of mathematics. Against this Spinozist and Deleuzian *multiplicity of the One* (Entheos through Pantheos) he posits *the multiplicity of emptiness* (Entheos through Atheos), an emptiness that is a non non-being. Only in this ontological equation of multiplicity and emptiness does Badiou see the possibility of correctly reflecting the nature of multiplicity. It is only when *somebody gets the energy from Atheos to formulate the truth* that the truth becomes an event.

We return to syntheism as the social theory of everything, and of course it accommodates both the Deleuzian and the Badiouian variants of *pathos*. Deleuze's entheist multiplicity takes its point of departure in *Pantheos*, while Badiou's entheist multiplicity takes its point of departure in *Atheos*. Deleuze is the pantheological prophet, Badiou is the prophet of atheology, and *entheology* is the oscillation between these two antipoles; a movement that is completed through the addition of *Syntheos* to the syntheological pyramid. In the midst of this earth-shattering oscillation, Deleuze and Badiou, the event's two prophets above all others, are in agreement that what is most important for the syntheist is the decision to enter at least one of the temples that is devoted to either Pantheos or Atheos and engage in its activities, while the ethically reprehensible thing to do is to remain passively outside. Both these temples are needed as foundations. Both these temples fill us with wonder and produce spiritual truth. Deleuze's pantheology moves in the direction of Entheos, Badiou's atheology reaches out towards Syntheos. It is pantheology that makes us appreciate the existential intensity of existence, *to further develop pantheism into entheism*, while it is atheology that drives us to long for the fulfilment of the utopia and which makes us *consummate atheism via its deepening in syntheism.*

In the second part of *the Futurica Trilogy, The Global Empire,* we describe in detail how the perceptive *eternalisation* of the mobilist chaos of existence is necessary in order for us to be able to act, while mobilism is eternalism's always present, demonic shadow. In that sense, ontology is the secondary eternalisation of the primary mobilism, the presentation of the unpresentable as a schematic model, the objectification of the emptiness of the void. This perception transforms the multiplicity into functional *fictives;* models that the mind must be allowed to tinker with in order to be able to mobilise an overview and organise a meaningful and relevant activity at all. Badiou puts the eternalisation of the phenomenon on an equal footing with the mathematisation of existence. Infinity takes precedence over finitude, ontology is the same thing as mathematics. He then continues to the need for *the situation*, Badiou's concept for *the structured presentation of the multiplicity*, a kind of consolidating theatrical performance of sundry fictives. Only in the right situation is *the truth event* possible, argues Badiou. He is inspired here by both St Paul and Vladimir Lenin: for these thinkers, *the timing* is not just a matter of strategic necessity: it also has a significant ethical dimension. Waiting for the right moment for the action faithful to the truth is an important component in Badiou's ethics: *the timing is a central aspect of the loyalty itself.*

So what then is the fundamental event – the event through which all other events are reflected – if not *death*? A longing for *immortality* – even if it is highly present in both Badiou and Meillassoux – is initially nothing other than a longing for *death as death*, in contrast to the will to *survival* as a longing for *life as life*. Only from its finality can anything at all gain a meaning, only through its transience can life be worth living. Without mortality, life and existence lose all intensity. The will to survival therefore oscillates between three poles: first a seeking of existential intensity, thereafter a desire for the prolongation of life in order to maximise this seeking. However, this seeking and this desire can only take place by virtue of the third pole's guarantee of life's indisputable finiteness. This guarantee of obliteration is thus in itself the third pole. In its full extent, eternity in the Abrahamic sense is namely an idea as unbearable as Hell itself, while life in its strongest intensity of the experience of here and now, seen against the backdrop of its transience as *the infinite now* – the syntheist event *par excellence* – is the holiest thing that exists. Thus consciousness always operates on the basis of death as the ultimate guarantor of the very will to life. *To live is to die.* But not at precisely this moment. Later.

Informationalism's obsession with the event – that is, informationalism's *the event* as the equivalent of monotheism's *eternity* and individualism's *progress* as the metaphysical engines that produce the dynamics within each of these paradigms – is driven by a greater fascination in the face of, and an obsession with, death than ever before in history. Regardless of whether we see Man's deepest longing as a quest for *survival* (the driving force behind Pantheos) or as a quest for *immortality* (the driving force behind Atheos), we return to our obsession with death. Death as a concept thus operates constantly in the oscillation between Pantheos and Atheos. But what then does our obsession consist of? What is it that drives Badiou to turn all forms of meaning into a meaning based on a suddenly arisen truth event, which in turn reflects death?

Convention says that death frightens us with all the pain, sorrow, loneliness, powerlessness and mystery with which it is associated. But even if the pain, sorrow and loneliness are factored out, the fascination still remains the same. Thus the powerlessness and mystery remain. In other words, death frightens us by how it reveals our powerlessness and lack of knowledge. It humiliates us all, not least those of us who have had power and social status during our lifetimes. It strips us of *anthropocentric internarcissism*. But death also reveals our existential banality, our entirely non-existent significance for the Universe. And what frightens us most of all is how death reveals our own lack of significance for the divine, that is, for *Pantheos*. At the deepest level, the Christian lie is that each and every one of us means something to God, that we are actually a desirable lot and cherished jewels for a god who thus has nothing better to do than to sit and coddle us and the likes of us (literally) in all eternity, like a dead robot god surrounded by dead rag dolls.

What death then reveals is of course how little we mean, how little we will be missed after our decease, how simply and almost offensively painlessly life goes on without us. And what we feel guilty about at the deepest level is *the lack of guilt when other people die* and disappear for good from our own lives. Life goes on: what else should it do? It is precisely here that death constantly chafes against our existential experience. We can never motivate for ourselves precisely why we should be so interesting and important for Pantheos that Pantheos would need to maintain us after death for Pantheos' own sake. It is not a desire for immortality that drives us; merely a banal fear of death as the definite singularity after which nothing is the same any more. The postponement of this event is *the will to survival*, and this will is formalised through all the other lesser events to which we ascribe a decisive importance during both our own history and the history of all of humanity.

Quentin Meillassoux formulates his radical utopianism in *L'inexistence divine*, a work published in instalments which, at the time of writing, is not yet complete. According to him, the history of the Universe contains three decisive leaps that cannot be understood as any originally built-in *phase transitions* – as totalists from Plato to Einstein imagine them to be – but rather as *contingent emergences* that suddenly appear from nowhere and out of anything, and which radically change existence, without thus having any mysterious qualities at all. Physics does obviously obey certain specific laws in our part of space–time, but *physics per se* does not obey any preordained laws whatsoever – it is instead radically contingent. For example, the Universe as a whole can evidently expand considerably faster than the speed of light, which the existence of *cosmic inflation* proves with abundant clarity. The laws of physics, or rather its *behaviour* or *habits*, can therefore change however and whenever, and without us being consulted about the matter. Otherwise, these behaviours would be compelled to precede the physics that they are deemed to regulate and the natural sciences have never found any support for any such *mystical non-material pre-existence of the laws of nature*. This is quite simply a matter of a somewhat embarrassing logical error, and a projection of this kind of bizarre metalaw of existence means if anything a depressing return to Newton's unfounded assumption of an external creator of the Universe, which this creator thus precedes (which of course constitutes the beginning of an unspeakably tedious and meaningless regression without end: who created the creator, who created the creator of the creator, and so on).

Meillassoux argues that the first singularity is *the genesis of existence per se*, the second singularity occurs at *the genesis of life* and the third singularity occurs at *the genesis of thinking*. He then takes a giant leap into the future and argues that in a contingent world a fourth revolution of the same importance is both possible, likely and above all desirable, and then in true syntheist spirit he casts God in the role of the fourth, and for mankind the final, step. We write in true syntheist spirit, not just because Syntheos is the created God placed in the future, but also because Meillassoux declares that his concept of God is to be understood based on the dogma that *a belief in God's existence does not entail that one believes in God, but that one believes in existence*. There is in Meillassoux, as in all syntheists, no way around or out of *the theological project*. Metaphysics is not a choice, but an absolute necessity that everything else is fundamentally dependent upon.

Meillassoux bases his philosophical system on four concepts: *potentiality, contingency, virtuality* and *chance*. These constitute two spheres of being. At the local level, potentiality is pitted against chance; at the global level virtuality is pitted against contingency. His Syntheos is *justice*, where justice consummates a history that runs via existence, life and thinking as the previous immanent *miracles*. Note that according to Meillassoux, a miracle is to be understood as proof that God does *not* exist. Rather, miracles open up the possibility of the Universe being God – a universe as a god that expresses itself to itself. But as the radical indeterminist that Meillassoux is, he opens the way for the possibility that justice never occurs (a reminder of the neutral position of Badiouian ethics). And above all, Meillassoux claims that justice can never occur *unless it is first desired*. His god is thereby the Marxist god *par excellence*. But it is a contingent Marxist god in an indeterministic world with a wide-open future, a singularity that Karl Marx himself would scarcely have understood.

However, we pose the question of whether the syntheist community shares Meillassoux's dream of the resurrection of the dead before a suddenly existing god whose essence is called *justice* really is the God that we long for, and which thereby can act as a utopian engine for us in our time. Do we ever actually desire something that actually later occurs? Is it not the case that both emergent and contingent phenomena occur only of their own accord – as both Hegel and Nietzsche maintain – and that we only afterwards place them in our value hierarchies? It appears undeniably as considerably more reasonable to speak of the *growth of the Internet* in the late 20th century as *the genesis of a – if only afterwards – desired god*, rather than as any form of justice as a god located in the distant future at the end of a road which in any case is filled with thousands and thousands of other paradigm-shifting events. Meillassoux's future is quite simply neither consistent with his radical contingency, nor sufficiently open to the future to be able to act as an *engine* for syntheist activism. However, it is unarguably a formidable *foundation* on which to build potential utopias.

Meillassoux's British colleague Simon Critchley defines the syntheist faith as a *pure faith* in his syntheist epic *The Faith of The Faithless*. Critchley argues that it is faith *per se* and not its object that is utopianism's innermost essence. He calls his conviction *mystical anarchism*, and this is of course identical with *the theological anarchism* that we formulate in this work. From this position, there is then nothing that stops us from taking one further step; from the pure faith of mystical anarchism to syntheism's *pure religion*, a spirituality in which the religious practice in itself is the innermost essence of the religion. In the spirit of Critchley, the pure religion's basic faith is in the idea that faith itself is necessary in order to make the impossible possible. Creativity runs from *Atheos* via *Pantheos* to *Entheos*, and the name of the enabled impossibility is of course *Syntheos*. Pure faith in a practised form is thus syntheism, the pure religion. As pure religion, religion is alienation's complete opposite and the only available weapon against *the cynical isolationism* in our contemporary world. Critchley's answer to the question of *what must be done* in our time is identical with syntheism's *subtraction* and its ensuing *monastisation*; he has had enough of the classical Left's bloody cultural revolutions – led by malicious and irresponsible tyrants and fanned by pompous and adventure-loving philosophers – who quite apart from wreaking great havoc and destruction, sooner or later are always absorbed by precisely the power structures that they purport to attack, and thereby in the long run actually strengthening rather than weakening them. This occurs since this sort of revolutionary, just like the quantum physics researcher, is internal and not external in relation to the relationalist society within which she acts. Subtraction must therefore always precede the revolution as truth as an act.

Meillassoux's contribution to syntheist thinking is obviously both welcome and exciting. This is true, not least of his concept *hyperchaos*: absolutely everything is contingent. Even the change *per se* is contingent. Existence has no sense. Instead *non-sense* rules. The world does not contradict itself, but operates within a permanent condition of non-sense and constant change in all directions and on all levels. At the same time, a universe that finds itself in hyperchaos might very well be consistent. Hyperchaos does not mean that the Universe must be unstable. Contingency is thus something completely different from just chance. Here Meillassoux, just like Badiou, gets inspiration from Georg Cantor's transfinite mathematics. The laws of physics can be suddenly changed, but as long as they function they are extremely stable. Here both Badiou and Meillassoux open the way for a new *realism*: mathematics can measure physics in such an exact way that we can experience the world around us almost precisely as it is.

Here mathematics distinguishes itself clearly from language, and here there is thus an opening of the door to the noumenal, the door that Kant believes he has closed. However, Meillassoux ends up in a return to the Paulinist dream of merging the Jewish religion with Greek philosophy and its main current, Platonism. This is apparent in his resistance to *the pagan circularity*, which for many syntheists is what drives the connection back to previous monist civilisations before the growth and spread of Abrahamic, dualist monotheism. Meillassoux has a fondness for referring to Paul, while other syntheists find a compact monism within quantum physics on which to build their world view and argue that anything else would be dishonest. When other syntheists welcome God *per se* as Syntheos rather than God as some kind of specific property – God's attribute is for them as secondary as the attributes of a beloved human being – he challenges us with his *God as justice*.

Meillassoux is inspired by both Badiou and Slavoj Zizek, who also build utopian systems around *the event*, informationalism's metaphysical centre. The event is a dramatically altering event that suddenly just happens and then changes the course of history in a decisive manner. Small events occur constantly in the dividual's life or in the local social arena, but the real singularities affect the future of both humanity and the planet for good. Events such as the invention of spoken language, written language, the printing press and the Internet have even generated completely new historical paradigms with new power structures, followed by new metaphysicists who have taken over the world and defeated old paradigms and narratives. Consequently with the advent of informationalism, we are compelled to rewrite all of history into *a history of event*s in order to make it comprehensible and relevant for ourselves and for future generations.

However much Meillassoux, Badiou and Zizek emphasise *the immanent* in their longed-for, utopian events, they all finally end up in a strong and culture-specific *transcendentalisation* of their imagined visions. In the spirit of Kant, the subject is still free from the object and tries to tame the object according to its own limited and above all closed fantasy in relation to the future. For Meillassoux, the utopia is *the arrival of justice* as a future divinity, but exactly what this justice consists of – and how it is related to Man's, until now necessary, focus on survival within a decisive existential experience of finality – this Meillassoux never succeeds in answering. It is therefore sometimes tempting to call him our time's version of *the beautiful soul* in Hegel's sarcastic sense, since Meillassoux likes to use fancy concepts that however lack a clear anchoring in modern Man's immanent reality. Meanwhile Badiou and Zizek mix the boys' room's fascination with war toys and violent video games with a romantic passion for macho tyrants and bloody revolutions, such as the 1960s' student protests in Europe. From this nostalgically coloured hybrid, they squeeze out the event as yet another bloody revolution.

For Zizek, *revolutionism* is even necessary on an ontological level. Just like his role model Lenin, Zizek claims that *revisionism* – the step-by-step transition to the Communist society – is impossible, since every step in the revisionist process salvages too much of what is reprehensible in the pre-revolutionary society, things that only the revolution can wipe out. Therefore the revolution is both desirable and necessary, and therefore, according to Zizek, it is the only authentic event. A radically immanent interpretation of the concept of revolution would however reply that both the bloody demonstrations on the streets and the realisations of a far-off personified justice – to the extent that they take place at all – actually are only marginal expressions among many others of the real, underlying revolution. This revolution is instead always a long drawn-out process, precisely a step-by-step but at the same time non-linear *revision* which starts with a revolutionary change of the material conditions (for example the Internet's emergence as the manifestation of Syntheos), followed by a revolutionary change in social practices (syntheism's high-tech participatory culture), which in turn is followed by a revolutionary change in intersubjective metaphysics (syntheism's subtraction, monastisation and psychedelic practices), which only thereafter can lead to the longed-for social event (the syntheist utopia, the syntheological pyramid's completion), where the power structure hopefully can be adjusted, more or less dramatically, in order to liberate the new paradigm's creative potential.

Badious' and Zizek's hero Hegel would be the first to criticise their bloody boys' room dreams as typical examples of shallow *internarcissism*. For Hegel, history is merely a long metahistory of constant re-writings of history, where an obsessive narrative production is a consistently failing but nonetheless necessary adaptation to an uncontrollable immanent flow. *The revolution* and *the event* must therefore be separated from each other. The revolution occurs in secret and its radicalness can only be attributed to it retroactively. The event assumes its dramatic and transforming consequences only a long time afterwards. As an example we might mention that Johannes Gutenberg invents the printing press around 1450. But the French Revolution was not launched until 1789. So there is a gap of all of 339 years between the immanent and transcendent revolutions in this case. And which of these we build our metaphysics on unfortunately has a decisive significance for where we will later arrive.

The real revolution is of course sparked as early as via the emergent arrival of the printing press, and then goes on until and even past 1789, when it suddenly expresses itself as an event in the bloody uprisings that only later assume the name *the French Revolution*. While it was actually going on, none of the actors were aware that they were participating in the French Revolution; the mythology in question was created and projected onto the events only afterwards, not least by the Russian revolutionaries who needed an event in the past to reflect themselves in, and from which they could derive both splendour and legitimacy, precisely as Hegel claims is always the case. From the perspective of the history of ideas, the choice is here between prioritising either *the immanent revolution* 1450–1789 – let us say with an emphasis on an information-technology writing of history – or else the spectacular event in 1789, which only afterwards is reified into a transcendent event within the capitalist-industrialist discourse with the purpose of turning it into a metaphysical inspiration rather than an immanent, narrated event. Thus it is about a cult of mysticism that old revolutionary romantics such as Badiou and Zizek, along with postmodern French nationalists, are reluctant to abandon.

At any rate, what is essential is that the Parisian street riots would be unthinkable without the printing press that became fully and widely accepted in society only after several transforming centuries. It first changed Europe and then the rest of the world beyond recognition, and the French Revolution's geographical domicile has much more to do with the fact that France was the first country where a majority of the population could read and write than them being extraordinarily innovative or clear-headed. For Badiou and Zizek, it appears necessary to first let the singularity take place, thereafter wait for it to generate a new power structure, only to then wait for a bloody conflict within the new power structure – where the otherwise obese and physically the worse for wear philosophers indeed promise to man the barricades themselves and throw Molotov cocktails at the authorities – only to thereafter be able to speak of a genuine revolution. Hegel would most likely not accept such a static and culture-specific idea of revolution. It was hardly the intention that Paris in 1789 would fix the meaning of the word revolution, which in fact is a metaconcept, for all eternity in the way that the essentially conservative revolutionary romantics Badiou and Zizek assume. That is, with *the revolution as the consistently failing, tragic repetition of the event in Paris in 1789*, moreover always carried out by angry young men with weapons in their hands and oppressed by an authoritarian tyrant whose boots they love to lick.

It seems, ironically enough, as though Badiou's and Zizek's nostalgic notion of revolution suffers from a glaring lack of, precisely, *the revolutionarity*. The syntheists, on the other hand, have their sights set on something much more radical. The singularity is the definitive event according to the criteria we use in this book. And there are already three parallel revolutions in progress – even if Badiou and Zizek with their conservative templates and blinkers appear unable to apprehend them – namely: *The expansion of the Internet, the relationalist paradigm shift within both physics and sociology* and last but not least *the chemical liberation*. The singularity that is our transition from humanity to transhumanity is one of the three revolutions' merging supraevents in a not too distant future. The fourth singularity in history is already waiting in the wings. All we need to do is take Critchley's advice which tells us to first build the syntheist temples and monasteries, where through our subtraction from the surrounding world we can enable the revolution as the truth as an act of our time. *We are ourselves the fourth singularity!*

Participatory culture, religious rituals and psychedelic practices

The sciences demand logical intelligence. The arts demand intuitive intelligence. Philosophy however requires both of these. Therefore philosophy is a narrow discipline as regards production, consumption and talent in general. Philosophical works are understandably not your typical bestsellers. But of course this does not make philosophy any less important. Philosophy heralds the advances that later reach both the sciences and the arts. Without a Nietzsche, there would never be an Einstein or a Picasso either. The time would not be ripe, as they say; there would be no resonance, no receptive environment that makes Einstein precisely an Einstein and Picasso precisely a Picasso.

From once having been an obscure philosophical idea, *emergence* with time has become a central concept within the sciences. The idea is that a specific system can change so dramatically in conjunction with a small shift in its degree of complexity – at a *tipping point* – that the system as a whole is transformed from one kind of phenomenon into something completely different, where *the new emergent phenomenon* appears with entirely new properties and qualities that entail that it must be classified as something entirely new in relation to the original system. According to relationalist physics, an emergence moreover means that *nature as a whole* goes through a change. The emergence has such a decisive ontological significance that a return from the new to the old *paradigm* is impossible after the emergence. Between different emergent phenomena with, in principle, the same component parts, there is a *hierarchy*. Every emergent transition forms a new level in the hierarchy. But because every suddenly arisen emergence has its own just as suddenly arisen laws and rules – this is quite possible as long as the newly created laws and rules do not threaten the existence of the actual hierarchy – it also changes *nature as a whole* for all time in a relationalist universe.

The syntheist biologist and complexity theorist Stuart Kauffman investigates the metaphysical significance of emergences in his book *Reinventing The Sacred*. Kauffman points out that there is nothing built into *physics* from the start that says that it should emerge and give rise to *chemistry*, in the same manner that there is nothing built into chemistry from the beginning that says that it should emerge and give rise to *biology*. Neither chemistry's nor biology's future births are in any mysterious way preprogrammed within *the Big Bang* at the genesis of the Universe. Rather, emergences tend to occur quite suddenly, and quite independently of all previously applying laws of nature. They thereby *add* an increased complexity to the Universe, rather than just *develop* something *built in* beforehand, as the totalist determinists from Plato via Newton to Einstein interpret the function of emergences.

Kauffman argues that the apparent presence of emergences means that *the principle of self-organisation* must be added to *Darwinian natural selection* in order for the sciences to hang together and provide a comprehensive picture of nature's various processes. Emergences and their self-organisation quite simply add something fundamental to the sciences that natural selection lacks, namely an idea of how *the pre-adaptive material,* which is later the basis of the success story of the evolutionary process, actually arises. The point is that *the emergence per se* is not a product of Darwinian natural selection; rather it is something as remarkable as a suddenly arisen and *self-organising phenomenon,* spontaneously emanating from a disorganised chaos, which later turns out to be a piece in the jigsaw puzzle with a perfect fit when circumstances in the otherwise Darwinian process change.

The emergence's potentiality is based on a single simple principle: however many *actualities* might exist in physics, the *potentialities* that precede these actualities are always still far more numerous. It is sufficient to go to every human being's genesis in order to establish that this is the case: for every dividual that is born, nature wastes millions and millions of sperm and also a large number of eggs, which are never made use of at all. And now we are just talking about the eggs and sperm that in spite of everything are actualised as precisely eggs and sperm – the virtual eggs and sperm are in turn many times more numerous. Out of this infinite multiplicity, the emergences stand out as the great winners, as the possibilities that an ultra-creative universe sooner or later must produce anyway, and they are impressive in their pre-adaptive ability to self-organise durable and stable complexities. It is not strange that people have allowed themselves to be carried away by nature's ability to generate emergences throughout history.

On the other hand, it is a mistake to imagine that in some mysterious way these emergences are givens, that they follow some kind of metalaw of nature – which in that case must exist even before the genesis of the Universe, which of course is an impossibility in *an internal self-creating universe* without a creating god that is both external and preceding. The Universe has namely not created itself in the past, *it is creating itself all the time.* In this, Kauffman breaks radically with *reductionism,* the fundamental axiom of the sciences since Newton's heyday. According to reductionism, everything can be deduced downwards in the hierarchy; as if everything that arises higher up and on a later occasion always lies fully pre-programmed at one of the lower levels on a previous occasion. According to reductionism for example, biology is really only an advanced form of chemistry, while chemistry is really only an advanced form of physics, and nothing more than this.

Reductionism quite simply assumes that the Universe and its history follow a preordained trajectory, which in some mysterious way is preprogrammed even in *the Big Bang*. Bizarrely enough, the actual creation of the Universe must therefore be both well-planned, immediate and long since concluded. Kauffman replies that this absurd idea – *the reductionist illusion* – arises because philosophers and scientists are fixated on only following the hierarchies from the top down, as if things cannot be anything other or more and greater than the sum of their constituent parts. But if one instead studies the hierarchies from the bottom up along the arrow of time – contrary to the masochistic fantasy of how spiritual power and thereby also physical existence must be structured from the top down – one discovers how suddenly arising emergences change the entire playing field once and for all through *contingently* introducing new phenomena into existence, which in turn *contingently* give rise to new paradigms in history. Emergences quite simply generate new laws and rules in at least their own region of the Universe, without these specific behavioural patterns having existed anywhere else previously. Thereby it is proven that *the arrow of time is real* – rather than illusory, as Plato, Newton and Einstein imagine it to be – and determinism is thus dead.

A dynamic system is regarded as *ergodic* if its behavioural patterns on average over time concur with its behavioural patterns on average in space. Scientists are fond of ergodic systems since they are relatively simple to turn into mathematics – they are of course, seen as totalities, comfortable constants rather than messy variables – and thereby even relatively simple to use as build-ing blocks. However we do not live in an ergodic universe, which reductionism persistently insists that we do. In fact, nothing occurs in the same way twice, every event is instead completely unique, every apparently identical repetition takes place in a completely new, specific context. Kauffman even claims that without the re-ductionist illusion, the metaphysical premise for *classical atheism* also falls down. The insight that we live in *a non-ergodic universe* must quite simply have dramatic consequences for metaphysics too. *An anti-reductionist explanatory model* is required that replaces the reductionist model. Existence is enormously much more com-plicated, the future is enormously much more open and harder to predict, and the Universe is enormously much more active than the reductionist illusion has led us to believe.

Kauffman points out that above all the Universe is characterised by an enormous, constant *creativity* – it is quite simply capable, in a pantheist spirit, of constantly giving rise to completely new phe-nomena with completely new laws and rules, right down to their metaphysical foundations. Therefore Kauffman draws the conclu-sion that the presence of emergences calls upon us to create a new religion – or to use his own parlance: he encourages us *to allow a new religion to emerge from our consciousness* – once the insight of the central roles of the emergence and self-organisation in relationist physics become widely accepted with full force in informationalist metaphysics. Decades of extensive complexity-theory studies have made Kauffman a convinced and almost militant syntheist. His book's title *Reinventing The Sacred* says it all.

With his theory of *the sum of all histories,* the physicist Richard Feynman proves that a particle can follow all sorts of potential paths from A to B. The vacuum's energy exhibits the least amount of energy in space, but is never at the zero level. A vacuum is always something and never nothing; it is filled with incessant fluctuations, there is never any passive condition of non-being anywhere. On top of this, Planck's constant is a kind of emergence engine of physics: below the Planck length there is pure chaos, above the Planck length organised cosmologies arise. Therefore the Planck length is the least relevant component in all physical measuring, it is the level where the organisation of existence first appears as *a discrete emergence* on top of which the ensuing higher emergences such as chemistry, biology and human consciousness have been able to arise entirely spontaneously.

If emergences within hierarchies are central for the sciences, there is no reason why our studies of mental and social phenomena should be facilitated by defining emergences within *mental and social hierarchies* as well. It is sufficient to note that a new level in a mental or social phenomenon is no longer reducible to its constituent parts, and we have thus identified an *emergence*. In this way Christianity is emergent in relation to Judaism, socialism is emergent in relation to liberalism, syntheism is emergent in relation to atheism, to name just three clear and close-at-hand examples. While interactivity is emergent in relation to the mass media, the mass media are in turn emergent in relation to written language, just as written language is emergent in relation to spoken language. Etcetera.

In accordance with the reasoning above, if we regard atheism as an emergent phenomenon in relation to theism, the fundamental dismissal of the concept of God no longer appears as such – that is, that which gives the position its name – as its most important theological achievement. No, atheism's most substantial achievement is its summation of all sorts of theist positions as a uniform and cohesive alternative to repudiate, that is, atheism's dialectical construction of *theism as an idea*. Seen as an emergent phenomenon in relation to atheism, as the historical and intellectual intensification of atheism, syntheism in turn is a *metareligion*, a faith that its practitioners unabashedly practice as a pure religion in itself. Thereby it also confirms and supports all other art forms' freedom to act from the metaperspective: art as art for art's sake, literature as literature for literature's sake, philosophy as philosophy for philosophy's sake, and so on. And therefore syntheism instinctively rejects all of individualism's calculations of utility. What syntheism seeks instead are the place and the time for itself as an event. This event is manifested within *love, art, science, politics* and *religion*: syntheology's five generic categories.

Syntheology is in turn the intensification of syntheism that is enabled when it sees itself as a *truth as an act* and focuses on one single wisely chosen eternalisation, in order to intensify the thinking based on this fundamental point. It is precisely this we mean when we say that correctly practised theology enables an intensification of philosophy. Syntheology's well-chosen eternalisation is neither God nor the Individual, as in the previous paradigms, but *religion per se as the network* before all others in the informationalist society. The term *religion* – in its original significance as a social phenomenon that connects people with each other – is in fact synonymous with the term *network*. This means that syntheism is the *metareligion* that binds together humanity through practising a truth that sees the network – that is, religion *per se* – as sacred. Syntheology thus realises what has always been the innermost dream of *a religion for religion's sake*.

When it comes to *the syntheist agent*, it is important to distinguish between the concepts *dividual* and *subject*. Informationalist Man is a dividual, but syntheism's ambition is, based on dividuality, to develop *an authentic subjectivity*. In order to go from the usual reactive dividuality to unique, active subjectivity, the dividual must be isolated from the surrounding world's constant distortions – be separated in order to be liberated from the lingering individualist ideology – which is enabled through purposeful spiritual work within the syntheist congregation's walls. In this isolated, conscious, enlightened environment, the dividual can develop genuinely critical thinking, understand and experience herself as the syntheist agent. Through the identification with herself as *an eternalised truth event*, the authentic syntheist subject appears. Syntheists call this state *clarification*, and fidelity to the clarification is manifested through the syntheist baptism which is called *the infinite now*. In this state, the mind focuses on a single point in space–time where there is serenity, where all existential tensions are finally released, where the subject creates a tranquillity which makes it possible *to quite simply be*.

The historical escalation from *eternity* via *progress* to *the event* as the metaphysical engine of the paradigm has put increasing pressure on the individual human being. The informationalist dividual hears a multitude of voices within herself – what Freud imagines as a solid unit that he calls the *superego* – which constantly calls for more, different and stronger efforts. But the dividual is also notoriously afraid of being disconnected from the reward system that is connected to these efforts, in particular the wordless meeting with the other and the other's gaze. What does the other want from her? What can she do to satisfy the other's desire? Even if only to avoid being confronted with her own desire and dependence on the other that the realisation of her desire threatens to entail.

Civilisation is in fact terrified of the threat of *disintegration*. The domestication of materials, plants, animals and, last but not least, Man himself, starts with magic and its invocations. Culture is ultimately the domestication of nature. Correspondingly, the informationalist dividual wrestles with the dread of *social isolation* as the Internet age's potential disintegration (if you are not located inside the networks, in practice, you cease to exist anymore). Modern Man experiences how questions and demands loom large to alarming levels. It is hardly strange that he lives under terrible stress. But then again, he is constantly busy with an incessant patching up of fracturing surfaces instead of doing something about deep spiritual needs, merely because modern Man has allowed himself to be convinced by the myth that says that such a credible course of action is impossible. Nothing could be further from the truth.

The syntheist community differs radically from the socialist idea of the collective that oppresses the dividual and forces her into submission. Here there is no talk of false consciousness. Rather, it is about the following: the less self-interest the dividual brings to the religious ceremony, the more powerful the spiritual experience. The spiritual work focuses on training the participants in a process that moves from the dissolution of the ego to a climb up the syntheological pyramid. Through this direct participation, the dividual becomes an active agent in and for the syntheist community, where the congregation is somewhat larger and more important than the separate dividual: the network of relations that gives the dividual context, meaning and existential weight in relation to herself. It is a matter of letting go of the ego fixation and allowing oneself to dissolve into the hierarchically higher collective emergence, where the community stands out as something greater than the sum of its constituent parts, as the most powerful agent. This is *the infinite now*, the immanent transcendence, the point where the connection to time and space disappears, where the dividual dissolves into something larger than herself, where Syntheos appears and completes the syntheological pyramid. The symbol for the infinite now is of course the lone *photon*, the light in eternity.

Ego fixation and its engine *narcissism* are strictly compensatory phenomena. These conditions are driven by fear and ignorance rather than by consciousness and reason. What gets the ego fixation to allow in the spiritual experience is the growth of ethical *self-love* as the correct way to confront the dramatic subjective experience. Self-love is thus the antipole of banal narcissism. The most common logical error about self-love is otherwise that it should require that one passively waits for an emotion. The background to this is the delusion that all forms of love are feelings and nothing but feelings. But at least self-love is different in comparison with other forms of love in several respects. Partly because it is a logical imperative and not a sought-after effect: there is one relationship in life that you can never opt out of, that you must learn to live with, and that is the relationship with yourself. Partly because self-love is fundamental for all other forms of love – it is *the passions' own Higgs field* – love of others and of life gets its power from self-love and not the other way around. On the other hand, narcissism is based on self-contempt and is nothing other than compensatory behaviour on top of this self-contempt – a clear sign of self-love that is deficient.

Self-love is naturally no guarantee for the genesis of any other love. On the other hand, the person who genuinely loves herself in the capacity of a syntheist agent within an intra-acting phenomenon has the ability to also love the rest of the world outside the subjective experience. World view and self-image are two sides of the same coin, the one being dialectically dependent on the other for its existence. This also applies of course to *the relationship to one's own reflection.* Therefore self-love is both a mental and physiological necessity for being able to love at all, including *amor fati*, the logically and ethically conditioned love of world history up until now. She who lacks self-love, who hates or is indifferent towards herself, is unquestionably unable to love anything else whatsoever. Moreover, she who hates herself must shift that hate onto some other person or some other object in order to be able to experience her *existence* without constantly being reminded of the hated self. However, the self-hating human being cannot love at all. Therefore she transfers this self-hatred onto the existential dissolution into *ressentiment* – bitterness against existence as a whole. This expresses itself as the idea that things could and should be different than they are, which they cannot and therefore are not going to be, which in turn can be experienced as comfortable by the self-hater who, without any doubt or reservations, can settle in permanently in his ressentiment.

This ressentiment expresses itself as blind submission to and worship of various external phenomena. The reason for this is that worship is a form of passion that does not require any love whatsoever; worshipping is driven by impulsive *ruthlessness* while loving is driven by long-term *benevolence*. Passionate but ruthless fascism is the self-hate ideology *par excellence*. When it comes to emotions, ressentiment can be every bit as passionate as love. It can create a dependence on more and be experienced as every bit as existentially satisfying as love. The American shopaholic in the department store, as well as the unscrupulous Nazi camp commandant and the Islamic fundamentalist who detonates bombs among innocent civilians, are extremely passionate beings, but their glowing passions stem from self-hatred, not from self-love. These are passions that seek destruction and an intense *enjoyment*, rather than love's search for playfulness and gratifying *pleasure*. It's about a twisted hatred which, just like all other forms of hatred, stems from *constitutional self-hatred*.

What is interesting, when we get closer to self-love and self-hatred, is their diametrically opposed logical premises. Contrary to the conventional image of love and hate, where love is presumed to be directed at *a thing* and hate directed at *a nothing*, it turns out on closer inspection that quite the opposite is actually the case. Self-love is always directed towards *Atheos*, the necessary void at the centre of the subject. All love is love for the void in the object of love, but this fact never stands out more clearly than in the very act of love, this truth as an act of blind faith without either substance or emotions, from which all passions then get their driving force. A person who loves does not know more precisely what it is that she loves about her beloved, since what she loves about the beloved is the void in the centre of the love object and the possibility of projecting love onto this object that this void in fact makes possible.

At the deepest level, love is a will to love without any ulterior motive, because the art of loving is the art of living. Wanting to love is wanting to live a life with *integrity*. Self-hatred, on the other hand, is always directed towards a *phantasmal substance* in the subject. Hatred must constantly find something concrete to hate in the hated one, since the subject itself as a void merely *absorbs* and never *resonates*. Atheos can only be loved or denied but never hated, since hatred is inevitably dissolved in the void. In contrast to unconditional love, hatred requires a concrete resonance from the hated object. Hatred does not want to give anything; it merely wants to temporarily dump self-hatred onto something else, and therefore hatred is conditional. Wanting to hate is wanting to die and wanting to take all life along with oneself into death. It is the total lack of integrity.

However, no resonance exists in a void. Therefore the self-hating human being must constantly find *something concrete within herself* to hate. Something that is not a void for the subject. Therefore self-hatred constantly locates new attributes in the hated subject that it objectifies and reifies in order to recast into an object of passionate hatred. Self-hatred is therefore to be regarded as an orgy of finding, reifying and subsequently mocking the shortcomings of the subject – based on an unattainable external template concerning how the subject *ought to be in order to pass muster as an object of worship*. As if it would ever be possible to love anything just because it is good enough according to an externally established norm. It is as the existential philosopher Hannah Arendt says: "Evil is banal". It quite simply gloats in its alienation vis-à-vis the world, in what antiquity's Zoroaster, as early as around 3,700 years ago, calls *druj*, the passionate enjoyment of existential lying.

According to syntheism, self-love is *truth as an act* above all others. Love yourself, without involving any emotions whatsoever, because you have no choice. Just act. Out of this conscious and logically cogent *self-love as truth as an act* flows love to everything else that exists in an intensely pulsating, creative Universe. The opposite of alienation-enjoying self-hatred could hardly be clearer. But self-love stands firm only in this fundamental conviction: that in essence love is a constitutional act without emotions and from which all other love passions later emerge. And this act in its purest form is self-love; the love of the encounter between the self and the divine where integrity arises. The moment when one's self-image and world view attain a harmonious reconciliation with each other is the event that the syntheists poetically call *the infinite now* or *the immanent transcendence*.

Thereby self-love, as truth as an act, is the obvious foundation for all syntheist rituals and ceremonies. It is the eternally recurring starting point for all spiritual work, whose ultimate purpose is to give the members of the congregation a strong and stable personal integrity without narcissistic elements. Since the self is in constant flux, and since all other emotions are dependent on the act of self-love, the act of self-love must be repeated time after time after time in the syntheist agent's life. This repetition – this cycle of difference and repetition, as Gilles Deleuze would express the matter – constitutes *the Nietzschean core* in the syntheistic spiritual life. A look at one's naked body in the mirror, followed by the decision to unconditionally accept this body as the current expression of Pantheos, as the Universe's construction for housing the subject and its consciousness and passions, as an object to love merely by virtue of an existential decision, a personal *primordial event*. "This is what I am, this is the body that houses my many dividual identities and I love this body in order to be able to love myself, in order to thereby be able to love anything at all. Because I identify myself with the will to love." Truth as an act cannot be expressed any more clearly.

Once the foundation of self-love is laid, the syntheist agent is open and receptive to the process that is called *transparency* within the community. The purpose of *transparentisation* is to maximise openness within the congregation, to bring its members closer to each other, to allow intimacy to develop, so that the collective manifestation of Syntheos is realised. Religion is about bringing people together and giving them an emergent, collective identity that is greater than the dividuals separately and greater than the sum of all the dividuals together. This occurs, for example, through the establishment of *sharing circles*, where the agents bear witness to their innermost thoughts and experiences in front of each other. However it is of the utmost importance that the transparentisation – in the spirit of the French philosopher Michel Foucault – follows the *ethics of interactivity* (see *The Body Machines*) and therefore is carried out from the *bottom up* rather than from the top down; that is, it is those who are strongest, most powerful, those most established who open themselves up first before the community in a process where everyone shares more and more of their innermost emotions and thoughts for every round of the sharing circle.

Through this transparentisation, *agentiality* in the phenomenon in question migrates from the separate dividuals to the community itself. This is what we call the manifestation of Syntheos. The ethics of interactivity are intimately connected with the identity of the subject. Therefore the syntheist agent – both as dividual and community – is very much *an ethical being*. And with conscious ethics as a generator of identity, the subject in turn becomes a formidable syntheist agent. Here we reconnect with Zoroaster's amoral but highly ethical ideal: "You are your thoughts, your thoughts govern your words; you are your words, your words govern your actions; you are your actions, your thoughts, words, and actions together constitute your ethical substance, they are and shall be your identity." At the same moment that the believer identifies fully with her thoughts, words and actions, Zoroaster's concept *asha* goes from being a phenomenological description of existence to becoming an ethical ideal. It is in this merging of phenomenology and ethics that the subject and *asha* become one with each other.

The obligation to love fate under all circumstances, Spinoza's and Nietzsche's ethical ideal *amor fati*, is a central concept in syntheism. The Universe is indifferent to our human cares and woes, does not give our species preferential treatment over someone or something else, accords no special status whatsoever to anyone or anything in relation to anyone or anything else. We can only forgive ourselves for our shortcomings as human beings precisely because we are human beings, not heroes. And in this self-forgiveness, *the now* plays a central part. Since, according to Spinoza's and Nietzsche's imperative, we are duty-bound to love all of history up until now – partly because it is the only history there is, partly because it is something that at any rate we cannot do anything about – we are also duty-bound to love our own life story up until now. And in this imposed love there also lies *self-forgiveness* as a logical obligation and not as a longed-for emotion. Syntheists create rituals in order to constantly return to the necessary self-forgiveness, including collective rituals to support the journey towards the insight of self-forgiveness, and then not least rituals that question and combat the enjoyment that is connected with *self-hatred*, the moralistic opposite of ethical self-forgiveness. There is in fact no place for self-hatred and its enjoyment within syntheist spiritual work.

The step from love to art is short. In his book *The Master and his Emissary*, British philosopher Iain McGilchrist pins his hopes for humanity on art and religion. According to McGilchrist, art and religion are the human expressions that can be used effectively in order to confront the big threat – what McGilchrist calls *the condition of anomie*. As is well-known, the term anomie was coined by the French sociologist Emile Durkheim in the late 19th century.

According to Durkheim, anomie starts with a total and irrevocable *internal* alienation and dissolution of values, which invokes an intense existential consciousness, which in turn generates a complete and devastating *external* paralysis. Durkheim expresses this by saying that the anomic human being can no longer see *the world*, but instead is *staring* back at existence; a blank stare that at once is both neurotically paralysing and psychotically megalomaniacal.

Consequently art plays a central role within syntheism. Art seeks to move away from alienation towards religion, not least when it investigates alienation itself, as if it were the only theme that remains for art to process. *Like syntheism in itself, art is implicit rather than explicit, ambiguous rather than monotonous, sensible rather than rational, and above all, always incarnated.* Therefore, really interesting art has always been *transrationalist*. Rationalist art would be unbearably banal and meaningless. Rather, art must be truer to life than life itself. Through art, Man can regain his gaze and abandon staring, and with this living gazing on the world there follows a living relationship with the surrounding world. McGilchrist claims that the key to this deeper artistic understanding of the terms of existence is *melancholy*. This is related to the fact that melancholy is the emotional consequence of a joyous acceptance, followed by a glorification of the multiplicity of existence. Thereby melancholy is the complete opposite of the Platonist simplification. Which possibly explains why melancholy, according to McGilchrist, was idealised during the Renaissance but despised during the Enlightenment, even by protosyntheists such as Spinoza and Leibniz.

This would mean that if syntheism were to be linked to the Renaissance and Romanticism, melancholy is also the key to syntheist art. Which of course also applies in the reverse direction: *for art, syntheism is the only possible way away from in-*

dividualistic isolationism towards the holism of network dynamics. But it also requires an artist who builds her work on *participatory pleasure* instead of *narcissistic enjoyment.* The artistic auteur is thus *yet another Napoleonic ideal* that must die in the informationalist society. The reason is that syntheist art is created by an artistic dividual who believes in the community's utopian possibilities, rather than by an artistic individual who revels in a ressentiment vis-à-vis her own time. And this must also occur without the art ever being allowed to fall into the trap of rationalist banality and lose its magic. Art must be constantly founded on and return to Atheos.

Syntheist art is not merely *participatory* and *dividual* rather than isolationist and individual; it is also *a metaphysical art* in the deepest sense of the term. With the advent of syntheism, art can leave *cynical and cultural relativist inquiry* which has been its axiomatic norm under late capitalism – from a Nietzschean perspective, what can be called *a voluptuous revelling in the death of God* – and instead devote itself *to a transcending and utopian creativity.* But this requires a distinct break with the late capitalist art world's eschatological mythology – history has not reached any ending in the sense that Francis Fukuyama speaks of – and its fixated, academic power structure. This in turn requires the artist's will to smash the individualist myth of the auteur as art's Napoleonic patriarchal genius. Syntheist art is in fact liberated from *the creator* of the art and his atomism – it formulates the idea and then insists that *the idea must be free.* It knows that it is a small but fundamentally *manifold* part of a greater *holistic phenomenon* – it does not act as the distanced rebel for the purpose of self-glorification, but serves an even greater utopian ideal – and it is art's relationship to this phenomenon, within which it acts as a cohesive agent, which is of interest.

Syntheist art operates either from an estimate of the anticipated influence on the wider phenomenon – even if this forecast naturally seldom or never hits the mark perfectly – or even more preferably based on its own emotional composition, as an *ethical art* which strives to be *a syntheist truth as an act*. It also strives to establish a relationship to *the universal* through *the particular*. Syntheist art does this within these extremely restricted arrangements in order to maximise its creative expression – isolation and limited resources have always been key ingredients for innovative creation – but these tendencies are further strengthened in a society characterised by a massive informational surplus. Therefore informationalist art is best produced and reproduced in environments such as *syntheist monasteries* and *participatory festivals*.

According to David Hume, *habit* is a necessity for the dividual identity. We call the religious habit *ritual*. Syntheist rituals are often or regularly repeated habits with the purpose of strengthening the particular identity of the dividual and social identity within the community. Since syntheism unites around *interactivity* as an ideal, syntheists first and foremost conduct *participatory rituals*. Participatoryism is a principle which entails the participants meeting in radical equality without any hierarchies whatsoever between them; a meeting where each and every one is assumed to take full responsibility for herself and his own well-being as well as to actively participate and co-create rather than passively receive and consume. This means that syntheism is a *radical egalitarianism*. From an intersubjective viewpoint, all people have as much (or as little) value, and there is continuous work within the community to maintain this radical ideal. This means that syntheist leadership serves the community from below rather than manipulating it from above. It is driven by a will to lead the community through the *mobilist* chaos of existence to a more profound *eternalist* understanding of the conditions and opportunities of existence, from which the ethics of interactivity can be applied through *truths as acts* which are determined and then carried out.

This explains why the syntheist ritual is always structured as *bottom-up* rather than *top-down*. At the same time, it is important to understand *the nature of the spiritual experience*. To begin with, it is not strange that spirituality is associated with the subject. Since spirituality must be experienced and cannot be thought – and thus even less so communicated as a spiritual experience *per se* – it is not just fundamental for *the syntheist subject*; it is also in the reverse direction very much *syntheistically subjective*. The experience is felt; it is not thought and it is not formulated: it really is felt if indeed it takes place at all. And it can only be described metaphorically afterwards; it cannot be conveyed as it is *per se*. Therefore by necessity spirituality is a practice rather than a doctrine. The doctrine can only discuss how the practice should be carried out and stimulate it, but the doctrine can never replace the practice. Spirituality is an *inner* and *transcendental* experience.

As early as during its first years of emergent self-organisation on the Internet – for example on collective web sites such as syntheism.org – the syntheist liturgy developed four different categories of rituals. The first category consists of *ceremonies that support and confirm transitions in life*, such as naming ceremonies, manhood rituals, baptism, confirmations of belonging, divorce rituals and burials. The second category is *periodic festivals* which are connected to the four seasons: *Atheos* is celebrated at the winter solstice and begins the *Athea* quarter; *Entheos* is celebrated at the spring equinox and begins the *Enthea* quarter; *Pantheos* is celebrated at midsummer and begins the *Panthea* quarter; and *Syntheos* is celebrated at the autumn equinox and introduces the *Synthea* quarter. The third category is *meditative techniques*, such as contemplation, meditation, yoga and contact improvisation. The fourth and last category comprises rituals focused on *the infinite now*, the transcendental experience, through structured shamanism and advanced psychedelic practices.

The syntheist liturgy at the dawn of the Internet age is very much about *desecularisation*, a historically necessary ambition to *sacralise* late capitalist Man's radically secularised lifeworld. For this reason, the syntheist liturgy has developed a nucleus consisting of two dividual components – a kind of spiritual lecture that is called a *homily*, and an often deeply personal *testimony*; as well as four collective components – a collective *sound-making* in order to manifest the affinity of the physical bodies present, a quiet phase of *contemplation* and *meditation*, a listening to carefully selected *music* which often is related to the theme of the current homily, and finally a closing *peace saluta-tion* where all those agents in the community who are present wish each other well. A less liturgical gathering is called an *act of worship*, and a large liturgical gathering is called a *mass*. The liturgy is led by a master of ceremonies, who is complemented by a lecturer and one or more personal witnesses, where the homily has a collectively consolidating and universally valid subject while the testimonies are particular in nature. The syntheist liturgy is of course not bound to a physical space: it can just as well be carried out as a virtual ceremony.

When we move from the oscillation between Atheos and Pantheos to the oscillation between Entheos and Syntheos, we are also in a deeper sense moving from the transcendent to the *immanent*. That which binds the Universe together, for example, is not that it *de facto* is a cohesive unit *per se* – over time different parts of the Universe may have developed completely different laws, substantially independent of one another – but that the Universe has a single common origin and since then has been tied together by cosmic time. This means that the void and the Universe as transcendental concepts are tied together by the immanent time line. However, this does not mean that the possibility of a credible transcendental experience must be ruled out. Through structured shamanism and advanced psy-chedelic practices – for each and every one as dividuals, or even better and more powerfully as a community – the possibility of *a transcendent experience* that we associate with Entheos is opened up; an acceptance and enjoyment within the entheist oscillation between Atheos and Pantheos, with the utopian focus directed towards Syntheos.

The syntheist religious experience is thus *a transcendental experience within an immanent world*, and absolutely not some kind of mystical excursion to some other parallel world in a dualist universe. Syntheism is of course *de facto* radically monist. We therefore speak of an immanent transcendentalism, a strongly emotional experience of both boundary-transcendence (Entheos) and entanglement (Syntheos) within and deeper down in a strictly immanent world (localised between Atheos and Pantheos). Instead of for example the Abrahamic ascendance to a supernatural Heaven, here we are talking about *a syntheist entry into immanent reality*. And since syntheism is a metareligion, with Syntheos constantly in its sights, it promotes and celebrates this connection of people.

In this, *the syntheist family* plays a central role. The Latin word *familia* can be found in every Indo-European language. This reveals that the concept of family has an extremely strong significance for human well-being, even if its detailed content has been altered throughout history. The family consists of those people who are closest to us, regardless of whether these are our biological relatives or not. This means that a living religion can hardly exist without a clear idea of the family, nor a sustainable idea of the family without a supporting metaphysics. In true relationalist spirit, the syntheist community's members are called *agents*. An agent can be anything from a dividual member in a human body to a complete congregation consisting of many separate dividuals. On the other hand, the self-appointed *victim* and his concomitant *victim mentality* has no place within syntheism, since the victim seeks isolation from and independence vis-à-vis all external forces and therefore constantly looks for scapegoats and excuses when confronted with immanent reality, that is, the exact opposite of syntheism's human-created gods and its quest for the sacred connection. The syntheist metaphysics around the family and the family's agents is of course based on *Syntheos*, the divine manifested as the community between people.

A necessary component in hypercapitalism – and its infiltration and colonisation of the human, existential experience – is the *hypersexualisation* of the social arena. Capitalism must commodify even the most sensitive and most intimate of human experiences in order to consummate itself. And capitalism cannot get there without first being liberated from both responsibility and shame concerning its own ruthless exploitation. This freedom from responsibility occurs through the creation of *the sexualist ideology*, not to be confused with *sexual liberation*, which in its capacity as a cultural predecessor to informationalism's relationalist view of humanity strives in the exact opposite direction. The problem is in fact that hypersexualisation requires a fundamental and deep-seated self-hatred, an all-encompassing conviction of inadequacy of the self, what Foucault calls "the internalised police", a kind of turbo-driven superego that arises as a necessary by-product to hyper-Cartesian self-centredness.

The internalised police in turn generates the internarcissistic culture that drives late capitalism's ultra-commercialised quest for identity and often expresses itself through an extremely tedious obsession with so-called self-fulfilment. The hypersexualised human being possesses and above all continuously changes more or less colourful *shells*, where weariness with the self and the presumed ability of these shells to attract booty in the form of high status, and affirmation in the form of a desired partner, determines the growing intensity in their constant changeovers. When we arrive at the historical *tipping point* where the dominant hyper-Cartesians are constantly chasing identities for their insatiable and immeasurable internarcissism, no obstacles remain for sexuality's takeover of the public sphere. Under severe pressure from myths – concerning the metaphysical potential of sexual desire, and concerning the free market's ability to satisfy eternally craving human desire – late capitalist society is hypersexualised. But it is precisely here, in exposing *the sexualist ideology*, that the door to syntheism and its genuine, and also sexual, liberation is opened.

Note that syntheism does not argue in favour of any form of abstinence or *asceticism*. Historical asceticism is an inheritance from the Platonist paradigm; it has no central place in a fundamentally monist and mobilist religion such as syntheism. Interestingly enough, *Zoroastrianism* is the only one of the classical world religions that lacks ascetic imperatives, and it is also the only monist and mobilist world religion before syntheism, seen as a whole. Thus there is not either any hostility to sex whatsoever within syntheism. There is nothing wrong with sex in itself – there is no kind of sex at all between consenting adults that is the least bit morally objectionable – it is just that sexualist ideology, and the hypersexualisation which is its consequence, has nothing to do with the sexual act itself. Its soul-poisoning individualist categorisations of people as interchangeable shells that constantly *put off* rather than *realise* sexual acts is, if anything, in fact hostile to sex rather than sex-affirming.

Sexualism's mistake lies in it changing sexuality from a free and creative, existential pleasure into a constrained and unconditionally moralist imperative that fans the escalating consumption of vapid identity. Hypercapitalism is quite simply driven by a moralistic order: *Enjoy!* Freedom and creativity are disconnected from the sex, which thus has been sexualised, that is, has been transformed into a destructive enjoyment of constantly postponed pleasure. Thus, the sexualist imperative is not to be interpreted as a "Be fertile and multiply" or even "Have sex!", but rather as a "Make yourself sexy, make yourself a passive self-contemptuous object, or die!", where it has become entirely irrelevant whether any sexual act ever occurs or not. Nothing could be more alien to syntheism. Sex is namely a highly natural, immanent phenomenon that is to be liberated from the bottom up, not a sacred transcendental activity that should be fenced in by a distancing, hierarchy-making set of rules from the top down, which historically has been the case, and which, under this offensive sexualism, is more so than ever.

The sought-after sexual liberation under capitalism if anything gets its follow-up in *the chemical liberation* (for a more exhaustive treatment, see *The Global Empire*) under attentionalism. The development of a post-atheist religiosity founded on the need for a new metaphysics, spurred on by globally collaborating syncretistic, religio-social practices, and not least the explosive flora of entheogenic substances, lays the foundation for a dissolution of the conflict between *theism* and *atheism;* a conflict that, in a Hegelian dialectical process, transitions into a synthesis in the form of *syntheism* as the metaphysics of the Internet age. At the same time, sexual liberation is displaced when its underbelly, *the hypersexualisation of the individual,* is exposed as the capitalist consumption society's underlying engine: sexualism ultimately became a straitjacket of the superego where chemical liberation offers the only possible way out. We do not lose liberated sexuality by returning to some kind of asceticism or abstinence with old-school religious overtones. We only gain access to means and ceremonies that finally enable us to start domesticating and mastering liberated sexuality to our long-term advantage. Indirect *desire* at last has the chance to balance the direct, vacuous, repetitive *drive*.

The attentionalist dividual uses the enormous offering of new chemicals to constantly modify and develop her creative multiplicity of personalities. Obviously, this may be an adaptive strategy vis-à-vis the demands and expectations of his surrounding world, but it can also be about subversive, revolutionary tactics in order to overthrow capitalism's restrictive *status quo*. When the chemicals set the classic constants of intelligence, gender and sexual orientation in motion, the foundation of obsolete individualism is eroded, and transitions into a concluding *hyperphase* as an escalating *consumtarian underclass phenomenon*. Therefore it is the consumtarian who, right to the bitter end, forces herself to constantly improve and refine herself and her own identity, to invoke a hotly desired underlying ego-essence, accompanied by tabloid culture's demands for consumption-generating self-frustration. The netocrat, on the other hand, has long stopped believing in a cohesive individual and instead cultivates innumerable different personalities, not uncommonly invoked by and developed with the aid of carefully designed chemical cocktails.

The myth of sobriety is crushed once and for all. Sobriety was invented in the newly-industrialised Europe in the 1830s with the purpose of keeping the factory workers in check. But of course no form of sobriety exists, and has never done so. The human brain is a battlefield for constant conflicts between lots of different hormones and chemicals. There is no sober ego: that we refrain from alcohol or other external stimulants, does not mean that a chemical equilibrium prevails in our brain, where all levels constantly vary wildly. Ask a woman who has been pregnant or a man who has lived with a pregnant woman. And we self-medicate all the time to the best of our abilities, carry out various actions in a more or less desperate hope that the brain's reward system will make us happy with sundry chemical kicks. This becomes evident at the same moment that the agent is divided and appears as *the first subject* who determines the mood of the agent, and as *the second subject* that experiences the mood that the first subject has decided on and administered. Thereby, chemical liberation fans the growth of dividualism. And late capitalism's bizarre, global quest for the enormously extensive, illegal drug trade appears to be the last exploding supernova in the tragicomic history of the myth of sobriety.

Syntheism is the home where psychedelic practices are carried out responsibly and with creativity with regard to what is best for the congregation and the participating agents. Where solid scientific facts meet reported spiritual experiences, a practice is constructed which is often carried out in defiance of prevailing norms and laws in the surrounding society. But psychedelic practice is an act of faith of the inquiring mind, a truth as an act, before which the syntheist never subordinates herself to the nation state and the narrow-minded and prejudiced norms of bourgeois society. This applies even if chemical liberation entails *a syntheist martyrdom*. The social arena is of course already filled with a host of different psychedelic practices. The Swedish historian Rasmus Fleischer also points to the fact that even pathologised psychological states such as eating disorders and other self-destructive behaviour must be regarded as psychedelic practices. Sexuality and entheogens are closely related to each other. This explains, for example, why it is extremely hard to be focused on both things at once. Both sexuality and entheogens are fundamentally a question of manifesting *the drive*, that is, to repeat what is meaningless *ad infinitum*. But through this meaningless repetition, meaning is created, where sexuality generates *eros* and the entheogens generate *philia*.

Practising *sensual actions* in the entheogenic state liberates the actions from all forms of sexuality; they can therefore advantageously assume a central role in the entheogenic ritual *without the ritual thereby being sexualised*. Entheogens namely make the subject aware of the meaningless emptiness of the sexual act, which means that the sensual act without sexuality – where Atheos transitions into Entheos – releases a powerfully transcendent *ecstasy* in the entheogenic state. Man constantly longs to get away from *extimacy* within himself towards *in-*

timacy with his closest friends. But intimacy is only possible when two or more agents really understand each other. Where language does not suffice to convey understanding, sensuality through *eros* and the entheogens through *philia* are used as precisely the spiritual tools that strengthen and maintain the intimacy between people. It is precisely because of their enormous existential and subversive potential that sexuality and the entheogens have regularly become the objects of the most false accusations, the most bizarre taboos and the most brutal persecutions throughout history. The forbidden fruit from the tree of knowledge is the oldest and probably best known euphemism for the psychedelic substance.

The reason for this moral panic and these eschatological propaganda campaigns is that sexuality and entheogens are associated with both *pure pleasure* and if possible even more so with subversive mysticism and its search for a mental, or if one prefers, a spiritual rather than a physiological pleasure. Under capitalism, sex and chemicals are regarded as incompatible with industrious work in the socio-economic-affluence-promoting factories. Sexual and chemical minimalism is therefore promoted for educative purposes and disseminated with vehement rabidness – as a kind of secular fundamentalism, with zero tolerance as the new utopian salvation – as soon as industrialism takes hold of Europe and North America during the 19th century. Pure and thus animalistic pleasure stirs up both envy and terror, for how does one go about domesticating unreserved pleasure? How does one accommodate it into civilisation's death worship without castrating, distorting, prohibiting and destroying it?

Subversive mysticism injects yet another threat, since its practitioners are not perceived as difficult to control in the same way as the sexually experimenting. Rather – which is even worse – they are experienced as if in some obscure manner they actually control the suspicious one himself. Therefore throughout history, this *eucharistiphobia* repeatedly expresses itself either through sexuality being made taboo if entheogens are tolerated in any way, or that entheogens are banned if liberated sexuality happens to be tolerated. Most paradigms and societies hate and attempt to minimise and if possible exterminate these two phenomena. The esoteric is equated with the satanic. Only in the syntheist utopia with its *theological anarchism* can the dream of liberated sexuality be found side by side with the dream of a free usage of entheogens – with the express ambition of realising the enormous potential for humanity of both of these dreams. For what is *the anarchist society* if not the very community where human pleasure is no longer restricted? And from the reverse perspective, what is *thought control* in its deepest sense, if not in fact a quest to control sex and drugs? Or to express the matter as a popular, countercultural t-shirt slogan: *Drug control is thought control.*

Revolutions are fundamentally material, not spiritual. Revolutions consist of new technological complexes, not of flocks of courageous heroes. The real revolution, as we said, is not the French Revolution in 1789, but the arrival of the printing press in the 1450s, without which what is called the French Revolution would have been an impossibility. The history of mankind is a dialectic between the constant *the body* and the variable *technology*. This dialectic was fundamentally changed with the genesis of 21st century human technologies, where even the body is technologised. This new human being, an *android*, a *cyborg*, is no longer human, but *transhuman*. The body is no longer a predetermined, fixed object to relate to, but an ongoing project that we ourselves are influencing and reshaping all the while, and in the long run also creating. Whether we want to or not, we have been cast into *the transhumanist revolution,* which is chemical liberation *par excellence.* But in order to place the transhumanist revolution in its correct context, we must define its relationship to *the informationalist event*.

So if revolutions only occur of their own accord – whether they are emergent or contingent phenomena – how can syntheists steer the three dramatic and parallel revolutions of our time towards a single common event: *the singularity*? In the world of physics, a singularity is a state where temperature, pressure and curvature are infinite at the same time. In such a singularity a universe, for example, can expand ten million times in a single moment, which makes possible, for example, the cosmic inflation in conjunction with the birth of our own universe. The singularity is a possibility for a universe such as ours to arise spontaneously. Precisely because the universal expansion is an expansion within nothing, it may be inflationary, far beyond the speed of light (which is otherwise the greatest possible speed *within* this universe). So how does syntheism relate to the Universe? What characterises the relationship between Man and his feared superior – the Universe?

An excellent theological starting point is the experience "the Universe rolled right over and crushed me, with colossal and indifferent weight, and this steam-rolling made me both religious and deeply grateful", a reaction that witnesses recount time after time after having, for example, gone through the *ayahuasca* and *huachuma* rituals in South America or the *iboga* rituals in Central Africa, which are considered the most powerful but also the most traditional psychedelic practices that humanity has developed. It becomes even more interesting when these recurring testimonies are followed by the words "And aside from this there is nothing in the experience that can be verbalised". This is the core of the syntheist spiritual experience. Its doctrine takes us the whole way to its practice. But the syntheist spiritual experience in itself can never be verbalised and it is precisely for this reason that it goes under the paradoxical name *the unnamable*. What we both can and should verbalise, however, is the logical insight that we attain after the life-altering meeting with the unnamable: The criminalisation of entheogenic substances must be regarded as the greatest and most tragic case of mass religious persecution in history. Rarely if ever has human evil been so simple-minded and banal. Therefore first and foremost syntheism strives for humanity at long last to have access to complete *freedom of religion*. It might be about time.

14

Syntheist temples and monasteries in the global empire

The will to know is Man's instinctive reaction to the trauma of extinction, his almost exorcistic attempt to expel this existential tormentor. At a deep level, the philosopher must realise that he is already dead; philosophy is not an affirmation of nor a justification for anything, but rather just one more by-product of the drive in its eternally revolving repetition of the same. But this does not prevent the will to know, the game of hide-and-seek with Pantheos, at some point from achieving a result that can influence the expression of the drive. The clearest example of such an effect of the will to know is technological development. Technology is what has developed most dramatically during the course of history; the development that has had the most far-reaching consequences, and is more a kind of ironic by-product with its origin in the incessant ravages of the drive. Technology quite simply changes the rules of the game in the social arena in a way that is, to say the least, radical. This is precisely what the books in *the Futurica Trilogy* are about. Now we are taking that argument one step further, and moreover in a new direction.

Religion is often accused of preaching the destruction of knowledge and for obsessively combating people's will to learn and reflect on new ideas, and unfortunately this is the way it has been during certain periods, which naturally is deeply reprehensible. Not least Christianity and Islam have a bulky register of sins in this respect. But from this one cannot conclude that every form of religion by definition is to be regarded as a kind of intellectual *escapism*, a form of social anaesthetic or perhaps a sedative. When Karl Marx claims that religion is the opium of the people, it is a generalisation without any appreciable precision. Moreover religion is much, much more for people, and serves a host of different and complex societal functions. In addition, there are religions and religions. Syntheism is – to take an example that is close at hand – in its capacity as a deepening of immanence rather than dissolution into transcendence – in fact the direct opposite of all forms of escapism. Rather, syntheism's pathos lies in what British poet Gerard Manley Hopkins in the 19th century calls *inscapism*, a quest for a stronger and deeper sincerity, a journey inwards and not an escape outwards or away in relation to reality. And inscapism not only wants to know, it also wants to give full expression to what it learns.

The distinction between escapist and inscapist religion becomes all the more important when the Internetified world – where all nations and cities of the world become intimately dependent on and entangled with each other – transitions from the patchwork of industrialism's sovereign nation states to the global empire of informationalism. It is important here to understand that *the global empire* is not some frictionless, synchronised, centralised millennial kingdom, but rather a fragmented and highly decentralised mishmash of social nodes. This mishmash is in turn subordinate to uncontrollable and ruthless flows of capital and information criss-crossing the old national borders, rather than being subordinate to some symbolically masterful central power with tangible or even discernible reach. Out of these flows, a decisive conflict emerges between on the one hand *the capitalist power structure* of nation states and the giant corporations – organisations that will do everything they can to halt, limit and above all attempt to domesticate the Internet's development and potential to their own advantage – and on the other hand the attentionalist power structure, created and celebrated by netocrats who are fighting for a free and open Internet in order to take over and control the world, driven by their vision of *theological anarchism*.

In its capacity as theological anarchism *par excellence*, syntheism is the netocracy's own built-in metaphysics. But the battle against the statist-corporativist establishment is neither simple nor has it any preordained result in a contingent and indeterminist world. At least not in the short term. There are trends and there are counter-trends. What many people forget is that nation states, which have long appeared to be so "natural" and God-given, actually were the result of never-ending bloody and hard-fought wars of religion in the old Europe. Consequently, the choice of strategy is entirely decisive for the outcome of this struggle. The global empire will borrow many features from, for example, Ancient Rome and Medieval Europe. The first Christian congregations, the Mithraic orders, the Masonic lodges, the cathedrals and monasteries that were built during the Middle Ages are therefore all excellent sources of inspiration for a rising elite who believe in the need for, and want to engage in the building of, *syntheist temples and monasteries in the global empire*.

When the netocrat atheist of the 3rd millennium takes a seat in a classical temple and is astonished at its inspiring beauty, the question arises of how hypercapitalism has succeeded in pacifying her and her generation's sisters and brothers to such a degree that they themselves have never realised any ideas of erecting equivalent buildings for spiritual purposes or even with a spiritual orientation. And in particular, not without some individual ulterior motives of some kind of capitalist gain in the long run. Through the historical extinction of religion, *ideality* has namely been lost and has been replaced by a blind and compact *instrumentality* in all relationships between human beings. All social activities and relationships in hypercapitalist society are assumed to revolve around value-destroying *exploitation* and never to be about value-creating *imploitation* (see *The Netocrats*). But the instrumentality view of one's fellow human being is an existential prison – Platonist alienation in its most manifest form – and the only way out of this prison is to negate the entire capitalist paradigm. Suddenly and in a very timely way, the Internet arrives as a potential lever to achieve the ideality renaissance. The Internet not only makes this longed-for revolution possible. According to the information-technology writing of history, it is the Internet that *de facto* is this revolution itself.

The building of syntheist temples and monasteries is preceded by the early 21st century's experimentation with *temporary autonomous zones*. The nation state is eroding in conjunction with, and as a result of, this ongoing paradigm shift. Since the resources for maintaining law and order are always limited, the regulatory framework of the nation state cannot be upheld during and in particular after a revolution of the magnitude that we are talking about when we talk about the Internet. We must prioritise, to a great extent we must pretend that we are upholding the old law in every respect. The ensuing anarchy turns into a *plurarchy* – a democracy in a real sense has never existed – which consists of an infinite number of smaller, competing and above all chaotically overlapping centres of power. The response to the plurarchy, which also constitutes its inherent opportunity and promise, is the establishment of temporary autonomous zones. These consist of everything from *eco villages* that are developing models for sustainable lifestyles that can later be copied and disseminated; to *participatory festivals* where attention is maximised through a generous sharing of resources, while capitalism is banned within the confines of the event with the purpose of *deinstrumentalising* and enlivening the relationships between human beings. The syntheist mission is consequently to build *temples* as *participatory art manifestations* and *monasteries as revolutionary cells* in the midst of the global empire's initial and most hectic chaos.

Since syntheism is the religion of the Internet age, syntheist temples and monasteries are both physical and virtual. In its capacity as a potential manifestation of Syntheos, the Internet is an excellent environment for spiritual work. When the temporary experiments are transformed into *permanent autonomous zones*, they will emerge as finished temples and monasteries. In relation to the alienated, chaotic surrounding world, these oases of authentic living and sustainability will shine with the power of attraction. But they will also demand from new members an honest distancing of themselves from capitalism's short-term and tempting superficial rewards; a distancing from *bourgeois individualism* and its fixation on exploitation in favour of *netocratic dividualism* and its quest for imploitation. This spiritual work must be carried out without the slightest instrumentality in human relations, without the least ulterior motive of any dividual gain for any single syntheist agent. Unlike the individual, the dividual is not the centre of existence, but subordinated to *the network* as the fundamental metaphysical idea. Dedication to the syntheist congregation is the bond to theological anarchism's practical execution, without beating about the bush or any caveats. This dedication is confirmed before the community as a truth as an act, for example, in the syntheist act of baptism: *the infinite now.*

Syntheism's sacred locales might just as well be dance floors on Saturday evenings as quiet rooms of contemplation on Sunday afternoons. Periods of unbridled carnival celebrations could be alternated to advantage with periods of meditation, yoga, fasting or quite simply just silence and concentration. The four quarters in the syntheist calendar – *Athea,* the three months after

Atheos (winter solstice), *Enthea* after Entheos (spring equinox), *Panthea*, the three months after Pantheos (summer solstice) and *Synthea* after Syntheos (autumn equinox) – open up possibilities of celebrating a host of different festivals and commemorative days, coupled with specific rituals and ceremonies. But the question is where the inspiration and guidance for the development of these rituals and ceremonies is sourced from. Traditionally, philosophy and theology have of course had that specific role. But at the dawn of the Internet age, these disciplines are in deep crisis. In fact, they have not even succeeded in predicting the arrival of the Internet age, the netocracy or syntheism, and now that these are established facts, both philosophy and theology are having difficulties in formulating relevant questions, never mind any credible answers. These disciplines are helplessly stuck in the past, fixated on increasingly irrelevant social antagonisms, unable to see and reflect on the utopian potential of the future.

Philosophy does not live up at all to its enormous potential during the 20th century. The most important reason for this is its academic marginalisation. Philosophy ceases to be a living, all-encompassing art form that is carried out by independent, risk-taking free thinkers who scrutinise society from its undefined margins. It is instead turned into a self-perpetuating and self-referencing academic activity and a system-affirming meal ticket among numerous others, with long and footnote-heavy repetitions and backward-looking references as its main activity. Thus, philosophy is no longer in dialogue with either other disciplines or society outside of academia. Neither Georg Cantor's new mathematics nor Niels Bohr's new physics have any impact worth mentioning within philosophy until after informationalism becomes widely accepted at the turn of the millennium, despite these two revolutions materially shaking up the world view of thinking people in the 20th century and shifting the mainstays of both ontology and phenomenology. The new relationalist ideas do of course pull the rug out from under the entire correlationist paradigm which has been regarded as axiomatic and unassailable ever since Kant presented his texts. But embarrassingly enough, philosophers are the last ones to understand and analyse this earth-shattering paradigm shift.

During the 20th century, academic philosophy is instead reduced to a stuffy, self-referencing loop. Like an old castrated monster, it behaves as though interactivity, the new physics and chemical liberation do not exist, nor can exist either. So why has philosophy got stuck in the suffocating grip of hermeneutics? How did it come to be impacted by postmodern paralysis? The answer can, once again, be found in the academic marginalisation of philosophy that occurred during the 20th century. From having been a dialogue between independent agents, between politically and artistically driven activists, philosophy was transformed during the 20th century into a politically controlled and socially castrated activity. Philosophy became a business exclusively practised at universities and on academic terms, and thereby creativity was weakened within the discipline, with some extremely rare but consequently also so much more important exceptions, for example psychoanalysis and pragmatism, which in principle also evolved precisely because they had access to their very own institutions.

The question is how it was imagined that philosophy would be treated in an intra-academic environment in the first place, controlled by the statist-corporativist establishment. Since it must then, of course, adapt itself in the service of the establishment, all that then remains for philosophy is to either produce material for a dreary, never-ending recycling of footnote-heavy formulaic language and a reactive, ruminating retelling without receivers anywhere outside their own institutions; or to flare up into career-strategic attacks on the same historical material, but without having one's own arrow of time directed forwards towards a potential utopia. Philosophical creativity is replaced by a kind of hermeneutic, presumed scholarliness. Based on this wider historical perspective, *deconstruction* during the second half of the 20th century is no triumph at all for philosophy; in the best case it is merely the least detrimental by-product from a century that, for the philosophical discipline, is to be regarded as substantially lost.

Just like all establishment-controlled and competition-shy monopolies, the academic world is extremely poor at rewarding genuine creativity; it is however tailor-made to question and dismantle philosophical discourse as such *in absurdum* and *ad infinitum*, which it does with full force through its highly-specialised ethics missions and the many vulgar-Nietzschean projects that dominated cultural studies at universities in the second half of the 20th century. The problem is that the philosophical institutions obviously never turn deconstruction onto those who really need it, namely the philosophical institutions themselves. In order to once again become relevant, philosophy must therefore leave the academic world's corrupting security and seriously question the prevailing ideological structure. Even at the price of thereby burning their own pay cheques. This is what is required if philosophy's interests as a discipline are to take precedence over the interests of the philosopher as a career-driven individual. Only then can philosophy recapture a faith in utopia. It must start by interacting with society and dealing with the issues of the time. It must become relevant.

Only in the 1990s does criticism begin to stir, and it is of course the rapid growth of the Internet and experimental metaphysics that open up the possibility of clearing a path out of postmodernist alienation. Historically and for obvious reasons, constructive criticism with the purpose of opening the way for expansive, creative thinking has always come from the outside. What academic philosophy has dismissed as an impossibility – the growth of a new metaphysics for the new Internet age, and thereby the construction of a new social theory of everything – is of course *de facto* made possible by the interactive conversations that are going on with frenetic intensity in extra-academic, virtual spaces. The netocrats are undermining the universities' monopoly on *metaphysical truth production* in the same way that the universities once undermined and razed the Church's monopoly on the same. The use of a constantly expanding Wikipedia is exploding while national encyclopaedias in fancy bindings are gathering an increasing amount of dust in bookshelves that nobody ever visits. History repeats itself when a new information-technology paradigm enables the growth of a new structure for truth production right under the very noses of the old, tired and corrupt elite, who are unable to intervene even if they had had the energy to do so, since the material conditions – and thereby the rules of the Darwinian punishment and reward system in the surrounding culture – have been fundamentally altered.

In spite of the fact that the Internet revolution is fundamentally and radically changing the conditions for human identity production and at the same time is directing a lethal attack on the capitalist power structure, initially it passed by relatively unnoticed: the capitalist entrepreneurs kept believing for a long time that the Internet revolution merely translated into an increased revenue flow which strengthened their position without resulting in any tangible problems. Because the philosophers are in fact still sitting in the academic chairs and are obediently serving the outgoing capitalist paradigm without any tangible desire or ability for radical questioning or ideological adventurousness. Giants such as Martin Heidegger have of course already established nostalgically that technology as such is evil. The striking parallel is naturally with how the clergy were left sitting inside church buildings vegetating in their internarcissistic, self-congratulatory homage to each other while the universities *in the name of science* expanded from the 17th century onwards, and in time took over truth production in society. Consequently, the philosophical innovative thinking that actually arises during the 20th century comes more or less entirely from alternative environments far out in the periphery in relation to academic philosophy, where Jacques Lacan's pioneering psychoanalytical school, which arises in a medical research environment, stands out as the singular most significant philosophical contribution of the 20th century.

Nowhere is philosophy's tragic academicisation as evident as in the servile acceptance of the discipline's own specialisation. Instead of taking some form of responsibility and attacking, or at least problematising, the fragmentation of the social arena that the academic and the professional hyperspecialisation of the 20th century gives rise to, philosophy heedlessly contributes to precisely this triumph of fragmentation by prostrating itself for this development and letting itself be split into lots of small, limited subject areas without any overarching critical discourse. Philosophy surrenders masochistically to hyperspecialisation, internalises it and produces texts that both embody and uncritically celebrate *the fragmentation per se*. This is most apparent in academic philosophy's escalating demonisation of metaphysics and its *metanarratives* under late capitalism.

However impressive, such a flow of specialism cannot however hide the glaring absence of a penetrating and visionary *generalism*. A multitude of loud-mouthed, self-satisfied voices – who have absolutely no consideration for nor show any understanding of *multiplicity as the One* – cannot of course produce any more meaningful narrative than the tragic *internarcissism* which is hypercapitalism's response to all issues in contemporary society. The result of this process of decline is the self-absorbed game by analytical philosophy of a kind of 'pick-up sticks' with the terms, and postmodernism's endless dissecting of the older generations' narratives about mankind and the world. The very attempt to create a new, cohesive metanarrative is branded as a mortal sin within philosophical discourse. Instead, everything is reduced to a regression of sign interpretation without end:

philosophy is finally completely paralysed and is thrust into *the hyperhermeneutical state*. For this reason, syntheism's serious attempt to create a new, credible metanarrative for the Internet age is a highly conscious, logical negation of the entire academic-philosophy paradigm. Philosophy returns to the essentials in the form of *syntheology*, instructed by independent, critical thinkers based on the interests of the burgeoning netocracy, where the logical follow-up question is what political expressions will grow out of the syntheological discourse.

If it was already built into the hyperhermeneutical state that it would come down to an intellectually sterilising banning of all metanarratives, how can syntheology respond to the glaring need for the return of utopianism? In order to understand at all how philosophical discourse is *politicised*, we must start by studying how political philosophy developed during the individualist and atomist paradigm. Capitalism is the constant carnival. The allure of the pay cheque is strictly limited, however. In his book *Drive*, Daniel Pink shows how an increased salary increases productivity only when it comes to boring, monotonous tasks similar to those that were carried out by industrial workers in the factories of the 19th century in Europe. However, productivity in late capitalism's knowledge-intensive jobs has no positive correlation with increased salary; the case is rather the reverse. Autonomy, having a vision, professional pride and social identity are the most important factors for maintaining and preferably even elevating the motivation and productivity of workers – not a fat pay cheque.

Here we see three clear movements: *constructivism* generates liberal democracy, *transcendentalism* generates totalitarian dictatorships and *genericism* generates theological anarchism. Constructivism uses people's differences as axiomatic and assumes that these differences create the necessary hierarchies. It regards universality as an illusion that appears in the form of an illusory antagonism every time it is time to hold democratic elections. Transcendentalism takes the hierarchisation one step further and launches and develops this axiom which says that when the authoritarian leader personifies the universality, when the leader and the party in some mysterious way become one and the party and the people become one, society is transcendentalised and history is realised. Genericism, however, sees history as an eternal repetition of the same with extremely minor variations for every loop, where people's similarity moves down to the dividual level: already from the start, all people are to be regarded as an expression of one and the same substance – the universality is already there.

The genericist imperative is therefore to create *the narrative of how the particular is already the universal*: and once that narrative exists, the universal is made visible through the realisation of the generic. Since constructivism and transcendentalism have already been tried thoroughly and have failed, it requires no great measure of reflection to understand why syntheism is investing its heart and its soul in genericism. *Political syntheism is a genericism*, and since genericism has still not yet been tested, from a sceptical perspective the utopia is also fully possible. But it requires a *truth as an act* to in order to be realised.

The original lie, the original crime, the phantasmic narratives that hold together the subject and the impossible gaze of the now: all this is part of syntheism's political ideology. The law is the third person present in all relations between dividuals. But syntheism is something much greater: it is instead the step outside of the eternal cycle of mythology production and incessant disappointment. In its capacity as a genericism, the syntheist political project must have *the universal singularity* as its point of departure. As networking dividuals, we no longer produce things, *we produce social life itself.* The question is who can play the role as the universal singularity during the introductory phase of the Internet age. How will this social production influence the emerging classes in the cyber world: *the netocrats* and *the consumtarians*? Will they be lured by the same capitalist temptations that seduced their individualistic predecessors, or will they succeed in seeing through these illusions? Or will they instead fall prey to entirely new illusions?

It is unreasonable to ask of the consumtarians that they should be able see through and be able to distance themselves from late capitalist consumption society. They are not even authentic social producers in a Foucauldian sense: rather, they are social consumers, thereof the tragic term *the consumtariat*. It is about a consumption proletariat which, in contrast to the classical workers' proletariat, is no longer united around a proud productivity, but has been reduced to an underclass that have the passive consumption of entertainment and identity production in prefabricated mass editions as their only cohesive factor. Resistance against the corrupt system must instead come from inside the netocracy, which constitutes *the subversive branch of social production*. However, there are no indications suggesting that the netocracy will stand united in the political struggle under informationalism, no more than the bourgeoisie were politically united under capitalism once it had managed to push through its formative struggle for liberal democracy.

The ideological cracks within the netocracy are already clearly discernible (see *The Netocrats*). The sole political project that is guaranteed to unite the netocracy under informationalism is the struggle for the free and open Internet, since this struggle *de facto* concerns its most fundamental conditions as a social class. Without a free and open Internet, the netocracy as a societal elite will not be realised, but will remain, in the best-case scenario, an odd group with interesting special skills on the outer fringes of the social arena. A conceivable, not to say likely, scenario is that a small minority within the netocracy first oppose the statist-corporativist power structure, adopt the absolute standpoint in the age of interactivity, break loose from the corrupt system and construct the parallel utopia. To begin with as a temporary autonomous zone, which subsequently with time is made permanent with the purpose of making the utopia and its potential visible; a visibility that inspires other aspiring netocrats to creatively imitate the utopia and thereby complete the information-technology revolution.

From a theological perspective, *the syntheist fall* occurs when self-love turns into narcissism. Therefore it is necessary for syntheism to steadfastly fight internarcissism. Narcissism is just as present in the self-appointed victim as in the person in power. *The syntheist hero* instead surrenders herself, unreservedly and anonymously, in a brotherly/sisterly communion with the syntheist community. Beyond this communion, ethics is born in the making of *agency*: as an agent, within and together with the syntheist congregation, the dividual seeks a strong ethical identity, an existential substance, which is realised when a promise becomes action. According to the amoral but incorruptibly ethical Zoroaster, ethics is a perpetually recurring feedback loop: You are what you think, what you think affects what you say; you are what you say, what you say affects what you do; you are what you do, what you do affects how you think, and so on. Only through identifying himself as a *syntheist agent* can the dividual enter into and complete the Zoroastrian ethical circle as an intra-acting phenomenon within the syntheist community.

The values and valuations of informationalism stem from what we call *the ethics of interactivity* (see *The Body Machines*). The network-dynamical effects must be the basis of the production of the values and valuations in a network society, where everything from physics and biology to artistic creation and religious practice is characterised by the obsession with intra-acting phenomena, and not least by their relations with each other. This is a world *where everything is always at least two*, as Friedrich Nietzsche expresses the matter, and often many times more than that. An agency for change in such a world is an extremely complex phenomenon in itself: multi-polar, multi-dimensional, multi-dependent and in all directions entangled with its environment. In a relationist society in a relationalist world, ethics must first be *interactive* and later also *intra-acting*.

The ethics of interactivity can and should be pitted against the hypersubjectivist ethics of the last great individualist ethicist, the Lithuanian-Jewish philosopher Emmanuel Levinas. According to Levinas, *the other* has lost all substance and has become an empty goal for the survival of ethics at all. With an almost psychotic conviction, Levinas claims that ethics is the primary philosophy, that it precedes and dictates ontology, epistemology and metaphysics. Justice is the promise to remember the victims of the past and the quest to act justly in the future. Levinas pursues his ethical fundamentalism by reducing the other to merely a face, in the presence of which Levinas claims to experience a blind existential love of almost biblical proportions.

Without this blind ethics there is no subject for Levinas. Only in the meeting between strangers does metaphysical infinity appear. The relationship between the isolated subject and the isolated object, as its emotionally overburdened target, can hardly be made clearer than with Levinas. And what in fact was individualism's built-in logical terminus if not this fundamentally banal mystification of the other? The only discernible way out is to make a clean break with individualism, as syntheism is doing. There is no cohesive subject which experiences itself as a permanent essence, either in itself or as a bizarre by-product of the romantic worship of the other. Instead *the entanglement* is primary. And in that entanglement, something entirely different from Levinas' individualist *infatuation,* with its Abrahamic nostalgia, arrives.

Syntheism opens the way for an ethics of interactivity, based on the entangled, outstretched phenomenon's quest for its own survival, its will to intensity and expansion. It is not in ethics and what the subject feels for the other that the primary arises. The primary is instead the existence of the Universe and how this existence manifests itself for itself by setting people in motion towards and with each other. Levinas' individualistic infatuation is replaced by the manifestation of Syntheos in the encounter between people. This encounter does not get its existential substance via a certain emotion or a holy sacrifice in only one direction between two subjects isolated from each other, as Levinas imagines it, but in a conscious joint act between two equal agents – *at once both entangled and autonomous* – who realise that, through an act of will, they actually can and therefore choose to let *agape* into the relationship between them, who thus *choose* to sacralise the encounter and the joint action. Syntheos quite simply arises when love between people is established as a joint *truth as an act*.

The sacralisation in question can be strengthened to advantage through the sharing of LSD, mescaline, MDMA, psilocybin or any other of many conceivable fraternisation chemicals in a sacred ceremony. Already in his *The Birth of Tragedy*, Nietzsche describes how the narcotic experience constitutes the re-establishment of the Dionysian world view, the joining of Man with Nature, the religious experience of existence as a whole. Nietzsche's vision of the spiritual possibilities of narcotics is fulfilled at a rapid pace during the 20th century: Albert Hoffman synthesises LSD for the first time in 1938 and later recounts his dramatic spiritual experiences under the influence of the drug; Aldous Huxley writes extensively about his own religious experience of mescaline in 1953; while Alexander Shulgin synthesises MDMA, uses it with his close friends, and recounts their spiritual experiences of it in 1976.

Both nature and the creative arsenal of Man himself are full of these *entheogens* – the term was coined by the historian Carl Ruck, as a more factual replacement for the erroneous term hallucinogens, and it is of course derived from syntheism's *Entheos*, the god within ourselves – which have always been used for spiritual purposes. This was the case despite many nation states, on the pretext of the most bizarre and prejudiced excuses, assiduously trying to stop the use of entheogens in what must be regarded as the current paradigm shift's most obvious form of bourgeois *religious persecution* of the emerging netocracy's metaphysical lifestyle choice. It is from *this radical equality*, in this literally syntheist procedure, that the ethics of interactivity is born and developed – not in Levinas' sentimental and anti-Nietzschean self-sacrificing romanticism.

If Emmanuel Levinas is an Abrahamic atheist, the French-Jewish philosopher Jacques Derrida is an atheist syntheist. When we move from Levinas to Derrida, we are moving from *the Messianic as immortality* to *the Messianic as survival*, as the Swedish philosopher Martin Hägglund insightfully includes in his pioneering reading of Derrida in his book *Radical Atheism*. The promise is always a promise against a backdrop of an open future and can therefore always be broken; it is part of the nature of the promise. This threat is already built into the promise from the start. Even the strongest will to include will therefore always exclude someone, which sets the political in constant motion, which in turn puts democracy into a state of constant reassessment. There are quite simply no objectively valid hierarchies between people. If people are special because they are strong, then it follows from this that some people are stronger than others. If 1 exists, 2 also exists, and 2 is greater than 1. Thus the ethical objective value must be 0 in order for us to attain equality. The problem is that, ever since the widespread acceptance of feudalism, Man has built hierarchies in order to maximise power for the fortunate and for the sake of its aggregated effect. Hierarchies blossom in the worlds of transcendental metaphysicists. It is only through breaking with transcendentalisation and introducing *an immanent metaphysics* that we can achieve a genuinely egalitarian society. *Syntheism is radical egalitarianism par excellence.*

Against Levinas' *transcendentalist ethics vis-à-vis the other* we can posit Alain Badiou's *genericist ethics vis-à-vis the same.* Badiou argues that what is constantly recurring is what characterises existence, and it is only in the recognition of the constantly recurring – the universal in the particular – that ethics is possible. The genericism of Badiou is pitted against the constructivism of Levinas. Badiou's anarchist ethics is pitted against Levinas' Abrahamic moralism. Badiou's ethics is a duty based on chance – quite simply because chance takes us precisely where we end up – there is no external meaning attached to anything, but once we have arrived where chance has actually taken us, it is still our duty to live ethically. Why? Because ethics makes us what we are as contingent beings. It is our agential essence.

Compared to Badiou, Slavoj Zizek takes yet another stride away from Levinas when he stands firm with their common antecedent Jacques Lacan and *the psychoanalytical ethics.* According to Zizek, ethics is only possible as a fidelity to the crack in the current view of the world, rather than as a fidelity to any decision made blindly. Only by holding onto *the sinthome* – the importunate little disturbance that constantly reminds us of the illusoriness of our world view, its incompleteness and thereby necessary, constant variability – are we able to use this world view in any way to orient ourselves, and then a sustainable ethics must be pinned to the sinthome and nothing else. We can never trust our world view, we cannot even trust ourselves: the closest we come to something we can actually trust, which we have to trust, is the sinthome itself, *the real* from both the internal and external reality that we are capable of experiencing at all. From a syntheological perspective, both Zizek and Badiou, of course, are located inside the syntheological pyramid, at opposite ends of the oscillation between *Atheos* (Zizek) and *Pantheos* (Badiou).

In sexuality, desire always desires itself, that is, it cannot attain the mental excitement without a considerable element of prohibition. This is what Lacan calls *the closed subject*. Even our identity for ourselves is built on total prohibition. You can only feel yourself as an identity that is closed and forbidden in relation to itself. You feel yourself through not being able to feel yourself, and thereby you arise as a *phenomenon in the face of itself* since in other respects you are a pure illusion. You do not really exist. Sex does not really exist. What exists is a body that lures itself into touching other bodies in the belief that it thereby satisfies a desire which, however, it thereby displaces in order to keep the desire for itself, and for *the other*. It would be more correct to describe life as bizarre theatre rather than as something that even resembles linear logic.

However, beyond the ethics of interactivity a landscape opens up for a pure syntheist ethics. It is an ethics where human actions can occur without any imagined observer, where *the other* as a target disappears from the equation. The Nietzschean *übermensch does whatever should be done merely because it should be done* and without any ulterior motive whatsoever. We can describe this as *an ethical vacuum state*. It is a case of a *metaethics*; a constantly ongoing investigative study of how the syntheist agent is changed by acting this way or that way. The artist that bases her whole creativity on her own desire and nowhere else is an early example of a syntheist ethicist. But there is really nothing to prevent all human behaviour in the syntheist utopia from taking as its point of departure such *an ethics of intra-acting* rather than an ethics of interactivity – because the ethics of intra-acting follows logically from the development of the syntheist agent as a human ideal.

Individualist metaphysics is based on a hierarchisation of different phenomenal states. For the individual to be able to be positioned – anthropocentrically and internarcissistically – as the ruler at the centre of existence, a mythology must be constructed around the individual as *the crowning achievement of creation*. The steps up to this status as the crowning achievement of creation are however lined with different existences of gradually ascending value. Furthest down are the minerals, above them the plants, above them the animals, and then at the very top, Man. The first difference between the minerals and the plants requires a fundamental metaphysical mythology, namely the narrative of *life as sacred*. The second difference between the plants and the animals requires an additional metaphysical mythology, namely the narrative of *the body as sacred*. The third difference between the animals and Man requires yet another additional mythology, namely the narrative of *consciousness as sacred*, or the soul as we used to call it.

Note that outside the anthropocentric fantasy, this entire mythological construction is in a worthless limbo. It is only within the capitalist fantasy, which revolves around the centrality of the individual and the substantiality of the atom and the insurmountable gap between them, that these mythological assertions can be distorted into categorical axioms. The sacralisations of life, the body and consciousness are by-products of the massive *internarcissism*; the collective self-glorification, which in turn is a consequence of fully implemented alienation. The truth is, however, that life, the body and consciousness are emergent phenomena in an open and contingent universe; phenomena that are characterised by constantly higher degrees of *complexity*, rather than by any form of *sacredness*. That which one can relate to in a deeper sense is not these three anthropocentric projections in themselves, but the common underlying variable; the constantly higher *intensities* of the current emergences. To a syntheist, concepts such as life, body or consciousness are not fundamental; rather, these must be regarded as secondary and precisely as anthropocentric projections onto the rich, creative ability of the Universe to produce hosts of different intensities. And it is *the intensity* that is sacred. The name of the intensity is *Entheos*.

Postmodernism is dominated by fear of conflict and its ideology, *cultural relativism*. In the furious animosity towards fixed values, cultural relativism still fixes a value in itself, namely the fixed value *per se* that all values are flexible. Thereby it immediately falls on its own sword (see *The Body Machines*). Cultural relativism is replaced in the information chaos of the Internet society by the search for *qualitative intensities*. All assertions are not as equally true or false. An assertion is strengthened intersubjectively and is accorded scientific credibility if it can be verified. It quite simply has a higher *truth intensity* than an unfounded fabrication. The energetic atheist Christopher Hitchens is quite right when he writes that what can be asserted without any evidence whatsoever also can be dismissed without evidence. The question is whether this truth intensity is *a specific intensity* (as though truth were a special spectrum within the intensity from the beginning), or a pure intensity (as though the intensity precedes the truth and the truth is derived temporarily from the intensity in its entirety as an ethical act). Is there any kind of objectively valid hierarchy between the various spectra within the intensity, or should the intensity be understood exactly as it is in its entirety?

Let us go to the history of philosophical vitalism in order to seek an answer. The difference between the individualist and the dividualist paradigms could not be any clearer than the difference that exists between the otherwise closely-related French philosophers Henri Bergson and Gilles Deleuze. Bergson's classical vitalism steadfastly sticks to the idea of *the sacredness of life* as an ontological foundation. For Deleuze however, the celebration of life becomes yet another banal anthropocentrism in a Cartesian universe that has been closed off and anaesthetised for no good reason. Instead, he sees *the active intensity itself* as the Universe's fundamental expression for its existence in relation to itself. Deleuze's *pantheist* rather than anthropocentric *vitalism* therefore remain – in the narrative about the Universe's magnificent capacity for creativity and multiplicity – as much with the marvellous in quantum physics and cosmology as with the marvellous in plants and animals. Therefore it seems quite reasonable that Karen Barad's, Manuel De Landa's and Robert Corrington's intensity-fixated variants of *relationalism* start from Deleuzian rather than Bergsonian vitalism. It is nature and not what is most closely related to Man that is *the vital*, and nature is vital in itself based on its own intensity. Therefore Deleuze, Barad and De Landa are *naturalist* philosophers. The self-confessed syntheist Corrington even calls his philosophical orientation *ecstatic naturalism*.

Process philosophy is fundamentally descriptive rather than prescriptive. Nietzsche builds a *genealogy*, Foucault compiles an *archaeology*, Derrida calls his method *deconstruction*, we ourselves describe our own work in previous volumes as a *meteorology* since we – as do the weather forecasters – study the future as a gigantic information complex that is difficult to grasp as a whole. The background to process philosophy's descriptive methods is that Nietzsche sees through his predecessor Kant when he traces an even deeper *will to fabricate* behind the latter's stated *will to truth*. Nietzsche does not see any other possibility at all for the writing of history than fabrication, even among philosophers. The difference thus does not lie in a will to fabricate pitted against a will to truth, but rather in the varying level of quality of different attempts at fabrication. All truths are a kind of myth, but all myths are not equally functional in the recurring confrontation with existence around us. Some myths are truer than others, which can and must be tested in the interaction with the surrounding world.

Violence is constantly present in all relations. The glorification of violence is predominantly a modern phenomenon. The further we distance ourselves from the society where direct physical violence was tantamount to power, the more naked violence is glorified by precisely those who believe themselves to be robbed of power when violence is built into the system or loses its obvious function as a bearer of power. Even the ambition to reduce violence requires further violence. Pacifism is therefore a perfect example of a false radicality. All systems contain built-in violence. A society without violence would be an impossibility, since a society without *antagonisms* can never can exist. The dream of absolute peace is the dream of absolute assault. Jean-Paul Sartre points out that pacifists in all societies always end up on the side of the oppressors, since it is through pacifism that the oppressed are denied the possibility of resistance. Pacifism implemented is of course in practice the smoothest way to maintain the *status quo* in a society where structural violence and oppression reign: repression with an ingratiating smile.

Via a parallel development, the avoidance of pain and suffering has become late capitalism's primary obsession. This avoidance has become a widespread social game. The result is a restless and deeply ignorant citizen who seeks immediate rewards, while avoiding everything that requires the least bit of patience and postponement of the reward. Postmodern popular culture is permeated by this strategy, which is designed to always take the shortest route to this or that objective on every occasion. Nothing may require anything, bad news must be silenced and repressed, complex truths must be hidden, for if the situation actually requires something of the consumer, she might of course turn in the doorway and quite simply choose to go to a more ingratiating competitor. However, this strategy requires that nature is in a permanent state of balance without antagonisms. But this balanced state in nature is a myth. Syntheist ecology therefore begins with the insight that everything in existence, including nature, is *process* and constant motion, as the syntheist philosopher Alfred North Whitehead expresses the matter. Stability is in the best case a parenthesis; in the worst case – and most probably – a pure delusion. Solidarity through organic unity is pitted against mechanical instrumentality.

An important component in all thinking around consciousness is the concept of *intelligence*. Intelligence, however, does not arise as a superfluous asset for the owner's amusement, but as a necessary instrument of survival in a system that otherwise would not survive, at the same time as intelligence is attractive in itself and results in procreative advantages. Like everything else that develops in a Darwinian way, intelligence develops as both a mutation-conditioned response to harsh circumstances, and as a human equivalent to the tail feathers of the peacock (wisdom, talent and humour attract potential partners: see *The Body Machines*). This means, for example, that the idea of God as an intelligent being is absurd. An omnipotent creature, who does not need to risk bumping into any obstacles worth mentioning in his quest to get his own way – and this applies as we know to both the Abrahamic father gods and syntheism's projected divinities – thus needs no intelligence. Omnipotence suffices perfectly well; it covers most things.

On closer inspection, intelligence is actually a symptom of a limitation or a weakness, a final weapon against another, greater power (and often one blissfully void of intelligence). Or to carry the matter to its extreme: If God had been in need of intelligent design in order to create the world – that is, a blueprint marked by an intelligence that must be followed by God and the angels of heaven, in the same way that construction workers relate to their instructions from the hopefully intelligent architect – God would instead be an expression of a lack of power and above all reveal his total lack of omnipotence. An omnipotent Universe therefore is not intelligent in the real sense of the word, since it emerges spontaneously. *Intelligence is thus a human trait, originating from our complex limitations and inflicted powerlessness, and definitely not some divine property.*

Since syntheism is fundamentally *relationalist*, it follows that *syntheist ethics* also must be relationalist. To begin with, ethics is always a matter of prioritisations. Nothing in itself has any kind of objectively valid value. In a greater objective sense, everything is meaningless, since no external god exists who cares about giving anything a value that endures regardless of the prevailing conditions. It is only a being whose existence is characterised by recurring deficits and limitations, and consequent necessary prioritisations, who is in need of a values system. A state of complete plenty – such as the *Universe in itself* – however needs no values at all. All argumentation around what Man values in the form of things and actions consequently revolves around the relationships of these things and actions to, and their significance for, himself as a creature inhibited by deficits and limitations.

That things and actions have a value for Man from the point of view of his possibilities of survival is not particularly surprising. But what makes Man's valuation special is that he also bestows value on things and actions that he has no evident use for whatsoever. Man experiences instead an emotional connection, a feeling of expanded identity, in relation to what he values. Thus there is every bit as much existential as utilitarian subjective valuation. Fetishistic valuation has its foundation in the subconscious conviction that if nothing is valued, one's own existence is worthless: therefore something must always be valued, and this valuation is consequently hysterical rather than logical, dividual rather than universal. What has been valued on purely fetishistic grounds often gets enormous value, since the process is linked to the narcissistic impulse – if this thing or this action gets a value, *then I get a value as well through my intimate relationship with the fetish*, and thereby life and existence get a value. Everything valuable hangs together and, through this very entanglement, creates a value. The world is thus saved by *the fetish* and Man can heave a sigh of relief.

The great illusion in this context is that it is perfectly possible to participate in a corrupt system by simultaneously building up an internal, emotional distance to the system. This is the great lie of the distanced indifference of postmodernism, preached by both cynical liberals and Californian Zen masters. The problem is that human creativity is lured into pouring all its energy into maintaining the system; this even applies to the theorists who are critical of the system. Only by stepping off, taking a position on the side-lines and *constructing a world in parallel outside the system* can the syntheist utopia be realised. *A revolution always starts with a subtraction.* We must retire to the position where, at long last, we can see the social entirety and then only act on the basis of this entirety, rather than devote ourselves to patching up a fundamentally defective system. For what is a revolution? What is a genuinely radical change? Revolutions occur in societies characterised by chaos, where the power has already discretely shifted from the formal power position in order to subsequently appear in a completely new, not yet defined position. And in a completely new guise, shaped by the new conditions that prevail. The superficial revolution with its rioting in the streets is merely a latter-day symptom of the underlying, authentic revolution, which takes place in a completely different place and at an earlier time. The link between the printing press and the storming of the Bastille is just one of many obvious examples.

The strategic prophet of the previous paradigm shift, G W F Hegel, defines his philosophical project as the construction of a bridge between *the sacred* and *the secular.* He distinguishes between three different spirits with the following characteristics: the objective, the subjective and the absolute spirit. What is important in our turbulent age here and now is to take Hegel's advice and set aside the objective and subjective spirits to instead assume the vantage point of the absolute; to first equip ourselves thoroughly for the coming struggle between the bourgeoisie and the netocracy and then position ourselves on the battlefield, conscious of and in accordance with *the radical truth as an act in the new paradigm*. The paradigm shift is namely occurring right under the very noses of the old power elite; it establishes a completely new power system in a completely different place than the previous one (see *The Netocrats*) and thereby offers historically unique possibilities for a radical and genuine change in society's orientation and organisation. But the paradigm shift can only be apprehended in the necessary detail from a position permeated by *subtraction*. Therefore the syntheist temples and monasteries are far more than merely exotic oases for some kind of collective spiritual pleasure. They are, in fact, the necessary points of departure, the revolutionary cells, in the subversive utopian project that goes under the name of *the Syntheist Movement*. It is there that new thoughts are being thought.

And all this is happening right now.

Glossary

agency the agent's capacity for emergent experience of the self, including the feverish, affirmative meaning creation that follows from this fundamentally traumatic experience. Agency arises when a series of dividualities interact around a necessary, primordial void (*Atheos*) and project a dividual identity onto this (*Entheos*), with the ambition of constructing an ethical substance in the void between the history in question (*Pantheos*) and the potentially utopian future (*Syntheos*), in *the infinite now*.

agent the subjective identity that arises within the active agency, as a mental emergence within a physical body as a relationalist phenomenon. *The syntheist agent* replaces *the Cartesian individual* as the human ideal at the transition from capitalism to informationalism.

alienation the systematic separation of people with the purpose of exercising power, partly as *external alienation* that isolates people from each other, partly as *internal alienation* that divides the dividual agency and generates self-contempt and narcissism as a result. See, by way of comparison, its opposite *religion*.

amor fati love of fate in Latin, the ethical-logical acceptance of everything that has happened in history up until the current moment and submission to everything waiting in the future that the agent cannot influence anyway in any respect. The concept was launched by the German philosopher Friedrich Nietzsche in the 19th century and is a fundamental principle for syntheist ethics. Note that the principle does not comprise any welcoming of future repetitions of past events no matter how ethically loved (or hated). Rather the reverse: *amor fati* is a welcoming of *the repetition of the constant change* and nothing else, and the concept is consequently strongly linked to the syntheist divinity *Entheos*.

anthropocentrism a world view with Man at the centre of existence. The capitalist paradigm is dominated for example by *humanism*, an anthropocentric metaphysics. See, by way of comparison, *universocentrism*.

atheism the conviction that a specific God concept lacks existential substance and/or social-psychological relevance. According *to the principle of explanatory closure,* atheism can never be directed towards all theological concepts at the same time; it can thereby never be universally valid but merely particular. It is always a particular god that atheism cannot believe in; it can never deny all gods simultaneously. See, by way of comparison, *theism, monotheism, polytheism* and *syntheism*.

Atheos the god that does not exist in Greek and which precisely therefore exists as an empty concept, as the god that does not exist; the virtual non-existence from which the current existence arises. Atheos is the first of the four divinities in *the syntheological pyramid,* symbolised by the void or the black hole and can be regarded as the primordial origin of everything, for both the material phenomenon and for the mental agent. Atheos is celebrated at midwinter and is followed by the quarter *Athea*.

atomism the conviction that existence seen at its deepest level consists of indivisible, fundamental building blocks of a kind which also comprise the complete, future potential for all higher hierarchies that follow through history, depending on the God-given, intrinsic, mystical properties of atoms. Atomism does for the object what humanism does for the subject: the two isms are therefore two sides of the same coin (*individualism*) and with the same progenitors from the European age of Enlightenment, above all Isaac Newton and Immanuel Kant.

attention a value that is calculated by multiplying medial credibility with medial awareness for one and the same meme, dividual, community or brand: the higher the attentional value, the greater the power and influence in the Internet society.

attentionalism a society where the accumulation of attention is more important with respect to power than the accumulation of capital. The complete paradigm shift from a capitalist to an attentionalist society is complete at the same historical moment that the amount of capital which follows attention surpasses the amount of attention which follows capital. According to Google's search engines, this shift has already occurred a long time ago.

The Body Machines the third of three books in *The Futurica Trilogy* by Alexander Bard & Jan Söderqvist with the focus on the Internet age's new, built-in, monist view of humans.

capitalism the third of the four information-technology paradigms that arises when both literacy and virtual value transfer are disseminated with devastating efficiency by the advent of the printing press. This paradigm shift enables a rapid economic and population growth through the focus being shifted from the countryside, agriculture, the monarchy and monotheism to an information-technology higher social emergence based around the city, industry, democracy and humanism. The concept is often used synonymously with *industrialism*.

chemical liberation the conviction that the extensive availability of chemical substances for radical alteration of the mind in turn fundamentally changes the idea of what it means to be a human being; partly through Man's evident discovery of himself as a strictly chemical-hormonal phenomenon, partly through the division between the first subject that decides what chemicals should be added and when this should happen and the second subject which then experiences the radical alteration of the mind *per se*. The concept can be compared to *sexual liberation* and *transhumanism*.

communication society one of the three classical concepts to describe the Internet age, to be compared with *information society* and *network society*. According to the information technology writing of history, all paradigms through history should be categorised as communication societies; it is only the degree of communication that separates them.

consumtariat the Internet age's pathetic underclass, those who are left behind or outside the digital world, isolated in their minimal social activities and reduced to mainly devoting themselves to the Internet society's lowest common denominator: the vulgar, passive consumption of mass produced goods and services.

correlationism the conviction that Man only has access to *the correlation* between thinking and being but never direct access to thinking or being by themselves. Correlationism dominates Western thinking from Immanuel Kant and onwards but according to Bard & Söderqvist is set aside by *model-dependent realism* which is first launched by Niels Bohr within physics and is later completed by Karen Barad within philosophy.

death drive according to Sigmund Freud, the drive in its most brutal form, as a longing for death, self-extinction and a return to the inorganic. The death drive in everyday life manifests itself as a life without life or as living as though life were dead, as an unwillingness to achieve or appreciate anything at all. See, by way of comparison, *ressentiment*.

desire is what the mind seeks but flees from attaining since desire seeks itself most deeply as a *metadesire* wherefore consummation of the desire would result in not just its satisfaction but also its death. To follow one's own desire is nevertheless the paradoxist foundation of psychoanalytical and thereby also for syntheist ethics. See, by way of comparison, *drive* and *libido*.

determinism the conviction that every occurrence is strictly bound by laws of nature that in some mysterious way are encoded in the Universe even before the Big Bang. The future is therefore closed and both time and all forms of will and choice are deeply illusory. Determinism dominates the Western history of ideas from Plato to Einstein but collapses at the same moment that there arises a single chance event anywhere or at any time in the Universe and, according to Niels Bohr, this occurs within quantum physics every time that potentialities are actualised. See, by way of comparison, the Bohrian opposite *indeterminism*.

dialectic(s) an ongoing logical system where the opposites thesis and antithesis are dissolved and transform into a synthesis which however must not be viewed as a kind of compromise between the thesis and antithesis but instead is the necessary exit from the antithesis, primarily by virtue of the aspect of the thesis that the antithesis lacks. Dialectics are first and foremost associated with their founder Heraclitus in ancient Greece and modern master G W F Hegel.

dialectic between eternalism and mobilism is a complete syntheist onto-epistemology developed by Bard & Söderqvist in the book *The Global Empire*. Existence is fundamentally chaotic or mobilist and becomes tangible, gaining meaning only by being frozen and in an illusory way fixed in space–time, thereby being *eternalised* by perception. It means that *chaos* is noumenal and analogous while *the Cosmos* is phenomenal and digital in a Kantian sense, which according to Bard & Söderqvist ironically makes Immanuel Kant's own *correlationism* superfluous. The completely mobilist nature of the Universe is namely, with its ancestral independence of Man's existence, an indisputable fact and is thereby all in all as a whole an eternalised phenomenon, process religion's *the One*, syntheology's divinity *Pantheos,* the point of departure for the universocentric world view that is directly accessible to Man.

dividual the opposite of an individual, an infinitely divisible human being or phenomenon, rather than an incorruptibly indivisible human being or object. See, by way of comparison, *agent*.

dividualism the opposite of individualism, the conviction that people and things are irreducible multiplicities that cannot be described as separate cohesive *phenomena* other than as radically intensity-reduced *eternalisations*.

drive the search for satisfaction that Man shares with animals; for example, the needs and longing for food, drink, sleep, sex and power. See, by way of comparison, *desire, libido* and *death drive*.

ecological apocalypse the dystopian conviction that the global socio-economic system under capitalism is heading towards the consumption of the Earth's finite resources and environmental destruction on such a scale that it radically worsens human life on the planet or even makes it impossible. According to syntheism the direct interconnection between all the inhabitants of the world and the phenomena in their environment through the sacred *Internet* is the only logical if utopian possibility of avoiding the ecological apocalypse.

emergence the conviction that existence is indeterministic and the future thereby is open, which enables various conditions to suddenly change so radically as to cause laws and rules for both states themselves and their surroundings, including so-called laws of nature, to fundamentally change. Often cited examples are that chemistry as a phenomenon is emergent in relation to physics and biology as a phenomenon is emergent in relation to chemistry. Note that emergences in principle only take place once in history and for example cannot be replicated in experiments, since they do not obey any laws of nature whatsoever preceding their genesis. Note also that emergences such as the Darwinian evolution cannot possibly arise in a determinist universe.

entheism the conviction that existence arises and can best be described as differences on top of differences and that duration, as a yardstick for the genesis and consummation of these differences, is absolute and must constitute the foundation for both the material and the spiritual world view. Entheism is fundamental to Taoism in China, as well as to the philosophical schools of Zoroaster, Heraclitus, Baruch Spinoza, Friedrich Nietzsche, Alfred North Whitehead and Gilles Deleuze, to take some examples, all of them of enormous value to syntheism.

entheogen a narcotic substance that gives rise to strong visions and feelings, often described by the users in question as deeply religious experiences. Examples of entheogens are preparations such as LSD, DMT, *ayahuasca,* mescaline, psilocybin mushrooms and MDMA. The concept entheogen is of course closely related to the syntheist divinity *Entheos.*

Entheos originally means the god within in Greek and refers to the divine that the syntheist *agent* derives from inside herself, the third of the four divinities in the syntheological pyramid. Entheos for difference and distinction, and thereby also for time, duration, change, multiplicity and ecstasy. Entheos is celebrated at the spring equinox, which is followed by the quarter *Enthea.*

epistemology the philosophical discipline that studies knowledge and the (im)possibility of knowledge. For a deeper understanding of a syntheist epistemology. See, by way of comparison, *dialectic between eternalism and mobilism, transrationalism* and *the principle of explanatory closure.*

eternalisation freezing or fixation of the mobilist chaos, an existential necessity for perception to be able to create a satisfactory order from the chaos of existence and give the incipient consciousness a functional world view within which the subject can arise and build an identity of its own. The problem is that the eternalisation is not reality; it has so to speak ceased to exist in the same moment that it is produced. It is thus not the ideas that are real in contrast to the chaos of existence, as Plato claims, but exactly the reverse is the case: mobilism precedes and is always primary in relation to eternalism in the dialectics between them.

eternalism the conviction that a world view can only be constructed from the temporary eternalisations produced by perception within the *dialectic between eternalism and mobilism*, which means that a world view is never permanent but must be constantly reassessed, modified and, at paradigm shifts, also rejected and replaced from scratch. Note that this state of affairs does not give any *carte blanche* for cultural relativism's claim that all histories are of equal value. According to eternalism, inter-subjectively and pragmatically rejected histories have for example no value whatsoever and there are great differences in *truth quality* between various assertions depending on their pragmatic utility and sustainability in the syntheist community.

ethics from the Greek *ethos*, originally customs: values based on intention in relation to expected processes of cause and effect. In contrast to their opposite *morals*, they lack both an external agency of judgement and any references whatsoever to different emotional states, for example empathy, as if these were relevant in terms of value. Ethics therefore only refers to the syntheist agent herself, who thereby gets her ethical substance by identifying completely with her libidinal intentions.

event a spectacular occurrence with dramatic consequences for a particular phenomenon or a specific region of the Universe. See, by way of comparison, *singularity*.

feudalism the second information-technology paradigm, made possible through Man's development of written symbols for the storage and transfer of information around 5,000 years ago and dominated by *written language*.

fiction a cohesive memetic narrative, which temporarily yet resolutely gives the *memes* their seemingly logical place within the prevailing *memeplex*. The fiction can be divided into smaller *fictives* to great effect and several fictions piled on top of each other support a subconscious *ideology* which enables the gradual growth of a cohesive paradigmatic *metaphysics*.

fictive the smallest component in Bard & Söderqvist's extensive memetics, and the unit to which every little aspect of a meme is attributable. See, by way of comparison, *fiction*, *ideology* and *metaphysics*.

The Futurica Trilogy the first three books by Alexander Bard & Jan Söderqvist: *The Netocrats*, *The Global Empire* and *The Body Machines*.

The Global Empire the second of the three books in *The Futurica Trilogy* by Alexander Bard & Jan Söderqvist focusing on the new, built-in, integrated world view of the Internet age. The global empire is the idea of a world where all socio-economic systems are completely, mutually dependent on each other for their own survival and thereby in practice no longer are separate, but have been transformed into one single, fragile system – a global empire – with or without a conscious centre, but based on an unfounded, subconscious, cohesive ideology, prominent under concepts such as *individualism, atomism, humanism, capitalism* and *statism*.

God the name of all the dreams of humanity projected onto one single point. In Bard & Söderqvist's philosophy the God concept is used exactly as the philosopher G W F Hegel uses it, that is, as an empty concept binding together all loose threads within metaphysics to one cohesive, ideological unit, without the concept thereby requiring any relevance whatsoever outside the metaphysical equation itself.

humanism the religious conviction that the human being rather than God is the centre of existence, its objective and meaning. This conviction was originally formulated by the French philosopher René Descartes and later consummated ideologically by the German philosopher Immanuel Kant. See, by way of comparison, *individualism* and *atomism*.

ideology a set of conscious or even more often subconscious memes that together generate a sense of context and mutual dependence on each other, regardless of whether this really is the case or not. An ideology thus does not need to be the least bit coherent; all human thinking stems from one or more ideological platforms, symbolised through *fictions* consisting of *fictives* and in the final analysis attributable to a prevailing *metaphysics* within the current information-technology paradigm.

indeterminism the conviction that the arrow of time is real, the Universe is constantly recreating itself, with laws and rules in a constant state of flux, the future wide open, and Man, just like all other phenomena, more or less influencing all the processes that he is part of. According to indeterminism's principles, it is fully possible that God has never existed, but it is definitely not possible to guarantee that God never will exist.

individual a thing or a human being that is indivisible, that exists as a solid substance. This is in contrast to a *dividual*, a phenomenon or a human being that is an irreducible multiplicity. The individual is the human ideal of capitalism and also its divinity, while the dividual is the human ideal of informationalism but in contrast to the individual lacks divine implications, as syntheism is *universocentric* rather than *anthropocentric* like capitalism.

individualism the religious conviction that Man rather than God is the centre of existence, its objective and meaning and that everything in existence consists of fundamental solid entities, *individuals*, of which everything else consists and to which everything else returns, without anything thereby being fundamentally changed. This *anthropocentric* ideology was originally formulated by the French philosopher René Descartes and later consummated by the German philosopher Immanuel Kant. The concept is synonymous with *humanism* within the social sciences and *atomism* within the natural sciences.

industrialism the socio-economic structure that arises when both literacy and virtual value transfer is disseminated with devastating efficiency through the arrival of the printing press. The paradigm shift in question enables a rapid economic and population growth through the focus being shifted from the countryside, agriculture, the monarchy and monotheism to an information-technology higher social emergence based on the city, industry, democracy and humanism. The concept is often used synonymously with *capitalism*.

infinite now the most sacred, most transforming and most ecstatic experience in syntheist religious practice; the infinite now is in itself immanent but is experienced as transcendental. As the condition is impossible to maintain over time without transitioning from ecstasy to agony, it is not the experience in itself but the memory of the experience that is the driving force existentially and ethically. The ecstasy thereby gets its true value as an eternalisation, which explains its paradoxical name. The infinite now can be executed for example as a mutual act of baptism or as a psychedelic ritual.

information society one of three classical concepts for describing the Internet age, to be compared with the *communication society* and the *network society*. According to the information-technology writing of history all paradigms through history should be categorised as information societies, it is only the degree of information processing that separates them.

information-technology writing of history the hypothesis where Man is the constant and technology is the variable through history and that history therefore can be best and most deeply described as a series of information-technology emergences and their ensuing revolutions within communication and information processing. According to the information-technology writing of history, at the end of the day power is always power over the information flows in every given society (see *The Netocrats*).

informationalism the fourth information-technology paradigm, made possible through the arrival of the Internet and dominated by interactive communication.

intensity within physics the measure of the concentration of energy within a given, delimited area. In relationalist physics, intensity replaces the old substance as the yardstick of everything; in social relationalist sociology attentional intensity replaces the old growth of the economy as the yardstick of everything; in syntheist ethics ecstatic intensity in *the infinite now* replaces all the old maxims for the existential experience and *the memory from the infinite now* is the fundamental identity-generating reference through life. See, by way of comparison, *relationalism* and *social relationalism*.

interactivity the fourth way for human beings to communicate with each other, arising chronologically after spoken language, written language and the mass media in turn, starting in the 1980s and onwards. Since interactivity requires and encourages an entirely different kind of talent than the previously dominant mass media, the arrival of interactivity will continue to turn all earlier truths on their head and cause a dramatic paradigm shift with a concomitant power shift from capitalism's *bourgeoisie* to informationalism's *netocracy*. The concept is synonymous with *participationism*.

internarcissism a displacement of the narcissistic pathology where two or more narcissists consciously or subconsciously act obsessively with each other instead of with themselves in order to thereby conceal the probably even stronger narcissism that *de facto* is active beneath the surface. Since narcissism is fundamentally a form of repressed self-contempt, the internarcissistic society is extremely alienating in nature.

Internet the divinity that arises when more than seven billion people and hundreds of billions of other phenomena across the globe are interconnected directly with each other in real time. According to Bard & Söderqvist the Internet is a clear and apparent manifestation of *Syntheos* and can also be regarded as a late realisation of Christianity's *the Holy Spirit*, but without the accompanying Father and Son.

Internet Age the epoch that is launched when all of humanity is directly interconnected with itself in real time around the world, whereupon the insight of the Internet's divine potential starts to spread.

ironic polytheism faith in or the practice surrounding two or more gods. Syntheism is not a form of polytheism in any classical sense, but is however definitely an *ironic polytheism*, since the recognition that gods can and should be created does not place any limits on how many of these divinities there can or should be.

irreducible multiplicity the conviction that all phenomena in existence are fundamental multiplicities that thereby cannot be reduced to any individual, delimited objects whatsoever. Clearly exemplified through Friedrich Nietzsche's declaration that nothing in the world is reducible to less than the number two. Within syntheist ontology, the irreducible multiplicity is unavoidable since ontology must always begin with a brutal write-off of information at the dialectical transition from mobilism to eternalism as the necessary, dramatic introduction to the perception process.

libido life energy, will to power, will to intensity, will to expand. Libido is often associated with sexual energy but according to both Sigmund Freud and Carl Gustav Jung is a considerably broader concept which comprises all sorts of life energy, in both liberated and sublimated form. Libido thus comprises both *desire* and *drive*, the two focal points for Jacques Lacan's psychoanalytical methods. This means that the alpha and omega of syntheist ethics are finding, following and liberating both the agent's and the community's libido. See, by way of comparison, *the infinite now*.

memeplex a cluster of memes that can be spread to great effect in the form of an experienced, cohesive unit. A memeplex can therefore be regarded as emergent in relation to dividual memes, as something greater and more complex than the constituent memes separately, which enables an anti-reductionist memetics.

memetics the study of how ideas or *memes* are formed, disseminated, stored and changed between people and media. Memes in these studies are regarded as *replicators*, as mental equivalents of a kind to the biological genes, and the parallels between memetics and *genetics* are therefore extensive. See, by way of comparison, *semiotics*.

metaphysics originally the philosophical studies of that which transcends physical reality, is comprised of the disciplines *ontology*, *cosmology* and *epistemology* within philosophy. Bard & Söderqvist also use the concept metaphysics as the top emergence in the hierarchy *fictives*, *fictions*, *ideologies* and *metaphysics*, in the sense of conscious or subconscious metaideological memeplexes. The concept of metaphysics is here synonymous with both *religion* and *world view*.

mobilisation to set in motion anew the eternalisations themselves within the *dialectic between eternalism and mobilism* after these have been consummated; thereby existence once again becomes a mobilist chaos but this time on the *metalevel*, whereupon new eternalisations at the metalevel are produced by perception in an eternal dialectical feedback loop.

mobilism in part the process-philosophy reality in the *dialectic between eternalism and mobilism*, a constantly mobile chaos in all directions and also within itself, which attains cosmic serenity only as *the One*, the Universe as an entirety, as one single cohesive phenomenon, syntheology's *Pantheos*; partly a frequently used synonym for *process philosophy*, particularly when relativism and relationalism are referred to jointly. In this capacity, mobilism constitutes the opposite of *totalism* in the history of philosophy.

monasteries sacred buildings for the execution of esoteric, religious rituals closed to or limited for the general public, often associated with temporary or permanent cohabitation for the participants. See, by way of comparison, *temples*.

monotheism the belief that all gods are false except one; alternatively that behind all the various gods people have proclaimed throughout history, simply hide one and the same god. Monotheism can thus be described an atheism with one small reservation.

morals from the Latin *morales*, customs; values and valuations attributable to an active or passive external judge who is to be obeyed without question and where the obedience is rewarded by for example material success or an eternal life. Both the Abrahamic religions and the capitalist nation states rest on moralist value foundations, for example *the Ten Commandments*, where the State and God respectively play the role of the external judge. See, by way of comparison, *ethics*.

narcissism compensatory self-obsession founded in a subconscious and impenetrable self-contempt, the modern consumer society is based on a continuously cultivated and encouraged *hypernarcissism* which often expresses itself in the form of a more concealed but precisely therefore even more destructive exchange of narcissistic obsession; see *internarcissism*; narcissism must absolutely not be mistaken for its opposite: *self-love*.

netocracy the new upper class of the Internet age, the social monsters who call the shots in the digital world through maximising their attention. Under the ongoing paradigm shift from capitalism to informationalism the netocracy is fighting for power over society against the old and increasingly vulnerable *bourgeoisie*. See, by way of comparison, *consumtariat*.

The Netocrats the first of three books in *The Futurica Trilogy* by Alexander Bard & Jan Söderqvist with the focus on the Internet age's new, built-in, information-technology writing of history.

network dynamics studies of how networks arise and are changed over time. Bard & Söderqvist launched their philosophical career in the 1990s with pioneering studies on the network dynamic effects of the Internet on the rest of society, summarised in *The Netocrats*. See, by way of comparison, *social relationalism*.

network society one of three classical concepts to describe the Internet age, to be compared with *information society* and *communication society*. According to the information-technology writing of history all paradigms throughout history should be categorised as network societies, it is only the degree of networking that sets them apart.

nihilism the conviction that existence lacks objective value since it lacks an external, objective value assigner. According to Bard & Söderqvist, nihilism must both logically and historically undergo three phases: first *naive nihilism*, where the nihilist is still not conscious of her nihilism; then *cynical nihilism*, where the nihilist pretends that objective values still exist in spite of an inner insight that this is not the case; and finally *affirmative nihilism*, where the lack of objective values is reinterpreted dialectically as the agential freedom to create one's own, subjective values that can take the place of the lost objective values. *Affirmationism* at present is of course the value creation's own *metavalue* and according to syntheology an example of the manifestation of *Entheos*.

ontology the metaphysical studies of being, becoming, existence and reality. Syntheism is based on a process philosophy ontology. See, by way of comparison, *process philosophy*.

Pantheos from the Greek *pan-theos*, everything is God and God is everything. The second of the four divinities within syntheology, pantheism regards everything that exists as one single cohesive phenomenon, *the One*, which thereby is tantamount to God himself. Represented within the history of philosophy by among others Baruch Spinoza and Asian doctrines such as Brahmanism and Zoroastrianism; is celebrated at midsummer and is followed by the quarter *Panthea*.

paradigm a world view that is used and defended by the prevailing power structure right up until a new technological complex produces a new, parallel power structure with a new metaphysics that is experienced as more relevant for the new, burgeoning elite and therefore compels a paradigm shift. According to the philosopher Thomas Kuhn, a paradigm is patched up and defended until it becomes untenable and a new paradigm appears, which is why the paradigm shifts through history tend to occur suddenly, dramatically and often tend to be bloody.

paradoxism the conviction that language arises as a way of dealing with paradoxical aspects of existentially formative traumas. The deepest truths about existence can therefore only be expressed as consciously constructed paradoxes, or not at all. The ancient paradoxism is represented by among others Heraclitus while Western paradoxism reaches its height with G F W Hegel's monist ontology.

participatory culture temporary or permanent events where all participants are expected to construct the event together from start to finish. Participatory culture is exploding with the growth of the Internet and is exemplified by festivals such as Burning Man in the United States, Going Nowhere in Spain and Africa Burn in South Africa. According to syntheism, participatory expressions of culture may be regarded to great effect as manifestations of *Syntheos*, the divinity that arises when people create things together for the sake of the community itself.

phenomenology the philosophical studies of experiences and consciousness; an illuminating and detailed example of a syntheist phenomenology is the *dialectic between eternalism and mobilism*.

phenomenon from the Greek *phainomenon*, to show, shine, arise, manifest itself. In syntheist onto-phenomenology the phenomenon replaces the classical object as the material point of reference in relation to the Universe as a whole. This phenomenon distinguishes itself from the object through primarily being a field consisting of equally primary relations and completely lacking the object's conceived substance and essence. All the phenomena influence and overlap more or less all other contemporary phenomena in the Universe, the boundaries of the phenomena are therefore always abstract and flowing rather than concrete and fixed as is the case with the objects.

philosophy the art of creating new concepts with the purpose of understanding the world better.

plurarchy from the Latin *pluralis* for multiplicity and the Greek *archos* for government. The chaotic condition in the political sphere that follows the collapse of democracy at the paradigm shift from the mass medial one-way communication and its efficient control of viewpoints to the interactive multi-way communication with its unfathomable and unruly information flows. See, by way of comparison, *theological anarchism*.

pragmatism a philosophical school founded by Charles Sanders Peirce and William James in the United States in the 19th century receiving a European equivalent through the legacy from Friedrich Nietzsche's existentialist philosophy. Pragmatism is the relativist school *par excellence* in the history of philosophy and it is from pragmatism that the first relationalist philosophy is developed by syntheism's primordial father Alfred North Whitehead in the 1920s. According to Bard & Söderqvist, pragmatism is also the political ideology that ought to dominate until *theological anarchism* can be implemented.

primitivism the first information-technology paradigm, made possible by Man's development of the speech organs in the larynx around 200,000 years ago and dominated by *spoken language*.

the principle of explanatory closure the insight that the Universe is expanding enormously makes an *ontic* rationalism impossible in the same way that the correspondingly enormous expansion of the amount of information in society makes an *ontological* rationalism impossible for exactly the same reasons. The human brain can never embrace what it does not have time to process. The principle of explanatory closure is therefore the death knell for Kantian rationalism.

process philosophy also called the ontology of becoming, a conviction that equates the metaphysical reality with difference and change *per se*. Is first developed in its radical, contemporary form by the British philosopher Alfred North Whitehead in the beginning of the 20th century and later inspires among other Niels Bohr's understanding of the fundamental conditions of physics. Process philosophy is represented within syntheology by Entheos and according to Bard & Söderqvist is a basic prerequisite for syntheist ontology.

process religion a religious conviction based on process-philosophy metaphysics where syntheism of course is the process religion *par excellence*. Note that the concept should not be confused with the admittedly Whitehead-inspired yet post-Christian school called *process theology*, which is represented by Charles Hawthorne among others.

psychedelia a subculture around the usage of various psychedelic drugs such as LSD, 'magic' mushrooms, mescaline and MDMA. The concept includes both art, music and various metaphysical schools. Syntheism is both tolerant and affirmative but absolutely not stipulative in terms of the use of psychedelic drugs within religious practices. Drugs should in any case be handled with knowledge and responsibility and possible health risks connected with them should be treated according to the principle of long-term harm reduction and not with the unscientific anti-drug variety of moralism.

psychoanalysis the history of philosophy applied by an analyst to a particular person, an analysand. The technique was first launched by the pioneers Sigmund Freud and Carl Gustav Jung and later developed in the most painstaking detail by Jacques Lacan, the main figure of modern psychoanalysis. If a psychotherapist strives for a patient's successful inclusion in society, the psychoanalyst's work aims to engender a critical questioning and truth-seeking in the analysand concerning the pitfalls of the ideological structure.

radical atheism the idea that classical atheism taken to its ultimate conclusion dialectically transforms into *syntheism*. The idea is investigated by philosophers such as Jacques Derrida, Simon Critchley and Martin Hägglund, before Bard & Söderqvist delve even deeper into it.

rationalism the conviction that Man is born with the capacity to mentally and intellectually understand and embrace the world logically in its entirety. Interestingly enough rationalism offers no logic for its own basic assumption: that the world can be grasped and understood through logic. See, by way of comparison, *transrationalism*.

reductionism the conviction that even the most complex of phenomena can be disassembled into their smallest components without any content whatsoever being lost. According to reductionism, all forms of *emergence* are illusory and seemingly emergent phenomena are nothing other than unusually complex *phase transitions*. Note that in spite of its extended popularity reductionism is incompatible with Darwinian evolution, for example.

relationalism a radicalisation of the relativist world view, where even the objects themselves are dissolved and set in motion vis-à-vis themselves and where there are no longer any reference points in relation to anything other than *the One*, that is, the Universe as a whole. Relationalism was first developed by the British philosopher Alfred North Whitehead only to be consummated later by the great master of quantum physics Niels Bohr. Bard & Söderqvist claim that relationalism not only takes relativism to the next level but once and for all kills off Kantian correlationism and thereby gives Man a direct contact with the physical surrounding world. Furthermore, relationalism can just as easily be applied to the social sciences as to the natural sciences, which Bard & Söderqvist do by developing *social relationalism* and its practical application *network dynamics*.

relativism a world view where all objects in existence are set in constant motion in relation to each other without the possibility of being frozen in space–time. The objects are thus fixed within and before themselves, but are completely background-independent in relation to their surrounding world. Examples of relativist ideologies are Friedrich Nietzsche's ontology and Albert Einstein's physics.

religion memes and social practices that bring people together and make them experience agential wholeness and meaning. The opposite of *alienation*.

ressentiment a hatred or contempt directed towards human existence and its prerequisites, merged with a conviction of the simultaneous birthright to freely cultivate and spread this hatred. Ressentiment thereby unconditionally includes an instinctive self-contempt and, according to syntheist ethics, locks its practitioner into a downward, self-destructive spiral where the ressentiment becomes self-fulfilling and finally is turned against and annihilates not just anything that comes in its way but also its memetic host.

schizoanalysis an anarchist response to the Lacanian psychoanalysis that was developed above all by Felix Guattari and Gilles Deleuze in France in the 1970s, aiming at a growing dividual heterogeneity in every way rather than the individual homogeneity that the schizoanalysts consider themselves to have found in their predecessors Freud and Lacan. Schizoanalysis becomes newly topical in Bard & Söderqvist who in the 21st century connect it to the growing Internet society with its oceans of schizoid identity production.

self-love the ethical self-acceptance of one's own body and its physiological and mental prerequisites and expressions. Self-love is a logical decision and not an emotional feeling and it has nothing to with *narcissism* but is rather the complete opposite of narcissism. See, by way of comparison, *amor fati*.

semiotics studies of how meaning is created and disseminated between people, animals and plants, also called *semiology*. See, by way of comparison, *memetics*.

sexual liberation the ambition that Man can and should be liberated from inhibitions and social norms in order to be able to live in full harmony with his own desires and drives. See, by way of comparison, *libido* and *chemical liberation*.

singularity an extraordinary historical event that immediately changes world history at a fundamental level. From an anthropocentric perspective, the genesis of the Universe, life and consciousness qualify as singularities. Since a singularity to a high degree is an emergent phenomenon that can never be predicted, according to syntheism there is no other word for a potential fourth, future singularity than the name *God*.

social relationalism the conviction that the principles presented by Niels Bohr for relationalist physics are just as applicable to the social sciences, particularly when the social is anyway just one of several emergences based on a fundamentally physical universe. According to social relationalism, multiplicity not only invariably precedes the dividual, the dividual is always fundamentally *de facto* illusory.

social technology techniques to control people in any given society and manipulate them in a direction desirable for the power structure. Social technologies can comprise everything from ideology production to radio broadcasts, censorship legislation to declarations of war, and can be exploited both consciously and subconsciously by the current people in power. See, by way of comparison, *socioanalysis*.

socioanalysis if psychology is applied as maximisation of happiness for each person and has its equivalent in the social arena in the form of sociology, psychoanalysis as truth maximisation for the dividual person has its equivalent in the social arena in the form of socioanalysis. See, by way of comparison,

*social technology.***sociography** mapping of social relations between dividuals and communities, for example through sociograms that show who knows and communicates with whom in the Internet society.

sociometry compilation and demonstration of social status and attentional power in the Internet society.

syntheism from the Greek word *syntheos* with the meaning created god or god that arises where it is man who creates: The historical as well as ideological dialectical dissolution of the dichotomy between theism and atheism; the conviction that God is Man's most important concept, the name of all of his visions and dreams, and thereby always has been created, will be created, and also should be created by Man, rather than the other way around, as classical atheism maintains.

syntheological pyramid three-sided graphical construction with Atheos, Pantheos and Entheos as the three corners at the bottom with lines drawn up to the eponymous top Syntheos. The three-sided pyramid consequently occurs frequently within syntheist symbolism.

syntheology syntheist theology, constructed around virtual divinities.

Syntheos from Greek, created god or god that arises where it is man who creates, the fourth, concluding and comprehensive concept in the syntheological pyramid, celebrated at the autumn equinox and introducing the quarter *Synthea*.

temples sacred buildings for the execution of open and public religious rituals. See, by way of comparison, *monasteries*.

theism the conviction that one or more gods physically or spiritually exist independently of Man's fantasies.

theological anarchism the conviction that the Internet society offers a unique historical opportunity to realise the anarchist utopia and thereby the power of the collective libido unleash fully. The concept is synonymous with the British philosopher Simon Critchley's ideal *mystical anarchism.*

totalism the conviction that existence can be comprehended both in totality and in the minutest detail and that history thereby can be summed up and concluded with the aid of the rationality of the philosophical genius. The history of totalism is launched by Plato in ancient Greece and is consummated with G W F Hegel's *ironic totalism* in 19th century Germany. After Hegel, totalist claims are namely pleaded by historians such as Francis Fukuyama and scientists such as Stephen Hawking, but they are seldom or never taken seriously in the world of philosophy. According to Bard & Söderqvist, because of *the principle of explanatory closure* all forms of totalism are both ontically and ontologically impossible. See, by way of comparison, *mobilism* and *transrationalism.*

transhumanism a broad virtual subculture with a great influence on for example Californian *counterculture,* revolving around ideas of a posthuman state as a growing consequence of an extensive, escalating technological development. Popular transhumanist subjects include immortality, cryonics, artificial intelligence, chemical liberation and anarcho-libertarian utopianism.

transrationalism the conviction that the human being is a Darwinian product that has developed a consciousness for the sake of her own survival and not in order to be able to logically grasp the world as a whole. All rationality must therefore comprise the insight of rationality's own built-in limitation. See, by way of comparison, *rationalism* and *the principle of explanatory closure.*

truth as an act an ontological and ethical concept devised by the French philosopher Alain Badiou with inspiration from the father of existentialism, the Danish philosopher Sören Kierkegaard, where the truth never finds the time to be tested through the drawn-out intersubjective processes that Karl Popper and Jürgen Habermas imagine, but rather appears as a decision based on intuition, taken agentially, followed by the incorruptible loyalty of the agent in question to the decision. According to Bard & Söderqvist, the concept is the *epistemological* cornerstone of syntheist ethics.

Universe everything that has existence regarded as one cohesive phenomenon. Used also as a synonym for *the Cosmos* and the syntheist divinity *Pantheos*.

universocentrism a world view starting from the Universe in its entirety as the centre of existence. Syntheism is based on a universocentric metaphysics, which is in contrast to, for example, capitalist *humanism* which is an *anthropocentric* religion.

the World State socio-economic interconnection between all the states of the world in such a way that the mutual dependence between them is so strong that the system in its entirety stands or falls on the continuation of this mutual dependence. The concept is used as synonymous with *The Global Empire* in the books of Bard & Söderqvist.

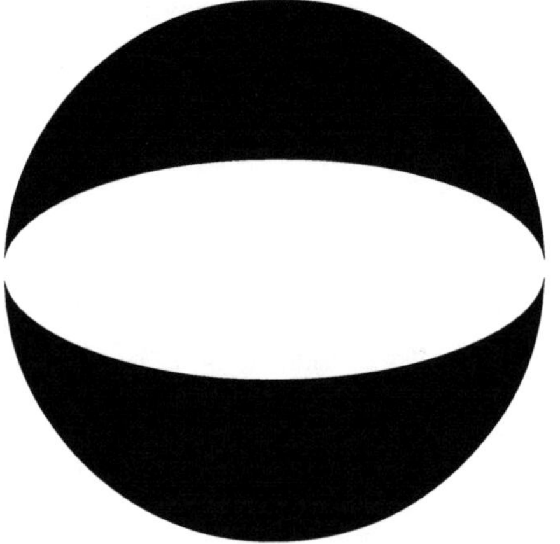

21739778R00257

Made in the USA
San Bernardino, CA
04 January 2019